The Young Hegelians

HUMANITIES PAPERBACK LIBRARY

Published

Commentary to Kant's "Critique of Pure Reason"
Norman Kemp Smith

The Foundations of Metaphysics in Science
Errol E. Harris

Fundamentals of Philosophy
Errol E. Harris

Hegel's Science of Logic
Translated by A. V. Miller

Hypothesis and Perception
The Roots of Scientific Method
Errol E. Harris

Karl Jaspers: Basic Philosophical Writings
Karl Jaspers; edited and translated by Edith Ehrlich, Leonard H. Ehrlich, and George B. Pepper

Philosophy and Truth: Selections from Nietzsche's Notebooks of the Early 1870's
Friedrich Nietzsche; edited and translated by Daniel Breazeale

The Principal Upanisads
Edited with Introduction, Text, Translation and Notes by S. Radhakrishnan

Reason and Revolution
Herbert Marcuse

The Worlds of Existentialism: A Critical Reader
Edited, with Introductions and Conclusions by Maurice Friedman

The Young Hegelians: An Anthology
Edited by Lawrence S. Stepelevich

The Young Hegelians

An Anthology

Lawrence S. Stepelevich

HUMANITIES PRESS
NEW JERSEY

First published in 1983

This paperback edition first published in 1997 by
Humanities Press International, Inc.
165 First Avenue, Atlantic Highlands, New Jersey 07716

Library of Congress Cataloging-in-Publication Data

The young Hegelians : an anthology / [edited by] Lawrence S. Stepelevich.
p. cm. — (Humanities paperback library)
Originally published: New York : Cambridge University Press, 1983, in series: Texts in German philosophy.
Includes bibliographical references and index.
ISBN 0-391-04017-0 (paper)
1. Philosophy, German—19th century. 2. Hegel, Georg Wilhelm Friedrich, 1770-1831—Influence. I. Stepelevich, Lawrence S., 1930-
B2741.Y68 1997
193—dc21 96-52981
CIP

Printed in the United States of America

10 9 8 7 6 5 4 3 2 1

In Memory of my Father
Stanley Stepelevich
(1903–1975)

Contents

Preface

A distinction must be made between being a Hegelian philosopher and a student of Hegelian philosophy, for the practice of this philosophy extends well beyond the mere scholarly recollection of that thought. To philosophize, as a Hegelian, is to take up, develop, and apply the dialectical methodology of Hegel to a point that would extend beyond the limits found in Hegel himself. Hegel once remarked that 'we can be Platonists no longer', and by the same token we can be Hegelians no longer – if by that is meant we would philosophize in the same terms and imagery, and seize upon those same problems which reflected only Hegel's time and place in history. Again – in Hegel's words – 'as every individual is a child of his time; so philosophy too is its own time apprehended in thoughts'. This restricting of philosophy to its own age rests upon the most fundamental of Hegelian principles: that philosophy is nothing other than the continuing development of the same self-reflective spirit driving ever onward to transcend the confines of any fixed system of thought. The historical series of philosophical systems which are treated in the history of philosophy are, to Hegel, but a 'series of successive spiritual forms . . . the moments of the one Spirit, of the one self-present Spirit'. In sum, that 'one self-present Spirit' which found birth in the consciousness of the first to properly claim the name *philosopher*, and which from that time developed in a self-consciousness of itself in the philosophy of Hegel, must – if philosophy is to continue – go beyond Hegel.

Those earliest followers of Hegel who understood Hegelianism in this manner, and who sought to develop the spirit of philosophy beyond Hegel, even to the point of contradiction, have come to be known as the Young Hegelians. And – as if out of respect for the laws of the dialectic – there were also those who held Hegelianism as a final revelation of the philosophic spirit, the actual *end* of philosophizing. These were known as the 'Old Hegelians', and shortly thereafter, the 'Right-wing Hegelians'. Karl Löwith notes of these that 'they preserved Hegel's philosophy literally...but they did not reproduce it in a uniform manner beyond the period of Hegel's personal influence. For the historical movement of the nineteenth century they are without significance. In contrast with these Old Hegelians, the designation "Young Hegelians"...arose.' In sum, the Young Hegelian movement rests upon the belief that Hegelianism did not die with Hegel.

Some years ago a so-called 'Hegel-renaissance' developed. This renewed interest centered – and in large measure still does – upon the recovery and reappreciation of Hegel's original contribution to philosophy, and of his role as a major thinker whose influence and importance extends well beyond his well-publicized role as Marx's teacher. In 1958, German scholars responded to this quickening interest in Hegel by establishing a permanent 'Hegel-Archiv', which set as its main task the publication of a complete and critical edition of Hegel's writings. Some suggestion of the extent of and effort involved in this project can be gained by knowing that the critical edition is not expected to be completed before the first quarter of the next century. Exactly a decade after the formation of the Hegel-Archiv, North American scholars also reacted to the growing interest in Hegel by incorporating the Hegel Society of America, which, within a few years, can now claim over 300 members. In 1980, the Hegel Society of Great Britain was formed.

But any 'renaissance' deserving of the name must – just as did the original Italian – expand beyond a merely reverential collection of past truths and go on to generate its own world. If it does not, it is not a true renaissance, but an ever more empty and formal exercise devoted to a dead system, which in this case would become nothing else than a noxious autopsy upon the Hegelian corpus. Young Hegelianism, which drew its spirit directly from Hegel, is – as this anthology reveals – far from resting content with such autopsies. As the immediate heirs of Hegel, they operated within its spirit, as a living philosophy. In this, insofar as they did not take Hegelianism as a finished and inactive collection of thought, but as the *first* self-conscious movement in the history of the philosophical spirit, they can be considered as the first Hegelian philosophers, as the exponents of the authentic direction of philosophy after Hegel. To accept this, and so to construe Hegelianism as the inner dynamic of reason itself, as that living thought which eludes the mere external analysis of scholars, is to be a Young Hegelian. In this perspective, Young Hegelianism is as much a mode of philosophical apprehension as a form of philosophy to be apprehended, and as much a methodology as a passing historical event. The following collection of writings from this school illustrates both features.

In the early 1960s, concurrent with the rise of the 'Hegel-renaissance', a series of English-language studies turned to the 'Young Marx'. Robert C. Tucker's *Philosophy and Myth in Karl Marx* (1961) and Eric Fromm's *Marx's Concept of Man* (1961) – which contained a translation of Marx's *Economic and Philosophic Manuscripts of 1844* – were among the most popular and influential of these new studies. Not unexpectedly, in the course of this recovery of the early Marx, the other members of the Young Hegelian school were brought into an unaccustomed appreciation as being his ideological comrades. Just as the Hegelians, the Marxists also recognized the need for an evaluation of these hitherto ignored thinkers. David McLellan's *The Young Hegelians and Karl Marx* (1969) considered his work as marking a new concern with what he perceived as an 'increasingly evident gap in the history of ideas'. And so, the Marxists, in seeking the origins of Marxism, and the Hegelians who sought to understand the legacy of Hegel met within the circle of the Young Hegelians. It is perhaps time to understand this circle as more than a mere link between Hegel and the present or as simply the matrix in which Marxism was formed, but as an authentic school of philosophy in its own right. The following collection can at least serve as an introduction to that school, and in so doing serve not only the students of that school, but the students of Hegel and Marx as well, and indeed anyone interested in that seminal and radically unstable mixture of religion, politics, and philosophy which tormented Germany prior to the Revolution of 1848.

As the Introduction to this anthology indicates, the individual members of the Young Hegelian school were faced with a galling set of political and social circumstances that permitted them neither the time nor the conditions for an unimpeded development of their inherited philosophy. It is not surprising that their writings generally appear to be hurried and incomplete. There is truth in the remark of Löwith that they wrote 'manifestos, programs, and theses, but never anything whole, important in itself'. But if their angers and frustrations rise to mark, and sometimes mar, the course of their logic, this signals the vitality of their thought and the adversity of their times.

The texts included in this collection were chosen not only because they reflect the thought of the individual, but also because they accorded to the general movement of Young Hegelianism itself. The Introduction has presented that movement as following a subtle inner logic which fully articulated itself within the course of two decades, from Feuerbach's optimistic 1828 letter to Hegel to 1846 and the cynical and cryptic work of Karl Schmidt, *Das Verstandestum und das Individuum*. As the developing logic of the school fitted itself to the history of the times, the selections have been chronologically ordered.

This collection is not only the first English-language text devoted to the writings of the Young Hegelians, but it is the first to contain English translations of a number of important writings by the major figures of this school. Here, for the first time, Arnold Ruge, Edgar Bauer, Moses Hess, and Karl Schmidt are introduced to the English-speaking reader, and highly significant essays by August von Cieszkowski, Bruno Bauer, and Max Stirner appear here in English for the first time. Each of the newly-translated sections, as well as those drawn from previously translated sources, have been introduced by the editor, and annotated by the translator of the particular selection.

Writings which had appeared earlier in print were selected in the light of their accuracy and readability. The Editor wishes to acknowledge the permission of Doubleday and Company for the use of Zawar Hanfi's translation of Feuerbach's 'Towards a Critique of Hegel's Philosophy' taken from their publication *The Fiery Brook: Selected Writings of Ludwig Feuerbach* (Garden City, 1972); permission to use material from *Readings in Modern Jewish History*, ed. by Ellis Rivkin; *Bruno Bauer: The Jewish Problem*, trans. by Helen Lederer (Hebrew Union-Jewish Institute of Religion, Cincinnati, Ohio); permission of Progress Publishers to use their translation of Friedrich Engels' *Outline of a Critique of Political Economy*, found in their *Engels: Collected Works*, *II* (Moscow, 1975). The translation of the *Introduction* to Marx's *Contribution to the Critique of Hegel's 'Philosophy of Right'* by Annette Jolin and Joseph O'Malley appeared in 1970 as a publication of Cambridge University Press.

The translations which here appear for the first time are not only the result of a rare facility on the part of these translators to set nineteenth-century German political and philosophical prose into modern English, but are also the products of scholars recognized for their interest and knowledge in the history and persons comprising Young Hegelianism. They not only knew *how* to translate, but, more importantly, knew *what* they were translating.

Professor Marilyn C. Massey, of Duke University and presently at Harvard Divinity School, selected and annotated the material from David F. Strauss' *Life of Jesus*, and although the standard translation of the fourth edition of that work by Marian Evans has been used as a base, Professor Massey has added critical material that had been deleted from the first edition of the Life. This restored and more radical text, the text familiar to the Young Hegelians, has added a significant new dimension to our understanding of the relationship holding between Strauss and his contemporaries.

It is difficult, if not impossible, to imagine a more highly qualified translator of August von Cieszkowski than André Liebich, of the Université du Québec à Montréal. Professor Liebich has already published a comprehensive study of Cieszkowski, *Between Ideology and Utopia: The Politics and Philosophy of August Cieszkowski* (Dordrecht, 1979), as well as a set of translations of this provocative thinker, *Selected Writings of August Cieszkowski* (Cambridge, 1979). Professor Daniel O. Dahlstrom, of The Catholic University of America, having published on Feuerbach, and interested in the subject of the relationship of Hegel to Feuerbach, was most qualified to translate Feuerbach's important essay 'The Provisional Theses for the Reformation of Philosophy'.

With the exception of Helen Lederer's translation of *The Jewish Problem*, Michael Malloy, of Georgetown University, was the first, in a special issue of *The Philosophical Forum* (VIII, 1978) to introduce English-language readers to Bruno Bauer.

Professor James A. Massey, of the University of Louisville, has had a long interest in the Young Hegelian school, an interest manifested in both articles and books, the most recent being a translation of Feuerbach's *Thoughts on Death and Immortality* (California, 1981). He has been preparing a full study of the influence of Arnold Ruge upon the Young Hegelian school.

Eric von der Luft, of Bryn Mawr College, presently completing his doctoral studies there with a dissertation focused on Hegel's philosophy of religion, is preparing a first English translation of H. F. W. Hinrichs' *Die Religion im inneren Verhältnisse zur Wissenschaft* (1822).

Finally, the assistance and encouragement of Professor Hans-Martin Sass, of Bochum University, was deeply appreciated by the editor.

This Hegelian would be much amiss were he not to mention those happily necessitated moments of his concrete personality, his wife and children.

Introduction

As an identifiable philosophic movement, Young Hegelianism endured for less than two decades, from 1830 to 1848. It first appeared in Feuerbach's ignored treatise, *Gedanken über Tod und Unsterblichkeit*, and it made its last coherent expression in Karl Schmidt's *Das Verstandestum und das Individuum*. This last work appeared anonymously in 1846, and caused as little concern as Feuerbach's introductory work. By 1848, 'the struggles of the school were ended, and it collapsed into itself, becoming insignificant in both intellectual and political life'.[1] In sum, the school existed between two politically eventful poles, being born in the revolutionary year of 1830, and dying in the revolution of 1848. At its rise, it shared the optimism of its older literary brother, Young Germany, for at that time the rebellion of the French against the reactionary visions of their King, Charles X, had sent a spasm of romantic hope throughout the whole European intellectual community. German intellectuals were no exception, and Heine recalled that when the news of the revolution was received, 'each item was a sunbeam, wrapped in printed paper, and together they kindled my soul into a wild glow... Lafayette, the tricolor, the Marseillaise – it intoxicates me. Bold, ardent hopes spring up, like trees with golden fruit... '[2] The long-delayed promises of the first French revolution were finally to be realized. Certainly, the students of Hegel were prepared to accept his charge that they 'grasp the spirit of the time, and each in his own place – consciously to bring it...from its lifeless seclusion into the light of day'.[3]

[1] Hans-Martin Sass, *Untersuchungen zur Religionsphilosophie in der Hegelschule: 1830–1850* (Ph.D. diss., Münster, 1963), p. 200. This compares with David McLellan's statement that 'by the end of 1844 the Young Hegelian movement was dead as a coherent force' if the writing of Karl Schmidt is taken into account. See McLellan's *The Young Hegelians and Karl Marx* (London, 1969), p. 47.

[2] Heinrich Heine, *Sämmtliche Werke* (Hamburg, 1867), 12, p. 83.

[3] Hegel, *Lectures on the History of Philosophy*, trans. by E. S. Haldane and F. H. Simson (London, 1955), 3, p. 553.

In 1830, all who were to become the central figures of the Young Hegelian school were young men. At 28, Arnold Ruge was their senior member, Ludwig Feuerbach was 26, Max Stirner 24, David Strauss 22, Bruno Bauer 21. The rest, August von Cieszkowski, Karl Schmidt, Karl Marx, Friedrich Engels, and Edgar, the brother of Bruno Bauer, were yet children. Of these, only the youngest members – as communists – would survive 1848 with some measure of social idealism. The older members, as their biographies indicate, found whatever solace they could in a pragmatic pessimism. Hegelianism itself would fade away, leaving only a trace in the persons of some prudent 'Old Hegelians', such as Johann Erdmann, who, in 1866, half-humorously referred to himself as the 'letzten Mohikaner'.[4]

The hopes of these Hegelians to engage in a free-flowing theological and cultural dialogue was tempered, then turned into bitter anger or sour silence in the face of an adamant union between a defensive Church and a reactionary Monarchy. The German revolution of 1848 came too late for the Young Hegelians, and as it was not born out of hope but of despair, it left all sides dissatisfied. In this view, Young Hegelianism is not seen in its usual light – as a confused extrapolation of Hegel's original thought carried on by visionary disciples of little originality – but rather as a graduated philosophic response to a debilitating union of religious dogmatism and political power.

Hegel himself lived only long enough to experience the first few external criticisms and inner developments of his thought, a system of thought by which he had intended – against Kant – to restore the dignity of metaphysics, the ideal content of religion, and the primacy of civil order. And so, what then had been understood to be a 'Restoration philosophy'[5] had yet to reveal its revolutionary potential. This unwelcome revelation of the esoteric 'absolute'[6] revolutionary character of Hegelianism was the vocation of Young Hegelianism.

Just as Hegel's original thought explicitly focused upon the restoration of metaphysics, speculative theology and conservative social and political theory, so the first arguments concerning the worth of Hegel's legacy followed serially upon these same three features. A few years before and after Hegel's death, until 1835 – the publication date of Strauss' *Leben Jesu* – the debate over the value

[4] Johann Erdmann, *Grundriss der Geschichte der Philosophie* (Berlin, 1866), 2, p. 663.

[5] *Ibid.*, p. 596.

[6] Friedrich Engels, *Ludwig Feuerbach and the Outcome of Classical German Philosophy* (New York, 1941), p. 12.

of Hegelianism turned upon its metaphysical worth. After the *Leben Jesu*, and until shortly after Friedrich Wilhelm IV ascended the Prussian throne in 1840, attention fixed upon the theological implications of Hegelianism. By the early 1840s, the religious debate suddenly gave way to arguments concerning the political and social intent of original Hegelianism. By 1848, Hegelianism was no longer a subject deemed worthy of any further interpretive efforts.

And so, within two decades, the 'decomposition' – as Engels would have it – of the original Hegelian corpus was complete. It could well be that even Hegel, particularly the young Hegel of the *Phenomenology of the Mind*, would see in this dissolution a sad, yet comforting testimony to the 'portentous power of the negative'. Certainly, if not the young Hegel, then the Young Hegelians – for they had much in common.[7] Be that as it may, it is a fact that the old Hegel was among the first to join in the defense of his doctrines against some early objections. He set out, in the *Berliner Jahrbücher*, to refute five separate attacks on his metaphysical teachings.[8] He soon tired of the game, having replied, somewhat contemptuously, to only two detractors, and excused himself by remarking – 'must I quarrel with such rabble?'[9] As to whether or not he would have continued to remain aloof is a question that his unexpected death left unanswered. The task of defending the Master fell upon his disciples, the 'epigoni', as they were first called,[10] and they faced an ever more formidable opposition, an opposition which in time did not hesitate to use the power of the Prussian state to make its point.

Among these first defenders, none was more loyal than Carl Friedrich Göschel. He had come to Hegel's defense in 1829, with a work entitled *Aphorismen über Nichtwissen und absolutes Wissen*. The *Aphorismen* is remarkable by reason of its exalted view of Hegel's thought, a vision which saw in Hegelianism the highest speculative expression of spiritual life, of Christianity itself. Christianity and Hegelianism were related as premise to conclusion, and to be a true Christian was to be a Hegelian. Indeed, for Göschel, becoming a Hegelian was not unlike undergoing a religious conversion, a philosophical 'Pentecost', for 'without a re-birth no one can rise from the sphere of natural understanding to the speculative height of the

[7] Two authors who suggest an affinity are Jürgen Gebhardt, *Politik und Eschatologie* (München, 1963), p. 33; and Karl Löwith, *From Hegel to Nietzsche* (New York, 1964), p. 71.

[8] For a detailed study, see Erdmann, *Grundriss*, 2, pp. 665ff.

[9] *Sämtliche Werke*, Jubiläumsausgabe, 20, 362.

[10] Karl Immermann, *Werke*, ed. Robert Boxberger (Berlin, n.d.), 5, *Die Epigonen*. Also, Gebhardt, pp. 49ff.

living notion'. Further, as the reward of attention, God's word could be esoterically discerned in the language of philosophy, and to find out that word, one must

> willingly and fully transport thyself into the concepts of philosophy;...be only first disposed to endure and to accept them, and thou shalt experience in thy heart their life and truth, that is, their total agreement with the word of God, whose restatement [*Übersetzung*] they are.[11]

Finally, and more significantly for the future of Hegelianism, it was defined as 'the highest product of Christianity'. In this equation, Hegelianism is not the source of new truths, a 'praxis' as von Cieszkowski will have it, but the fulfillment of past truths. On this point, Hegelianism divided into two schools, the 'Old' and the 'Young'. Hegel's lavish praise[12] of Göschel's work not only insured Göschel's primacy in the orthodox school of Hegelianism, but proved that Hegel himself was an 'Old' Hegelian.

On this matter, Hegel is – just as Göschel – sensitive to the complaints of both rationalists and theologians that speculative philosophy, i.e., Hegelianism, would 'by means of the Notion...create another truth'. This, as Hegel notes, is a totally mistaken view,

> for in this higher sphere of thought is understood that which constitutes the innermost truth – the untruth of the difference between form and content, and that it is the pure form itself which seeks content.[13]

This essential unity of philosophical form and spiritual content, of Hegelianism as formulated Christianity, is the principle of conservative Hegelianism, of that which came to be known as 'Old Hegelianism'. In this conservative perspective, original Hegelianism stood as the conclusion of thought, and not as a premise for future action. Karl Michelet, who stood in the 1840s 'on the dividing line between Old and Young Hegelians',[14] tried to diplomatically unite them in order to lead them. To this end, he appealed to both sides that philosophy was not only 'the Owl of Minerva' which introduced a night in which form and content joined, but equally a 'cockcrow' which proclaimed a new dawn. But the schism had endured too long, and reached back into the very core of Hegelianism itself. Michelet failed to reconcile the 'hostile brothers'.

Young Hegelianism can be said to have made one of its earliest appearances in a letter that Ludwig Feuerbach sent to Hegel in November of 1828. The letter was enclosed along with a copy of his

[11] *Aphorismen* (Berlin, 1829), p. 160.

[12] *Werke*, 20, 309.

[13] *Ibid.*, p. 298.

[14] *Geschichte der letzten Systeme der Philosophie in Deutschland von Kant bis Hegel* (Berlin, 1837–8), 2, p. 623.

recent doctoral dissertation, *De Ratione, une, universali, infinita*, and both testify to their author's indebtedness to Hegel.[15] Feuerbach was no less fulsome than Göschel in his praise of Hegel's thought, expansively declaring it to be the 'Incarnation of the pure Logos'. But still, Feuerbach took the opportunity to introduce his own perception of the import of Hegelianism. To Feuerbach, the knowledge gained through the study of Hegel should not merely

> be directed to academic ends, but to mankind – for at the least, the new philosophy can make the claim that it is compelled to break through the limits of a school, and to reveal itself as world-historical, and to be not simply the seed in every spirit of a higher literary activity, but rather to become the expressed universal spirit of reality itself, to found, as it were, a new world-epoch, to establish a kingdom. ... There is now a new basis of things, a new history, a second creation, where... reason will become the universal appearance of the thing.

To Feuerbach, Spirit, after 'having worked for centuries upon its completion and development', has finally revealed itself in Hegel's philosophy. It is now the mission of Spirit, acting through its disciples – the Hegelians – to rationalize the world. In theological terms, which always seem natural in a Young Hegelian context, the redemption of the world by incarnate reason is now at hand, and from Feuerbach on, this 'apocalyptic tone, this sense of historical revolution, was the essential ingredient of Young Hegelian metaphysic'.[16]

The style of Feuerbach's letter preludes the whole of Young Hegelian literature. Its glimpse of an ideal future provoked a stylistic brilliance that was simply absent in the staid commentaries of the Old Hegelians. But this same apocalyptically inspired enthusiasm, as magnified in their later literature, threatened to degenerate into noisy propaganda, fitted for 'manifestos, programs and theses... '.[17] On the other side, the Old Hegelians ran the equal but opposite risk of falling into a cryptic, flat *réchauffé* of original Hegelianism. As being charged to preserve, rather than act upon the truth of Hegelianism, they had little to say for themselves. These Old Hegelians, such as von Henning, Hotho, Forster, Marheineke, Hinrichs, Daub, Conradi and Schaller,

> preserved Hegel's philosophy literally, continuing its individual historical studies, but they did not reproduce it in a uniform manner beyond the period

[15] *Briefe von und an Hegel*, ed. J. Hoffmeister (Hamburg, 1954), 3, pp. 244–8. Letter of Nov. 22, 1828.

[16] William J. Brazill, *The Young Hegelians* (New Haven, Conn., 1970), p. 56.

[17] Karl Löwith, *Die Hegelsche Linke* (Stuttgart, 1962), p. 10.

of Hegel's personal influence. For the historical movement of the nineteenth century they are without significance.[18]

The literary style of the two Hegelian schools mirrored their interests, and so, as the Old Hegelian, H. F. Hinrichs observed in 1842, 'The style [*Darstellungweise*] of the right side is mostly aphoristic, that of the left, pamphleteering'.[19]

In the early 1830s, Göschel found a willing ally in his defense of Hegel's metaphysical coherence in the person of Georg Andreas Gabler. Gabler could claim the honor of being once Hegel's student in Jena, and would be further honored, in 1835, by being appointed to Hegel's former chair at Berlin. Together they formed the nucleus of the Old Hegelian school, and both were pleased to find, in the young theologian Bruno Bauer, an energetic and talented defender of Hegel's theological orthodoxy. Bauer, who had first heard Hegel lecture in 1828, was then – and for a decade thereafter – convinced that Hegelian metaphysics formed the rational core of traditional Christianity. His skill in defending this view was put to the test when he was selected by the Old Hegelians to be the first among them to confront, and so confute, Strauss' newly-published *Leben Jesu.* This work put an end to the convoluted argumentation over the merits and demerits of Hegel's metaphysics. The arguments were becoming, to be blunt, simply boring to all contenders. As one of the contestants, Johann Erdmann, more delicately remarked, 'the interest in metaphysics – that is, the first point in which Hegel had shown himself to be a restorer, was on the wane... the question of a logical foundation and of dialectical development was... soon regarded with perfect indifference'.[20]

The second set of arguments, concerning the relationship of Hegelianism to orthodox Christian belief, insofar as it touched directly upon the existing theological-political nexus, determined the future course of Hegelianism, and its echoes are still being heard.[21] To Bauer, Christianity was the proper content of Hegelian form; revelation found its most adequate rational expression in Hegelian thought. The content of Christian belief found its proper form in Hegelian philosophy. In short, Christian revelation and Hegelian reason were perfectly fitted to one another. To Strauss, on the other hand, representing a new, irreverent, and so 'Young' Hegelianism, the relationship was one of pictorial representation against philoso-

[18] Löwith, *From Hegel to Nietzsche*, p. 54.

[19] *Jahrbücher für wissen. Kritik*, 52 (March, 1842), p. 414.

[20] *Grundriss*, 2, p. 649.

[21] E.g., Alexandre Kojève, 'Hegel, Marx and Christianity', *Interpretations*, 1 (Summer, 1970), pp. 21–42.

phic comprehension, of *Vorstellung* against *Begriff*. What Christianity portrayed was but the inkling of what Hegelianism comprehended, and to stay at the noetic level of Christianity in the face of Hegelianism was to decide in favor of ignorance.

After the appearance of Strauss' work, Hegelianism could no longer, without being suspect, play its old humble role of being the philosophic handmaid to Lutheran theology. With the *Leben Jesu* Hegelianism was transformed, in the eyes of a younger generation of philosophers, into at least the rival, if not the actual destroyer, of Christian orthodoxy. The work advanced with the same confident tone found in Feuerbach's letter to Hegel, and it presented its conclusions with a blunt clarity. The conclusions were both simple and shocking: the Christ of the gospels was a myth generated out of the messianic longings of the Jews. Jesus actually existed, and his personality drew upon him the mantle of the Christ, but beyond that, little more can be said of Jesus. Finally, mankind is the actual Christ insofar as it is its own savior. It is this last optimistic, humanistic, and irreverent thesis which reveals Strauss as a Young Hegelian. The incarnation of the Logos, the *Geist*, was not restricted to the particularity of Jesus but was received into the total human race. The messianic ideal of a redemption of mankind

> does not squander its fullness on one individual in order to be stingy to everybody else. Its desire, rather, is to distribute its wealth among the multiplicity of individuals... Is not the idea of the unity of divine and human natures a real one in a more lofty sense when I regard the entire human race as its realization than if I select one man as its realization? Is not the incarnation of God from eternity more true than an incarnation limited to one point in time?[22]

In commenting upon this passage, William Brazill summarizes – 'as there could be no man without God, so there could be no God without man. Humanity was the Christ.'[23]

Given Strauss' theoretic perspective, avowedly Hegelian, there could be no other practical consequence but that the individual, to be saved, i.e., to overcome his alienation, should consciously enter into the secular equivalent of the Christ, the community. The individual was called upon to participate fully 'in the divine-human life of the race'.[24] And so, at this early moment in its development, the dominant theme of Young Hegelianism is in evidence – a secularization of eschatological Christianity.

[22] *Leben Jesu*, 2, p. 734.
[23] Brazill, p. 112.
[24] *Leben Jesu*, 2, p. 735.

By a fine dialectical turn of fate, Bruno Bauer was chosen as the champion of Old Hegelianism, dialectical because within a few years he would be recognized as the leader of the Young Hegelians.[25] Bauer's first counter-arguments appeared in the *Jahrbücher für wissenschaftliche Kritik*,[26] then known less reverently as the 'Hegel Gazette'. Bauer maintained that Hegelianism did not lead to a new quasi-religious truth, but provided the metaphysical foundation for tradition Christianity. In this, for example, the Incarnation could be understood as 'the result of the encounter of receptivity and creative necessity and in this encounter all physiological questions are irrelevant'.[27] Göschel and Gabler, among others, also contributed their criticisms of Strauss' Hegelianism, Gabler in his inaugural address of 1835 as he accepted his chair at the University of Berlin, and Göschel, first with an essay and then with a book.[28]

But the Young Hegelians, those who were to agree with Strauss – and at that time they could even number a very young Friedrich Engels[29] – had seized the initiative. The Old Hegelians soon ceased to be a significant philosophical force since their arguments encountered extreme speculative difficulties, and in addition, the orthodox Lutherans and pietists had never asked for nor accepted their proffered help. These conservatives, led by the Berlin preacher Ernst Wilhelm Hengstenberg, now saw in the shocking *Leben Jesu* only what they had always suspected of Hegelianism: atheism and Jacobinism. Indeed, Strauss had at least been an honest Hegelian, and even Hengstenberg could ironically remark that the *Leben Jesu* was 'one of the most pleasing contributions in the field of recent theological literature'.[30] This first judgment has been echoed by more recent commentators, such as John T. Noonan, who holds that Strauss' *Leben Jesu* is properly Hegelian, in fact, even more than that – 'more courageous than Hegel, Strauss is the better Hegelian'.[31] In short, by the opponents of Hegel, Strauss' *Leben Jesu* has been taken as the authentic theological expression of original Hegelianism. The

[25] Bauer was recognized as such by his contemporaries, e.g., Karl Rosenkranz, *Aus einem Tagebuch* (Leipzig, 1853), p. 113.

[26] The first volume of the *Leben Jesu* was reviewed in Numbers 110–13 (December, 1835); the second volume in Numbers 86–8 (May, 1836).

[27] *J. W. Kritik*, December, 1835, No. 112, p. 897.

[28] *Beiträge zur spekulativen Philosophie* (Berlin, 1838).

[29] Letter of Engels to Graeber, June 15, 1839; Marx-Engels *Werke* (Berlin, 1965), Ergänzungsband, Zweiter Teil, p. 401.

[30] *Evangelische Kirchenzeitung* (1836), p. 382. See also Horton Harris, *David Friedrich Strauss and His Theology* (Cambridge, 1973), pp. 78–9.

[31] 'The Dialectic and the Gospels', *The Catholic Biblical Quarterly*, 12 (April, 1950), p. 144.

political influence of the pietists and orthodox Lutherans, which peaked in the reactionary reign of Friedrich Wilhelm IV, insured that Hegelianism would soon lose all of its previous academic and political influence. A Hegelian would soon be forced to choose to remain prudently silent on political and religious issues and so remain without influence, as the Old Hegelians, or to speak out and suffer academic and political repression, as the Young Hegelians. Only a very few of the latter escaped this repression, and that long series of imprisonments, exiles, impoverishments and rejections which marked their collective careers, was shared by Strauss when he was removed from his teaching post at Tübingen.[32]

In 1837, Strauss took up his own defense by writing a set of rejoinders to his numerous critics.[33] In introducing that section of his work dealing with the objections of the Hegelians, Strauss established a new mode of classifying the Hegelians. Borrowing the terms used to designate the relationships of the French politicians to the *Ancien Régime*, Strauss classed all Hegelians as either of the 'right', or the 'center', or the 'left'.[34] This philosophical-political classification was popular from its inception, and has remained so to this day.[35] Strauss used it in an exclusively theological context, with the right-wing Hegelians, such as Bauer, Göschel, and Gabler, accepting both the unity of the divine and human nature in Jesus as well as the factuality of the miracle-stories. Those on the left – such as Strauss – would deny both. As for the center – men such as Rosenkranz – they would hold only to the divinity of Jesus, and follow Strauss in other matters. On the whole, however, as Horton Harris has commented, 'the classification was confusing, for this difference was solely a question of definitions, and the line between centre and left was extremely ill-defined.'[36]

Whatever virtues such a schema might possess have been purchased at the cost of provoking a category mistake. The political categories of 'left' and 'right' cannot simply be superimposed upon Young and Old Hegelianism. In this regard, it can be noted that the liberal or

[32] Harris, pp. 58–65.

[33] *Streitschriften zur Verteidigung meiner Schrift über das Leben Jesu und zur Characteristik der gegenwärtigen Theologie* (Tübingen, 1837). This work is divided into three sections, the first dealing with the criticisms of the quasi-rationalist theologians Steudel and Eschenmayer, the second directed against the publicist Menzel, and the third part mainly against the pietists such as Hengstenberg and the Hegelians – Göschel, Gabler and Bauer.

[34] *Ibid.*, 3, p. 95.

[35] As in Robert S. Hartman's introduction to Hegel's *Reason in History* (Indianapolis, Ind., 1953).

[36] Harris, p. 81.

socialistic interpretations of Hegelianism did not openly begin until the 1841 appearance of Arnold Ruge's *Deutsche Jahrbücher*. Prior to that time, and from the publication of the *Leben Jesu*, Young Hegelianism had developed within a theological context. Strauss himself, as a matter of fact, was politically a conservative, as were all of the Young Hegelians up until 1840 – unless Moses Hess is considered, whose socialistic *Die heilige Geschichte der Menschheit* appeared in 1837.

However, this theological context of early Young Hegelianism did fall within a larger political context, and in that same year in which the *Leben Jesu* appeared the Mainz Commission, established by the Frankfurt Diet, had condemned the Young German movement for 'attacking the Christian religion and the social order'.[37] The conservative equation of the two would insure the censure of Young Hegelianism as well.

In retrospect, perhaps the most striking feature of the *Leben Jesu* is not its content, but its intention. Strauss had – with that particular *naiveté* found in youthful genius – imagined that the religious clique which gathered in the Royal court would gladly respond to the evidently well-meaning rationality of his work. As he concluded in a lengthy letter defending his teaching post:

> If all those who have accepted the critical and sceptical elements of the time wanted to resign from the ministry, only the unscientific faith would finally remain to it; the critical doubting would devolve onto the educated in the congregation and the Church would have to split into two halves between which, finally, agreement would be no longer possible; but as against this, so long as the sceptical and critical direction remains represented in the ministry, such a mediation, and therewith a continuing progress of religious and theological education is assured.[38]

Such candor and confidence regarding the therapeutic effects of criticism had little effect upon his judges, as he was removed from his teaching post. He had repeated Feuerbach's imprudence of 1830, who, being warned that to publish his speculations on death and immortality would ruin his career, proceeded to do both.

An extended controversy between Bauer and Strauss never occurred, for although Bauer was still eager to debate, Strauss took Bauer's 'foolish piece of pen-pushing'[39] as unworthy of reply. With this, Strauss' contribution to the Young Hegelian movement came to an end. By 1840, after unsuccessfully attempting to regain respectability with a compromising third edition of the *Leben Jesu*,

[37] Frederick B. Artz, *Reaction and Revolution* (New York, 1963), p. 278.
[38] Letter of Strauss to Karl C. Flatt (July 12, 1835); Harris, p. 63.
[39] Harris, p. 80.

and after a short and disastrous attempt to teach at Zürich, he turned to a career of writing unorthodox theological treatises.

For his part, Bauer continued to exercise his Hegelianism in the cause of religious orthodoxy. However, in 1839, Bauer – displaying an innocence equal to Strauss – took it upon himself to question Hengstenberg's biblical interpretations. Hengstenberg was not at all prepared to receive a rebuke from a young Hegelian *Privatdozent*, and Bauer was persuaded, for his future well-being, to accept a post at the University of Bonn. At Bonn, Bauer's faith in both Christianity and his fellow academics was lost. His loss of faith was precipitated not only by the immanent logic of his own theological principles, but by his confrontation with the *Leben Jesu*. In 1840, Bauer recalled that prior to this work, the disciples of Hegel 'had lived like the blessed gods with patriarchal calm in the realm of the Idea', but with it, 'the lightning of thought struck into the kingdom of the Idea and disturbed the dream'.[40] This dream, of course, being the old Hegelian one of the unity between history and the Idea, between events and Hegelian philosophy. Bauer not only lost his faith, but his hope in conducting critical and free-ranging theological discussions within the context of the Prussian university system. In June of 1841, he had the temerity – or again, innocence – to send a first copy of his most infamous work, the *Kritik der evangelischen Geschichte der Synoptiker*, to the reactionary culture minister, J. G. Eichorn. The Minister sent a letter to the theological faculties of all Prussian universities asking two simple questions: was Bauer a Christian? and should he be allowed to teach on a theological faculty? The answers were mixed, but overall negative. In March of 1842, Bauer was formally forbidden to teach at any Prussian university. The reaction of the authorities is understandable in the light of what Bauer had maintained in the *Kritik*. His general conclusions were similar to those of Strauss – that humanity was divine – but he went beyond Strauss' reduction of Jesus to mere humanity by considering him as a fictional entity. In sum, the gospels were nothing but the further offshoots of an original literary fiction by an unknown author who had simply intended to present his own philosophic viewpoint in the person of a fictional Jesus.

Bauer's highly publicized removal established him as the 'spiritual leader'[41] of the Berlin Young Hegelians. Engels celebrated Bauer's return with an anonymous mock-epic, *Der Triumph des Glaubens*.[42]

[40] *Die evangelische Landeskirche Preussens und die Wissenschaft* (Leipzig, 1840), p. 2.

[41] Gustav Mayer, 'Die Anfänge des politischen Radikalismus im vormärzlichen Preussen', *Zeitschrift für Politik* (Berlin, 1913), 6, p. 46.

[42] Marx-Engels *Werke*, Ergänzungsband, Zweiter Teil, pp. 280–316.

Besides permitting an insight into the pre-Marx Engels, and the notorious Young Hegelian circle of *Die Freien*, the poem is a fine example of the literary course being taken by intellectuals out of favor with the established powers: it is marked by a reckless, almost desperate bravado. Here, in 1842, the course of the school had already turned from optimism and willing orthodoxy into an ironic pessimism that could only terminate in a sour compliance or outright rebellion. The vision of a bright future marked by the progressive incarnation of reason, as projected in August von Cieszkowski's 1838 *Prolegomena to the Wisdom of History* was replaced by the decision to engage in an 'unrestrained criticism of everything established'.[43] By 1842, the repressive policies of Friedrich Wilhelm IV had taken full effect, although he had ascended the throne with the good will, if not the blessings, of the Young Hegelians. Certainly some, such as Friedrick Köppen, the lifelong friend of Marx,[44] had first enthusiastically welcomed the new king as Frederick the Great *redivivus*.[45]

The new King indicated his philosophic inclinations early in his reign, when he invited the ageing Schelling to Berlin. In November of 1841, the lecture series began, a pleasant focus for the anti-Hegelians, such as Henrich Leo and Karl Schubarth, and an insult against 'free philosophy' according to the Young Hegelians.[46]

In that same year of 1841, four literary events of great significance occurred within the Young Hegelian school: the publication of Feuerbach's *Essence of Christianity*, the publication of Bauer's *Trumpet of the Last Judgment Against Hegel the Atheist and Anti-Christ*, the publication of Moses Hess' *The European Triarchy*, and the first issue of Ruge's *Deutsche Jahrbücher*. With each event, a decisive turn was marked in the relationship of Young Hegelianism to Christianity, Hegelianism, Socialism, and Prussian Nationalism.

The Essence of Christianity theologically concluded that Strauss had doctrinally initiated, the absolute reduction of God to Man, the transformation of theology into anthropology. Henceforth, theological issues would be translated into human issues, and theological criticism would be replaced by social criticism. Marx, in 1843, summed up the matter in a famous passage:

For Germany, the *criticism of religion* has been largely completed; and the criticism of religion is the premise of all criticism.

[43] Letter of Marx to Ruge, September, 1843; in *Deutsch-französischen Jahrbüchern*, see *Werke*, 1, p. 344.

[44] Helmut Hirsch, 'Karl Friedrich Köppen', *International Review for Social History* (Leiden, 1936), 1, pp. 311–70.

[45] *Friedrich der Grosse und seine Widersacher* (Leipzig, 1840).

[46] Engels, 'Schelling und die Offenbarung', *Werke*, Ergänz., Zweiter Teil, pp. 171ff.

> The *profane* existence of error is compromised once its celestial *oratio pro aris et focis* [prayer for altars and hearths – cf. Cicero, *Cat.* 4. 11. 24] has been refuted. Man, who has found in the fantastic reality of heaven, where he sought a supernatural being, only his own reflection, will no longer be tempted to find only the semblance of himself – a non-human being – where he seeks and must seek his true reality.[47]

The second event, the publication of Bauer's *Trumpet*, set about – by selectively employing the actual texts of Hegel – to demonstrate that the 'Philosopher of the Restoration' was a covert atheist and revolutionary. This 'unmasking', a familiar Young Hegelian conceit, destroyed the possibility of any future *rapprochement* between them and the conservatives – be they religious, political, or philosophical. After the *Trumpet*, the disciples of Hegel would be compelled to choose between two warring camps: that of the conservative and Christian wing, and that of the revolutionary atheists. The line which presently separates Hegelians such as Marcuse, Kojève, and Lukács from others such as Findlay, Knox, and Kroner, was first drawn by Bruno Bauer.

With Hess' *The European Triarchy*, Germany's first introduction to socialist theory, Young Hegelianism made its fateful link with the emerging proletarian class. After Hess, it was no longer possible to limit the influence of philosophy to issues isolated from the harsh, but actual, world of class struggles. Through Hess, both Marx and Engels were led to a greater appreciation of how a 'Philosophy of Action' could generate a new ordering of human society, and Young Hegelianism – as a whole – found in Hess a crossroad which offered the choice between theoretical exhaustion or world-transforming practice.

In line with Feuerbach's radical humanism, Bauer's radical criticism, and Hess' 'Philosophy of Action', there was yet one factor needed to complete the full formulation of mature Young Hegelianism: political radicalism. This fourth element was contributed by Ruge, who, in 1841, set forth in the Preface to the first issue of the *Deutsche Jahrbücher* a call for all Hegelians to enter into political struggle. The rejection of doctrinal servility in both theology and philosophy must complete itself in the rejection of political servility, the pre-condition for all free criticism. His call was heeded by the most radically politicized, and provoked Mikhail Bakunin – in a later issue – to make his famous declaration that 'The urge to destroy is a creative urge!' But because of the expanding inner divisions within the frustrated group, and the constant pressure of governmental censorship and academic rejection, Ruge's efforts to form a political

[47] 'Zur Kritik der Hegelschen Rechtsphilosophie', *Werke*, I, p. 378; E.t., *Marx-Engels Reader*, ed. R. C. Tucker (New York, 1972), p. 11.

party around the banner of Young Hegelianism soon failed. In 1843, the *Jahrbücher* was prohibited to be published even in liberal Saxony, and the ill-fated *Deutsch-französiche Jahrbücher*, so-edited with Marx in the Spring of 1844, marked an end to Ruge's political effectiveness.

Given the four declarations of 1841, from Feuerbach, Bauer, Hess, and Ruge, the Young Hegelian movement had set itself against the full spectrum of orthodoxy – religious, philosophical, economic, and political. The insurrection failed on all counts, and after the abortive revolution of 1848, Germany entered into a period of reaction whose signs are yet in evidence.

In the Fall of 1844, Max Stirner's singular masterpiece, *Der Einzige und sein Eigentum* [*The Ego and Its Own*], made its appearance. With this, Young Hegelianism reached a final and angry impasse. As 'le dernier maillon de la chaîne hégélienne',[48] Stirner made a clean sweep of everything, leaving only naked self-assertion. With Stirner, Hegelianism, as a system, had reached a dialectical limit and had been transformed into its opposite.[49] The optimistic drive to rationalize the whole of reality which had motivated the earliest of the Young Hegelians had finally withered into an irrational egoism. But Nicholas Lobkowicz has stated the matter with the greatest possible clarity:

> Hegel had *idealized* the existing world. His disciples from Strauss to Marx felt forced to translate Hegel's idealizing *description* of the world into a language of *ideals to be achieved*. In the course of this development they also tried to concretize Hegel's abstract idealizations by translating talk about religion into talk about mankind, talk about the state into talk about existing bourgeois society, etc. Stirner might be described, and in any case was understood by Marx as the man who made the final step in this development – a step which leads beyond Hegelian idealism and negates it. For Stirner achieved the final concretization of Hegelianism by reducing all Hegelian categories to the naked individual self; he denounced not only a certain type of ideal, but all ideals whatsoever.[50]

But even after Stirner, the logic of Hegelianism and the logic of events had to produce yet one final statement, a statement upon the school by one who had followed the course of criticism to the point where criticism rejected itself, to a point beyond Stirner – who could retain the title of the 'final critic'. This last judge upon the school was Karl Schmidt, who wrote an extraordinary and now-forgotten

[48] Henri Arvon, *Aux Sources de l'existentialisme: Max Stirner* (Paris, 1954), p. 177.

[49] See my article 'Hegel and Stirner: Thesis and Antithesis', *Idealistic Studies*, 6, No. 3 (September, 1976), pp. 263–78.

[50] 'Karl Marx and Max Stirner', *Demythologizing Marxism*, ed. Frederich J. Adelmann (The Hague, 1969), p. 85.

work, *Das Verstandestum und das Individuum.* In it, Schmidt traced his, and the whole Young Hegelian *via dolorosa* from beginning to end. In retrospect, Schmidt recognized that throughout the whole history of the school an uncritical dogmatism had prevailed, a dogmatism that led its possessor into an unconscious apotheosis of his particular ideals. Even the hypercritical Stirner 'stands with his enemies on the same ground. He is just as these, an idealist. He revels in his ideals and dreams thereby of a world full of egoists, of an egoistic world which should come to pass.'[51] Schmidt has passed through Young Hegelianism only to arrive at one certain truth: 'I am only myself.'[52] With this modest conclusion, the movement called Young Hegelianism came to an end.

[51] Karl Schmidt, *Das Verstandestum und das Individuum* (Leipzig, 1846), p. 237.
[52] *Ibid.*, p. 308.

I

David Friedrich Strauss

1808–1874

David Friedrich Strauss

It has generally been agreed that Strauss' *Life of Jesus Critically Examined* was not only the first major work of what was to become known as 'Young Hegelianism', but that it might well be considered as the most influential of all those that were to follow. It is now difficult to believe that such a dense theological study could exercise any widespread and decisive effect upon the course of our political and social life, yet such was the effect of the *Life of Jesus* upon its age. The intellectuals of that time, the intellectuals of the German *Vormärz*, not only perceived the *Life* as destroying the possibility of any *rapprochement* between philosophy and biblical theology, but as also setting the rational state forever against the Christian governments of Metternich's Europe.

In essence, the *Life* defended the thesis that the miraculous biblical narratives regarding Jesus were ultimately grounded in a shared mythic consciousness of their authors, a consciousness so excited by messianic expectations that it set a series of totally unhistorical supernatural episodes about the natural historical personage of Jesus. This thesis, which Strauss developed by a brilliant recourse to other biblical and theological authorities, was cast into the matrix of Hegelian dialectic. This alone would have caused sufficient embarrassment to those conservative and Christian 'right-wing' Hegelians – as Strauss first labeled them – but he went beyond the limits of official toleration when he declared that 'from its onset, my critique of the life of Jesus stands in profound relationship to the philosophy of Hegel'. With this, the orthodox and pious believers who clustered about the thrones of Europe were now – through the free and open confession of a Hegelian – convinced of what they had always suspected: that Hegelianism was an atheistic philosophy bent upon the overthrow of civil order. The subsequent course of Young Hegelianism gave them no further reason to doubt their judgment.

Strauss, who wrote the *Life* while but a twenty-seven-year-old instructor at Tübingen University, was immediately cast into irrevocable notoriety. From 1835, the publication date of the first volume of the *Life*, until his death, he was never permitted to occupy another teaching post, and although some of his later works, such as his last, *The Old Faith and the New* (1872), were often to evoke loud acclaim or damnation they could not surpass the height of influence and scandal once reached by his *Life*. His subsequent career, passed in prolific theological and biographical studies, and marked by occasional political activity, exercised no deep effect upon the course of either German history or culture.

Strauss has been recognized as one of the finest prose stylists of his time, and this style was transformed into English by the young and talented genius of George Eliot – Marian Evans. Although Eliot's translation assured the widespread fame of the *Life* in English-speaking countries, it obscured its significance for the history of Hegelianism. This is so because Eliot worked from the fourth (1839) German edition which differed from the first (1835) edition, most notably in the deletion of key Hegelian passages. What follows is a translation of the first edition. Professor Marilyn Chapin Massey, who selected the passages, has translated the deleted parts of the first edition. These have been added to portions of the Eliot translation that do correspond with the text of the first edition. Within the Eliot translation, Professor Massey has re-translated select words and phrases and has interpolated German words in order to make their Hegelian references more evident. The following passages are: the preface, paragraphs 1 and 12 from the introduction, and paragraphs 140, 143, and 145–6 from the conclusion. Professor Massey's translations (found in sections 12 and 147) and her notes appear in brackets. Strauss' own notes, which she has annotated, appear without marks.

For a further study of Strauss, the editor recommends Horton Harris' *David Friedrich Strauss and His Theology* (Cambridge, 1973).

The Life of Jesus

PREFACE
TO THE FIRST GERMAN EDITION

It appeared to the author of the work, the first half of which is herewith submitted to the public, that it was time to substitute a new mode of considering the life of Jesus, in the place of the antiquated systems of supernaturalism and naturalism. This application of the term antiquated will in the present day be more readily admitted in relation to the latter system than to the former. For while the interest excited by the explanations of the miracles and the conjectural facts of the rationalists has long ago cooled, the commentaries now most read are those which aim to adapt the supernatural interpretation of the sacred history to modern taste. Nevertheless, in point of fact, the orthodox view of this history became superannuated earlier than the rationalistic, since it was only because the former had ceased to satisfy an advanced state of culture, that the latter was developed, while the recent attempts to recover, by the aid of a mystical philosophy, the supernatural point of view held by our forefathers, betray themselves, by the exaggerating spirit in which they are conceived, to be final, desperate efforts to render the past present, the inconceivable conceivable.

The new point of view, which must take the place of the above, is the mythical. This theory is not brought to bear on the evangelical history for the first time in the present work: it has long been applied to particular parts of that history, and is here only extended to its entire tenor. It is not by any means meant that the whole history of Jesus is to be represented as mythical, but only that every part of it is to be subjected to a critical examination, to ascertain whether it has not some admixture of the mythical. The exegesis of the ancient church set out from the double presupposition: first, that the gospels contained a history, and secondly, that this history was a supernatural one. Rationalism rejected the latter of these presuppositions, but only to cling the more tenaciously to the former, maintaining that these books present unadulterated, though only natural, history. Science cannot rest satisfied with this half-measure: the other presupposition also must be relinquished, and the inquiry must first be made whether in fact, and to what extent, the ground on which we stand in the gospels is historical. This is the natural course of things, and thus far the appearance of a work like the present is not only justifiable, but even necessary.

It is certainly not therefore evident that the author is precisely the individual whose vocation it is to appear in this position. He has a very vivid consciousness that many others would have been able to execute such a work with incomparably superior erudition. Yet on the other hand he believes himself to be at least possessed of one qualification which especially fitted him to undertake this task. The majority of the most learned and acute theologians of the present day fail in the main requirement for such a work, a requirement without which no amount of learning will suffice to achieve anything in the domain of criticism, namely, the internal liberation of the feelings and intellect from certain religious and dogmatical presuppositions; and this the author early attained by means of philosophical studies.[1] If theologians regard this absence of presupposition from his work, as unchristian: he regards the believing presuppositions of theirs as unscientific. Widely as in this respect the tone of the present work may be contrasted with the edifying devoutness and enthusiastic mysticism of recent books on similar subjects; still it will nowhere depart from the seriousness of science, or sink into frivolity; and it seems a just demand in return, that the judgments which are passed upon it should also confine themselves to the domain of science, and keep aloof from bigotry and fanaticism.

The author is aware that the essence of the Christian faith is perfectly independent of his criticism. The supernatural birth of Christ, his miracles, his resurrection and ascension, remain eternal truths, whatever doubts may be cast on their reality as historical facts. The certainty of this can alone give calmness and dignity to our criticism, and distinguish it from the naturalistic criticism of the last century, the design of which was, with the historical fact, to subvert also the religious truth, and which thus necessarily became frivolous. A dissertation at the close of the work will show that the dogmatic significance of the life of Jesus remains inviolate: in the meantime let the calmness and insensibility with which, in the course of it, criticism undertakes apparently dangerous operations, be explained

[1] [It is the promise of the Hegelian philosophy to reconcile scientific knowledge and Christian faith that provides for Strauss not only the liberation of the feelings and intellect from dogmatic presuppositions but also the confidence that what he calls the essence (*inneren Kern*) of Christian faith will not be damaged by the free exercise of criticism made possible by this liberation. (Tr.)]

solely by the security of the author's conviction that no injury is threatened to the Christian faith. Investigations of this kind may, however, inflict a wound on the faith of individuals. Should this be the case with theologians, they have in their science the means of healing such wounds, from which, if they would not remain behind the development of their age, they cannot possibly be exempt. For the laity the subject is certainly not adequately prepared; and for this reason the present work is so framed, that at least the unlearned among them will quickly and often perceive that the book is not destined for them. If from curiosity or excessive zeal against heresy they persist in their perusal, they will then have, as Schleiermacher says on a similar occasion, to bear the punishment in their conscience, since their feelings directly urge on them the conviction that they understand not that of which they are ambitious to speak.

A new opinion, which aims to fill the place of an older one, ought fully to adjust its position with respect to the latter. Hence the way to the mythical view is here taken in each particular point through the supernaturalistic and rationalistic opinions and their respective refutations; but, as becomes a valid refutation, with an acknowledgment of what is true in the opinions combated, and an adoption of this truth into the new theory. This method also brings with it the extrinsic advantage, that the work may now serve as a repertory of the principal opinions and treatises concerning all parts of the evangelical history. The author has not, however, aimed to give a complete bibliographical view of this department of theological literature, but, where it was possible, has adhered to the chief works in each separate class of opinions. For the rationalistic system the works of Paulus remain classical, and are therefore preeminently referred to; for the orthodox opinions, the commentary of Olshausen is especially important, as the most recent and approved attempt to render the supernatural interpretation philosophical and modern; while as a preliminary to a critical investigation of the life of Jesus, the commentaries of Fritzsche are excellently adapted, since they exhibit, together with uncommon philological learning, that freedom from prejudice and scientific indifference to results and consequences, which form the first condition of progress in this region of inquiry.

The second volume, which will open with a detailed examination of the miracles of Jesus, and which will conclude the whole work, is already prepared and will be in the press immediately on the completion of the first.

THE AUTHOR

Tübingen, 24th May, 1835

1. Inevitable rise of different modes of explaining sacred histories

Wherever a religion, resting upon written records, prolongs and extends the sphere of its dominion, accompanying its votaries through the varied and progressive stages of mental cultivation, a discrepancy between [the spirit and form of those ancient records and the more advanced mental cultivation of those who refer to them as sacred books] will inevitably sooner or later arise. In the first instance this disagreement is felt in reference only to [the inessential (*Unwesentliche*) and the formal (*Formelle*)]: the expressions and delineations are seen to be inappropriate; but by degrees it manifests itself also in regard to [the essential content (*Inhalt*)]; the fundamental ideas and opinions in these early writings fail to be commensurate with a more advanced civilization.[2] As long as this discrepancy is either not in itself so considerable, or else is not so universally discerned and acknowledged, as to lead to a complete renunciation of these Scriptures as of sacred authority, so long will a system of reconciliation by means of interpretation be adopted and pursued by those who have a more or less distinct consciousness of the existing incongruity.

A main element in all religious records is sacred history; a history of events in which the divine enters, without intermediation, into the human; [divine purposes (*die Ideen*) seem to be immediately materialized]. But as the progress of mental cultivation mainly consists in the gradual recognition of a chain of causes and effects connecting natural phenomena with each other; so the mind in its development becomes ever increasingly conscious of those mediate links which are indispensable to [the actualization (*Verwicklung*) of the Idea (*Idee*)]; and hence the discrepancy between the modern culture and the ancient records, with regard to their historical

[2] [This statement of the problematic of a modern religion based on ancient texts is notable for the *absence* of the Hegelian distinction between the form of religious representations (*Vorstellungen*) and philosophical concepts (*Begriffe*) central to *The Philosophy of Religion*. Only at the end of the introduction (in §12) does Strauss refer directly to this distinction. He later reported this distinction to be that with which he was concerned when he decided to write the *Life*. See David Friedrich Strauss, *Streitschriften zur Vertheidigung meiner Schrift über das Leben Jesu und zur Charakteristik der gegenwärtigen Theologie* (Tübingen: C. F. Osiander, 1837), pt. 3, pp. 57–60. The terms used here – 'the inessential' (*Unwesentliche*), which Strauss relates explicitly to the 'formal' (*Formelle*), and the 'essential' (*Wesentliche*), which he implicitly relates to the 'content' (*Inhalt*) – are general, not specifically Hegelian, terms. However, when coupled as they are here with references to immediacy and mediation in the actualization (*Verwicklung*) of the idea (*Idee*) they suggest that Strauss was formulating the religious problematic with the categories of Hegel's *Logic* on which he had given lectures at Tübingen just before writing the *Life*. (Tr.)]

portion, becomes so apparent that the immediate intervention of the divine in human affairs loses its probability. Besides, as the humanity of these records is the humanity of an early period, consequently of an age comparatively undeveloped and necessarily rude, a sense of repulsion is likewise excited. The incongruity may be thus expressed. *The divine cannot so have happened*; (not immediately, not in forms so rude, or, *that which has so happened cannot have been divine*: – and if a reconciliation be sought by means of interpretation, it will be attempted to prove, either that the divine did not manifest itself in the manner related – which is to deny the historical validity of the ancient Scriptures; or, that the actual occurrences were not divine, – which is to explain away the absolute contents (*Inhalt*) of these books. In both cases the interpretation may be partial or impartial: partial, if undertaken with a determination to close the eyes to the secretly recognized fact of the disagreement between the modern culture and the ancient records, and to see only in such interpretation the original signification of these records; impartial, if it unequivocally acknowledges and openly avows that the matters narrated in these books must be viewed in a light altogether different from that in which they were regarded by the authors themselves. This latter method, however, by no means involves the entire rejection of the religious documents; on the contrary, the essential may be firmly retained, whilst the unessential is unreservedly abandoned.

12. Arguments for and against the mythical view of gospel history[3]

In adopting the mythical point of view as hitherto applied to Biblical history, our theologians had again approximated to the ancient allegorical interpretation. For as both the natural explanations of the Rationalists, and the jesting expositions of the Deists, belong to that form of opinion which, whilst it sacrifices all divine meaning in the sacred record, still upholds its historical character; the mythical mode of interpretation agrees with the allegorical, in relinquishing the historical reality of the sacred narratives, in order to preserve to them an absolute inherent truth. [The fundamental viewpoint of the

[3] [This section, ending the introduction to the first edition, differs significantly from Strauss' treatment of arguments over myth and his description of the criteria for identifying myth in subsequent editions. In 1835, he was more Hegelian than later in two ways: first, he structured his treatment of theoretical arguments about myth to end with the distinction between representations and philosophical concepts; secondly, he chose to be a 'phenomenologist' and let his criteria for judgment unfold as he reviewed the history of Jesus' life recorded in the gospels instead of merely testing each part of that life against predetermined criteria. (Tr.)]

mythical and the allegorical (as well as the moral) modes of interpretation is that the historian relates that which is apparently historical; but the historian, whether conscious of it or not,[4] is influenced by a higher spirit preparing this history as the mere shell of a trans-historical truth or meaning.] The only essential distinction therefore between these two modes of explanation is, that according to the allegorical this higher [spirit] is the immediate divine agency; according to the mythical, it is the spirit of a people or a community. (According to the moral view it is generally the mind of the interpreter which suggests the interpretation.) Thus the allegorical view ascribes it to that *natural* process by which legends are originated and developed. To which it should be added, that the allegorical interpreter (as well as the moral) may with the most unrestrained arbitrariness separate from the history every thought he deems to be worthy of God, as constituting its inherent meaning; whilst the mythical interpreter, on the contrary, in searching out the ideas which are embodied in the narrative, is controlled by regard to conformity with the spirit and modes of thought of the people and of the age.

This new view of the sacred Scriptures was opposed alike by the orthodox and by the rationalistic party. From the first, whilst the mythical interpretation was still restricted to the primitive history of the Old Testament, Johann Jacob Hess (1741–1828) on the orthodox side, protested against it.[5] The three following conclusions may be given as comprising, however incredible this may appear, the substance of this book, a work of some compass; upon which however it is unnecessary to remark further than that Hess was by no means the last orthodox theologian who pretended to combat the mythical view with such weapons. He contends: [1.] that mythi are to be understood figuratively; now the sacred historians intended their writings to be understood literally: consequently they do not relate mythi. [2.] Mythology is something [pagan]; the Bible is a Christian book; consequently it contains no mythology. The third conclusion is more complex, and, as will appear below, has more meaning. If, says Hess, the marvellous were confined to those earliest Biblical

[4] [In the first edition Strauss noted, 'According to Philo, Moses was aware of the deeper sense of his writings and also according to origin the prophets had a certain consciousness of the deeper meaning of their words and narratives. According to the mythical view the writers, as reporters, were not *clearly* conscious of the idea materialized in their narrative; rather, they were conscious of it only in the form of that narrative.' (Tr.)]

[5] [The criteria of what is myth, etc., and what is actually history. See Johann Jacob Hess, *Bibliothek der heiligen Geschichte*, 2 parts (Zürich: Orell, Gessner, Füssli and company, 1791–2) 2:155ff. (Tr.)]

records of which the historical validity is less certain, and did not appear in any subsequent writings, the miraculous might be considered as a proof of the mythical character of the narrative; but the marvellous is no less redundant in the latest and undeniably historical records, than in the more ancient; consequently it cannot be regarded as a criterion of the mythical. In short the most hollow natural explanation, did it but retain the slightest vestige of the historical – however completely it annihilated every higher meaning, – was preferable, in the eyes of the orthodox, to the mythical interpretation. Certainly nothing could be worse than Johann Gottfried Eichhorn's (1752–1827) natural explanation of the fall. In considering the tree of knowledge as a poisonous plant, he at once destroyed the intrinsic value and inherent meaning of the history; of this he afterwards became fully sensible, and in his subsequent mythical interpretation, he recognized in the narrative the incorporation of a worthy and elevated conception.[6] Hess however declared himself more content with Eichhorn's original explanation, and defended it against his later mythical interpretation.[7] So true is it that supranaturalism clings with childlike fondness to the empty husk of historical semblance, though void of divine significance, and estimates it higher than the most valuable kernel divested of its variegated covering.

If the orthodox were displeased at having their historical faith disturbed by the progressive inroads of the mythical mode of interpretation, the rationalists were no less disconcerted to find the web of facts they had so ingeniously woven together torn asunder, and all the art and labour expended on the natural explanation at once declared useless. Unwillingly does Dr H. E. G. Paulus (1761–1851) admit to himself the presentiment that the reader of his Commentary may possibly exclaim: 'Wherefore all this labour to give an historical explanation to such legends? how singular thus to handle mythi as history, and to attempt to render marvellous fictions intelligible according to the rules of causality!'[8] Contrasted with the toilsomeness of his natural explanation, the mythical interpretation appears to this theologian merely as the refuge of mental indolence, which, seeking the easiest method of treating the gospel history, disposes of all that is marvellous, and all that is difficult to com-

[6] [Johann Gottfried Eichhorn, *Einleitung in das Neuen Testament*, 2nd ed. 3 vols. (Leipzig: Weidmann, 1820, 1810, 1812) 1: para. 6. (Tr.)]

[7] [Hess, *Bibliothek* 2: 251f. (Tr.)]

[8] [Heinrich Eberhard Gottlob Paulus, *Exegetisches Handbuch über die drei ersten Evangelien*. Wohlfeile Ausgabe. 3 parts (Heidelberg: Winter, 1830–3) 1: sec. a: 1 and 71. (Tr.)]

prehend, under the vague term – mythus, and which, in order to escape the labour of disengaging the natural from the supernatural, fact from opinion, carries back the whole narration into the *camera-obscura* of ancient sacred legends.[9]

Still more decided was Johann Christian Greiling's (1765–1840) expression of disapprobation, elicited by Wilhelm Krug's (1770–1842) commendation of the *genetic* – that is to say, mythical theory;[10] but each stroke levelled by him at the mythical interpretation may be turned with far greater force against his own natural explanation. He is of the opinion that among all the attempts to explain obscure passages in the New Testament, scarcely any can be more injurious to the genuine historical interpretation, to the ascertaining of actual facts and their legitimate objects (that is, more prejudicial to the pretensions of the natural expounder) than the endeavour to supply, by aid of an inventive imagination, the deficiencies of the historical narrative. (The inventive imagination is that of the natural interpreter, which suggests to him collateral incidents of which there is no trace in the text. The imagination of the mythical interpreter is not inventive; his part is merely the recognizing and detecting of the fictitious.) According to Greiling the *genetic*, or mythical mode of explaining miracles, is a needless and arbitrary invention of the imagination. (Let a groping spirit of inquiry be added, and the natural explanation is accurately depicted.) Many facts, he continues, which might be retained as such are thus consigned to the province of fable, or replaced by fictions the production of the interpreter. (But it is the *historical* mythical mode of interpretation alone which substitutes such inventions, and this only in so far as it is mixed up with the natural explanation.) Greiling thinks that the explanation of a miracle ought not to change the fact, and by means of interpretation, as by sleight of hand, substitute one thing for another; (which is done by the natural explanation only,) for this is not to explain that which shocks the reason, but merely to deny the fact, and leave the difficulty unsolved. (It is false to say we have a fact to explain; what immediately lies before us is a statement, respecting which we have to discover whether it embody a fact or not.) According to this learned critic the miracles wrought by Jesus should

9 [See above, paragraph 1 [on the relation of the natural to the supernatural]. (Tr.)]

10 [J. C. Greiling, 'Psychologischer Versuch über die psychische Kur des tobsüchtigen Gergaseners', *Museum für Religionswissenschaft in ihrem ganzen Umfange* 1 (1803) 620–54, written as a reaction to an article in the same volume of the *Museum* (pp. 395–413) by Wilhelm Krug entitled 'Versuch über die genetische oder formelle Erklärungs art der Wunder'. (Tr.)]

be naturally, or rather psychologically, explained; by which means all occasion to change, clip, and amplify by invention the recorded facts, till at length they become metamorphosed into fiction, is obviated (with how much justice this censure may be applied to the natural model of explanation has been sufficiently demonstrated).[11]

[Everywhere misunderstanding and circular reasoning characterize the arguments of the rationalists and the supernaturalists against the mythical view.[12] What can one say, for example, about the introduction to Paulus' exegetical handbook, in which he declares joyfully that the Gospel of Luke assures us rightly in its Prologue that the facts reported there are authentic and that the reporter was a careful investigator? What can one say when Paulus confidently poses the hypothetical question – What can be more certain than that we will find no myth in *this* Gospel? Since no one would begin a mythical piece of writing with such a *Foreword*, then only pure facts will be found in Luke's Gospel. This whole way of arguing is destroyed by a simple distinction. Certainly Luke could not speak as he did if he recognized that what he was about to narrate was myth. However, it is entirely possible that he would begin this way if he did not know it was myth. And given the spirit of his age, it is a good probability that he did not know his narrative material was myth. Just as shaky is Paulus' second argument. He reasons that it is inconceivable that Luke, who was true to Paul's theology, would accept myth into his Gospel since his teacher Paul condemned so often and so vehemently Jewish myths (*I Timothy* 1.4; 4.7 and *Titus* 1.14). Even granting the Pauline authorship of the cited letters and the close relationship between Luke and Paul, this argument fails. It is readily evident that the myths condemned in these letters were obviously of a different type from those in the Gospel; the former were debasing offsprings of Jewish or Christian Gnosis and the latter were the most edifying expressions of Christian and Jewish ideas. Simply, Paul's aversion to myth could not keep Luke from accepting into his Gospel mythical narratives that he did not recognize as such. The problem is that Paulus accepts as a definition of myth with regard to the New Testament only *intentional* form (*Einkleidung*). Thus Luke would *have had to be conscious* of accepting myth into his Gospel. Paulus props up one wrong proposition with another even more distorted proposition.

[11] [Greiling, 'Psychologischer Versuch', pp. 621ff. (Tr.)]

[12] [All of the following selection on myth is from the first edition. Some of the arguments here were recast for later editions but the clarity, brevity and irony of the first edition was lost in them. Only the editor's interpolations will be bracketed in the remaining footnotes to Paragraph 12. (Tr.)]

Paulus asserts then that the word myth should not be used to refer to the Gospel history, because if it is to be used here, it would have to have an entirely different connotation than its ordinary and indeed original use conveys.[13] Paulus is right in his definition of ancient classical mythology. In it the presupposition of an intervention of a higher essence into the affairs of humans is not mere form (*Einkleidung*) and it is not a pious deception. It was not as if the ancient human, and especially the writer, knew accurately the visible and natural sources of the facts narrated and then added an account of supersensible causes only in order to ennoble the event. No, all, including the writer, believed so deeply in the existence and the efficacy of the invisible essence that to them it seemed visible. Paulus, however, distinguished the birth narratives in the New Testament from this classical mythology. In the former, the word myth *does* mean form (*Einkleidung*) and refers to the later intentional embellishment of the very earliest and little known events of Jesus' life. This myth in the Gospels cannot as in classical mythology be considered an unconscious, unwilled creation; it must be considered conscious and intentional.

Who grants this famous exegete the right to put forward such a distorted concept of myth – as if myth is the artistic product of an intentional–poetic process? This definition of myth has been rejected by all those who have seriously studied it in the sacred history.[14] Paulus, of course, thinks he has solid reasons. He declares that in ancient classical times the mythical was a product of psychological illusion about the presence of the supersensible, that is, about forces speaking or acting on matter that, however, could properly be explained as due to natural causes. In contrast, the myths found in the New Testament contain the recollections of those living later in history about *past facts* and they therefore cannot be explained as merely delusions about natural causation. But what Paulus gives as evidence for this interpretation of pagan mythology – the inspiration of the poet by the Muses, God speaking in dreams, etc. – are only mythological representations (*Vorstellungen*), not myth proper. These,

[13] [Paulus, *Exegetical Handbuch*, pp. 2ff. (Tr.)]

[14] [See above, para. 8, 'The Rise of the Mythical Mode of Interpretation in Reference to the Old Testament', especially the notes to 'Über Mythen, historische Sagen und Philosopheme der ältesten Welt', in H. E. G. Paulus' *Memorabilien: Ein Philosophische-Theologische Zeitschrift* 5 (1793) part S, pp. 1ff. and Wilhelm Martin Leberecht De Wette, *Kritik der Israelischen Geschichte* Part 1: *Kritik der Mosaischen Geschichte* (Halle: Schimnelpfenning, 1807), Introduction, pp. 10ff. Hess commits the same error as Paulus in this regard when he wants to be able to prove that because the biblical authors want to be properly understood their narratives are not myths. (Tr.)]

for example, the mythical narratives of the Argonauts' expedition of the Trojan war and so forth, Paulus would find hard to explain as psychological illusions of contemporaries. Indeed he would have to understand them then as representations (*Vorstellungen*) of later generations reflecting on past history and thus to treat them just as he does the myth he recognizes in the New Testament.

Hardly worth mentioning is the following argument against myth which is nevertheless often repeated: since Christianity is an historical religion, then one cannot find any myth in its sources. As if our representation of the historical character of Christianity did not have to be determined by the previously discovered character of the sources! This argument presupposes that polytheism is the only form of religion that is mythological; monothesim is anti-mythological. For the people who have myths, everything in religion is a search for a higher, single Godhead. Thus mythological concepts cannot be used in the Old Testament and the New Testament because in them the doctrine of the true God is found.[15] (Certainly, mythology expresses a seeking and a struggling that is not satisfied, but this is not a search for a content (*Inhalt*), which is now found in Christianity, but for a form (*Form*) that of the clear concept (*Begriff*).[16] This clarity of concept was still not present in the first Christian community, and thus, notwithstanding its knowledge of the fundamental religious truths, it could still manifest a need for a mythological presentation (*Darstellung* of that truth).

Another argument is that the alleged mythological narratives in the New Testament are too precise and give too many minute details for any one to have invented them.[17] However, Georg Konrad Horst (1767–1838) has shown that exactly this multiplicity and minuteness of detail in a narrative is characteristic of sagas and poetic creations because the first writer of history is seldom so lucky to receive along with an account of events a description so pure that it was like a painting with the most subtle shading of colors.[18] Moreover, you only

[15] [Christoph Gottlieb Werner, *Geschichtliche auffasung der drei ersten Kapitel des ersten buchs Mose* (Tübingen: Osiander, 1829). (Tr.)]

[16] [This is Strauss' most direct reference to Hegel's philosophy of religion in the introduction to *The Life of Jesus*. He implies agreement with Hegel's assertion that the content of the absolute religion is made present in history with the appearance of Christianity. The form adequate to that content, however, is the philosophical concept and that was not available to ancient Christians. Thus they could express the truth of what is indeed fulfilled religion in mythological form. (Tr.)]

[17] [August Ludwig Christian Heydenreich, *Ueber die Unzulässigkeit der mythischen Auffasung des Historischen im Neuen Testament und im Christenthum*. 2 parts. (Frankfurt: Streng, 1831–33), pt. 1, p. 87. (Tr.)]

[18] [G. K. Horst, 'Über die beyden ersten Kapitel im Evangelium Lukas': *Müseum für Religionswissenschaft* 1 (1803), p. 705. (Tr.)]

have to turn a few pages in the works of the authors of this argument to find the exact opposite argument, that is, that a fictitious legend would not have been accepted into the Scripture because in such everything has to manifest itself expressly and in an embellished way.[19] In these arguments then, the narrative of the evangelists are considered now too expressive, then too little expressive, at one time too precisely delineated even to the smallest detail, at another time not colored enough, to be considered mythical. The opponents of the mythical view know how to make use of opposites. Thus one can see that their own contradiction refutes their position. Moreover, a cogent response to this last argument rests on Matthias Schneckenberger's (1804–1848) work in which he asserts that more or less detailing is to be found in myths according to the period in which they are written.[20] In the primary period healthy products, such as the canonical gospels, marked by an excellent simplicity, appear. In the secondary period, sick offspring, such as the New Testament Apocrypha, marked by the unnatural and the exaggerated appear. More to the point is Friedrich Wilhelm Schelling's (1775–1854) triumphant proclamation against those opposed to the mythological character of ancient sagas: there is no artistry in it, it is much too simple, it makes too meager a hunt for the miraculous, for one to call it a myth. Expressed directly, it is too profane![21]

Karl Heinrich Heydenreich (1764–1801), one of the newest opponents of the mythological view, proposes obsolete arguments against the aversion to the miraculous as the principal source of the older view of the naturalists and the newer view of the mythologists.[22] Moreover, this argument is dangerous for his own supernaturalist position. He calls to mind a forgotten view of the world when he says that the truth that God usually acts mediately on the world does not exclude the possibility that he could take exception to this mode of acting and act immediately on the world if he found it necessary to the accomplishment of a special purpose and referring to each of the divine attributes in succession he shows how such a direct intervention does not contradict any of them. He demonstrates that each single miracle is a peculiarly appropriate exercise of divine power. But Heydenreich goes on, following Johann Gottfried Herder's (1774–1803) example, to consider many miracles to be symbolic examples. He asserts that through the miracles in physical and

[19] [Heydenreich, *Ueber die Unzulässigkeit*, p. 91. (Tr.)]

[20] [Matthias Schneckenburger, *Ueber den Ursprung des ersten kanonischen Evangeliums. Ein kritischer Versuch* (Stuttgart: C. W. Löflund, 1834), p. 72. (Tr.)]

[21] [Cited in Paulus, *Memorabilien*, in the conclusion. (Tr.)]

[22] [Heydenreich, *Ueber die Unzulässigkeit*, pp. 46ff. and 61ff. (Tr.)]

sensible images is presented what Jesus reflects spontaneously in his humanity. When Jesus healed bodily sickness and raised the dead, he was symbolizing the healing of the sick soul and the giving of new life to the morally dead soul and he awakened the desire for spiritual help. Obviously with this interpretation, Heydenreich raises the possibility that the symbolic character of the miracles could be explained by the following: the spirit of the first Christian community attempted to bring to consciousness *precisely* those ideas, but they used a symbolic shell (*Hülle*) of a history that did not actually happen.

The most weighty, or rather the only serious charge, brought against the mythological view by its opponents is that two Gospels were written by eyewitnesses and that the other two were so closely related to eyewitness sources that the inclusion of unhistorical tales in them is unthinkable.[23]

...by New Testament myth are to be understood as nothing other than the history-like forms (*Einkleidungen*) of early Christian ideas (*Ideen*), formulated in sagas without conscious intention in the poetic process.[24]

...Further criteria by which an element of the gospel history could be proven to be myth might well be expected here. Since, however, these principles and criteria could only be abstracted from thoroughly worked out application in individual cases, and since apart from this application these could not be seen with the requisite clarity, it is probably better to interweave their exposition with the course of this investigation....][25]

140. Necessary transition from criticism to dogma

The results of the inquiry which we have now brought to a close, have apparently annihilated the greatest and most valuable part of that which the Christian has been wont to believe concerning his Saviour Jesus, have uprooted all the animating motives which he has gathered from his faith, and withered all his consolations. The boundless store of truth and life which for eighteen centuries has been the aliment of humanity, seems irretrievably dissipated; the most sublime levelled with the dust, God divested of his grace, man of his

[23] [A lengthy refutation of the assertions linking the Gospels directly with eyewitnesses of Jesus' life follows. (Tr.)]

[24] [This is Strauss' own definition of myth put forward at the end of his introduction. (Tr.)]

[25] [The subtle interweaving of which Strauss speaks here gave a power and integrity to the first edition that he himself admits is lost in the later editions. (Tr.)]

dignity, and the tie between heaven and earth broken.[26] Piety turns away with horror from so fearful an act of desecration, and strong in the [illimitable self-certainty (*unendlichen Selbstgewissheit*)] of its faith, pronounces that, let an audacious criticism attempt what it will, all which the scriptures declare, and the Church believes of Christ, will still subsist as eternal truth, nor needs one iota of it to be renounced. Thus at the conclusion of the criticism of the history of Jesus, there presents itself this problem: to re-establish dogmatically that which has been destroyed critically.

At first glance, this problem appears to exist merely as a challenge addressed by the believer to the critic, not as a result of the moral requirements of either. The believer would appear to need no re-establishment of the faith, since for him it cannot be subverted by criticism. The critic seems to require no such re-establishment, since he is able to endure the annihilation resulting from his own labours. Hence it might be supposed that the critic, when he seeks to rescue the dogma from the flames which his criticism has kindled, acts falsely in relation to his own point of view, since, to satisfy the believer, he treats what is valueless for himself as if he esteemed it to be a jewel; while in relation to the believer, he is undertaking a superfluous task, in labouring to defend that which the latter considers in no way endangered.

But on a nearer view the case appears otherwise. To all belief, not built on [scientific knowledge (*Wissen*)], doubt is inherent, though it may be developed; the most firmly believing Christian has within him the elements of criticism as a latent deposit of unbelief, or rather as a negative germ of knowledge (*Keim des Wissens*), and only by its constant repression can he maintain the predominance of his faith, which is thus essentially a re-established faith. And just as the believer is intrinsically a sceptic or critic, so, on the other hand, the critic is intrinsically a believer. In proportion as he is distinguished from the naturalistic theologian, and the free-thinker, – in proportion as his criticism is conceived in the spirit of the nineteenth century, – he is filled with veneration for every religion, and especially for the substance of the sublimest of all religions, the Christian, which he perceives to be identical with the deepest philosophical truth; and hence, after having in the course of his criticism exhibited only the differences between his conviction and the historical belief of the Christian, he will feel urged to place that identity in a just light.[27]

[26] [In the first edition Strauss noted: 'Theologians, who have used similar phrases against me in reviews (of the first volume) see here that I am fully aware of the consequences of my study and do not need to be reminded of them.' (Tr.)]

[27] [Although there is no explicit Hegelian language here, this is an expression of

Further, our criticism, though in its progress it treats of details, yet on becoming part of our internal conviction (*Bewusstsein*), resolves itself into the simple element of doubt, which [the believing consciousness (*das glaubige Bewusstsein*)] neutralizes by an equally simple *veto*, and then spreads anew in undiminished luxuriance all the fullness of his creed. But hereby the decisions of criticism are only dismissed, not vanquished, and that which is believed [is not truly mediated (*vermittelt*) but rather remains in its immediacy (*Unmittelbarkeit*)]. Criticism cannot but direct itself against this [immediacy], and thus the controversy which seemed ended is renewed, and we are thrown back to the beginning of our inquiry; yet with a difference which constitutes a step forward in the discussion. Hitherto our criticism had for its object the [content (*Inhalt*)] of Christianity, as historically presented in the evangelical records; now, [this content] having been called in question in [its] historical form, [assumes] that of a mental product, and finds a refuge in the soul of the believer; where they exist, not as a simple history, but as a reflected history (*in sich reflectirte Geschichte*), that is, a confession of faith, a received dogma. [Against this dogma appearing in its immediacy (*Unmittelbarkeit*), criticism, as a force of negativity and of the struggle for mediation (*Vermittlung*), must certainly arise, just as it must arise against any immediacy. Thus this criticism is no longer historical but rather dogmatic. It is only after faith has passed through both types of criticism that it is truly mediated or that it becomes scientific knowledge (*Wissen*).]

This second process through which the faith has to pass, ought, like the first, to be made the subject of a distinct work: I shall here merely give a sketch of its most important features, that I may not terminate an historical criticism without pointing out its ultimate object, which can only be arrived at by dogmatical criticism as a sequel.

143. The Christology of rationalism

The Rationalists, rejecting the doctrine of the Church concerning Christ, his person, and his work, as self-contradictory, useless, nay, even hurtful to the true morality of the religious sentiment, propounded in its stead a system which, while it avoided all contradictions, yet in a certain sense retained for Jesus the character of a divine manifestation, which even, rightly considered, placed him far higher, and moreover embodies the strongest motives to practical piety.[28]

Strauss' Hegelian purpose – to demonstrate the identity of the content of Christianity as the absolute religion and Hegelian philosophy. (Tr.)]

[28] [Compare with what follows especially Johann Friedrich Röhr, *Briefe über Rationalismus. Zur Berichtigung der schwankenden und zweideutigen Urtheile, die in neuesten*

According to them, Jesus was still a divine messenger, a special favourite and charge of the Deity, inasmuch as, furnished by the disposition of Providence with an extraordinary measure of spiritual endowment, he was born in an age and nation, and guided in a career, the most favourable to his development into that for which he was destined: and, especially, inasmuch as he was subjected to a species of death that rendered possible his apparent resurrection, on which depended the success of his entire work, and was encompassed by a series of circumstances which actually brought that resurrection to pass. The Rationalists hold that their idea of the Christ is not essentially below the orthodox one, as regards his natural endowments and his external destiny, for in their view also he is the greatest man that ever trod the earth – a hero, in whose fate Providence is in the highest degree glorified: while, as regards the internal development and free agency of Jesus, they believe their doctrine essentially to surpass that of the Church. The Christ of the Church, they contend, is a mere automaton, whose manhood lies under the control of his Godhead like a lifeless instrument, which acts with moral perfection because it has no power to sin, and for this reason can neither have moral merit, nor be the object of affection and reverence: according to the rationalistic view, on the contrary, Jesus had implanted in him by God the natural conditions only of that which he was ultimately to become, and his realization of this destiny was the result of his own spontaneity. His admirable wisdom he acquired by the judicious application of his intellectual powers, and the conscientious use of all the aids within his reach; his moral greatness, by the zealous culture of his moral dispositions, the restraint of his sensual inclinations and passions, and a scrupulous obedience to the voice of his conscience: and on these alone rested all that was exalted in his personality, all that was encouraging in his example.

As regards the work of Jesus, the rationalistic view is, that he has endeared himself to mankind by this above all else, that he has taught them a religion to which for its purity and excellence is justly ascribed a certain divine power and dignity; and that he has illustrated and enforced this religion by the brilliant example of his own life. This prophetic office of Christ is with Socinians and Rationalists the essence of his work, and to this they refer all the rest, especially what the doctrine of the Church comprehends under the office of high

dogmatischen Consequenz-Streitigkeiten über denselben gefällt worden sind. (Aachen: J. Frosch, 1813), pp. 372ff. – This work was published anonymously – and Julius August Ludwig Wegscheider, *Institutiones Theologiae Christianae dogmaticae* 7th ed.: (Halle: Sumtibus Librariae Gebaueriae, 1833), para. 128, 133, and 140. (Tr.)]

priest. With them the so-called active obedience has value solely as an example; and the death of Jesus conduces to the forgiveness of sins, solely by furthering the reformation of the sinner in one of these two ways: either, as a confirmation of his doctrine, and a type of the devoted fullfilment of duty, it serves to kindle a zeal for virtue; or, as a proof of the love of God to man, of his inclination to pardon the converted sinner, it invigorates moral courage.[29]

If Christ was no more, and did no more, than this rationalistic doctrine supposes, it is not easy to see how piety has come to make him her special object, or dogmatism to lay down special propositions concerning him. Consistent Rationalists have in fact admitted, that what the orthodox dogma calls Christology, forms no integral part of the rationalistic system, since this system consists indeed of a religion which Christ taught, but not of a religion of which he is the object; that, viewing Christology as the doctrine of the Messiah, it is merely an accommodation to the Jewish mind, – that even taken in a more noble sense, as the doctrine of the life, the actions, and the fate of Jesus as a divine messenger, it does not belong to a system of faith, for the universal truths of religion are as little connected with our ideas concerning the person of him who first enunciated them, as are the philosophical propositions in the systems of Leibnitz and Wolf, of Kant, Fichte, and Schelling, with the opinions we may happen to form of the persons of their authors; that what relates to the person and work of Jesus belongs, not to religion itself, but to the history of religion, and must either be prefixed to a system of religious doctrine as an historical introduction, or appended to it as an elucidatory sequel.[30]

Thus, however, Rationalism enters into open war with the Christian faith, for it seeks to thrust into the background, nay, to banish from the province of theology, that which is its essential point, and corner-stone. But this very opposition is decisive of the insufficiency of the rationalistic system, proving that it does not perform what is demanded from every system of religious doctrine: namely, first, to give adequate expression to the faith which is the object of the doctrine; and secondly, to place this expression in a relation, whether positive or negative, to science. Now the Rationalists, in the effort to bring the faith into harmony with science,

[29] [For the different views, see Carl Gottlieb Bretschneiders' *Handbuch der Dogmatik der evangelisch-lutherischen Kirche*. 3rd. ed. 2 vol. (Leipzig: J. A. Barth, 1828), 2: 353 and *Systematische Entwicklung aller in der Dogmatik vorkommender Begriffe nach den symbolischer Schriften der evangelisch-lutherischen Kirche und den wichtigsten dogmatischen Lehrbüchern ihrer Theologen.* (Leipzig: J. A. Barth, 1819), p. 107. (Tr.)]

[30] [Röhr, *Briefe über Rationalisms*, pp. 36, 405ff. (Tr.)]

restrict its expression; for a Christ who is only a distinguished man creates indeed no difficulty to the understanding, but is not the Christ in whom the Church believes.

145. Christology interpreted symbolically – Kant, De Wette

The attempt to retain in combination the ideal (*Urbildliche*) in Christ with the historical, having failed, these two elements separate themselves: the latter falls as a natural residuum to the ground,[31] and the former rises as a pure sublimate into the ethereal world of ideas. Historically, Jesus can have been nothing more than a person, highly distinguished indeed, but subject to the limitations inevitable to all that is mortal: by means of his exalted character, however, he exerted so powerful an influence over the religious sentiment, that it constituted him the ideal (*Ideal*) of piety; in accordance with the general rule, that an historical fact or person cannot become the basis of a positive religion until it is elevated into the sphere of the ideal (*des Idealen*).[32]

Benedict Spinoza (1632–77) made this distinction when maintaining, that to know the historical Christ is not necessary to felicity, but only to know the ideal Christ, namely, the eternal wisdom of God, which is manifested in all things, in the human mind particularly, and in a preeminent degree in Jesus Christ – that wisdom which alone teaches man what is true and false, good and bad.[33]

According to Immanuel Kant (1724–1804), also, it ought not to be made a condition of salvation to believe, that there was once a man who by his holiness and merit gave satisfaction for himself and for all others; for of this the reason (*die Vernunft*) tells us nothing; but

[31] [The reference here is to the subject matter of paragraph 144, the christology of Friedrich Schleiermacher (1768–1834), the noted theologian who was Hegel's colleague at the University of Berlin. Schleiermacher had asserted that historical science could discover that Jesus had a perfect consciousness of God. This perfection of God-consciousness is the absolute fulfillment of human religiosity making possible fulfillment for all other humans. Thus Christ was both historical and ideal (*Urbildlich*). Strauss held that historical science could not reach the evidence necessary to posit a *perfection* of Jesus' consciousness. (Tr.)]

[32] [Heinrich Schmid, *Ueber Schleiermacher's Glaubenslehre mit Beziehung auf die Reden über die Religion* (Leipzig: F. A. Brockhaus, 1835), p. 267. (Tr.)]

[33] [Benedict Spinoza, Epistle 21 to Oldenburg in *Corpus philosophorum optimae notae, qui ab restauratione litterarum ad Kantium usque floruerunt*, ed. August Friedrich Gfrörer (Stuttgart: J. B. Mezleri, 1830), p. 556: *dico, ad salutem non esse omnino necesse, Christum secundum carnem noscere; sed ed æterno illo filio Dei, h.e. Dei æterna sapientia, quæ sese in omnibus rebus, et maxime in mente humana, et omnium maxime in Christo Jesu manifestavit, longe aliter sentiendum. Nam nemo absque hac ad statum beatitudinis potest pervenire, utpote quæ sola docet, quid verum et falsum, bonum et malum sit.* (Tr.)]

it is the duty of men universally to elevate themselves to the ideal of moral perfection deposited in the reason, and to obtain moral strength by the contemplation of this ideal. Such moral faith alone man is bound to exercise, and not historical faith.[34]

Taking his stand on this principle, Kant proceeds to interpret the doctrines of the Bible and the Church as symbols of the ideal. It is humanity, or the rational part of this system of things, in its entire moral perfection, that could alone make a world the object of divine Providence, and the end of creation. This idea of a humanity well-pleasing to God has existed in God from all eternity; it proceeds from his essence, and is therefore no created thing, but his eternal Son, the Word, through whom, that is, for whose sake, all things were created, and in whom God loved the world. As this idea of moral perfection has not man for its author, as it has been introduced into him even without his being able to conceive how his nature can have been susceptible of such an idea, [the Archetype (*Urbild*)] may be said to have come down to us from heaven, and to have assumed the human nature, and this union with us may be regarded as an abasement of the Son of God. This ideal of moral perfection, so far as it is compatible with the condition of being dependent on necessities and inclinations, can only be conceived by us under the form of a man. Now just as we can obtain no idea of the amount of a force, but by calculating the degree of resistance which it can overcome, so we can form no estimate of the strength of the moral disposition, but by imagining hard conflicts in which it can triumph: hence the man who embodies the perfect ideal must be one who would voluntarily undertake, not only to perform every duty of man on his own behalf, and be precept and example to disseminate the good and the true around him as extensively as possible; but also, though tempted by the strongest allurements, to submit to all sufferings, even to the most ignominious death, for the welfare of mankind.

In a practical relation this idea (*Idee*) has its reality completely within itself, and it needed no exemplification (*Vorbild*) in experience in order to become a model binding on us, since it is enshrined as such in our reason (*Vernunft*). Nay, this ideal (*Urbild*) remains essentially confined to the reason, because it cannot be adequately represented by any example in outward experience, since such an example would not fully disclose the inward disposition, but would only admit of our forming dubious inferences thereon. Nevertheless, as all men ought to be conformed to this ideal, and consequently must-

[34] [Immanuel Kant, *Die Religion innerhalb der Grenzen der blossen Vernunft* (Königsberg: Friedrich Nicolovius, 1794), part 1, section 1, p. vii. (Tr.)]

be capable of such conformity, it is always possible in experience that a man may appear, who in his teaching, course of life, and sufferings, may present an example of a man well-pleasing to God: but even in this manifestation of the God-man, it would not properly be that which is obvious to the sense, or can be known by experience, which would be the object of saving faith; but the ideal lying in the reason, which we should attribute to this manifestation of the God-man, because he appeared to us to be conformed to it – that is, indeed, so far only as this can be concluded from outward experience. Inasmuch as all of us, though naturally generated men, feel bound, and consequently able, ourselves to present such an example, we have no reason to regard that exemplification of the ideal man as supernaturally generated, nor does he need the attestation of miracles; for besides the moral faith in the idea, nothing further is requisite than the historical conviction that his life was conformed to that idea, in order to accredit him as its personification.

He who is conscious of such a moral disposition, as to have a well-founded confidence that under temptations and suffering similar to those which are attributed to the ideal man, as a touchstone of his moral disposition, he would adhere unalterably to this exemplar, and faithfully follow his steps, such a man alone is entitled to consider himself an object of the divine complacency. To elevate himself to such a state of mind, man must depart from evil, cast off the old man, crucify the flesh; a change which is essentially connected with a series of sorrows and sufferings. These the former man has deserved as a punishment, but they fall on the new: for the regenerated man, who takes them on himself, though physically and in his empirical character, as a being determined by the senses, he remains the former man; is morally, as an intellectual being, with his changed disposition, become a new man. Having by this change taken upon him the disposition of the son of God, that which is strictly a substitution of the new man for the old, may be represented, by a personification of the idea, as a substitution of the Son of God, and it may be said, that the latter himself, as a substitute, bears for man, for all who practically believe in him, the guilt of sin; as a redeemer, satisfies supreme justice by suffering and death; and as an intercessor, imparts the hope of appearing justified before the judge: the suffering which the new man, in dying to the old, must perpetually incur through life, being conceived in the representative of mankind, as a death suffered once for all.[35]

[35] [*Ibid.*, part 2, Division 1, part 3, section 1. (Tr.)]

Kant, like Friedrich Schleiermacher (1768–1834) (whose Christology in many respects recalls that of Kant),[36] carries his appropriation of the Christology of the Church no farther than the death of Christ: of his resurrection and ascension, he says, that they cannot be available to religion within the limits of reason alone (*blossen Vernunft*), because they would involve the materiality of all existences. Still, in another light, he employs these facts as symbols of the ideas of the reason; as images of the entrance into the abode of blessedness, that is, into communion with all the good: while Johann Heinrich Tieftrunk (1759–1837) has yet more decidedly given it as his opinion, that without the resurrection, the history of Jesus would terminate in a revolting catastrophe; that the eye would turn away with melancholy and dissatisfaction from an event, in which the pattern of humanity fell a victim to impious rage, and in which the scene closed with a death as unmerited as sorrowful; that the history requires to be crowned with the fulfilment of the expectation towards which the moral contemplations of every one are irresistibly drawn – with the passage into a compensating immortality.[37]

In the same manner, Wilhelm M. L. De Wette (1780–1849) ascribed to the evangelical history, as to every history, and particularly to the history of religion, a symbolical, ideal character, in virtue of which it is the expression and image of the human mind and its various operations. The history of the miraculous conception of Jesus represents the divine origin of religion; the narratives of his miracles, the independent force of the human mind, and the sublime doctrine of spiritual self-reliance; his resurrection is the image of the victory of truth, a foreshadowing of the future triumph of good over evil; his ascension, the symbol of the eternal majesty of religion. The fundamental religious ideas which Jesus enunciated in his teaching, are expressed with equal clearness in his history. This history is an expression of devoted enthusiasm, in the courageous ministry of Jesus, and in the victorious power of his appearance; of resignation, in his contest with the wickedness of men, in the melancholy of his premonitory discourses, and above all in his death. Christ on the cross is the image of humanity purified by self-sacrifice; we ought all to crucify ourselves with him, that we may rise with him to new life.

[36] [This is shown by F. C. Baur, in *Die christliche Gnosis; oder*, *Die christliche Religions-Philosophie in ihrer geschichtlichen Entwicklung* (Tübingen: Osiander, 1835), pp. 660ff. (Tr.)]

[37] [Johann Heinrich Tieftrunk, *Censur des christlichen protestantischen Lehrbegriffs nach den Principien der Religionskritik* 2nd ed.: 3 parts (Berlin: Königl. Preussichen Akad. Kunst- und Buchhandlung, 1794–6), 3: 180. (Tr.)]

Lastly, the idea of devotion was the keynote in the history of Jesus, every moment of his life being dedicated to the thought of his heavenly Father.[38]

At an earlier period, Horst presented this symbolical view of the history of Jesus with singular clearness. Whether, he says, all that is narrated of Christ happened precisely so, historically, is a question indifferent to us, nor can it now be settled. Nay, if we would be candid with ourselves, that which was once sacred history for the Christian believer, is, for the enlightened portion of our contemporaries, only fable: the narratives of the supernatural birth of Christ, of his miracles, of his resurrection and ascension, must be rejected by us as at variance with the inductions of our intellect. Let them however only be no longer interpreted merely by the understanding as history, but by the feelings and imagination, as poetry; and it will be found that in these narratives nothing is invented arbitrarily, but all springs from the depths and divine impulses of the human mind. Considered from this point of view, we may annex to the history of Christ all that is important to religious trust, animating to the pure dispositions, attractive to the tender feelings. That history is a beautiful, sacred poem of the human race – a poem in which are embodied all the wants of our religious instinct; and this is the highest honour of Christianity, and the strongest proof of its universal applicability. The history of the gospel is in fact the history of human nature conceived ideally, and exhibits to us in the life of an individual, what man ought to be, and, united with him by following his doctrine and example, can actually become. It is not denied that what to us can appear only sacred poetry, was to Paul, John, Matthew and Luke, fact and certain history. But it was the very same internal cause which made the narratives of the gospel sacred fact and history to them, which makes those narratives to us a sacred mythus and poetry. The points of view only are different: human nature, and in it the religious impulse, remains ever the same. Those first Christians needed in their world, for the animating of the religious and moral dispositions in the men of their time, history and fact, of which, however, the inmost kernel consisted of ideas: to us, the facts are become superannuated

38 [Wilhelm Martin Leberecht de Wette, *Ueber Religion und Theologie. Erlaüterung zu seinem Lehrbuche der Dogmatik*. 2nd ed. (Berlin: Reimer, 1821), second section, Chapter 3. Compare this with W. M. L. de Wette, *Lehrbuch der christliche Dogmatik, in ihrer historischen Entwicklung dargestellt.* Part I: *Biblische Dogmatik Alten und Neuen Testaments; oder kritische Darstellung der Religionslehre des Hebräismos, des Judenthums und Urchristenthums* and Part II: *Dogmatik der evangelisch-Lutherischen Kirche nach den symbolischen Buchern und dem älteren Dogmatikern*, 3rd ed. (Berlin, Reimer: 1831) I, para. 255 and II, para. 64ff. (Tr.)]

and doubtful, and only for the sake of the fundamental ideas, are the narratives of those facts an object of reverence.[39]

This view was met immediately on the part of the Church by the reproach, that instead of the riches of divine reality which faith discovers in the history of Christ, is palmed upon us a collection of empty ideas (*Ideen*) and ideals (*Ideale*); instead of a consolatory work effected (*Sein*), an overwhelming obligation (*Sollen*). For the certainty, that God once actually united himself with human nature, the admonition that man ought to obtain divine dispositions, offers a poor compensation: for the peace which the redemption completed by Christ brings to the believer, it is no equivalent to put before him the duty of freeing himself from sin. By this system, man is thrust out of the reconciled world in which Christianity places him, into an unreconciled world, out of a world of happiness into a world of misery; for where reconciliation has yet to be effected, where happiness has yet to be attained, there is at present enmity and unhappiness. And, in truth, the hope of entire deliverance from these conditions, is, according to the principles of this system, which only admits an infinite approximation towards the idea, a deceptive one; for that which is only to be reached in an endless progression, is in fact unattainable.

But not faith alone, [scientific knowledge (*Wissenschaft*)] also in its newest development, has found this system unsatisfactory. [Scientific knowledge (*Wissenschaft*)] has perceived that to convert ideas simply into an obligatory possibility (*blossen Sollen*), to which no reality (*Sein*) corresponds, is in fact to annihilate (*aufheben*) them; just as it would be to render the infinite finite, to represent it as that which lies beyond the finite. [Scientific knowledge (*Wissenschaft*)] has conceived that the infinite has its existence in the alternate production and extinction (*im Setzen und Wiederaufheben*) of the finite; that the idea is realized only in the entire series of its manifestations; that nothing can come into existence which does not already essentially (*an sich*) exist; and, therefore, that it is not to be required of man, that he should reconcile himself with God, and assimilate his sentiments to the divine, unless this reconciliation and this assimilation are already virtually effected (*an sich shon vollbracht ist*).

39 [See G. K. Horst 'Ideen über Mythologie' in *Neues Magazin für Religionsphilosophie, Exegesis und Kirchengeschichte* 6 (1802), 454ff. Compare with the material in *Museum* 3 (1806–9), 455. (Tr.)]

146. The speculative Christology[40]

Kant had already said that the good principle did not descend from heaven merely at a particular time, but had descended on mankind invisibly from the commencement of the human race; and Schelling laid down the proposition: the incarnation of God is an incarnation from eternity.[41] But while the former understood under that expression only the moral instinct, which, with its ideal of good (*Ideal*), and its sense of duty (*Sollen*), has been from the beginning implanted in man; the latter understood under the incarnate Son of God the finite itself, in the form of the human consciousness, which in its contradistinction to the infinite, wherewith it is nevertheless one, appears as a suffering God, subjected to the conditions of time.

In the most recent philosophy this idea has been further developed in the following manner.[42] When it is said of God that he is [Spirit (*Geist*)], and of man that he also is [Spirit (*Geist*)], it follows that the two are not essentially distinct. [It is the essential characteristic of Spirit to remain identical with itself in the distinction (*Unterscheidung*) of itself from itself, that is, to possess itself in others. Thus, to speak more precisely, it is given with the recognition of God as Spirit that God does not remain as a fixed and immutable infinite (*Unendliche*) outside of and above the finite (*Endlichen*) but enters into it, posits finitude, nature, and human spirit, merely as his alienation (*Entäusserung*) of self from which he eternally returns again into unity with himself.] As man, considered as a finite spirit, limited to his finite nature, has not truth; so God, considered exclusively as an infinite spirit, shut up in his infinitude, has not reality (*Wirklichkeit*). The infinite spirit is real only when it discloses itself in finite spirits; as the finite spirit is true only when it merges itself in the infinite. The true and real existence (*Dasein*) of spirit, therefore, is neither in God by himself (*für sich*), nor in man by himself (*für sich*), but in the God-man; neither in the infinite alone, nor in the finite alone, but

[40] [This should have been titled Hegelian christology. Here the editor has altered Eliot's translation to make the Hegelian position more evident. (Tr.)]

[41] [Friedrich Wilhelm Joseph Schelling, *Vorlesungen über die Methode des akademischen Studiums*. (Tübingen: J. G. Cotta, 1803), p. 192. (Tr.)]

[42] [G. W. F. Hegel, *Die Phänomenologie des Geistes* (Bamberg & Würzberg, J. A. Goebhardt, 1807), pp. 561ff. and *Vorlesungen über der Philosophie der Religion*, ed. Phillipp Marheinecke, in (18 vols.) *Werke: Vollständige Ausgabe durch einen Verein von Freunden des Verewigten* 2 vols. (Berlin: Duncker and Humblot, 1832) 2: 234ff.; Philipp Marheineke, *Die Grundlehren der christlichen Dogmatik als Wissenschaft* 2nd ed. (Berlin: Duncker und Humblot, 1827), pp. 174ff.; and Karl Rosenkranz, *Encyclopädie der Theologischen Wissenschaft* (Halle: C. A. Schwetschke, 1831), pp. 38ff. and 148ff. (Tr.)]

in the interchange of impartation and withdrawal between the two, which on the part of God is revelation, on part of man religion.

If God and man are in themselves one, and if religion is the [developing consciousness (*Bewusstsein*) of this unity]: then must this unity be made evident to man in religion, and become in him consciousness and reality. Certainly, so long as man knows not that he is a spirit, he cannot know that God is man: while he is under the guidance of nature only, he will deify nature; when he has learned to submit himself to law, and thus to regulate his natural tendencies by external means, he will set God before him as a lawgiver. But when, in the vicissitudes of the world's history, the natural state discloses its corruptions, the legal its misery; the former will experience the need of a God who elevates it above itself, the latter, of a God who descends to its level. Man being once mature enough to receive as his religion the truth that God is man, and man of a divine race; it necessarily follows, since religion is the form in which the truth presents itself to the popular mind, that this truth must appear, in a guise intelligible to all, [as sense certainty (*sinnliche Gewissheit*)]: in other words, there must appear a human individual who is recognized as the visible God. This God-man uniting in a single being the [otherwordly (*jenseitige*)] divine essence and the [earthly (*diesseitige*)] human personality, it may be said of him that he has the Divine Spirit for a father, and a woman for his mother. His personality reflecting itself not in himself, but in the absolute substance, having the will to exist only for God, and not at all for itself, he is sinless and perfect. As a man of Divine essence, he is the power that subdues nature, a worker of miracles; but as God in a human manifestation, he is dependent on nature, subject to its necessities and sufferings – is in a state of abasement. Must he even pay the last tribute to nature? Does not the fact that the human nature is subject to death preclude the idea that that nature is one with the Divine? No: the God-man dies, and thus proves that the incarnation of God is real, that the infinite spirit does not scorn to descend into the lowest depths of the finite, because he knows how to find a way of return into himself, because in the most entire alienation (*Entäusserung*) of himself, he can retain his identity. Further, the God-man, in so far as he is a spirit reflected in his infinity, stands contrasted with men, in so far as they are limited to their finiteness: hence opposition and contest result, and the death of the God-man becomes a violent one, inflicted by the hands of sinners; so that to physical degradation is added the moral degradation of ignominy and accusation of crime. If God then finds a passage from heaven to the grave, so must a way be discoverable for man from the grave to heaven: the death of the prince of life is the life of mortals. By his entrance into the world as God-man, God showed himself reconciled [with the world]; by his dying, in which act he cast off [his state of naturalness (*Natürlichkeit*)], he showed moreover the way in which he perpetually effects that reconciliation: namely, [by remaining identical with himself throughout his alienation into the natural state and his subsequent sublation (*Wiederaufhebung*) of the same]. Inasmuch as the death of the God-man is merely the [sublation (*Aufhebung*) of his alienation and lowliness], it is in fact an exaltation and return to God, and thus the death is necessarily followed by the resurrection and ascension.

The God-Man, who during his life stood before his contemporaries as an individual distinct from themselves, and perceptible by the senses, is by death taken out of their sight; he enters into their [representation (*Vorstellung*)] and memory; the unity of the divine and human in him, becomes part of the general consciousness; and the [community (*Gemeinde*)] must repeat spiritually, in the souls of its members, those events of his life which he experienced externally. The believer, finding himself environed with the conditions of nature, must, like Christ, die to nature – but only inwardly, as Christ did outwardly, – must spiritually crucify himself and be buried with Christ, [that through the sublation (*Aufhebung*) of the natural state (*Natürlichkeit*) he may become identical with himself as Spirit], and participate in the bliss and glory of Christ.

147. Last dilemma

Thus by a higher mode or argumentation, from the [concept (*Begriff*)] of God and man in their reciprocal relation, the truth of the [representation (*Vorstellung*)] which the Church forms of Christ appears to be confirmed, and we seem to be reconducted to the orthodox point of view, though by an inverted path: for while there, the truth of the conceptions (*Begriffen*) of the Church concerning Christ is deduced from the correctness of the evangelical history; here, the veracity of the history is deduced from the truth of those conceptions. That which is rational (*das Vernünftige*) is also real (*wirklich*); the idea (*die Idee*) is not merely the moral imperative (*Sollen*) of Kant, but also an actuality (*ein Sein*). Proved to be an idea of the reason (*Vernunftidee*), the unit of the divine and human nature must also have an historical existence (*Dasein*). The unity of God with man, says Philipp Conrad Marheineke (1780–1846), was really and visibly manifested (*offenbar und wirklich als ein Geschehensein*) in the person of Jesus Christ;[43] in him, according to Karl Rosenkranz

[43] [Marheineke, *Dogmatik*, para. 326. Marheineke, a professor of theology in Berlin from 1811, was the most famous of the Hegelian theologians. Strauss heard him

(1805–79), the divine power over nature was concentrated, he could not act otherwise than miraculously, and the working of miracles, which surprises us, was to him natural.[44] His resurrection, says Kasimir Conradi (1784–1849), is the necessary sequel to the completion of his personality, and so little ought it to surprise us, that, on the contrary, we must rather have been surprised if it had not happened.[45]

But do these deductions remove the contradictions which have exhibited themselves in the doctrine of the Church, concerning the person and work of Christ? We need only compare the strictures, which Rosenkranz in his Review has passed on Schleiermacher's criticism of the Christology of the Church, with what the same author proposes as a substitute in his *Encyclopaedia*, in order to perceive, that the general propositions on the unity of the divine and human natures, do not in the least serve to explain the appearance of a person, in whom this unity existed individually, in an exclusive manner (*auf ausschliessende Weise individuell*). Though I may conceive that the divine spirit in a state of [alienation (*Entäusserung*)] and abasement becomes the human, and that the human nature in its return into and above itself becomes the divine; this does not help me to conceive more easily, how the divine and human natures can have constituted the distinct and yet united portions of an historical person. Though I may see the human mind in its unity with the divine, in the course of the world's history, more and more completely establish itself as the power which subdues nature; this is quite another thing, than to conceive a single (*einen einzelnen*) man endowed with such power, for individual (*einzelne*), voluntary acts. Lastly, from the truth, that [the sublated natural state (*die aufgehobene Natürlichkeit*)] is the resurrection of the spirit, can never be deduced the bodily resurrection of an individual (*Individuums*).

We should thus have fallen back again to Kant's point of view, which we have ourselves found unsatisfactory; for if the idea (*Idee*) have no corresponding reality (*Wirklichkeit*), it is an empty obligation and ideal (*Sollen und Ideal*). But do we then deprive the idea of all

lecture and felt that he did not solve the problem of whether Hegel intended to assert that the historical accuracy of the gospel narratives belonged to the essential content of Christianity and thus was necessitated by the philosophical content or whether the assertion of historical truth was merely part of the *form* of the religious representation. See Strauss, *Streitschriften* 3: p. 57. (Tr.)]

44 [Rosenkranz, *Encyclopädie*, p. 160. Karl Rosenkranz was a Hegelian philosopher at Königsberg who became Hegel's biographer. Strauss, although differing from Rosenkranz, respected him as did Arnold Ruge. (Tr.)]

45 [Kasimir Conradi, *Selbstbewusstseyn und Offenbarung, oder Entwickelung des religiösen Bewusstseyns* (Mainz: F. Kupferberg, 1831), pp. 295f. (Tr.)]

reality? By no means: we reject only that which does not follow from the premises. If reality (*Realität*) is ascribed to the idea of the unity of the divine and human natures, is this equivalent to the admission that this unity must actually have been once manifested, as it never had been, and never more will be, in one individual (*in einem Individuum*)? This is indeed not the mode in which Idea realizes itself (*die Idee sich realisirt*); it is not wont to lavish all its fullness on one exemplar (*in ein Exemplar*), and be niggardly towards all others: it rather loves to distribute its riches among a multiplicity of exemplars which reciprocally complete each other – [in the alternate positing and sublating of individuals (*im Wechsel sich setzender und wieder aufhebender Individuen*)]. And is this no true realization of the idea (*Wirklichkeit der Idee*)? Is not the idea of the unity of the divine and human natures a real one in a far higher sense, when I regard the whole race of mankind as its [actualization (*Verwirklichung*)], than when I single out one man as such a realization? is not an incarnation of God from eternity, a truer one than an incarnation limited to a particular point of time?

This is the key to the whole of Christology, that, as subject of the predicate which the Church assigns to Christ, we place, instead of an individual, an idea (*statt eines Individuums eine Idee*); but an idea which has an existence in reality, not in the mind only, like that of Kant. In an individual (*einem Individuum*), a God-man, the properties and functions which the Church ascribes to Christ contradict themselves; [in the idea of the human species (*der Idee der Gattung*)], they perfectly agree.[46] Humanity is the union of the two natures – [the incarnate God, the infinite Spirit alienated (*entäusserte*) in the finite and the finite Spirit recollecting (*sich erinnerde*) its infinitude]; it is the child of the visible Mother and the invisible Father, Nature and Spirit; it is the worker of miracles, in so far as in the course of human history the spirit more and more completely subjugates nature, both within and around man, until it lies before him as the inert matter on which he exercises his active power. [Humanity is the sinless one because the course of its development is blameless. Pollution cleaves to the individual only; in the human species and its history, pollution is sublated.] It is Humanity that dies, rises, and ascends to heaven, for from the [negation of its natural state (*Negation ihrer Natürlichkeit*)]

[46] [Here Strauss is following the movement of Hegel's Logic. Strauss replaces traditional logic's syllogism, whose members are the particular, the individual, and the universal with speculative thought's syllogism whose members are Nature, Spirit, and Idea. The Idea is the Idea of life; it is given 'a reality that is itself simple universality' in the *species*. See G. W. F. Hegel, *Hegel's Logic*, trans. William Wallace (Oxford: Clarendon Press, 1975), pp. 281–2. (Tr.)]

there ever proceeds a higher spiritual life; [from the sublation of its finitude] as a personal, national, and terrestrial spirit, arises its union with the infinite spirit of the heavens. By faith in this Christ, especially in his death and resurrection, man is justified before God: that is, by the kindling within him of the idea of Humanity, the individual man participates in the divinely human (*gottmenschlichen*) life of the species. Now the main element of that idea is, that the negation of the [natural state (*Natürlichkeit*)], which is itself the negation of the spirit, (the negation of negation, therefore,) is the sole way to true spiritual life.

This alone is the [absolute content (*Inhalt*)] of Christology: that it is annexed to the person and history of one individual, is a necessary result of the historical form which Christology has taken.[47] [That this content appears joined together with the person and history of one individual (*eines Einzelnen*) has only subjective bases: (1) This individual through his personality and his fate became the *occasion* for the elevation of that content into the universal consciousness (*das allgemeine Bewusstsein*), and (2) the stage of the spirit of the ancient world and of the people of that time could perceive (*anschauen*) the *idea of humanity* only in the concrete figure of an individual. In a time of the deepest inner strife (*Zerrissenheit*) and of the most extreme bodily and spiritual need, a pure individual revered as a divine messenger, sank down into suffering and death, and soon belief in his resuscitation developed. Then it must occur to everyone that this matter is of personal import, and Christ appear as the one who, as Clement of Alexandria said in a somewhat different sense, 'takes on himself the drama of Humanity'. If, in his suffering the external necessity which oppressed humanity was concentrated and the internal strife was illustrated, then in his resuscitation lay the consolation that does not lose itself, but rather preserves itself, in such sufferings of the spirit. That consolation does not deny itself through the negation of the natural state but affirms itself in a higher manner. If God willed his prophet, indeed his loved one and son, to undergo such misery because of the sins of humanity, then also this most extreme limit of finitude was recognized as a moment in the divine

[47] [This section was deleted from subsequent editions. It is important to Strauss' Hegelian position because it links, as Feuerbach was to do later, the limitations of religious *Vorstellungen* with a subjective, non-universal stance. Indeed Strauss does assert that scientific knowledge (what Feuerbach called objective knowledge) recognized the divine attributes of Christ as belonging to the human species. The difference between this 1835 conclusion of *The Life of Jesus* and the 1839 *Essence of Christianity* by Feuerbach is that Strauss does grant with Hegel that the subjective religious standpoint possesses the truth in a popular form while Feuerbach denies truth to the religious standpoint. (Tr.)]

life, and the human oppressed by necessity and sin learned to feel himself taken up into the divine freedom. The early Christian community formed its image of Christ just as the God of Plato formed the world looking at the ideas. Stimulated through the person and fate of Jesus, it framed the picture of its Christ, having in mind unconsciously the idea of humanity in its relationship to Divinity.

The scientific knowledge of our time, however, can no longer repress the consciousness, that the tie of the content of Christology to one individual belongs to a temporally and culturally conditioned form of this doctrine. Schleiermacher was quite right when he foreboded that the speculative view would not leave much more of the historical person of the Saviour than was retained by the Ebionites.[48] The phenomenal history of the individual, says Hegel, is only a starting point for the [Spirit (*Geist*)]. Faith, in her early stages, is governed by the senses, and therefore contemplates a temporal history; what she holds to be true is the external, ordinary event, the evidence for which is of the historical, forensic kind – a fact to be proved by [sense certainty (*sinnliche Gewissheit*)], and the moral confidence inspired by the witnesses. But mind having once taken occasion by this external fact, to bring under its consciousness the idea of humanity as one with God, [perceives (*anschaut*) the movement of this idea in that history); the object of faith is completely changed; instead of a sensible, empirical fact, it has become a spiritual and divine idea, which has its confirmation no longer in history but in philosophy. When the mind has thus gone beyond the sensible history, and entered into the domain of the absolute, [the former will be sublated (*aufgehoben*) as the essential and placed at a subordinate level], above which the spiritual truths suggested by the history stand self-supported; it becomes as the faint image of a dream which belongs of the spirit which is absolutely present to itself.[49] Even Luther subordinated the physical miracles to the spiritual, to the truly great sick people in Galilee, than in the miracles of intellectual and moral life belonging to the history of the world – in the increasing, the almost incredible dominion of man over nature – in the irresistible force of ideas, to which no unintelligent matter, whatever its magnitude, can oppose any enduring resistance? Shall isolated incidents, in themselves trivial, be more to us than the universal order of events, simply because in the latter we presuppose, if we do not perceive, a natural cause, in the former the contrary? This would be a direct contravention of the more enlightened

[48] [Friedrich Schleiermacher, *Zweites Sendschrieben in Sammlung zerstreuter, theologischer Aufsätze des Freidrich Schleiermacher* (Reutlingen, 1830) (Tr.)]

[49] [Hegel, *Philosophie der Religion* 2: pp. 263ff. (Tr.)]

sentiments of our own day, justly and conclusively expressed by Schleiermacher. The interests of piety, says this theologian, can no longer require us so to conceive a fact, that by its dependence on God it is divested of the conditions which would belong to it as a link in the chain of nature [would be sublated]; for we have outgrown the notion, that the divine omnipotence is more completely manifested in the interruption of the order of nature, than in its preservation. Thus if we know the incarnation, death and resurrection, the *duplex negatio affirmat*, as the eternal circulation, the infinitely repeated pulsation of the divine life; what special importance can attach to a single fact, which is but a mere sensible image of this unending process? Our age demands to be led in Christology to the idea (*Idee*) in the fact (*Factum*), to the [species (*Gattung*)] in the individual (*Individuum*): a theology which, in its doctrines on the Christ, stops short at him as an individual, is not properly a theology, but a homily.

II
August von Cieszkowski
1814–1894

August von Cieszkowski

In 1835, Strauss' *Life of Jesus* recast Hegelianism into a radically new role: that of an unorthodox and critical philosophy. Three years later, Cieszowski's *Prolegomena to Historiosophy* completely re-orientated Hegelianism, transforming it from a doctrine considered to be merely retrospective and theoretical into a program cf fundamental social change. Prior to the *Prolegomena*, Hegelian categories had been exercised upon the analysis of the historical past, but this work revealed that it was possible to apply Hegelianism to the interpretation and construction of future history. The Owl of Minerva which had set forth at the twilight of an age had been dialectically transformed into the Eagle of Apollo[1] – flying into the dawning sun of a new age. The *Prolegomena* marked the change from impotent theory to world-revolutionizing praxis, from philosophic contemplation to social action. It became a seminal work upon which later Young Hegelians – such as Karl Marx and Moses Hess – and later political activists – such as Alexander Herzen – were to develop their plans for the rationalization of the real.

Cieszkowski envisioned his task to be the correction of two fundamental mistakes in Hegelianism: its undialectical articulation of the moments of world history, and its disregard for the future. In place of the unseemly four-fold passage of world history set out of Hegel – the Oriental, Greek, Roman, and Christian-Germanic – Cieszkowski proposes a proper triadic paradigm: Antiquity, Christianity, and the Future. These three moments were dialectically entailed, with the *feeling* of antiquity passing into the antithesis of Christian *thought*, and then both fusing into a future of *praxis* – of activity incorporating both the ancient feeling of beauty with the wisdom of Christianity.

Here, just as in the case of all Young Hegelians, Cieszkowski sought to carry forth what he considered to be the veridical principle of Hegelianism even if it meant confuting Hegel himself. In this regard, a recent remark concerning Strauss is appropriate – that being 'more courageous than Hegel, Strauss is the better Hegelian'.[2] Undoubtedly, Cieszkowski, with

[1] [For a brief history of this unique conceit, i.e, the transformation of Hegel's Owl of Minerva into either a rooster heralding 'a newly breaking day' or an eagle seeking the sun see Stuke's *Philosophie der Tat*, p. 64. (Ed.)]

[2] [John T. Noonan, 'Hegel and Strauss: The Dialectic and The Gospels', *Catholic Biblical Quarterly*, XII, No. 2 (Apr. 1950), p. 144. (Ed.)]

similar thoughts, must have considered his revision of Hegel to have made him 'the better Hegelian'.

Cieszkowski, with the respect and leisure granted to him in virtue of being a Polish nobleman, soon turned from philosophical interests to matters more literary and political, and eventually became the least 'young' of the Young Hegelians. He never suffered the social and financial difficulties which beset all of the others. In 1838, he moved to Paris, and there associated with a number of French political radicals, such as J. P. Proudhon and V. Considerant, and even encountered Karl Marx – a meeting which left both apparently unimpressed. In Paris he wrote *Du crédit et de la circulation* (1839), a treatise on monetary reform, and *De la pairie et de l'aristocratie moderne* (1844) on legislative reform. In 1842, he wrote *Gott und Palingenesie* as a rebuttal of Karl L. Michelet's views regarding Divine personality and personal immortality, but shortly joined Michelet in establishing the Berlin *Philosophische Gesellschaft* – a pro-Hegelian society which endured into the 1890s. In 1848, Cieszkowski returned to Prussia to defend Polish political interests, but by the 1860s, tiring of politics, he retired in Prussian Poland[3] to devote himself to what he considered to be his greatest work, the *Our Father*, a series of volumes – left unfinished at his death – which sought to prove that the Lord's Prayer was actually but a concealed prophecy that foretold of a future age of harmony and love among men. At his death, he was mourned as one of Poland's most honored personages – a public mourning that was far different from the unmarked passages of his fellow Young Hegelians.

The following section from the work of Cieszkowski is the third chapter of his *Prolegomena to Historiosophy*. It is here, for the first time, translated in its entirety by Professor André Liebich, who followed, in part, an earlier draft by Mr Michael Malloy.

All footnotes, unless otherwise indicated, are those given by Cieszkowski. Bracketed numerals refer to the pagination of the original edition, published in Berlin by Veit und Co., 1838.

For the reader who might wish to know more of Cieszkowski, no better work can be recommended than Liebich's *Between Ideology and Utopia: The Politics and Philosophy of August Cieszkowski* (Dordrecht: D. Reidel, 1979); and for those wishing to read more of Cieszkowski a representative selection is now available in Professor Liebich's *Selected Writings of August Cieszkowski* (Cambridge University Press, 1979).

[3] [Cieszkowski's return to Prussia and then to Poland suggests that he moved from one place to another. In fact, he settled in Poznań, the Polish part of the Prussian crown lands, in the 1840s and remained there until his death. (Ed.)]

Prolegomena to Historiosophie

CHAPTER 3
TELEOLOGY OF WORLD HISTORY

> The Spirit aids! From anxious scruples freed
> I write: in the *end* will be the deed!
>
> Goethe

...[78] The teleology of world history also must pass through a course of development and establish the determinate stages of the idea particularly and by degrees. Here we must again seek to discern the organic structure of these stages; that is, the completely speculative course of the teleology.

The idea in its immediacy – in its first externally natural form – is the idea of the beautiful and of art. This is quite correctly comprehended by Hegel in the doctrine of the absolute spirit, although not logically derived with such [79] clarity. This immediacy remains the true place of the beautiful and of art, even if one later tried, as for example Weisse did, to assign another place to their idea, and even if on the other hand one wanted to view the idea of beauty as the speculative unity of the idea of the true and the good, thus as the synthesis of the theoretical and the practical. That error, arising from the wish to vindicate the priority of thinking, insists that beauty must have truth as its precondition. In fact, the situation is quite the reverse, for truth is a further and higher determination, though standing in opposition to the first. This has already been quite correctly shown by Hegel in the passage from art to philosophy. The second error, however, undoubtedly originated from the misunderstanding of what Hegel says in the *Aesthetics*, where he characterizes the beautiful as the union of the two viewpoints of the finite intelligence and the finite will, which it really is, but the beautiful is only this, and in no way the unity of the absolutely true and good. In other words, this conception is still to a certain extent correct if it takes the beautiful to be such a [80] unity, but with the difference that this is an immediate, undeveloped and therefore thetical unity, but in no way a synthetic and absolutely mediated one. This unity is only in-itself; it constitutes only a natural indifference which still has not undergone the process of differentiation.

Therefore, it is the essence of the idea to establish the idea of the beautiful as the first stage of the teleological process of world history. Its more specific determination is in world-historical terms: culture, humanity, the aesthetic formation of the human race. The first thinker who fixed the teleological standpoint of history also came forward at the same time with these concepts. Even if the idea of culture was established prior to Herder by Iselin, it occurred in such an indeterminate way that only an honourable mention can be given him as his share in the presentation of the development of historical teleology. But what Iselin brought into world history indeterminately, abstractly, and at the same time instinctively, Herder has distinctly, concretely and consciously brought through the empirical stuff of world history, until at last Schiller brought it out speculatively and entirely ideally – and, in [81] bringing it out, at the same time brought it forward to a higher and broader standpoint. Before we proceed to this second thinker, we must briefly make ourselves familiar with the significance of the first.

Since art constitutes the first reconciliation of the spirit with nature and generally of the radical and fundamental opposition within the universe, the aesthetic formation and humanity, corresponding to it in world history is the first determination of mankind. That is the core of the Schillerian and Herderian world view, which is itself entirely consciously expressed in Schiller.[1] The absolute demand of this standpoint is the reconciliation, already really synthetic, which accords to both sides of the opposition their due – 'hence it should always express a deficient development, if the moral character maintains itself only by the sacrifice of the natural'.[2] This reconciliation meanwhile, even if already absolute, but yet the first and most immediate in this absoluteness, must bring itself into existence in the form of the natural particularity. [82] It could not happen otherwise for the philosophers of 'immediate knowledge' which starts from 'perceived truth' and from 'belief, as a result of experience, which reason has to obey', just as for the poet-philosopher, whose philosophical world view always had to form itself poetically and artistically. The 'coincidence of opposites' is admittedly taken at this stage as the culmination point of history, but, as the expression itself shows, it is affected with contingency and particularity. That is, it is only coincidence, but in no way a speculative identity. Therefore, this unity is made and found in experience in a natural and sensible way. Cultural formation is merely the cultural formation of partic-

[1] In his so very important, and yet – in this important respect – often misunderstood work *Concerning the Aesthetic Education of Man.*

[2] *Aesthetic Education*, Letter 4; *Outlines of a Philosophy of the History of Man.*

ulars. This is why Herder, disregarding the substantiality of the state, deals only with individual humanity. This is why the further development of mankind into this humanity has been treated as accidental, as one which could really have happened otherwise; but if man enters society, this is because he is born into it.[3]

[83] This object of mankind is furthermore derived from the physical and sensible organization of man. The organization is for him [i.e. Herder] the work of art from which he derives its teleological significance – The highest is present in the sensible, and every minute detail of the sensible organization is the most suitable expression or hint for the determination of mankind. – This (we must acknowledge it) is the genuine standpoint of art carried over into world history.

Analogously, Schiller demands for nations what Herder demands for the individual, but he further elevates this artistic view to higher universality when he says that 'totality of character must therefore be present in the people'.[4] With the artistic formation of the nation we find that the call to preserve all the differences among nations represents a demand that the same artistic criterion be applied to the world spirit, which Hirt[5] affirmed for the beautiful in general and which, formally and abstractly, is correct. But Schiller does not stop there. He proceeds to the content which he [84] finds in the reconciliation of the universal antagonism through art. Here we see him already falling in with Schelling.

But we have to grasp not merely the teleological world view of these subjective thinkers at this first stage. This would only be an end in itself, a presupposed end; rather, this view is still to be exhibited in reality as posited. The world spirit at the stage of art is the Grecian spirit; Greek history and Greek life are classical *par excellence*. This artistic standpoint in history as something already past is likewise interpreted by Schiller, and thus he says quite truly, 'the appearance of Greek mankind was incontestably a maximum which at this stage could neither persist nor rise higher. Not persist, since the understanding, through the resources which it already had, had to be inevitably compelled to separate itself from sensation and intuition and to aspire to clarity of perception. Not even to rise higher, since only a certain degree of clarity can exist together with a certain fullness and warmth. The Greeks had attained this degree, and if they wanted to progress to a higher development, then they had to [85]

[3] *Outlines of a Philosophy of the History of Man*, Bk 4, Ch. 3.

[4] *Aesthetic Education*, Letter 1.

[5] [Aloys Hirt (1759–1836), author of *The History of Ancient Architecture; The History of Ancient Pictorial Art*. (Tr.)]

like us, abandon the totality of their essence and pursue truth along separate paths.'[6]

While Schiller so very clearly perceived that this naturally present unity had to open itself up and fall into contradiction, he did not remain at that position. After he had viewed contradiction as the fate of the present, he demanded of the future a new, higher unity and he assigned it the goal of developing a higher art in the place of the first which had been destroyed.

When viewed with our present-day consciousness, this demand is as follows. The beautiful and the artistic standpoint of the world spirit in Greece was a natural condition. Subjectivity did not act at all in its production and maintenance, because it was itself not yet developed. It was therefore a purely objective condition which precisely for this reason only *was* and which, as soon as it began to be *thought*, thereby disintegrated in itself. But now thinking has thought itself through. It has reconciled itself with being, because it itself becomes [86] being, not as condition, but rather as development which has brought forth an art already permeated by thinking, and therefore mediated. The artistic life of the past thus relates to that of the future as fact to act (factum to actum).[7] A. W. Schlegel quite appropriately calls the Greek culture a perfect natural development. After its disintegration, therefore, an artistic development must be set up. An actual and active artistic development is to replace a factual one. This is the supreme end which Schiller wishes to attain and it really would be supreme, if art as such could be the supreme and highest end.

In this way the foundations of the true aesthetic of world history are established by Herder and Schiller. At this stage the life of mankind is an aesthetic development, states and individuals are works of art, and great men are ultimately public artists. But as we now pass into the second stage, we shall first encounter the true philosophy of world history at which stage the life of mankind is again a perfecting of [87] consciousness, states are ideas, and great men are ultimately (and we mean this not at all ironically) philosophers of the state. Here therefore aesthetic development must give way to philosophical development.

Again an expression of Schiller's serves us as a transition. He himself comes to the consciousness of the insufficiency of his standpoint, and seizes this as a means and a transition. He states: 'Beauty is that through which one approaches freedom.'[8] This quotation is at

[6] *Aesthetic Education*, Letter 6.

[7] See first chapter of these *Prolegomena*.

[8] *Aesthetic Education*, Letter 2.

the same time quite true and quite false. To view beauty only as a transition would mean to detract from art. But the aesthetic development of mankind is not only a means, but also an end in itself, a real determination of the world spirit. But it is an end in itself in an as yet immediate and therefore inadequate form, and again this is the truth of the passage. Art is already this absolute reconciliation, this high synthetic determination which is not merely a means and a point of passage but rather a real teleological determination. But the synthesis itself is a totality, which again contains in itself various stages of development, the first of which for our case here, that is, [88] for world history, is aesthetic development. Therefore, although it is already in itself the highest, yet it points to something still higher, and thus it is that the universally highest then differentiates itself, while it yet contains in itself both the lower and the higher.

[89] While beauty thus no longer grasps itself as sufficient, since it is only the lowest of the highest, it must dialectically turn into its opposite. Now the change happens through the emphasis on that which is the essential in it, and since this exhibited itself to be inadequate, its opposite must conversely emerge as adequate. The essential element of beauty and of art is precisely immediacy, natural and artistic externality, in which the highest comes into existence spontaneously, but not self-spontaneously (i.e., quite spontaneously in the sense of *generatio spontanea*, but not *sua sponte*). From that arises, therefore, the need for the opposite principle, for the reflected-for-itself, for the supersensible interiority, in which this highest now has to develop itself in the form of thought and of consciousness. Thus the beautiful really becomes the point of transition, which relation Hegel describes quite correctly[9] when he says that the work of art stands in the middle between immediate sensibility on the one hand [90] and ideal thought on the other. Hegel thus could first express the clear consciousness of the preceding stage; that is why he perceives the artistically beautiful as 'one of the means which dissolved and led back to unity that opposition and contradiction between the spirit resting abstractly in itself and nature'.[10]

No less than Schiller, Hegel also does not stop at this retrospective perception. Rather, he proceeds forward to the further center, which will later appear to us as the center of the centers. In it 'the form which is higher in relation to sensually concrete representation, i.e. thought – admittedly abstract in a relative sense – must not be one-

[9] *Lectures on Aesthetics*, 51 [In F. P. B. Osmaston's translation of Hegel's *The Philosophy of Fine Art* (New York: 1975), vol. 1, p. 52. (Ed.)]

[10] *Ibid.*, p. 71. [Osmaston, vol. 1, 68. (Ed.)]

sided but concrete thought in order to be true and rational thought'.[11]

That is just the point which we wanted to reach for the present. It is precisely this which for our subject shapes the foundation of the true philosophy of history, as opposed to the previous aesthetic of history. As with the first teleological standpoint, history was only [91] conceived according to its individual and natural foundation, so it is now conceived according to its objective universality. Beauty is carried over into truth, the artistic life of mankind has been absorbed into its philosophical idea. The true consciousness of the spirit as an 'end in itself of the world',[12] is expressed by its freedom, instead of by its humanity and beautiful culture.

This second standpoint of the teleology of history, the truly philosophical one, which is first stated in perfect clarity by Hegel, must first of all be acknowledged and perceived in its truth in opposition to the first aesthetic one, so that it is afterwards itself transgressed and dissolved into a third, and higher standpoint. But the essence of this standpoint is generally comprehended quite easily since it is the present standpoint of science itself. ...We need only take into consideration Hegel's definition [92] of world history which is found on page 22 of his *Lectures on the Philosophy of History* to comprehend the whole standpoint in its perfect clarity. It runs as follows: 'World history is the progress in consciousness of freedom – a progress which we have to perceive in its necessity.' The analysis of this definition and its comparison with the previous stage will open up for us the whole system. This definition of Hegel's standpoint is thus an excellent one.

(a) At the previous stage we found the perception of a natural, sensible and external progress in beautiful culture; here we find conversely the perception of the progress in consciousness, which (to explain this definition through another quotation) is 'the impulse of the spiritual life in itself to break through the bond of naturalness, sensibility and estrangement, and to come to the light of consciousness, that is, to itself'. The opposition here is so literal that one can add nothing more.

(b) At the previous stage we further found the acceptance of the contingency of this progress. This further development of culture could, according to Herder, [93] turn out thus or otherwise. The totality of the characteristic peculiarities, according to Schiller, is essential. Here, to the contrary, Hegel requires the perception of the necessity of this progress, which is in no way merely a gallery of

[11] *Ibid.*, pp. 93–4. [Osmaston, vol. 1, 98. (Ed.)]

[12] Hegel's *Lectures on the Philosophy of History*, p. 20, and other places.

individual works of art, but rather an apodictic concatenation of universal ideas.

(c) Finally, in regard to freedom, its concept, as Hegel himself acknowledges, is so very much subject to misunderstanding that here we must present a few illustrations. We hope to prevent one of these misunderstandings from the very beginning through the logical determination of freedom. This determination is in no way a one-sided member of an opposition and thus in contradiction with an opposite as, for example, with necessity. Rather it is already, in itself, a true synthetic determination, in that it contains the accomplished identity of contingency and necessity, and so at a higher stage the dissolution and actual reconciliation between arbitrary will and compulsion. That false acceptance of the meaning of freedom is deeply rooted in common sense; and it is upon this which most incongruities hinge. A further misunderstanding is to grasp the concept of freedom itself as a [94] totality set against itself, whereupon it inclines itself against the various trends constituting it, in order to come, in the end, truly and purely to itself and to grasp itself firmly. It will therefore surprise none, though it may be taken as contradictory, if we divide freedom itself into: (a) contingent freedom; (b) necessary freedom; and (c) free freedom. In these terms, it is true, there clearly appear to lie contradictions, but, speculatively grasped, the contradictions are already dissolved. Thus, in order to determine this more closely, we may say that spirit is free (a) while it produces works of art, which is certainly free, but its freedom here is a contingent one, because it contingently depends (α) subjectively, on the individual genius and the idiosyncrasies of the artist, and (β) objectively, on the various qualities of the sensible material. (b) Here, on the contrary, while the spirit does produce thoughts, it is indeed no less free, but its freedom is a necessary one, for it necessarily depends on the speculative dialectic of the object – on the universal objectivity of thought. However, on both sides it is a dependent freedom and a free dependence, and although they are the same in this regard, they are – that notwithstanding – [95] yet opposed to each other. That free freedom which unites necessity and contingency in itself *par excellence* will be spoken of later.

The freedom of Hegel is therefore a true and real freedom which is yet encumbered with a preponderance of necessity, whose basis lies in the principle of absolute idealism itself, which we shall soon discuss. It stands in abstract opposition to the freedom of Schiller, which is encumbered with immediate contingency. The whole point of the well-known polemic against Hegelian freedom may be reduced to the perception of this issue. But the criticism is misguided insofar as it attacks not the result but the principle. This is so because a freedom based upon thought must be understood as thoroughly incapable of not being. However, in that Hegel's freedom is still affected by necessity, and thus even if, properly speaking, concrete, it yet remains partially one-sided. But this is so well known that we need not dwell on it any longer.

Thus, at this stage, thought is the highest form of the spirit. Reason is the leading and objectively true principle of history. [96] Finally, the consciousness of this is the highest goal and need of mankind. It is connected with that which, initially, might be taken as contingent: that the development of the world spirit in history would be interpreted as a corollary of the phenomenological development of consciousness, and hence, the development of the world spirit would be naturally joined to the critique of consciousness. In Hegel consciousness is the Alpha and Omega, and in general he derives the entire system of his philosophy from consciousness and he subordinates the entire process of world history to consciousness. This is, by the way, what constitutes the great significance of the *Phenomenology* in the history of philosophy; namely, that the spirit, in developing itself under the form of thought, has reached with this work, with this genesis of consciousness, precisely to consciousness *par excellence*. The standpoint of Hegel has assumed that place in the history of philosophy in general which consciousness as such assumes in the system of philosophy itself. This is why consciousness is the specific core of Hegelian philosophy. Although its development itself accompanies the whole process of history [97] *in extenso*, still it coincides intensively with itself for the first time in Hegel, and thus consciousness is here consciousness *par excellence*. This coincidence can well fall apart once more, but the result of the achieved coincidence is already an attained result. Hence, the separation will not become a falling apart any more but rather a continuation out of itself, that is, a separation which will always remain identical with itself. But with that the seed of the dissolution of this standpoint is already given, and with that at the same time it also suggests why we are even now at a world-historical turning point in the conversion of facts into acts. That is, consciousness occupies a distinct place in the true system of philosophy; thus the universe is not therefore closed with it. What lies before it (according to thought) is unconscious, i.e. fact, but what follows from it must develop itself consciously, and that is the deed.

Thus, through the absolute conquest of consciousness the spirit will henceforth unfold itself with a wholly other determination in its extending movement. It will, from now on, find itself at home in objective and absolute metamorphoses.

But, as in the past stage of [98] historical teleology we were not content with the exhibition of a presupposed view, but rather perceived it as posited in reality developing itself, in the form of beauty in the ancient and principally in the Greek world, so also, the same must be done for this stage although it must be clearly evident from what has just been said that the corresponding development of the spirit at this stage is the modern one. It is true that for philosophy in general this sphere already has its beginning in the Aristotelian *thought of thought*, νόησις νοήσεως, but also no more than its beginning. Only Christian philosophy, the philosophy of thought was in a position to accomplish in its true inner element the further and absolute implementation of this sphere. The second Aristotle of our own time has recently completed its actual end and actual execution. Thus, just as classical antiquity, and especially Greece, was the world of art and immediate beauty, so too is the modern Christian epoch the world of thought, of consciousness, and of philosophy. This world, which Aristotle revealed as thinking of thinking, Hegel has consumated concretely with the thought of the identity of thought and being, since [99] this is, from Hegel's standpoint, the highest definition of philosophy.[13] But this world must dissolve itself as abstraction and as a harsh contrast to the previous one, and find its formal transition in the postulate of a third world. As has been said, the content of this transition lies in the perception that consciousness is not the Highest but rather goes beyond itself – and even more correctly, must proceed out of itself. The transition represents itself as the demand for a substantial unity of thought and being which must not only be in and for itself, but must also produce a substratum out of itself.

For the sake of this transition, however, we must exchange the more specialized considerations of historiosophy for a more universal and much more comprehensive one.

When Aristotle said: 'Theory is the most excellent thing', precisely by that expression, he gave the death-blow to art. Admittedly, this was stated out of an entirely different consideration; [100] nevertheless, its absolute spiritual significance was to set art back and after this setback followed the enthronement of philosophy in its place. Thus, as art ceased to be supreme for the spirit of mankind, this significance (i.e., to be the Highest) fell to inner thought, to theory, with a word, to philosophy.[14]

[13] Even if not stated literally it is nonetheless truly Hegel's. Moreover, the definition given that 'philosophy is the science of reason insofar as the latter is conscious of itself as all being' accords perfectly with the preceding one.

[14] One cannot speak of religion here; a true comprehension of religion, as Hegel understands it in paragraph 554 of the third edition of the *Encyclopedia* and as Richter has brought out very clearly more recently in his *Lehre der letzten Dingen*,

This high significance of philosophy has maintained itself until our time, in which the epoch of intelligence has attained its apogee. This is perceived even by those who can give no clear account of the [101] essential task which remains for philosophy after the discovery of the absolute method. The absolute method is now attained, and this is the core of philosophy. Thus it would really be called an understatement of Hegel's greatness and world-historical significance not to see in him at least (to borrow Weisse's use of Talleyrand's *bon mot*) the beginning of the end of philosophy, just as in Aristotle, we see, if not its true beginning, that at least the end of the beginning. Indeed, in Hegel thought has solved its essential task. Even if its course of development is no way terminated thereby, it will nevertheless recede from its apogee and partially yield to the rising of another star. Just as art, when it had attained the classic form, proceeded beyond itself and dissolved itself in the romantic form af art, but also at the same time ceded world dominion to philosophy, so also has philosophy itself attained such a classic point where it must go beyond itself and thereby at the same time must cede true world dominion to another. From this viewpoint we first perceive that both those who still promise quite a few changes and developments in philosophy, [102] and those who demand, with consciousness of the importance of the attained standpoint, an absolute self-sufficiency for it, are mutually correct. Since transformations in philosophy are still to be expected, even very important ones (though the most important are past), the more philosophy will progress, the more it will alienate itself and become distant from its classicality. Nevertheless, this will be an advance of the spirit, just as Romanticism, vis-à-vis ancient art, was also really an advance of the idea of the beautiful.

The dissolution of the present standpoint will result as soon as we have grasped it clearly. To that end we want to make use here of the entirely appropriate words of Professor Michelet, who says that 'the universal character of all new systems of philosophy is not only in general the intimate penetration of being and thought, subject and object, but rather such a penetration where thought or the idea is recognized as principle, and according to an Aristotelian expression

encompasses the whole absolute sphere of the spirit in which art, philosophy, etc. are only particular stages. Religion is thus in no way assimilated or subordinated to them; it is precisely the highest substantiality of the whole sphere and it governs these stages absolutely, reflecting itself constantly in them and not *separating* itself from them as something *different*, as Hegel and his school normally assume. If we say that in Antiquity art was supreme we mean religion as art, just as the later opposition of philosophy to art expresses itself also in the form of religion since the Christian religion appears vis-à-vis that of Antiquity as philosophical, meditated, believed and conscious.

as the most excellent of the two moments standing in relation to each other – so, the particular character of every one of these systems can therefore [103] be interpreted only as the forming of an idealism of this or that sort... It was finally Hegel, who... in uniting idealism with realism most intimately, led philosophy in a height of development where it can be given the name of absolute idealism.'[15]

Here, the one-sidedness of this standpoint emerges in its full light, for it is expressly said that this identity of being and thought is not only generally such but is affected by the predominance of thought, one member of this opposition. It therefore remains an idealist identity, even if this idealism is characterized as absolute. It is quite absolute, but it is absolute in its sphere, for itself, and thus only as idealism. Precisely for that reason, because it remains idealism, it cannot be the absolute absolutely. In this, the one-sidedness is not even concealed, but is openly expressed and praised as an advantage. This, of course, has its justification in the necessary internal opposition of the absolute idealism of philosophy to the immediately absolute realism of art. For insofar as we have defined philosophy as 'the thought [104] of the identity of being and thought', so again in contrast to that, the truest definition of art is the being of the identity of being and thought. Thus, on one hand, art is higher as the abstract finite being, in that it is not merely an existing thing in general, but rather a being which corresponds entirely to its inner concept. But, on the other hand, philosophy is higher as the abstractly finite thought, since it is not merely a thing which is thought in general, but precisely a thought which possesses the most concrete objectivity. There are, therefore, on both sides superior synthetic determinations which nevertheless yet remain encumbered with the one-sidedness of opposition.

[105] As we have earlier distinguished the very concept of freedom in itself, and as we have exposed the internal antitheses in this synthetic determination, as we let teleology itself, which constitutes the highest point of world-historical consideration [106] develop itself yet again in lower and higher stages, so here again the question is to establish this differentiation and this developmental process in the light of the highest and most absolute synthesis. Although the highest identity is already from its very beginning what it should be according to its concept, yet as it develops its various stages from itself, so it always becomes higher, more perfected and more concrete. Thus a mistake can easily originate when one contents oneself with the

[15] Michelet's *Geschichte der letzten Systeme der Philosophie von Kant bis Hegel*. Pt. 1, pp. 33–6.

achievement of the synthetic standpoint in general, without distinguishing again within this standpoint itself, and allowing it to proceed to make the synthesis itself more synthetic. Therefore we have to distinguish even in the absolute synthesis the moments of thesis, antithesis and synthesis as such. Art is already this Highest, this absolute synthesis which, however, remains at the stage of thesis. It is only a struggling identity. Conversely, philosophy is at the same time this absolute synthesis, but at the stage of antithesis, which reposes in its abstract element freed from the sensible immediacy of art. [107] Do not misunderstand us as intending to debase philosophy to an empty abstraction; just the reverse, for we have said that both it and art were already absolute, concrete identities. However, one must differentiate this concreteness itself and so recognize the predominance of one or the other opposing members.

Hegel himself says: 'In reality philosophy stands in the province of thought, it thereby has to deal with universals. Its content is abstract but only according to the form, the element, but in itself the idea is essentially concrete – the unity of differentiated determinations.' This is precisely what we aim at in differentiating the highest synthesis. Just as philosophy itself is affected in a one-sided and abstract way with the predominance of one side (namely, that of thought and idealism), so also is art conversely one-sided, since [108] according to its element it is abstractly sensible and immediately natural. Art thus has to do with particularities – although essentially concrete itself – and is the unity of various determinations.

And so, the new demand which we have to make is to resolve the contradiction of art with philosophy – to cancel the predominance of being and of thought in identity and to develop a substantial identity from the formal one. Finally, the highest synthesis itself must be synthesized and raised to its third true power.

Art is a matter of representing the internal, i.e., the objectification of meaning. But philosophy, on the contrary, is a matter of the meaning of objectivity. Thus art as well as philosophy is the identity of thought and being, of internal and external, of subject and object. But in art this identity is still insufficient, precisely because it is the first, and so a sensibly natural one. In philosophy, on the contrary, this identity is completed a second time and precisely because of this is also deficient, because it forms only the reflected antithesis of the first standpoint and is one-sided in its suprasensibility one-sidedness. Thus art stands to philosophy in harsh contradiction, [109] but this contradiction could not be emphasized until now, for on one hand the second member of the opposition (philosophy) had not yet developed to its classical maturity, and so could not be situated at the same relative height as already developed art. But, on the other hand, the more concrete and elevated an opposition is, the less glaringly it stands out in appearance. Thus the contradiction reigning between art and philosophy is not as visibly sharp as we observe it in its lower stages, since in the poorest and most immediate determinations the members of the opposition are at the furthest from one another. But the higher we climb, the more important and harder they become. At the same time, however, they differ from one another all the less, so that at the absolute stage they preserve their highest significance but also at the same time their infinitely smallest difference. Accordingly, they would at once coincide for the understanding in abstract, immediate, and natural unity. (Thus also from the standpoint of the understanding it is said: in God nothing contradictory is present; for speculation, on the contrary, these contradictions are pressed to their highest extremes. But precisely by this they are resolved into the highest unity, without [110] renouncing the power of their differentiation. Thus, speculation can say in this regard that God abounds in contradictions, since He is the highest unity and the ground of all contradictions.) If, therefore, the contradiction reigning between art and philosophy is less apparent than other lesser contradictions it is yet more important, for it lays claim to such high interests of the spirit and contradictions here are only of the lowest order when they appear to be the highest.

To resolve this contradiction and at the same time to fill up the chasm just mentioned is the destiny of the highest, practical, social life which will animate anew both a decadent art, and a somewhat fossilized philosophy.

In order to fill up the chasm, we must ask: [111] What has philosophy decisively negated in art? Where is the turning point of one-sidedness? For further progress the task will be to negate this negation itself and to integrate again the earlier one-sidedness. The immediate sensibility of art has passed into the suprasensibility of thought, and thought has revenged itself in philosophy at the expense of being for its earlier injuries inflicted by art. Thus in order to resolve the contradiction and to abolish the one-sidedness a return to the first standpoint is required, but a return which is no longer burdened with contradiction and preponderance, but rather one which will be an harmonious identification of the two members. This identification must develop itself not only formally, as a neutral indifference, but also substantially, as an affirmatively new formation. Absolute thought must therefore return to absolute being, yet without at the same time alienating itself. This re-begotten being will be unlike the first passively present being; rather it will be a newly created being produced with consciousness, the absolute deed. The talk is now no longer a mere identity of thought and [112] being, but rather an identity expressing itself according to its substrate in a new affirmation, the only true and actual identity. Thus, after immediate artistic praxis had ceased to be the most excellent and this predicate had fallen to theory so now theory cedes to synthetic post-theoretical praxis, whose vocation is to be ground and truth both of art and philosophy. The absolutely practical, social action, political life (which one should take care not to confuse with finite actions and practices) becomes from now on the determining factor, whereas art and philosophy considered until now as the highest identities, will be reduced to the significance of abstract premises of political life. Being and thought must therefore dissolve in action, art and philosophy in social life, in order to emerge and truly flourish anew, for the first time in conformity to their final determination.

The same reproach which Hegelian philosophy makes against Kantian philosophy (namely, that as soon as it attains objective rational cognition it again falls back upon subjective [113] one-sidedness) one must make against Hegelian philosophy itself, but on a higher and more comprehensive plane. This is, the question here is no longer at all, as with Kant, of the opposition of subject and object, of transcendent and transcendental, of noumenon and phenomenon, etc., because these oppositions are already overcome at this stage. Rather, here the question is again about the chief opposition of thought and being, which, even if most satisfactorily resolved in and for itself, still does remain abstract. On the other hand, it does not come from itself and produces from its identity nothing substantial; on the other hand – and this is the analogy made with the reproach leveled at Kantian philosophy – it again collapses back into absolute idealism, and thus always impairs the side of being to the advantage of thought. That is precisely the truth of this banal and trivial accusation against Hegel, that he dissolves the entire content of reality in the logical idea. This assumption is fundamentally false. Hegel, far from reducing everything to the logical, quite to the contrary allows the logical to develop itself into the most concrete reality. [114] But where he errs, what he does one-sidedly, what makes up the concrete basis of this certainly felt but not clearly conscious deficiency and of this assumption of his opponents, is precisely this holding fast and putting at the pinnacle consciousness for-itself, over which there should be nothing higher. It is precisely this which forms the one-sided relapse into idealism (even if an absolute one). Just as we see Kant often arrive at the speculative height and again and again fall back into his restrictedness, so also the same is the case with Hegel. With Hegel reason may manifest itself as the most objective and absolute, yet it always remains only reason. For philosophy it is the highest, but not for the absolute Spirit as such. The absolute will should now be raised upwards to such a height of speculation, as reason has already known, and in this respect very deep hints are already found in the elder Fichte. However, these hints, weighty as they are, always remain only hints, analogous to the truly speculative hints which are in Kant, and whose true, complete discovery we owe only to Hegel. We have already noted in the first chapter that both [115] in philosophy and in life no new great movements can be initiated, and no important discovery completed unless it has previously announced itself like a meteor. This is also true of the new movement which the spirit now has to initiate. Here philosophy, abandoning its most particular and proper standpoint, passes beyond itself into a truly alien territory, one which thoroughly determines its further development, namely, into the absolutely practical territory of the will. We shall see this sphere as that frequently announced by the more recent philosophers. In the developmental process of philosophy itself, it will constitute what Romanticism signified for art. Truth, the idea and reason: that is in general the most proper core of philosophy. Even while philosophy has now arrived at the absolute classical development of this core, it now goes beyond this core. Indeed, for philosophy itself one could say that this constitutes a fall, but for the spirit in general this is an enormous upswing.

Hegel has led the spirit simply to the in- and for-itself. But the in-itself and the for-itself only have their full truth in the from-itself, not to be mistaken [116] for the outside-itself, which for its part would be very immediate and abstract in comparison with this so high and concrete category. That is, the from-itself comprises production out of itself, yet without alienating itself, and thus in no way any going out or remaining outside itself. Thus the from-itself is precisely the result of the in-itself and the for-itself, the substantial and continual unity of these premises which themselves are abstractions in relation to it, but are in no way excluded or abstracted by it. The from-itself indeed reflects itself also as the third sphere in the normal course of thought itself. Speculative reason as this third stage is itself not merely thought-in and for-itself, but rather thought from itself in general. Precisely in this way thought becomes truly active and self-active.

The spirit is only spirit, when it is itself. This selfness is the specificity of the spirit, as otherness is the specificity of nature. Thus the principal forms of the spirit are:

(a) self-being:
(b) self-thought; and,
(c) self-acting.

(a) As in-itself, the spirit is self-being. [117] i.e., ideal living individuality, which first separates itself from nature and has in itself its center. That is the first natural stage of the spirit, its sense certainty.
(b) As for-itself, the spirit is self-thought, i.e., consciousness, which is the stage of reflection of the spirit.
(c) As from-itself, however, the spirit is self-acting, i.e., free activity as such, which is the most concrete evolution of the spirit.

Nature, on the contrary, can only attain in- for- and from-anotherness. Its being is an alien one; thus, it is a means. Its thought is the consciousness of another concerning it. Finally, its activity is posited from the outside; thus, it is subordinated to physical laws. This is why no miracle can originate in nature. Only the spirit is capable of miracles, because only it is autonomous. This autonomy of self-acting is the highest predicate of the absolute.

From that it follows that the spirit is not at all activity alone, but indeed activity in general. That is, thought in its purest element is the logical as such. Being, [118] on the contrary, is in the element most proper to it, the physical: thus, acting is the particular element of the spiritual, and the spirit is activity *par excellence*. As was said, the spirit is first sense certainty in itself and this is the side of being in it. Then it is consciousness for itself, and that is the side of thought in it. But it is finally free activity and this is its third most particular determination. Thus, Hegel is perfectly correct in saying that the spirit is first of all one and immediate and that it then doubles itself, since it becomes for itself through consciousness. Only one must add that its further determination is to triple itself, since it must practically, reproduce consciousness from itself, and translate thought into being. This reproduction and translation constitute in no way only a moment of consciousness (like the practical vis-à-vis the theoretical), but rather just the opposite, they constitute a specifically higher stage than consciousness. This is the stage into which consciousness flows and to which the spirit must raise itself precisely in order to satisfy its true determination. This it cannot do with theory as such. I know quite [119] well that I thereby reduce the significance of theory itself and that I will be accused of falling back into the already historical opposition of theory and praxis. But the present extension of the significance of theory is an anomaly which could only persist as long as theory itself was the most excellent, and as long as it was reputed to be the universally predominating and determining force. In other words, as long as the highest synthesis had developed itself only in the form of thought. But as to the eventual opposition, one should still guard against confusing identity with indifference. The important statement of Spinoza's, '*Voluntas et intellectus unum et idem sunt*', [Will and intelligence are one and the same] is to be grasped precisely in the former but not in the latter significance. The difference between these two meanings must be posited as nothing but the difference between developmental stages so that praxis is related to theory as speculative to reflected thought. Hegel,[16] who himself perceived so profoundly the essence of the practical, has nevertheless contributed the most among modern thinkers to this misunderstanding. This is not to say that it is a misunderstanding properly speaking, but rather only a perception not yet matured. [120] That is, in Hegel the practical is still absorbed by the theoretical. It has not yet distinguished itself from it. It is still, so to speak, viewed as a tributary of the theoretical. Its true and particular determination is, however, to be separated, specific, indeed even the highest, stage of the spirit...According to Hegel, the will is only a particular mode of thought, and this is the false conception. Rather, thought is a merely integral moment of the will, since thought, which again becomes being, is just will and act. According to Hegel, all spiritual activity has only this goal: to become conscious of the union of the subjective and the objective side.[17] [121] Taken abstractly this is true, but taken phenomenologically it would be much more correct to reverse the relationship entirely and say: all intellectual consciousness has only one goal, to realize this union actively from itself. Phenomenologically[18] the completely correct expression, '*Nihil est in intellectu, quod non fuerit in sensu*', [Nothing is present in the intellect which was not in the senses] will now be pushed up one stage of the spirit to read: 'Nihil est in voluntate et actu, quod prius non fuerit in intellectu.' [Nothing is present in the will and act which was not previously in the intellect.]

16 As, for example, in the introductory paragraphs to *The Philosophy of Right*.

17 *Ibid.*, p. 38.

18 We use the term 'phenomenological' intentionally here because, as Hegel shows from another point of view, the inverse is also true. Phenomenologically considered, however, Locke's formulation is correct. Our statement too can be thus translated, for nothing can be generated in thought which we do not *want* to think. In the normal development of the spirit, however, thought must precede conscious realization.

Thus, the actual identity of knowing and willing is maintained without damaging their difference. Consciousness in all its activity, which, as has been said, is the principal attribute of the spirit and which must therefore manifest itself at each of its stages, is not yet pure activity and still remains affected with passivity. Its activity is therefore still a passive activity which, we hope, will no longer be considered a contradiction [122] any more than necessary freedom. Active activity (which according to what has been said is no pleonasm but rather expresses activity *par excellence*, affected with no alien influence) will first develop itself in the future

(a) Subjectivity, through the adequate formulation of the will;
(b) Objectivity, through the adequate formation of political life of the state; but,
(c) absolutely, through the attainment of the substantial and highest identity of being and thought which is absolute action.

Thus the will must go through its phenomenological process, as reason has already done. For its part, political life must assert its universal dominion just as art and philosophy have done one after the other. Finally, absolute action must bear witness to its teleological character *par excellence*, since it is essentially process. It has struggle constantly within itself, continuously goes through obstacles and constantly achieves victory. Thus the struggling and the still synthesis passes into the creating one. That the synthesis of art was an insufficient and only struggling one is proven de facto by its destruction. However, we believe we have shown theoretically that the synthesis of philosophy is likewise still deficient [123] by showing its one-sidedness and abstraction even as we recognize its relative concreteness. As for the second synthesis (i.e. that of philosophy) to make this relation more graphic we may compare it to the magnet, whose two poles are perceived to be identical, but where nevertheless the north pole is held, quite one-sidedly, to be more important than the south pole and is the only indicative pole. In the Hegelian identity, thought is the indicative pole, and its method is also the compass, where the north pole enjoys more recognition, although one does not ignore the fact that south pole is quite equally authoritative. But as in the further electro-magnetic process the north pole is deprived of the prevailing authority which it still possesses in the compass, and is acknowledged, with the south pole, to be quite equally authoritative dynamically, so also in the future formation of philosophy the prevailing polarity of thought will be stripped away and normally transferred into the process of action.

The transition from the classical standpoint of philosophy, which is precisely that of absolute idealism, to a new, still alien, territory which, however, will be totally its own, but broader, [124] is entirely analogous to the transition from classical to romantic art. Just as art has lost its highest significance and universal domination through this transition, so also philosophy now has to expect the same fate. However, just as this in no way prejudiced the further progress of art, so too the abdication of philosophy as such should be only a step in its development. To demonstrate this, we can best make use of a statement close to Hegel's own in relation to art, merely with some alterations, required by the difference of the object and the shifting of the synthesis to a higher stage. Thus, if you compare what follows next with what is found in the *Lectures on Aesthetics*, then you will be required to confess that we really draw on Hegel in order to give his own testimony.

Absolute idealism has attained the highest point which philosophy is able to fulfill. If there is something deficient in absolute idealism then it is only a defeciency of philosophy itself and of the restrictedness of the philosophical sphere. This restrictedness is located in the fact that philosophy makes the universal, the spirit (according to its concept, infinitely concrete and in general [125] active) an object in suprasensible abstract form. In absolute idealism the completed interaction of thought and being is merely represented as one-sided mediation in itself. But in this identity the spirit does not yet in fact attain its true and highest determination, its highest identity. Since the spirit is not simply absolute interiority, it is also not able to shape itself freely in itself, for itself and from itself, so long as it remains tied to this interiority as its appropriate mode of being. From this principle the future form of philosophy again abolishes that speculative unity of idealism because it has obtained a content which exceeds idealism. Now the higher stage consists of the action of this unity which is in and for itself, as the content of the absolutely idealist form of philosophy consists of this unity completed in thought. However, this elevation of the in-itself and for-itself in self-determined action produces an enormous distinction. It is the infinite distinction which separates, for example, the abstract man in general from the man who has appropriated the concrete development of his determinations in the highest spheres of the spirit, i.e. the distinction which [126] separates the still relatively abstract ego from the ego which is destined for the most concrete personality from itself. Now in such a way the in-itself and the for-itself of the earlier stages become the highest synthesis, raised on the one hand from a merely immediate unity and then on the other hand from a merely conscious one to a third self-achieved unity, so the specific element corresponding to the reality of this content is no longer

(a) the sensual, immediate being of the spiritual, e.g. the corporeal human form, as natural exteriority;

and also no longer

(b) the self-conscious interiority, as the abstract supra-sensibility;

but rather,

(c) the first actual penetration of the exterior and the interior in the process of absolute action, by which the exterior recollected in the interior again expresses itself without alienating itself.

Thus, the unity of human divine nature ceases to be; on the one hand, merely a sensibly individual one (which standpoint has already long since been overcome), and, on the other hand, merely a unity only known, and only realized through intellectual knowledge and in the mind. Rather, it now becomes a self-achieved unity through [127] the intellectual will in the process of absolute action. The new content obtained thereby is therefore no longer bound to the sensible representation, as the one corresponding to it. It is also no longer merely freed from this immediate being which had to be posited negatively, overcome and reflected in spiritual unity. Rather, it is, thirdly, a content produced from itself which, to be sure, again manifests itself in sensibility, but not immediately as in the first stage. Rather, it enriches itself through mediation. This will be the true rehabilitation of matter and the absolute, substantial reconciliation of the real and the ideal equally founded and legitimate on both sides. In this way future philosophy will be the surpassing of philosophy beyond itself, yet within its own territory and in the form of philosophy itself. In short we can therefore conclude that the object of this third stage is the free concrete spirituality which should develop itself as spirituality for the spiritual interior and exterior. Hence, philosophy in accord with this object can no longer work merely for intellectual thought, but rather for the reality which coincides with its concept as well with itself. [128] It must work for the subject-objectivity, the speculative will, which, inasmuch as it is spiritual, strives from itself toward freedom, and which finally seeks and possesses its reconciliation in absolutely spiritual actuality. This recollected yet still newly produced world will constitute the content of the future. Thus it will adequately represent itself as this interior in the exterior. Thus will be celebrated the absolute peace of interiority with exteriority and this will, both in the exterior and the interior, allow their mutual victory to appear, whereby worthlessness is removed from sensible appearances.

Thus we have described the transition in Hegel's own terms and we have only altered the results thereof. Stated more properly, we have shifted these to a higher stage, since what in Hegel was already the result and wanted to pass as the last stage, has been used by us merely as a mediate link and is legitimated only as the penultimate stage. We have thus perceived it as conceived in contradiction. Thus originated the demand to proceed to a further synthesis. We therefore announce to philosophy as such a new epoch which will amount to a progress of the spirit even if philosophy abandons its most proper element and its [129] standpoint. But on the other hand, just as art still had to give way to the rising sun of thought and of philosophy as soon as it had gone beyond itself – though raised up to a higher stage – and had to exchange its former absolute value for itself for a subjection to the interiority of thought, so too must philosophy in the future suffer itself to be chiefly applied. And just as the poetry of art stepped over into the prose of thought, so must philosophy descend from the height of theory to the plane of praxis. To be practical philosophy, or (stated more properly) the philosophy of praxis, whose most concrete effect on life and social relations is the development of truth in concrete activity – this is the future fate of philosophy in general. ...Just as thought [130] and reflection surpassed the fine arts, so now the deed and social activity will surpass the true philosophy. Therefore, precisely at this moment consciousness hastens to penetrate everything and hardly having attained itself it now seeks to precipitate the deed. This phenomenological circumstance is the reason why in one blow both the past and the future become clear precisely in this epoch. Consciousness has come to maturity, it has opened the eyes of its Janus head.

You will perhaps object that to the contrary instead of dying out in this fashion, philosophy now appears to be establishing its world dominion and to be flourishing. But this would be the same error, as if one wanted to take the zenith of the sun for its dawn. When Greece enjoyed the work of a Phidias, the hour of art was nearly over. Hegel is the Phidias of philosophy. He has thought over the universe in general, and without asserting that nothing more remains to be explored further in the field of speculation, we must confess that the essential is already disclosed. The [131] discovery of the method is truly the long-yearned-for discovery of the Philosophers' Stone. Thus now it is a question of producing the wonders which lie in the power of this stone. Philosophy will still discover much, but it has already discovered itself and precisely for this reason it is outliving itself at this moment. Moreover, the epoch of philosophy has not been impaired at all in the development of the world spirit, since it has been celebrating its prime from Aristotle to Hegel. If therefore thought now attains its culmination point and has resolved its essential problem, progress itself calls for thought to step back, i.e. to pass from its purity into an alien element. Thus, we do not want to shy away from expressing the fact that philosophy will from now on begin to be applied. In itself it always remains thereby an end-in-itself, like art, but, when it ceases to pass as the most important center of the spirit, its relative subordination begins. Its next destiny is to popularize itself, to transform its esoteric character into an exoteric one. In a word, if we might be allowed an antinomic expression, it must become shallow in the depths. All are called to it, [132] and everyone who wants to think is chosen for it. Now therefore its normal influence on the social relations of mankind will begin, in order to develop the absolutely objective truth, not merely in existing reality, but also in self-created reality. On the basis of this, one can grasp the rage which has risen to the status of a monomania in our epoch for building social systems and constructing society *a priori*, and which otherwise would be only a hollow presentiment of a requirement of the times which has not yet matured to clear consciousness. But should one call this an abnormality? According to the content, by all means, but according to the form, not in the least. Formally consciousness now feels it is entitled to guide true deeds and no longer to merely acknowledge existing reality, but rather to determine it as known and willed. But since it merely felt this until now, and thus found itself only at the stage of perception and intuition, it could not yet arrive at the true content and, therefore, the content is still anomalous. However, as consciousness now steps out of itself, it will make its way into the rich plains of the objective spirit. Its discoveries in this new path will [133] be precisely the result of the future direction of philosophy. But to the contrary, it might be a gross blunder if, out of love of philosophy, we failed to recognize the normality of the present-day, generally practical world tendency.[19]

[19] These considerations regarding the absolute development of the spirit in general and its specific principal forms were indispensable in order to attain the third, as yet not established, teleological standpoint of world history. Although I have given here only fleeting elements of a discussion to be held in the future, still I believe I have said enough to call forth possibly the grossest misunderstandings. Namely, the determinations which we have stated for the determining of the future direction have until now been neglected or even falsely understood because they will only be worked out in a definite form in the future. Hence, certainly, a multitude of scientific prejudices will struggle against innovation. So, for example, the will probably shall be understood in its mere subjectivity, indeed

All that was said up to now may be formulated accordingly in the following representation of the principal stages of the spirit.

[135] (1) The stage of beauty, where the interior (the concept) corresponds to the exterior (objectivity), but as the particular, as the immediate this, as particularity, external thing, etc.

(2) The stage of truth, where conversely objectivity corresponds to the concept. There the receptacle of this union is no longer the

even in its particularity and contingency. Thus the good shall be considered as something practical in a paltry way, at which point the useful will be declared as supreme, and the good will be burdened with the contradiction of the theoretical and the practical.

With the deed one perhaps will not be able to attain clarity in the beginning, since it will be viewed as something alien in comparison with the past objects of philosophy. Moreover, I am still certain that such false explanations themselves can proceed from speculative heads which, after they have borrowed their conception from us, then will endeavor to oppose far and wide what they have imagined to be our opinion. That is, those who are at a considerable height of speculation sometimes have such a case of dizziness that they see clearly only what is exactly at their level, not what [134] really remains lower and through which they had to wend their way. But what really towers over them they transpose through an optical illusion to a lower region, and with the firmest consciousness they take it to be *bona fide* something which they have already long since surmounted indeed, this consciousness appears to be so clear to them that they are even in a position to determine adequately the number of steps whereby they tower over it.

Against so peculiar a delusion there is no other remedy than to wait for several years of progress which will clarify the correct relationship of these stages. I know quite well that delusion can take place on both sides. On the other hand, those who can articulate a particular position according to their system and according to the developmental process of consciousness itself (a position where the presumptive error should be found) can draw from this consciousness just so much negative power as to resist this innovation considered as something old. But on the other hand, I cannot help but remark that this abstractly systematic assignment of positions and this seemingly reliable accounting cannot be grounded on concepts but rather on preconceived opinions and presuppositions. These prejudices have their foundation in a philosophical content which has still not been worked out absolutely. However convinced a present philosopher can be of the importance of the discovered method, certainly no one will maintain that the system of philosophy is already absolutely constituted. Therefore, wherever gaps or even falsely alleged determinations occur there may be hidden the basis for treating truth as error, and conversely, for treating error as the higher truth.

However I dislike anticipatory polemics, I nevertheless see myself compelled to enter into them in order to save my eventual opponents from absurd objections. Every positive writing is, according to my view, soiled by the polemical, but only [135] thinkers who are firmly grounded in and protected by science can abstract totally from this because their already recognized power as well as the pupils they have raised protect them sufficiently from attacks. But we young growths on the field of science must often arm ourselves with thorns in order fully to resist the grazing of the ruminating *servum pecus* [servile herd].

exterior but rather the universal itself, no longer a determinate this or that, a thing and so forth, but rather everything actual, the essence, the idea.

(3) The stage of the good in its highest significance, in no way merely opposed to the true, but rather the highest identity of the concept with objectivity which appears

(a) no longer merely externally in something determinate as particularity, and

(b) not internally in everything as universality, but rather

(c) internally and externally as a concrete individuality and this individuality [136] is simply its self-creating agent.

It is therefore no longer the immediate, and so the insufficient, as mere correspondence in relation to the other. It is also no longer something merely mediated itself, something which has clearly arrived-at-itself in relation to itself, but rather it is that which is most concrete, absolutely mediated, self-operating from itself. Precisely thereby it comprehends the former in itself. Thus it is thoroughly in and for itself at the same time. The good – the deed – the will, this is therefore the core of the direction newly taken.

Thus in art the identity of thinking and being is already completed for the first time but in a one-sided fashion – immediately – in a sensible mode. Likewise in philosophy it is completed for the second time – but conversely in a suprasensible mode, reflectively, thus also in a one-sided way. In social life and work, however, this unity becomes completed for the third time, *par excellence*, in an all-round absolutely mediated mode. And this at the expense of the ought, since precisely at this stage the ought will pass into reality through the act – from thinking, into being. In the great reasoning of the universe, [137] therefore, the act will appear as the *terminus medius* although in another respect the syllogism can also shape itself otherwise.

However, in order to return to our specific investigation, we can formulate our new teleological standpoint of world history in the following definition:

World history is the developmental process of the spirit of mankind in sensibility, in consciousness and in the practice of the beautiful, the true and the good, a developmental process which we have to perceive in its necessity, contingency and freedom.

The analysis of this definition will disclose to us the entire standpoint. Since this is a third position, it is, in general, synthetic; i.e., it does not content itself with the statement of one specific principle which would be distinguished from the earlier ones, although it had developed from them. Rather, it raises these earlier ones speculatively; i.e., it integrates them in itself as moments of itself. Thus we do not restrict ourselves in this definition to the supervening element, but rather we let it reflect itself in the past stages themselves, just as conversely we also [138] maintain the reflection of the former stages in the new one. From these, nine factors have arisen which are to be found in the definition and which we have to combine reciprocally as follows:

(A) The ancient world is the world of immediate sense perception and beauty, truth and freedom developed in this form of the spirit as first totality.

(a) Beauty was at home in this form, since art is precisely the sensibly immediate stage of the synthesis – but antiquity is the period of being.

(b) Truth, however, manifested itself to us by way of anticipation. Hence, there philosophy is either patchwork, like the oriental and ancient Greek, or artwork, like for example the Platonic philosophy. Thus it was until Aristotle, who, properly speaking, opened the new era in the field of thought, which in the real realm of historical events actually dates from the migration of peoples. Or, finally, philosophy was accidental and passive imitation, like the Roman.

(c) The practical good is anticipated to an even greater extent. Since, however, this third moment includes a return to the first immediately, in the ancient world it is thus endowed with a natural beauty. [139] Thus the states of antiquity are in general natural states with which character even the Greek state remains affected, since Greek customary morality is an innate, presupposed, instinctive morality and not at all mediated through the subjectivity of thought. Hegel therefore expressed himself incorrectly when he said that the consciousness of freedom was first awakened in Greece. We maintain to the contrary that it was only the sensation of freedom, whereas consciousness thereof slumbered until Christianity. And in fact Greek freedom is a freedom of particularities and of unconscious immediacy – not man as man (i.e., according to his abstract universality) was known as free (i.e., as an end-in-itself) which is the highest teleological good, but rather only he who by accident of nature was born a Greek. The same is the case in Rome, but with the difference that the spirit cast itself outwards immediately, whereas the Greek spirit was satisfied with itself. However, particularity and contingency is precisely the form of sensation, whereas universality and necessity fall to true consciousness. Consciousness is certainly to be found in sense perception but only in-itself, not consciousness as such, [140] which attains its proper significance and development only in knowledge.

(B) The consciousness of world history is only awakened with the Christian era.

(a) At first its relation to the beautiful was that of the surpassing to the surpassed. Art in its flowering was for it something belonging to the past. This is why the interior (the concept) has overtaken the exterior (objectivity), and the plastic has turned into a thinking romanticism. But since the purely adequate relation of classicism was destroyed, consciousness positioned itself in opposition to sensation. Thus the immediate praxis of art, i.e. subjectively speaking, inspiration, turned into its theory and the world spirit produced aesthetics instead of art works.

(b) On the other hand, here consciousness finds itself in its normal relation to truth for the modern world is the period of thought. With the Christian era the world spirit went into itself. Religion itself accepted the form of thought and perception. Belief was established as the source of bliss, and Christianity has revealed to us the highest truth. Therefore, it was entirely appropriate that in the beginning thinking of thinking [141] (i.e., philosophy) entered into the service of theology. There it attained true content in its complete fullness. Its later detachment from theology was only for the sake of the higher unification which now makes itself known. The truth which emerged with the Christian era in the immediate form of religious representation was now led up through speculation to the summit of thought, which acknowledges this as its unique and full content. Finally, consciousness has worked up to its apogee and, as has been said, thought has established itself as the dominant principle of world synthesis.

(c) However, in relation to the good, consciousness still stands as a premiss to its conclusion. Its place does not correspond concretely, but only abstractly. Thus freedom, whose concept requires it to be absolutely concrete, has stepped forward here only in its most ideal abstraction. At the awakening of consciousness only the abstract man is acknowledged as free; i.e., according to his mere universality in contrast to the particular element of antiquity. At this stage, therefore, freedom is merely ideal, whereas at the earlier stage it was only real, which is insufficient in both cases. [142] The abstraction of this standpoint has been driven to the highest point through that subjectivity which is its leading element and this is what called forth Protestantism in the sphere of religion and liberalism in the sphere of politics. However, these two forms of religious and political life are merely the peaks of abstract subjectivity. This one-sidedness, which affects the one as well as the other, as well as the emptiness arising from it, is precisely what conservatives and authoritarians struggle against.

Selfhood is certainly this great motor principle which the most recent times have elicited and whose justification constitutes what is true in this sphere. However, the untrue consists of remaining at this relative emptiness. The self must become concrete, and this it becomes through the process of action. In thought, however, even at its most speculative-concrete stage, it remains abstract in relation to the universe. Thus the abstract man, as only general self, is abstract so long as he is not yet a proprietor. Only as proprietor is man a particular and real man. This is the most immediate stage of his concreteness, which we take here not at all in the abstractly legal [143] sense, but rather in the highest moral one.

One is entirely correct, therefore, in stating that the revolutionary movements of our time have resulted from philosophy. However, one should have added that, after philosophy had attained its classicity, a contrary evolution was to be expected from it which will mediate the abstractness directly deriving from it. It will develop into the positively concrete. By that we do not mean a return onto the old beaten tracks. This is so because whatever world history has passed judgment upon can never be reanimated. Rather, the question here is one of acknowledging the positivity of the abandoned standpoint and the relative emptiness and abstraction which the purely theoretical produced in the practical. As soon as this is speculatively comprehended, we shall arrive at the third standpoint; namely,

(C) at the real application of all earlier elements which itself will, in turn, be the dominant orientation of the future. At this stage the world spirit will be related:

(a) to the beautiful, as Schiller requires, in establishing the real teleology of world history on the standpoint of art. The [144] absolute artistic development of mankind will shape a return to the ancient world to a certain extent, without alienating itself from the modern. It will be an exhilaration of life without loss of its deep-set interiority. Only the disunion is abolished which has caused so many pains, but also so many inner pleasures of mankind. It will therefore not be a return and descent to the natural life, but rather a withdrawal and elevation of the life of nature to us. But since this is accompanied by consciousness, this fresh life of nature should change itself into a still richer life of art. To the contrary, our present life is quite an artistic life, but not that true life of art for which we have been longing hitherto. But since we must confess that our life is really *dénaturé*, our longing for nature must not be defined by the well known expression '*Rétournons à la nature*', but rather much more by the following: 'Let us raise nature up to ourselves.' It is thereby said that the development of nature must mature to the point where it will appear as the adequate receptacle for the spirit and that the gradual reconciliation of the spirit with nature, totally analogous to the reconciliation of [145] man with God in the past stages of revelation, should attain its absolute stage.

Here in all that follows, the 'ought' is not in the least a defect of speculation. The determinations which we establish are future ones but ones to which a very precise place in the process of the world spirit is assigned. All in all, only the act can prevail fully over the ought.

(b) On the other hand, the relation of the world spirit to the true will not be that of a return, since it is still precisely at this stage. Rather, it will consist (aside from the consciousness of its acts) principally in the translation of the truth from thought into act. The famed and infamous saying of Hegel's that everything rational is real and everything real rational, still demands the correction that both the rational and the real are only results of development. That is, at certain stages of the spirit the rational coincides with the real, so that afterwards, one goes beyond the other dialectically and reciprocally. From that the epochs of disunion in world history originate. The real constantly makes itself more suitable to the rational, [146] and this developmental process of both only separates itself into two parts, in order to coincide again at a higher stage.

Therefore if the rational has precisely now arrived at the solution of its inner contradictions, then this same victory must be celebrated in reality. Just as in the course of development of the spirit there is only one philosophy which is destined finally to come to itself and to comprehend itself organically, so too in reality there is only one normal unfolding of social life which can set out on its true career with the maturity of thought. Thus the really objective dialectic of life approaches its most highly mediated standpoint. The contradictions of the times emerge so glaringly only because they are maturing unto the point of their overturn and solution. I direct the attention of speculative thinkers to the system of Fourier, not that I should misunderstand the fundamental defects which make this system a utopia, but rather to show that an important step has been made towards the development of organic truth in reality. Certainly this organism still stands at the stage of mechanism, [147] but it is already an organism. Those who do not perceive the living seed, but rather still the dead husk, do not see this. As the immediate reconciliation of the Platonic principle with that of Rousseau, this utopia has an enormous import for the future. However, I say nothing more than immediate reconciliation. If it already were the highest reconciliation of these two opposed principles of world history which are prototypical of two epochs and if, moreover, it still let the organic seed develop organically, then it would also cease to be utopia. Therefore, one can say that Fourier is the greatest (but also the last) utopian. The chief defect of utopia is generally that it does not unfold itself with reality but wants to step into reality. That it can never do since as long as it is utopia, it finds an unbridgeable gap between itself and reality. Moreover, if the unfolding of the principle should not be utopian, then, as was said, the rational must coincide directly with the real. However, since consciousness now certainly has to outpace the dead, then one does not need to be too anxious at all about designing social [148] relations. What utopias lack is not at all the fact that they are too rational for reality, but rather, quite the contrary, that they are not rational enough. Utopia, even as it means to approach closest to reality, strays from it. To develop truth, one cannot be ideal enough, since the real good is only its other side. Fourier's system is therefore a utopia because it capitulates too much to a predetermined reality. Nevertheless, it is the most speculative statement that has been made concerning present circumstances of life, even if without speculative form or speculative consciousness. And everyone will see this who is in the position to perceive the speculative even when it is produced instinctively in an ocean of contingencies. Hence the future does not belong to Fourier's system, as he supposed, but the system itself belongs to the future. That is, it is an important moment towards the development of the true reality, but also only a moment, and in a very restricted sphere at that. Just as everything new never emerges into the world all at once, so also no utopia is ever realized in the world directly.

[149] Hence, if the rational is separated from the real, then they both must gravitate towards one another and approach each other more and more through imperfect reconciliations, until they finally coincide organically. Any one-sided retrieval is impossible.

Just as earlier with the beauty of life, its artistic development and the reintegration of nature, so here the truth of life, and the true solution of the social contradictions in reality, is the second demand which we make upon the future.

(c) However, from this standpoint the activity of the world spirit will be related to the good as to its most particular element. We saw in relation to the beautiful that the world spirit had to return to beauty first. On the other hand, in relation to the truth, in whose possession the world spirit finds itself, it has to translate truth into objective reality. The world (that is, the actually teleological) has to develop the positive good from itself. From the viewpoint of world history this is no longer and in no respect abstract, but rather most absolutely concrete and determined, since the world spirit passes from the former stage of becoming to that of a definite being. [150] From its own point of view, it still remains becoming, that is, ever developing being. This universal becoming, unfolding towards particular being through the particular chief forms of world history, is the positive result of the whole process, and its real creations, first as unconscious facts, then as conscious acts of mankind which are institutions.

The system of institutions is for the idea of world history what the system of individual arts is for the idea of beauty in general. The various directions of the world spirit, which often formed into contradictions, here attain unification. Every abstract element of the life of mankind finds in it the field appropriate to itself in objectivity where it can move autonomously. (This is so since this autonomy is synthetic. This is no longer comprehended in opposition, and consequently it already includes heteronomy.) This system of institutions, positive and organic in itself, is the first real, concrete freedom. Inversely, it is not in the least like that abstract, hollow, unilaterally, [151] subjectively originating thing which one still now honors with the name of freedom. Where there is no affirmative foundation, no definite being, one can even say, no reality restricted by concept (since everything real is restricted), there is also no speculative freedom. As freedom in general is synthetic, the *liberum arbitrium* is in no way its principle in general, it is only one of its principles. Therefore, if Leibniz ventured to say, '*Ex mero Dei arbitrio nihil omnino proficisci potest*' [From merely the will of God nothing at all can be produced], why do we want to let the good be produced '*ex mero hominis arbitrio*' [from merely the will of man]? Just as concrete freedom is the highest good, so abstract freedom is the highest evil, the real social original sin. It will be redeemed through the organic condition of mankind for humanity as it is already for the reborn individual.

The objectivity of freedom has gradually unfolded itself through the whole process of history. However, since until now we have gone through only two principal stages of the spirit, we are really only in possession of two abstract classes of institution, that is, the legal and the moral. The first already experienced its [152] totally mature development in Rome, thus even before Christianity, since the Roman legal system is and remains the most perfect in its abstractness and cannot be led any further beyond this point of maturity. The inner morality awakened by Christianity and prevailing through the whole Christian-Germanic period, has likewise already been absolutely developed. The moral principle, universal but still acting only in private relations and thus abstract in its bare interiority, has nothing higher to develop than what has already manifested itself in the world spirit. However, ethics had to emerge as the third concrete sphere in the two abstract spheres preceding it without finding a place corresponding to itself there. It is now destined for the first time to begin its true development and to appear in as adequate a form as is already the case for law and morality. Relations of the family, the civil society, the state, etc. were existent at every stage of the world spirit, but they were always affected with the one-sidedness and insufficiency of the respective premisses in which they appeared, so that the real and absolute consequence still [153] is left to be derived. That this is the real demand of the time we see already from the instinctive turmoil which manifests itself in the most important, spiritual as well as material interests of mankind. This turmoil can be called nothing other than a real elementary process of life which makes itself known through fermentation and even partially through putrefaction.

Man therefore plunges forth from his abstractness and becomes the social individual *par excellence*. The naked *I* abandons its universality and determines itself as the concrete person rich in relations.

The state likewise abandons its abstract separateness and itself becomes a member of humanity and of the concrete family of peoples. The natural state of peoples passes over into a social state of the same and the hitherto still very young law of nations develops itself ever more richly towards the morality and ethical life of nations.

Finally, mankind whose universality could barely be present in consciousness and in thought, comprehends itself concretely and vitally to become the organic mankind which could be called a church in its highest sense.

Thus the world spirit unites itself organically through the [154] activization of the beautiful, true and good and it unfolds itself from itself concretely in an articulated totality of real institutions.

However, in the total character of the world spirit will be produced the realization

(a) of the beautiful, in feeling – love;
(b) of the true, in knowledge – wisdom;
(c) of the good, in the will – the strength and omnipotence of life.

And so the life of mankind has to become part of these three highest terms of the absolute which will be precisely the highest transfiguration of the world spirit.

We still have to investigate the third class of the determining factors of our definition of world history, that is, the predicates of this process, and to characterize their role in history and historical writings.

(a) The contingency of the march of history is the most immediate view which one can have of the doings of the world spirit. In the epoch of the beautiful and of sensation, there is no other. This is precisely what constitutes its graceful and artistic [155] character. However, this contingency merely shapes the being of:

(b) necessity, which again is the essence of the developmental process. This second viewpoint had to change totally into its opposite with the transformation of the spirit, since necessity is the predicate of truth, of consciousness and of thought in general in the syllogism considered here. In the second principal sphere of world history occurs, therefore, the philosophical conception derived from St Augustine and brought to its summit by Hegel. This is where essence shapes itself necessarily in given events.

(c) However, for the essence the appearance is essential but the appearance in general, not this or that exclusive appearance. The appearance must be suitable throughout for the essence, but the range of suitability is wide, and necessity must have the fullness of adequate possibility present before it to enable it to emerge into reality. While we thus maintain the necessity of the essential process, we in no way impair contingency, and, on the contrary, we return to it. This is so simply because the mutual penetration of these moments [156] produces freedom, which is the real concept of the developmental process.

However, in the system of historiosophy the premises will be inverted. We proceed from thought as from the absolutely prior. We must establish *a priori* in the first speculative part the necessary laws of development, which are then proven *a posteriori* in the second empirical part, as they appear to emerge through an abundance of contingent events. Just as in the first part the concept of world history and its genesis are to be established apodictically, so too the second part will detail the actuality of this concept and analyze this reality. This, however, is precisely the problematical field of history. We have realized that the course of events is always contingent, but even in this contingency it must yet remain suitable to the Concept if we do not want to prejudice the freedom of the spirit in favour of necessity. And so, these principles of the first part, as necessary laws of thought, must be derived in a strict dialectical manner. They must emerge absolutely in appearance, i.e. in events. On the other hand, the principles which comprise the content of the second part must be depicted as entirely dependent upon nature, while yet recognizing [157] their guiding ideas. Finally, from these opposed modes of consideration there originates the third, synthetic part of historiosophy. In pursuing the idea of mankind in its speculative freedom through the principal trends of the Spirit, this part will develop an ever more suitable existence for the idea of freedom in concrete institutions.

III

Ludwig Feuerbach

1804–1872

Ludwig Feuerbach

Among the Young Hegelians, none – with the exception of Karl Marx and Friedrich Engels – has attracted more public attention than Ludwig Feuerbach. In his own time, Feuerbach was the most popular – or notorious – of them, and this by reason of his striking defense of an unqualified humanism as found in his major work, *The Essence of Christianity*. Karl Marx, who for a time was a disciple of Feuerbach, voiced the opinion of the majority of young German intellectuals when he asserted in his *Paris Manuscripts of 1844* that 'Feuerbach is the only one who has a *serious* and *critical* relationship to the Hegelian dialectic, the only one who has made genuine discoveries in this area. In general, he has truly overcome the old philosophy.'

The following translations not only encompass an important part of *The Essence of Christianity*, but two other studies which appeared shortly before and after that major work: the first being Feuerbach's case against Hegelianism; the second being his most concise proposal for a future philosophy. In sum, these three translations relate the central elements of Feuerbach's thought.

On its positive side, Feuerbach's philosophy is a radical humanism which posits the absolute priority of actual human experience, of the directly apprehended world of nature and society in which man lives. Negatively, it denies the relevance of either traditional speculative philosophy – exemplified in Hegelianism – or religion. Modern philosophy is, to Feuerbach, but an esoteric rational restoration of those commonplace and perverse religious notions that would degrade actual human life for the sake of illusory ideals – a God and a Heaven set over and against man and his sensuous earth.

Feuerbach's enthusiastic humanism – later ridiculed by Stirner as a 'pious atheism' – can be detected as early as 1830, with his unorthodox work *Thoughts Concerning Death and Immortality*. This work established Feuerbach as the first of the Young Hegelians. In it, the young philosopher denied both personal immortality and the transcendence of God. He published the work against the advice of his father, and so immediately fulfilled his father's dire prediction: Ludwig's academic career was ruined forever.

In 1839, with the publication of *Towards a Critique of Hegelian Philosophy* (*Zur Kritik der Hegelschen Philosophie*) Feuerbach established himself publicly a member of the 'Hegelian Left', and by the publication of *The Essence of Christianity*, in 1841, he assumed a paramount role in that movement. In 1843, his *Provisional Theses for the Reformation of Philosophy* (*Vorläufige Thesen zur Reformation der Philosophie*) set the stage for an apparently brilliant program of philosophical renewal and recovery – in humanistic terms – of the power and promise of original Hegelianism. But the promise was never fulfilled.

After 1844, with the exception of a short moment of activity within the Frankfurt Parliament of 1848, and a set of lectures delivered at Heidelberg that same year, Feuerbach withdrew completely from the fields of controversy, and – sedately married – settled into a growing obscurity and poverty which ended only with his death. Perhaps, as Engels thought, this final silence was merely due to his failure to obtain academic recognition – or, again, it might have signalled a radical change in his own thought; but, in any case, Feuerbach lost both his interest in and his influence upon the course of events. In 1888, Engels looked back upon the disappointing end of Feuerbach's philosophical life, and blamed it on 'the wretched conditions in Germany, in consequence of which cobweb-spinning eclectic flea-crackers had taken possession of the chairs of philosophy, while Feuerbach, who towered above them all, had to rusticate and grow sour in a little village'.

For the reader wishing to pursue a further study of Feuerbach's thought, the excellent recent work of Professor Marx Wartofsky is recommended: *Feuerbach* (Cambridge University Press, 1977). An extensive bibliography is appended.

The first of the three translations which follow is Feuerbach's 1839 *Towards a Critique of Hegelian Philosophy* which appeared in Arnold Ruge's *Hallischen Jahrbüchern*. It has been translated and annotated by Professor Zawar Hanfi, and is here reprinted by his permission. The second translation is that of George Eliot (Marian Evans) and is the first chapter of Feuerbach's most famous work, *The Essence of Christianity*. The third is of Feuerbach's 1843 *Provisional Theses for the Reformation of Philosophy* which appeared in Arnold Ruge's journal, the short-lived *Anekdota*. It is here translated and annotated by Professor Daniel Dahlstrom.

Towards a Critique of Hegel's Philosophy

German speculative philosophy stands in direct contrast to the ancient Solomonic wisdom: whereas the latter believes that there is nothing new under the sun, the former sees nothing that is not new under the sun; whereas oriental man loses sight of differences in his preoccupation with unity, occidental man forgets unity in his preoccupation with differences; whereas oriental man carries his indifference to the eternally identical to the point of an imbecilic apathy, occidental man heightens his sensibility for the manifold to the feverish heat of the *imaginatio luxurians*. By German speculative philosophy, I mean that philosophy which dominates the present – the philosophy of Hegel. As far as Schelling's philosophy is concerned, it was really an exotic growth – the ancient oriental idea of identity on Germanic soil. If the characteristic inner movement of Schelling's school is towards the Orient, then the distinguishing feature of the Hegelian philosophy and school is their move towards the Occident combined with their belittlement of the Orient. The characteristic element of Hegel's philosophy as compared to the orientalism of the philosophy of identity is *difference*. In spite of everything, Hegel's philosophy of nature does not reach beyond the involutions of zoophytes and mollusca to which, as is known, acephales and gastropodes also belong. Hegel elevated us to a higher stage, i.e., to the class of *articulata* whose highest order is constituted by *insects*. Hegel's spirit is logical, determinate, and – I would like to say – entomological; in other words, Hegel's is a spirit that finds its appropriate dwelling in a body with numerous protruding members and with deep fissures and sections. This spirit manifests itself particularly in its view and treatment of history. Hegel determines and presents only the most striking differences of various religions, philosophies, times, and peoples, and in a progressive series of stages, but he ignores all that is common and identical in all of them. The form of both Hegel's conception and method is that of exclusive time alone, not that of tolerant space; his system knows only *subordination* and *succession*; co-ordination and coexistence are unknown to it. To be sure, the last stage of development is always the *totality* that includes in itself the other stages, but since it itself is a definite temporal existence and hence bears the character of particularity, it cannot incorporate into itself other existences without sucking out the very marrow of their independent lives and without robbing them of the meaning which they can have only in complete freedom. The Hegelian method boasts of taking the same course as nature. It is true that it imitates nature, but the copy lacks the life of the original. Granted, nature has made man the master of animals, but it has given him not only hands to tame animals but also eyes and ears to admire them. The independence of the animal, which the cruel hand robs, is given back to it by sympathetic ears and eyes. The love of art breaks the chains that the self-interest of manual work puts around the animal. The horse that is weighed down under the groom's behind is elevated to an object of art by the painter, and the sable that is slain by the furrier for the purpose of turning its fur into a momentary ornament of human vanity is preserved by natural science so that it can be studied as a whole organism. Nature always combines the monarchical tendency of time with the liberalism of space. Naturally, the flower cancels the leaf, but would the plant be perfect if the flower only sat brightly on a leafless stem? True, some plants do shed their leaves in order to put all their energy into bringing forth the blossom, but there are other plants in which the leaf either appears later than the flower or simultaneously with it, which proves that any presentation of the totality of the plant requires the leaf as well as the flower. It is true that man is the truth of the animal, but would the life of nature, would the life of man itself be perfect if animals did not exist independently? Is man's relationship with animals only a despotic one? Do not the forsaken and the rejected find a substitute for the ingratitude, scheming, and unfaithfulness of their fellow human beings in the faithfulness of the animal? Does the animal not have a power that consoles and heals his broken heart? Is not a good, rational sense also part of animal cults? Could it not be that we regard these cults as ludicrous because we have succumbed to an idolatry of a different kind? Does not the animal speak to the heart of the child in fables? Did not a mere donkey once open the eyes of an obdurate prophet?

The stages in the development of nature have, therefore, by no means only a *historical* meaning. They are, indeed, moments, but moments of a simultaneous totality of nature and not of a *particular* and *individual* totality which itself would only be a moment of the universe, that is, of the totality of nature. However, this is not the case with the philosophy of Hegel in which only time, not space, belongs to the form of intuition. Here, totality or the absoluteness of a particular historical phenomenon or existence is vindicated as predicate, thus reducing the stages of development as independent entities only to a historical meaning; although living, they continue to exist as nothing more than shadows or moments, nothing more than homoeopathic drops on the level of the *absolute*. In this way, for example, Christianity – and, to be sure, taken in its historical-*dogmatic* development – is determined as *absolute* religion. In the interest of such a determination, however, only the difference of Christianity from other religions is accentuated, thus neglecting all that is common to all of them; that is, the *nature* of religion which, as the only absolute condition, lies at the base of all the different religions. The same is true of philosophy. The Hegelian philosophy, I mean the philosophy of *Hegel*, that is to say, a philosophy that is after all a particular and definite philosophy having an empirical existence – we are not concerned here with the character of its content – is defined and proclaimed as *absolute* philosophy; i.e., as nothing less than *philosophy itself*, if not by the master himself, then certainly by his disciples – at least by his orthodox disciples – and certainly quite consistently and in keeping with the teaching of the master. Thus, recently, a Hegelian – and a sagacious and thoughtful person at that – has sought to demonstrate – ceremoniously and, in his own way, thoroughly – that the Hegelian philosophy 'is the *absolute reality of the idea* of philosophy'.

But however sagacious the author is otherwise, he proceeds from the very outset uncritically in so far as he does not pose the question: Is it at all *possible* that a species realizes itself in *one* individual, art as such in *one* artist, and philosophy as such in one philosopher? And yet this is the main question; for what use to me are all the proofs that *this* particular person is the messiah when I do not believe at all that any messiah ever will, could, or must appear. Hence, if this question is not raised, it is quietly taken for granted that there must and does exist an aesthetic or speculative Dalai Lama, an aesthetic or speculative transubstantiation, and an aesthetic or speculative Day of Judgment. It is just this presupposition, however, that contradicts reason. 'Only all men taken together', says Goethe, 'cognize nature, and only all men taken together live human nature.' How profound – and what is more – how true! Only love, admiration, veneration, in short, only passion makes the individual into the species. For example, in moments when, enraptured by the beautiful and lovable nature of a person, we exclaim: he is beauty, love, and goodness incarnate. Reason, however, knows nothing – keeping in mind the Solomonic wisdom that there is nothing new under the sun – of a real and absolute incarnation of the species in a particular individuality. It is true that the spirit of the consciousness is 'species existing as species', but, no matter how universal, the individual and his head – the organ of the spirit – are always designated by a definite kind of nose, whether pointed or snub, fine or gross, long or short, straight or bent. Whatever enters into time and space must also subordinate itself to the laws of time and space. The god of limitation stands guard at the entrance to the world. Self-limitation is the condition of entry. Whatever becomes real becomes so only as something determined. The incarnation of the species with all its plenitude into *one* individuality would be an absolute miracle, a violent suspension of all the laws and principles of reality; it would, indeed, be the *end of the world*.

Obviously, therefore, the belief of the Apostles and early Christians in the approaching end of the world was intimately linked with their belief in incarnation. Time and space are *actually already* abolished with the manifestation of the divinity in a particular time and form, and hence there is nothing more to expect but the *actual end* of the world. It is no longer possible to conceive the possibility of history; it no longer has a meaning and goal. *Incarnation* and *history* are absolutely incompatible; when deity itself enters into history, history ceases to exist. But if history nevertheless continues in the same way as before, then the theory of incarnation is in reality nullified by history itself. The manifestation of the deity, which is only a report, a narration for other later times – and hence only an object of imagination and recollection – has lost the mark of divinity, and relinquishing its miraculous and extraordinary status, it has placed itself on an equal footing with the other, ordinary phenomena of history in as much as it is itself *reproduced* in later times in a *natural* way. The moment it becomes the object of narration, it *ceases* to be a miracle. It is therefore not without reason that people say that time betrays all secrets. Consequently, if a historical phenomenon were actually the manifestation or incarnation of the deity, then it must extinguish – and this alone would be its proof – all the lights of history, particularly church lights, as the sun puts out the stars and the day nocturnal lights; then it must illuminate the whole earth with its rapturous divine effulgence and be for all men in all times an absolute, omnipresent, and immediate manifestation. For what is supernatural must also act *as such beyond all limits of time*; and hence, what reproduces itself in a natural way – maintains itself only through the medium of either oral or written tradition – is only of mediated origin and integrated into a natural context.

The situation is the same with the theories of incarnation in the field of art and science. If Hegelian philosophy were the absolute reality of the idea of philosophy, then the immobility of reason in the Hegelian philosophy must necessarily result in the immobility of time, for if time still sadly moved along as if nothing had happened, then the Hegelian philosophy would unavoidably forfeit its attribute of absoluteness. Let us put ourselves for a few moments in future centuries! Will not the Hegelian philosophy then be chronologically a foreign and *transmitted* philosophy to us? Will it be possible for us then to regard a philosophy from other times, a philosophy of the past as *our* contemporary philosophy? How else do philosophies pass if it is not because men and epochs pass and posterity wants to live not by the heritage of its ancestors but by the riches acquired by itself? Will we therefore not regard the Hegelian philosophy as an oppressive burden just as medieval Aristotle once was to the Age of Reformation? Will not an opposition of necessity arise between the old and the new philosophy, between the unfree – because traditional – and free – because self-acquired – philosophy? Will not Hegelian philosophy be relegated from its pinnacle of the absolute reality of the Idea to the modest position of a particular and definite reality? But is it not rational, is it not the duty and task of the thinking man to anticipate through reason the necessary and unavoidable consequences of time, to know in advance from the nature of things what will one day automatically result from the nature of time?

Anticipating the future with the help of reason, let us therefore undertake to demonstrate that the Hegelian philosophy is really a definite and special kind of philosophy. The proof is not difficult to find, however much this philosophy is distinguished from all previous philosophies by its rigorous scientific character, universality, and incontestable richness of thought. Hegelian philosophy was born at a time when mankind stood, as at any other time, on a definite level of thought, when a definite kind of philosophy was in existence. It drew on this philosophy, linked itself with it, and hence it must itself have a definite; i.e., finite character. Every philosophy originates, therefore, as a manifestation of its time; its origin *presupposes its historical time*. Of course, it appears to *itself* as not resting on any presuppositions; and, in relation to earlier systems, that is certainly true. A later age, nevertheless, is bound to realize that this philosophy was after all based on certain presuppositions; i.e., certain accidental presuppositions which have to be distingjished from those that are *necessary* and *rational* and cannot be negated without involving absolute nonsense. But is it really true that the Hegelian philosophy does not begin with any presuppositions? 'Yes! It proceeds from pure

Being; it does not start from a *particular* point of departure, but from that which is purely indeterminate; it starts from that which is itself the beginning.' Is that really so? And is it not after all a presupposition that philosophy has to begin at all? 'Well, it is quite obvious that everything must have a beginning, philosophy not excepted.' Quite true! But 'beginning' here has the sense of accidental or indifferent; in philosophy, on the other hand, beginning has a *particular* meaning, the meaning of the first principle in itself as required by philosophical science. But what I would like to ask is: why should beginning be taken in this sense? Is the notion of beginning not itself subject to criticism? Is it immediately true and universally valid? Why should it not be possible for me to abandon at the start the notion of beginning and, instead, turn directly to that which is real? Hegel starts from Being; i.e., the notion of Being or abstract Being. Why should I not be able to start from Being itself; i.e., real Being? Or, again, why should I not be able to start from reason, since Being, in so far as it is thought of and in so far as it is an object of logic, immediately refers me back to reason? Do I still start from a presupposition when I start from reason? No! I cannot doubt reason and abstract from it without declaring at the same time that both doubting and abstracting do not partake of reason. But even conceding that I do base myself on a presupposition that my philosophizing starts directly from real Being or reason without at all being concerned with the whole question of a beginning, what is so harmful about that? Can I not prove later that the presupposition I had based myself on was only formally and apparently so, that in reality it was none at all? I certainly do not begin to think just at the point when I put my thoughts on paper. I already know how the subject matter of my thinking would develop. I presuppose something because I know that what I presuppose would justify itself through itself.

Can it therefore be said that the starting point taken by the Hegelian philosophy in the *Logic* is a general and an absolutely necessary starting point? Is it not rather a starting point that is itself determined, that is to say, determined by the standpoint of philosophy before Hegel? Is it not itself tied up with (Fichte's) *Theory of Science*? Is it not connected with the old question as to the first principle of philosophy and with that philosophical view-point which was essentially interested in a formal system rather than in reality? Is it not linked with the first question of all philosophy: what is the first principle? Is this connection not proved by the fact that the method of Hegel – disregarding, of course, the difference of content which also becomes the difference of form – is *essentially*, or at least generally, the method of Fichte? Is this not also the course described by the *Theory of Science* that that which is at first *for us* is in the end also *for itself*, that therefore the end returns to the beginning, and that the course taken by philosophical science is a circle? Is it not so that the circular movement, and indeed taken literally, becomes an inner need or a necessary consequence where method; i.e., the *presentation* of philosophy, is taken to be the essence of philosophy itself, where anything that is not a system (taken here in its narrow sense) is not philosophy at all? For only that which is a completed circle is a system, which does not just go on *ad infinitum*, but whose end rather returns to its beginning. The Hegelian philosophy is actually the most perfect *system* that has ever appeared. Hegel actually achieved what Fichte aspired to but did not achieve, because he concluded with an 'ought' and not with an end that is also beginning. And yet, systematic thought is by no means the same as *thought as such*, or *essential* thought; it is only self-*presenting* thought. To the extent that I present my thoughts, I place them in time; an insight that contains all its successive moments within a simultaneity in my mind now becomes a sequence. I posit that which is to be presented as not existing and let it be born under my very eyes; I abstract from what it is prior to its presentation. Whatever I therefore posit as a beginning is, in the first instance, that which is purely indeterminate; indeed, I know nothing about it, for self-presenting knowledge has yet to become knowledge. Hence, strictly speaking, I can start only from the notion of a starting point; for whatever object I may posit, initially it will always have the nature of a starting point. In this regard, Hegel is much more consistent and exact than Fichte with his clamorous 'I'. But given that the starting point is indeterminate, then moving onward must mean determining. Only during the course of the movement of presentation does that from which I start come to determine and manifest itself. Hence, progression is at the same time retrogression – I return whence I started, in retrogression I retract progression; i.e., temporalization of thought: I restore the lost identity. But the first principle to which I return is no longer the initial, indeterminate, and unproved first principle; it is now mediated and therefore no longer the same or, even granting that it is the same, no longer in the same form. This process is of course well founded and necessary, although it rests only on the relationship of self-manifesting and self-presenting thought to thought in itself; i.e., to inner thought. Let us put it in the following way. I read the *Logic* of Hegel from beginning to end. At the end I return to the beginning. The idea of the Idea or the Absolute Idea contains in itself the idea of Essence, the idea of Being. I therefore know now that Being and

Essence are moments of the Idea, or that the Absolute Idea is the *Logic in nuce*. Of course, at the end I return to the beginning, but, let us hope, *not in time*, that is, not in a way that would make me begin with the *Logic* all over again; for otherwise I would be necessitated to go the same way a second and a third time and so on with the result that my whole life will have become a circular movement within the Hegelian *Logic*. I would rather close the three volumes of the *Logic* once I have arrived at its end – the Absolute Idea, because I will then *know* what it contains. In the knowledge that I now have, I cancel the temporal process of mediation; I know that the Absolute Idea is the Whole, and I naturally need time to be able to realize for myself its processual form; however, this order of succession is completely indifferent here. The *Logic* in three volumes, i.e., the worked-out *Logic*, is not a goal *in itself*, for otherwise I would have no other goal in life than to go on reading it or to memorize it as a 'paternoster'. Indeed, the Absolute Idea itself retracts its process of mediation, *encompasses* this process *within itself*, and nullifies the reality of presentation in that it shows itself to be the first and the last, the one and all. And for this very reason, I, too, now shut the *Logic* and concentrate its spread into one idea. In the end, the *Logic* leads us, therefore, back to *ourselves*, i.e., to our inner act of cognition; mediating and self-constituting knowledge becomes *unmediated* knowledge, but not unmediated in the subjective sense of Jacobi because there is no unmediated knowledge in that sense. I mean a different kind of unmediatedness.

To the extent to which it is *self-activity*, thinking is an *unmediated* activity. No one else can think for me; only *through myself* do I convince myself of the truth of a thought. Plato is meaningless and non-existent for someone who lacks understanding; he is a blank sheet to one who cannot link ideas that correspond with his words. Plato in writing is only a *means* for me; that which is primary and *a priori*, that which is the *ground* to which all is ultimately referred, is understanding. To bestow understanding does not lie in the power of philosophy, for understanding is presupposed by it; philosophy only shapes my understanding. The *creation* of concepts on the basis of a particular kind of philosophy is not a real but only a formal creation; it is not creation out of nothing, but only the development, as it were, of a spiritual matter lying within me that is as yet indeterminate but, nevertheless, capable of assuming all determinations. The philosopher produces in me only the awareness of what I can know; he fastens on to my mental ability. In this sense, philosophy, issuing either from the mouth or the pen, goes back directly to its own *source*; it does not speak in order to speak – hence its antipathy against all pretty talk – but in order *not* to speak, that is, in order to *think*; it does not demonstrate – hence its contempt for all sophistic syllogistics – but only to show that what it demonstrates is *simply* in keeping with the very *principle* of all demonstration and reason, and that it is stringent thought; i.e., a thought that expresses to every thinking person a law of reason. To demonstrate is to show that what I am *saying* is *true*, is to lead expressed thought back to its source. The meaning of demonstration cannot, therefore, be grasped without reference to the meaning of *language*. Language is nothing other than the *realization of the species*; i.e., the 'I' is mediated with the 'You' in order, by eliminating their individual separateness, to manifest the unity of the species. Now, the element in which the word exists is air, the most spiritual and general medium of life. A demonstration has its ground only in the mediating activity of thought *for others*. Whenever I wish to prove something, I do so for others. When I prove, teach, or write, then I do so, I hope, not for myself; for I also know, at least in essentials, what I do not write, teach, and discuss. This is also the reason why one often finds it most difficult to write about something which one knows best, which is so perfectly certain and clear to oneself that one cannot understand why others should not know it as well. A writer who is so certain of the object he is to write about that he would not even take the trouble to write about it falls into a category of humor that is in a class by itself. He defeats the purpose of writing through writing, and jokes about proofs in his proofs. If I am to write and, indeed, write well and in a fundamental way, then I must doubt that the others know what I know, or at least that they know it in the same way as I do. Only because of that can I communicate any thoughts. But I also presuppose that they should and *can* know them. To teach is not to drum things into a person; rather, the teacher applies himself to an active capacity, to a capacity to learn. The artist presupposes a sense of beauty – he cannot bestow it upon a person – for in order that we take his works to be beautiful, in order that we accept and countenance them at all, he must presuppose in us a sense of art. All he can do is to cultivate it and give it a certain direction. Similarly, the philosopher does not assume that he is a speculative Dalai Lama, that he is the incarnation of reason itself. In order that we recognize his thoughts as true, in order that we understand them at all, he presupposes reason, as a common principle and measure in us as well as in himself. That which he has learned, we should also be able to know, and that which he has found we should also be able to find *in ourselves* with the help of our own thinking. Demonstration is therefore not a mediation through the medium of language between thought, in so far *as it is my thought*, and the thought of another person, in so far as it is his thought – where two or three people assemble in my name, I, reason, and truth am there among you – nor is it a mediation of 'I' and 'You' to know the identity of reason, nor, again, a mediation through which I verify that my thought is not mine, but is rather thought *in and for itself* so that it can just as well be mine as that of someone else. If we are indifferent in life as to whether our thoughts are understood and acknowledged, then this indifference is shown only to this or that man or to this or that class of men because we regard them as people who are full of prejudices, corrupted by particular interests and feelings, incorrigible. Their number does not matter here at all. It is of course true that man can be self-sufficient because he knows himself to be a whole, because he distinguishes himself from himself, and because he can be the other to himself, man speaks to and converses with himself, and because he knows that his thought would not be his own if it were also not – at least as a possibility – the thought of others. But all this indifference, all this self-sufficiency and self-concern are only exceptional phenomena. In reality, we are not indifferent; the urge to communicate is a fundamental urge – the urge for truth. We become conscious and certain of truth only through the other, even if not through this or that accidental other. That which is true belongs neither to me nor exclusively to you, but is common to all. The thought in which 'I' and 'You' are united is a *true* thought. This unification is the confirmation, sign, and affirmation of truth only because it is itself already the truth. That which unites is true and good. The objection that, hence, theft too is true and good, because here, too, men are united, does not deserve to be refuted. In this case, each is only for himself.

All philosophers we know have *expressed* – i.e., *taught* – their ideas either orally, like Socrates, or in written form; otherwise they could not have become known to us. To express *thoughts* is to teach; but to teach is to demonstrate the truth of that which is taught. This means that demonstrating is not just a relationship of the thinker to himself or of a thought that is imprisoned within itself to itself, but the relationship of the thinker to others. Hence, the forms of demonstration and inference cannot be the *forms of reason*[1] as such;

[1] Hence the so-called forms of logical judgments and conclusions are not active forms of thought, not causal relations of reason. They presuppose the metaphysical concepts of generality, particularity, individuality, of the whole and the part, of necessity, of cause and effect. They are thought of only through these concepts: hence, as forms of thought, they are posited, derived, and not original. Only metaphysical relationships are logical; only metaphysics, as the science of categories, is the true, *esoteric* logic. This is the profound insight of Hegel. The

i.e., forms of an inner act of thought and cognition. They are only *forms of communication*, modes of expression, representations, conceptions; in short, forms in which thought manifests itself. That is why a quick-witted person can be ahead of his demonstrating teacher; even with the first thought, he anticipates in no time the ensuing sequence of deductions which another person must go through step by step. A genius for thinking is just as much innate to man, and exists just as much to a certain degree in all men – in the form of receptivity – as a genius for art. The reason why we regard the forms of communication and expression as the basic forms of reason and thought lies in the fact that, in order to raise them to the clarity of consciousness, we present our fundamental thoughts to ourselves in the same way as we present them to another person, that we first teach ourselves these fundamental thoughts which directly spring from our genius for thinking – they come to us we know not how – and which are perhaps innate to our being. In short, the reason lies in the fact that we express and articulate our thoughts in thought itself. Demonstrating is therefore only the means through which I strip my thought of the form of 'mine-ness' so that the other person may recognize it as his own. Demonstrating would be senseless if it were not also *communicating*. However, the communicating of thoughts is not material or *real* communication. For example, a push, a sound that shocks my ears, or light is real communication. I am only passively receptive to that which is material; but I become aware of that which is mental only through myself, only through self-activity. For this very reason, what the person demonstrating communicates is not the *subject matter itself*, but only the medium; for he does not instil his thoughts into me like drops of medicine, nor does he preach to deaf fishes like Saint Francis; rather, he addresses himself to *thinking* beings. The main thing – the understanding of the thing involved – he does not give me; he *gives* nothing at all – otherwise the philosopher could really produce philosophers, something which so far no one has succeeded in achieving. Rather, he presupposes the faculty of understanding; he shows me – i.e., to the other person as such – my understanding only in a mirror. He is only an actor; i.e., he only embodies and represents what I should reproduce in myself in

so-called logical forms are only abstract and elementary forms of language; but speech is not thought, for otherwise the greatest chatterer would be the greatest thinker. What we normally call thought is only the translation into an idiom comprehensible to us of a highly gifted but more or less unknown author who is difficult to understand. The so-called logical forms have their validity only in this translation, not in the original. Hence, they belong not to the 'optics', but only to the 'dioptric' [belonging to the use of optical instruments. Tr.] of the spirit, a domain which is, of course, still unknown.

imitation of him. Self-constituting and systematic philosophy is dramatic and theatrical philosophy as opposed to the poetry of introspective material thought. The person demonstrating says and points out to me: 'This is rational, this is true, and this is what is meant by law; this is how you must think when you think truly.' To be sure, he wants me to grasp and acknowledge his ideas, but not as his ideas; he wants me to grasp them as generally rational; i.e., also as mine. He only expresses what is my own understanding. Herein lies the justification for the demand that philosophy should awaken, stimulate thought, and not make us the captives of its oral or written word – a communicated thought is precisely thought externalized into word – which always has a mentally deadening effect. Every presentation of philosophy, whether oral or written, is to be taken and can only be taken in the sense of a means. Every system is only an expression or image of reason, and hence only an object of reason, an object which reason – a living power that procreates itself in new thinking beings – distinguishes from itself and posits as an object of criticism. Every system that is not recognized and appropriated as just a *means*, *limits* and warps the mind for it sets up the indirect and formal thought in the place of the direct, original, and material thought. It kills the spirit of invention; it makes it impossible to distinguish the *spirit* from the *letter* for together with the thought – herein lies the limitation of every system as something external – it also *necessarily* insists on retaining the word, thus failing to capture, indeed denying completely the original meaning and determination of every system and expression of thought. All presentation, all demonstration – and the presentation of thought is demonstration – has, according to its *original* determination – and that is all that matters to us – the cognitive activity of the other person as its ultimate aim.

Moreover, it is quite obvious that presentation or demonstration is also an end *for itself*, since every means must, in the first instance, be an end. The form must itself be instructive, that is, objectively expressed. The presentation of philosophy must itself be philosophical – the demand for the identity of form and content finds herein its justification. The presentation is, of course, *systematic* to the extent to which it is itself philosophical. By virtue of being so, the presentation comes to have a value *in and for itself*. For that reason the systematizer is an artist – the history of philosophical system is the picture gallery of reason. Hegel is the most accomplished philosophical artist, and his presentations, at least in part, are *unsurpassed models of scientific art sense* and, due to their rigor, *veritable means for the education and discipline of the spirit*. But precisely because of this, Hegel – in keeping with a general law which we cannot discuss here – made form into essence, the being of thought for others into being in itself, the *relative goal* into the *final goal*. Hegel, in his presentation, aimed at anticipating and imprisoning the intellect itself and compressing it into the system. The system was supposed to be, as it were, reason itself; all immediate activity was to dissolve itself completely in mediated activity, and the presentation of philosophy was *not to presuppose anything*, that is, nothing was to be left over in us and nothing within us – a complete emptying of ourselves. The Hegelian system is the *absolute self-externalization* of reason, a state of affairs that expresses itself, among other things, in the fact that the empirical character of his natural law is pure speculation. The true and ultimate reason for all complaints about formalism, neglect of subjectivity, etc., lies solely in the fact that Hegel compresses everything into his presentation, that he proceeds abstractly from the pre-existence of the intellect, and that he does not appeal to the intellect within us. It is true Hegel retracts the process of mediation in what he calls the result, but in so far as form is posited as objective essence, one is again left in doubt as to the objectivity or subjectivity of the process of mediation. Hence, those who claim that the process of the mediation of the Absolute is only a formal one may well be materially right, but those who claim the opposite, that is, those who claim objective reality for this process, may not, at least formally, be in the wrong.

The Hegelian philosophy is thus the culminating point of all speculative-systematic philosophy. With this, we have discovered and mooted the reason underlying the beginning of the *Logic*. Everything is required either to present (prove) itself or to flow into, and be dissolved in, the presentation. The presentation ignores that which was known before the presentation: It must make an absolute beginning. But it is precisely here that the limits of the presentation manifest themselves immediately. Thought is prior to the presentation of thought. That which constitutes the starting point within the presentation is primary only for the presentation but not for thought. The presentation needs thought which, although always present within thinking, emerges only later.[2] The presentation is that which

[2] What the term 'presentation' connotes here is the same as 'positing' in Hegel's philosophy. For example, the concept is already a judgment, but not yet posited as such; similarly, the judgment is in itself a conclusion, but not posited, not realized, as such. That which precedes presupposes that which succeeds, but the former must nevertheless emerge as itself and for itself, so that the latter, which in reality is prior, may again be posited for itself. As a consequence of this method, Hegel also gives independent status to determinations that have no reality in themselves. This is what happens in the case of being at the beginning of the *Logic*. What other meaning can being have except that of real, actual being? What

is mediated in and for itself; what is primary is therefore never immediate even within the presentation, but only posited, dependent, and mediated, in that it is determined by the determinations of thought whose certainty is self-dependent and which are prior to and independent of a philosophy presenting and unfolding itself in time. Thus, presentation always appeals to a higher authority – and one which is *a priori* in relation to it. Who would think that this is not also the case with the 'being' of the Hegelian *Logic*? 'Being is that which is immediate, indeterminate, self-same, self-identical, and undifferentiated.' But are not the notions of immediacy and identity presupposed here? 'Being merges into Nothingness; it disappears immediately into its opposite: its truth is the very movement of its disappearing.' Does Hegel not take perceptions for granted here? Is disappearing a notion or is it rather a sensuous perception? 'Becoming is restlessness, the restless unity of being and nothingness; existence is this unity having come to rest.' Is not a highly doubtful perception simply taken for granted here? Can a skeptic not object that rest is a sensory illusion, that everything is rather in constant motion? What, therefore, is the use of putting such ideas at the starting point, even if only as *images*? But it may be objected that such assumptions as the notions of sameness and identity are quite evident and natural. How else could we conceive of being? These notions are the necessary means through which we cognize being as primary. Quite right! But is being, at least for us, immediate? Is it not rather that wherefrom we cannot abstract the Primary? Of course, the Hegelian philosophy is aware of this as well. Being, whence the *Logic* proceeds, presupposes on the one hand the *Phenomenology*, and on the other, the Absolute Idea. Being (that which is primary and indeterminate) is revoked in the end as it turns out that it is *not* the *true* starting point. But does this not again make a *Phenomenology* out of the *Logic*? And being only

therefore is the concept of being supposed to be as distinct from the concept of existence and reality? The same holds true for the forms of judgments and syllogisms, which, as special logical relationships, are given an independent character by Hegel. Thus the affirmative and negative judgments are meant to express a particular relationship; namely, that of immediacy, whereas singular, particular, and universal judgments are meant to express the relationship of reflexion. But all these different forms of judgments are only empirical modes of speech that have to be reduced to a judgment wherein the predicate contains the essential difference, the nature, the species of the subject before they can express a logical relationship. The same holds true for the assertive and problematic judgment. In order that the judgment inherent in the concept may be posited, these forms must also be posited as particular stages, and the assertive judgment must again be an immediate judgment. But what kind of logical relationship must lie at the base of these forms of judgments? Does this not lie at the base of the subject that makes judgments?

a *phenomenological* starting point? Do we not encounter a conflict between appearance and truth within the *Logic* as well? Why does Hegel not proceed from the true starting point? 'Indeed, the true can only be a result; the true has to prove itself to be so, that is, it has to present itself.' But how can it do so if being itself has to presuppose the Idea, that is, when the Idea has already in itself been presupposed as the Primary? Is this the way for philosophy to constitute and demonstrate itself as the truth so that it can no longer be doubted, so that skepticism is reduced once and for all to absurdity? Of course, if you say A, you will also have to say B. Anyone who can countenance being at the beginning of the *Logic* will also countenance the Idea; if this being has been accepted as proved by someone, then he must also accept the Idea as proved. But what happens if someone is not willing to say A? What if he says instead, 'Your indeterminate and pure being is just an abstraction to which nothing real corresponds, for real is only real being? Or else prove if you can the reality of *general* notions!' Do we not thus come to those general questions that touch upon the truth and reality not only of Hegel's *Logic* but also of philosophy altogether? Is the *Logic* above the dispute between the Nominalists and Realists (to use the old names for what are natural contraries)? Does it not contradict in its first notions sense perception and its advocate, the intellect? Have they no right to oppose the *Logic*? The *Logic* may well dismiss the voice of sense perception, but, then, the *Logic* itself is dismissed by the intellect on the ground that it is like a judge who is trying his own case. Have we therefore not the same contradiction right at the outset of the philosophical science as in the philosophy of Fichte? In the latter case, the contradiction is between the *pure* and the empirical, real ego; in the former, it is between the pure and the empirical, real being. 'The pure ego is no longer an ego'; but, then, the pure and empty being, too, is no longer being. The *Logic* says: 'I abstract from determinate being; I do not predicate of determinate being the unity of being and nothingness.' When this unity appears to the intellect as paradoxical and ridiculous it quickly substitutes determinate being by pure being, for now it would, of course, be a contradiction for being not to be nothingness as well. But the intellect retorts: 'Only determinate being is being; in the notion of being lies the notion of absolute determinateness. I take the notion of being from being itself; however, all being is determinate being – that is why, in passing, I can also posit nothingness which means "not something" or "opposed to being" because I always and inseparably connect "something" with being. If you therefore leave out determinateness from being, you leave being with no being at all. It will not be surprising if you then demonstrate that indeterminate being is nothingness. Under these circumstances this is self-evident. If you exclude from man that which makes him man, you can demonstrate without any difficulty whatsoever that he is not man. But just as the notion of man from which you have excluded the specific difference of man is not a notion of man, but rather of a fabricated entity as, for example, the Platonic man of Diogenes, so the notion of being from which you have excluded the content of being is no longer the notion of being. Being is diverse in the same measure as things. Being is one with the thing that is. Take away being from a thing, and you take away everything from it. It is impossible to think of being in separation from specific determinations. Being is not a particular notion; to the intellect at least, it is all there is.'

Therefore, how can the *Logic*, or any particular philosophy at all, reveal truth and reality if it begins by contradicting sensuous reality and its understanding *without resolving this contradiction*? That it can prove *itself* to be true is not a matter of doubt; this, however, is not the question. A twosome is needed to prove something. While proving, the thinker splits himself into two; he contradicts himself, and only after a thought has been and has overcome its own opposition, can it be regarded as proved. To prove is at the same time to refute. Every intellectual determination has its antithesis, its contradiction. Truth exists not in unity with, but in refutation of its opposite. Dialectics is not a monologue that speculation carries on with itself, but a dialogue between speculation and empirical reality. A thinker is a dialectician only in so far as he is his own *opponent*. The zenith of art and of one's own power is to doubt oneself. Hence, if philosophy or, in our context, the *Logic* wishes to prove itself true, it must refute rational empiricism or the intellect which denies it and which alone contradicts it. Otherwise all its proofs will be nothing more than *subjective* assurances, so far as the intellect is concerned. The antithesis of being – in general and as regarded by the *Logic* – is *not nothingness*, but *sensuous* and *concrete* being.

Sensuous being denies logical being; the former contradicts the latter and vice versa. The resolution of *this* contradiction would be the proof of the reality of logical being, the proof that it is not an abstraction, which is what the intellect now takes it to be.

The only philosophy that proceeds from no presuppositions at all is one that possesses the courage and freedom to doubt *itself*, that produces itself out of its *antithesis*. All modern philosophies, however, begin only with themselves and not with what is in opposition to them. They presuppose philosophy; that is, what they understand by philosophy to be the immediate truth. They understand by mediation only *elucidation*, as in the case of Fichte, or *development*, as in the case of Hegel. Kant was critical towards the old metaphysics, but not towards himself. Fichte proceeded from the assumption that the Kantian philosophy was the truth. All he wanted was to raise it to 'science', to link together that which in Kant had a dichotomized existence, by deriving it from a common principle. Similarly, Schelling proceeded from the assumption that the Fichtean philosophy was the established truth, and restored Spinoza in opposition to Fichte. As far as Hegel is concerned, he is a Fichte as mediated through a Schelling. Hegel polemicized against the Absolute of Schelling; he thought it lacked the moment of reflection, apprehension, and negativity. In other words, he imbued the Absolute Identity with Spirit, introduced determinations into it, and fructified its womb with the semen of the Notion (the ego of Fichte). But he, nevertheless, took the truth of the Absolute for granted. He had no quarrel with the existence or the objective reality of Absolute Identity; he actually took for granted that Schelling's philosophy was, in its essence, a true philosophy. All he accused it of was that it lacked *form*. Hence, Hegel's relationship to Schelling is the same as that of Fichte to Kant. To both the true philosophy was already in existence, both in content and substance; both were motivated by a purely 'scientific', that is, in this case, *systematic* and *formal* interest. Both were critics of certain specific qualities of the existing philosophy, but not at all of its essence. That the Absolute existed was beyond all doubt. All it needed was to prove itself and be known *as such*. In this way it becomes a result and an object of the mediating Notion; that is, a 'scientific' truth and not merely an assurance given by intellectual intuition.

But precisely for that reason the proof of the Absolute in Hegel has, in principle and essence, only a formal significance, notwithstanding the scientific rigor with which it is carried out. Right at its starting point, the philosophy of Hegel presents us with a contradiction, the contradiction between truth and science, between essence and form, between thinking and writing. The Absolute Idea is assumed, not formally, to be sure, but essentially. What Hegel premises as stages and constituent parts of mediation, he thinks are determined by the Absolute Idea. Hegel does not step outside the Idea, nor does he forget it. Rather, he already thinks the antithesis out of which the Idea should produce itself *on the basis of its having been taken for granted.* It is already proved substantially before it is proved formally. Hence, it must always remain unprovable, always subjective for someone who recognizes in the antithesis of the Idea a premise which the Idea has itself established in advance. The externalization of the Idea is, so to speak, only a dissembling: it is only a pretense and nothing serious – the Idea is just playing a game. The conclusive proof is the beginning of the *Logic*, whose beginning is to be taken as the beginning of philosophy as such. That the starting point is being is only a formalism, for being is here not the true starting point, nor the truly Primary. The starting point could just as well be the Absolute Idea because it was already a certainty, an immediate truth for Hegel before he wrote the *Logic*; i.e., before he gave a scientific form of expression to his logical ideas. The Absolute Idea – the Idea of the Absolute – is its own indubitable certainty as the Absolute Truth. It posits itself in advance as true: that which the Idea posits as the other, again presupposes the Idea according to its essence. In this way, the proof remains only a formal one. To Hegel, the thinker, the Absolute Idea was absolute certainty, but to Hegel, the author, it was a formal uncertainty. This contradiction between the thinker who is without needs, who can anticipate that which is yet to be presented because everything is already settled for him, and the needy writer who has to go through a chain of succession and who posits and objectifies as formally uncertain what is certain to the thinker – this contradiction is the process of the Absolute Idea which presupposes being and essence, but in such a way that these on their part already presuppose the Idea. This is the only adequate reason required to explain the contradiction between the actual starting point of the *Logic* and its real starting point which lies at the end. As was already pointed out, Hegel in his heart of hearts was convinced of the certainty of the Absolute Idea. In this regard, there was nothing of the critic or the skeptic in him. However, the Absolute Idea had to demonstrate its truth, had to be released from the confines of a subjective intellectual conception – it had to be shown that it also existed for *others*. Thus understood, the question of its proof had an essential, and at the same time an inessential, meaning: it was a necessity in so far as the Absolute Idea had to prove itself, because only so could it demonstrate its necessity: but it was at the same time superfluous as far as the inner certainty of the truth of the Absolute Idea was concerned. The expression of this superfluous necessity, of this dispensable indispensability or indispensable dispensability is the Hegelian method. That is why its end is its beginning and its beginning its end. That is why being in it is already the certainty of the Idea, and nothing other than the *Idea in its immediacy*. That is why the Idea's lack of self-knowledge in the beginning is, in the sense of the Idea, only an ironical lack of knowledge. What the Idea says is different from what it thinks. It says 'being' or 'essence', but actually it thinks only for itself. Only at the end does it also say what it thinks, but it also retracts at the end what it had expressed at the beginning, saying: 'what you had, at the beginning and successively, taken to be a different entity, that I am myself.' The Idea itself is being and essence, but it does not yet confess to be so; it keeps this secret to itself.

That is exactly why, to repeat myself, the proof or the mediation of the Absolute Idea is only a formal affair. The Idea neither creates nor proves itself through a *real other* – that could only be the empirical and concrete perception of the intellect. Rather, it creates itself out of a formal and apparent antithesis. Being is in itself the Idea. However, to prove cannot mean anything other than to bring the other person to my own conviction. The truth lies only in the unification of 'I' and 'You'. The Other of pure thought, however, is the sensuous intellect in general. In the field of philosophy, proof therefore consists only in the fact that the contradiction between sensuous intellect and pure thought is disposed, so that thought is true not only for itself but also for its opposite. For even if every true thought is true only through itself, the fact remains that in the case of a thought that expresses an antithesis, its credibility will remain subjective, one-sided, and doubtful so long as it relies only on itself. Now, logical being is in direct, unmediated, and abhorrent contradiction with the being of the intellect's empirical and concrete perception. In addition, logical being is only an indulgence, a condescension on the part of the Idea, and, consequently, already that which it must prove itself to be. This means that I enter the *Logic* as well as intellectual perception only through a violent act, through a transcendent act, or through an immediate break with real perception. The Hegelian philosophy is therefore open to the same accusation as the whole of modern philosophy from Descartes and Spinoza onward – the accusation of an unmediated break with sensuous perceptions[3] and of philosophy's *immediate* taking itself for granted.

The *Phenomenology* cannot be seen as invalidating this accusation, because the *Logic* comes *after* it. Since it constitutes the antithesis of logical being it is always present to us, it is even necessarily brought forth by the antithesis and provoked by it to contradict the *Logic*, all the more so because the *Logic* is a new starting point, or a beginning from the very beginning, a circumstance which is *ab initio* offensive to the intellect. But let us grant the *Phenomenology* a positive and actual meaning in relation to the *Logic*. Does Hegel produce the Idea or thought out of the other-being of the Idea or thought? Let us look

[3] There is, of course, an unavoidable break which lies in the nature of science as such; however, there is no necessity for it to be an unmediated break. It is mediated by philosophy by the fact that it produces itself out of non-philosophy.

at it more closely. The first chapter deals with 'Sensuous Certainty, the This and Meaning'. It designates that stage of consciousness where sensuous and particular being is regarded as true and real being, but where it also suddenly reveals itself as a general being. 'The "here" is a tree'; but I walk further and say: 'The "here" is a house'. The first truth has now disappeared. 'The "now" is night', but it is not long before 'the "now" is day'. The first alleged truth has now become 'stale'. The 'now' therefore comes out to be a general 'now', a simple (negative) manifold. The same is the case with 'here'. 'The "here" itself does not disappear, but remains in the disappearance of the house, tree, and so on, and is indifferent to being the house, tree, etc. Therefore, this shows itself again as *mediated simplicity* or *generality*.' The particular which we mean in the context of sensuous certainty is something we cannot even express. 'Language is more truthful; here, we ourselves directly cancel our opinions, and, since it is the general which is true in sensuous certainty and which alone is expressed by languages, we cannot possibly express a sensuous entity as intended.' But is this a dialectical refutation of the reality of sensuous consciousness? Is it thereby proved that the general is the real? It may well be for someone who is certain in advance that the general is the real, but not for sensuous consciousness or for those who occupy its standpoint and will have to be convinced first of the unreality of sensuous being and the reality of thought. My brother is called John, or, if you like, Adolph, but there are innumerable people besides him who are called by the same name. Does it follow from this that my brother John is not real? Or that Johnness is the truth? To sensuous consciousness, all words are names – *nomina propria*. They are quite indifferent as far as sensuous consciousness is concerned; they are all signs by which it can achieve its aims in the shortest possible way. Here, language is irrelevant. The reality of sensuous and particular being is a truth that carries the seal of our blood. The commandment that prevails in the sphere of the senses is: an eye for an eye and a tooth for a tooth. Enough of words, come down to real things! *Show* me what you are talking about! To sensuous consciousness it is precisely language that is unreal, nothing. How can it regard itself, therefore, as refuted if it is pointed out that a particular entity cannot be expressed in language? Sensuous consciousness sees precisely in this a refutation of language but not a refutation of sensuous certainty. And it is perfectly justified, too, because otherwise we would have to feed ourselves on mere words instead of on things in life. The content of the whole first chapter of the *Phenomenology* is, therefore, for sensuous consciousness nothing but the reheated cabbage of Stilpo, the Megarian – only in the opposite sense. It is nothing but a verbal game in which thought that is already certain of itself as truth plays with natural consciousness. Consciousness, however, does not let itself be confounded; it holds firmly to the reality of individual things. Why just the 'here' and not 'that which is here?' Why just the 'now' and not 'that which is now?' In this way, the 'here' and the 'now' will never become a mediated and general 'here', a mediated and general 'now' for sensuous consciousness or for us who are its advocates and wish to be convinced of something better and different. Today is now, but tomorrow is again now, and it is still completely the same unchanged and incorrigible now as it was yesterday. Here is a tree, there a house, but when there, I again say 'here'; the 'here' always remains the old 'everywhere' and 'nowhere'. A sensuous being, a 'this', passes away, but there comes another being in its place which is equally a 'this'. To be sure, nature refutes this individual, but it soon corrects itself. It refutes the refutation in that it puts another individual in place of the previous one. Hence, to sensuous consciousness it is sensuous being that lasts and does not change.

The same unmediated contradiction, the same conflict that we encounter at the beginning of the *Logic* now confronts us at the beginning of the *Phenomenology* – the conflict between being as the object of the *Phenomenology* and being as the object of sensuous consciousness. The 'here' of the *Phenomenology* is in no way different from another 'here' because it is actually general. But the real 'here' is distinguished from another 'here' in a real way; it is an exclusive 'here'. 'This "here" is, for example, a tree. I turn around and this truth has disappeared.' This can, of course, happen in the *Phenomenology* where turning around costs nothing but a little word. But, in reality, where I must turn my ponderous body around, the 'here' proves to be a very real thing even behind my back. The tree delimits my back and excludes me from the place it already occupies. Hegel does not refute the 'here' that forms the object of sensuous consciousness; that is, an object for us distinct from pure thought. He refutes only the logical 'here', the logical 'now'. He refutes the *idea* of 'this-being', *haecceitas*. He shows the untruth of an individual being in so far as it is determined as a (theoretical) reality in imagination. The *Phenomenology* is nothing but a phenomenological Logic. Only from this point of view can the chapter on sensuous certainty be excused. However, precisely because Hegel did not really immerse himself in sensuous consciousness, did not think his way into it because in his view sensuous consciousness is an object in the sense of an object of self-consciousness or thought; because self-consciousness is merely the externalization of thought *within* the self-certainty of thought; so the *Phenomenology* or the *Logic* – both have the same thing in common – begins with itself as its own immediate presupposition, and hence with an unmediated contradiction, namely, with an absolute break with sensuous consciousness. For it begins, as mentioned already, not with the 'other-being' of thought, but with the *idea of the 'other-being' of thought.* Given this, thought is naturally certain of its victory over its adversary in advance. Hence, the humor with which thought pulls the leg of sensuous consciousness. But this also goes to show that thought has not been able to refute its adversary.

Quite apart from the significance of the *Phenomenology*, Hegel started, as was already mentioned, from the assumption of Absolute Identity right from the earliest beginnings of his philosophical activity. The idea of Absolute Identity, or of the Absolute, was simply an objective truth for him. It was not just a truth for him, but absolute truth, the Absolute Idea itself – absolute, that is, beyond all doubt and above all criticism and skepticism. But the idea of the Absolute was, according to its positive meaning, at the same time only the idea of objectivity in opposition to the idea of subjectivity, as in the Kantian and Fichtean philosophy. For that reason, we must understand the philosophy of Schelling not as 'absolute' philosophy – as it was to its adherents[4] – but as the antithesis of critical philosophy. As we know, Schelling wanted in the beginning to go in an opposite direction to idealism. His natural philosophy was actually reversed idealism at first, which means that a transition from the latter to the former was not difficult. The idealist philosopher sees life and reason in nature also, but he means by them his own life and his own reason. What he sees in nature is what he puts into it; what he gives to nature is therefore what he takes back into himself – nature is objectified ego, or spirit looking at itself as its own externalization. Idealism, therefore, already meant the unity of subject and object, spirit and nature, but together with the implication that in this unity nature had only the status of an object; that is, of something posited by spirit. The problem was, therefore, only to release nature from the bondage to which the idealist philosopher had subjected it by chaining it to his own ego, to restore it to an independent existence in order to bestow upon it the meaning it received in the philosophy of nature. The idealist said to nature, 'you are my *alter* ego', while he emphasized only the ego so that what he actually meant was: 'you

[4] The Hegelian philosophy, too, can be correctly known, appreciated, and judged only if one realizes that, notwithstanding the fact that it has formally incorporated Fichteanism into itself, it constitutes the antithesis of Kantianism and Fichteanism in its content.

are an outflow, a reflected image of myself, but nothing particular just by yourself'. The philosopher of nature said the same thing, but he emphasized the 'alter': 'to be sure, nature is your ego, but your *other* ego, and hence real in itself and distinguished from you.' That is why the meaning of the identity of spirit and nature was also a purely idealistic one in the beginning. 'Nature is only the visible organism of our intellect.' (Schelling, in the Introduction to the *Project for a System of the Philosophy of Nature.*) 'The organism is itself only a mode of perception of the intellect.' (Schelling, in *The System of Transcendental Idealism.*) 'It is obvious that the ego constructs itself while constructing matter...This product – matter – is therefore completely a construction by the ego, although not for an ego that is still identical with matter.' (Ibid.) 'Nature shall be the visible spirit, and spirit, invisible nature.' (Schelling, in the Introduction to *Ideas for a Philosophy of Nature.*) The philosophy of nature was supposed to begin only from what is objective, but at the same time to arrive at the same result at which idealism arrived through and out of itself. 'The necessary tendency of all natural science is to arrive at the intellect from nature.' (Schelling, in *The System of Transcendental Idealism.*) 'The task of the philosophy of nature is to show the primacy of the objective and to derive the subjective from it! All philosophy must strive either to produce the intellect out of nature or nature out of the intellect.' (Ibid.) That is why the philosophy of nature, with all its integrity, left idealism undisturbed, for all it wanted was to demonstrate *a posteriori* what idealism had said of itself *a priori.* The only difference between the two lay in the course taken, in method. Nevertheless, basic to the opposite course, there was an opposite intuition, or at least it had to emerge unavoidably from this opposite course. It was bound to happen that nature thus received a meaning *for itself.* The object had already been released from the confines of subjective idealism in so far as it had also been posited as the object of a *particular* science. If not in itself, nature was nevertheless not something derivative or posited for natural science, but rather something primary and independent. In this way, nature received a meaning that was opposed to the idealism of Fichte. But even so the meaning which nature had in and for idealism – that is, one which was diametrically opposed to the meaning of nature in the philosophy of nature – was to retain its validity as if nothing had happened, and idealism was to continue to exist undiminished and with all its rights and pretensions. Consequently, we now have two independent and mutually opposed truths instead of the only absolutely decisive and autonomous truth of the Fichtean ego – the truth of idealism, which denies the truth of the philosophy of nature, and the truth of the philosophy of nature, which in its turn denies the truth of idealism. For the philosophy of nature it is nature alone that exists, just as for idealism it is only spirit. For idealism, nature is only object and accident, but for the philosophy of nature it is substance, i.e., both subject and object, something which only intelligence within the context of idealism claims to be. However, two truths, two 'Absolutes', is a contradiction. How do we find a way out of this conflict between a philosophy of nature that negates idealism and an idealism that negates the philosophy of nature? Only by turning the *predicate* wherein both concur into the *subject* – this would then be the Absolute or that which is purely and simply independent – and the subject into the predicate. In other words, the Absolute is nature *and* spirit. Spirit and nature are only predicates, determinations, forms of one and the same thing; namely, of the Absolute. But what then is the Absolute? Nothing other than this 'and', that is, the unity of spirit and nature. But are we really making any progress in taking this step? Did we not have this unity already in the notion of nature? For the philosophy of nature is a science not of an object that is opposed to the 'I', but of an object that is itself both subject and object – the philosophy of nature is at the same time idealism. Further, the connection between the notions of subject and object within the notion of nature was precisely the supersession of the separation – effected by idealism – between mind and non-mind, hence the supersession of the separateness of nature and spirit. What is it, therefore, through which the Absolute distinguishes itself from nature? The Absolute is the Absolute Identity, the absolute subject-object, whereas mind is the subjective subject-object. Oh, what brilliance! And how surprising! Suddenly, we find ourselves on the standpoint of idealistic dualism: We deprive nature at the same time of that which we give it. Nature is the subject-object with the *plus* of objectivity. That means that the positive notion of nature – provided that the *plus* gives us a notion whereby nature is not suspended into the *vacuum* of the Absolute, but still remains nature – is that of *objectivity*; and similarly the notion of the spirit – in so far as it is spirit – is not a vague, nameless entity, but the notion of *subjectivity* in as much as the *plus* of subjectivity constitutes its distinguishing feature. But are we the cleverer for this approach than we were initially? Do we not have to bear again the same old cross of subjectivity and objectivity? If the Absolute is now cognized, that is, if it is brought out of the darkness of absolute indeterminateness where it is only an object of imagination and phantasy into the light of the notion, then it is cognized either as spirit or as nature. Hence, there is no science of the Absolute as such, but either the science of the Absolute as nature or that of the Absolute as spirit; that is, either the philosophy of nature or of idealism, or if both together, then only in such a way that the philosophy of nature is only the philosophy of the Absolute as nature, while idealism is only the philosophy of the Absolute as spirit. But if the object of the philosophy of nature is the Absolute as nature, then the positive notion is just the notion of nature, which means that the predicate again becomes the subject and the subject – the Absolute – becomes a vague and meaningless predicate. Hence, I could just as well delete the Absolute from the philosophy of nature, for the Absolute applies equally to spirit as to nature; as much to one particular object as to another opposite object; as much to light as to gravity. In the notion of nature, the Absolute as pure indeterminateness, as *nihil negativum*, disappears for me, or if I am unable to banish it from my head, the consequence is that nature vanishes before the Absolute. That is also the reason why the philosophy of nature did not succeed in achieving anything more than evanescent determinations and differences which are in truth only imaginary, only ideas of distinctions but not real determinations of knowledge.

But precisely for that reason the positive significance of the philosophy of Schelling lies solely in his philosophy of nature compared to the limited idealism of Fichte, which knows only a negative relationship to nature. Therefore, one need not be surprised that the originator of the philosophy of nature presents the Absolute only from its real side, for the presentation of the Absolute from its ideal side had already occurred in Fichteanism before the philosophy of nature. Of course, the philosophy of identity restored a lost unity, but not by objectifying this unity as the Absolute, or as an entity common to and yet distinguished from nature and spirit – for thus understood, the Absolute was only a mongrel between idealism and the philosophy of nature, born out of the conflict between idealism and the philosophy of nature as experienced by the author of the latter – but only in so far as the notion of this unity meant the notion of nature as both subject and object implying the restoration of nature to its proper place.

However, by not being satisfied with its rejection of subjective idealism – this was its positive achievement – and by wanting itself to acquire the character of absolute philosophy, which involved a misconception of its limits, the philosophy of nature came to oppose even that which was positive in Idealism. Kant involved himself in a contradiction – something necessary for him but which cannot be discussed here – in so far as he misconceived the affirmative, rational limits of reason by taking them to be *boundaries*. Boundaries are arbitrary limits that are removable and ought not to be there. The philosophy of identity even rejected the positive limits of reason and philosophy together with these boundaries. The unity of thought and being it claimed to have achieved was only the unity of *thought* and *imagination*. Philosophy now became beautiful, poetic, soulful, romantic, but for that matter also transcendent, superstitious, and *absolutely uncritical*. The very condition of all criticism – the distinction between 'subjective' and 'objective' – thus melted into thin air. Discerning and determining thought came to be regarded as a finite and *negative* activity. No wonder then that the philosophy of identity finally succumbed, irresistibly and uncritically, to the mysticism of the Cobbler of Görlitz [i.e. Jakob Böhme].

It was in the context of this philosophy that Hegel's own philosophizing began, although Hegel was by no means a disciple bound to the originator of that philosophy. Rather, they were friends. Hegel restored philosophy by rescuing it from the realm of imagination. A Hegelian applies with perfect justification to Hegel what Aristotle remarked of Anaxagoras; namely, that he (Anaxagoras), as one among drunks, was the only sober thinker among the philosophers of nature. With Hegel the unity of thought and being acquired a rational meaning, which is not, however, above criticism. Hegel's principle is the thinking spirit. He incorporated into philosophy the element in which rationalism has its being; namely, the intellect. In spite of the assurance to the contrary, the intellect, both as a matter of fact and with respect to its own reality, was excluded from the idea of the Absolute; in Hegel, it became a moment of the Absolute itself. The metaphysical expression of this state of affairs is the statement that the negative, the other or that which is an object of reflection, is to be conceived not only as negative and finite, but also as positive and essential. There is therefore a negative and critical element in Hegel even if what really determines his thinking is the idea of the Absolute. Although he recognized that the Absolute lacked intellect or the principle of form – both are to him one and the same – and although he actually defined the Absolute differently from Schelling by attributing to it the principle of form, thus raising form to the level of essence, the fact remains that for Hegel form – and this is indeed necessarily included in its notion – simultaneously means something formal, and the intellect again means something negative. It was assumed that the content of the philosophy of the Absolute was true, speculative, and profound; all it lacked was the form of the notion. The notion – form or intellect – was posited as essential to the extent that its absence meant a defect. However, this defect must be only a formal affair if the content has been assumed as true – herein can be seen the proof of what we said earlier about the method of Hegel. This means that philosophy is not concerned with anything except notion or form. The content – even if it is to be produced internally by philosophy's self-activity inasmuch as it is contained in the form of the notion – is always given: the business of philosophy is solely to apprehend it by critically distinguishing the essential from the non-essential or from that which is contributed by the peculiar form of intuition or sensuousness. Philosophy in Hegel has therefore no genetico-critical sense, although it certainly has a critical one. A genetico-critical philosophy is one that does not dogmatically demonstrate or apprehend an object given through perception – for what Hegel says applies unconditionally to objects given immediately, i.e., those that are absolutely real and given through nature – but examines its *origin*; which questions whether an object is a real object, only an idea, or just a psychological phenomenon; which, finally, distinguishes with utmost rigor between what is subjective and what is objective. The genetico-critical philosophy is mainly concerned with those things that are otherwise called secondary causes. Indeed, its relationship to absolute philosophy – which turns subjective psychological processes and speculative needs, for example, Jakob Böhme's process through which God is mediated, into the processes of the Absolute – is, to illustrate by analogy, the same as the relationship of that theological view of nature which takes comets or other strange phenomena to be the immediate workings of God to the purely physicist or natural philosophical view which sees, for example, the cause of the gallnut in the innocent sting of an insect rather than looking upon it, as theology does, as a sign of the existence of the Devil as a personal being. The Hegelian philosophy is, uniquely, a rational mysticism. Hence it fascinates in the same measure as it repels. The mystical-speculative souls, for whom it is an unbearable contradiction to see the mystical united with the rational, find it repulsive because they find the notion disappointing, and destructive of the very mystical fascination they cherish. It is equally repulsive to rational heads who find the union of the rational and the mystical abhorrent. The unity of the subjective and the objective as enunciated and placed at the summit of philosophy by Schelling, a unity that is still basic to Hegel although placed by him – but only according to form – in the right place; namely, at the end of philosophy as the Result. This unity is both a fruitless and a harmful principle because it eliminates the distinction between 'subjective' and 'objective' even in the case of particulars, and renders futile the genetico-critical thought, indeed, negates the very question about truth. The reason why Hegel conceived those ideas which express only subjective needs to be objective truth is because he did not go back to the source of and the need for these ideas. What he took for real reveals itself on closer examination to be of a highly dubious nature. He made what is secondary primary, thus either ignoring that which is really primary or dismissing it as something subordinate. And he demonstrated what is only particular, what is only relatively rational, to be the rational in and for itself. Thus, as a consequence of the lack of a genetico-critical model of inquiry, we see nothingness – a conception that is extremely proximate to the idea of the Absolute – play its role right at the beginning of the *Logic*. But what is this nothingness? 'By the shadow of Aristotle!' Nothingness is that which is absolutely devoid of thought and reason.[5] Nothingness cannot be thought at all, because to think is to determine, as Hegel himself says. If nothingness were conceived, it would come to be determined, and hence it would no longer be nothingness. As has been rightly said, of the non-essent there is no knowledge.[6] We call nothingness that to which no concept corresponds (Wolf). Thought can think only that which is because thought is itself an essent, a real activity. The pagan philosophers have been criticized for not being able to overcome the eternity of matter and the world. However, to them, matter meant being; it was the sensuous expression of being. What they have been criticized for is that they *made use of thought*. But have the Christians really done away with the eternity; that is, the reality of being? All they have done is to place it into a particular being, into the being of God which they thought of as its own ground and as being without beginning. Thought can never go beyond being, because it cannot go beyond itself; because reason consists only in positing being; because only this or that being, but not the genesis of being itself, can be thought. The activity of thinking authenticates itself as a well-grounded and real activity precisely through the fact that its first and last notion is that of being without beginning. The Augustinian nothingness, which appears to be so impressive and profound to speculative thinkers precisely because there is nothing behind it, is simply an expression of *absolute arbitrariness* and *thoughtlessness*. This amounts to saying that I cannot conceive of any other ground of the world except absolute arbitrariness; that is, I cannot conceive of any other ground except no ground at all, except as just an empty act of will. But in a mere act of will reason disappears and I do not advance something which

[5] Hegel designates nothingness as privative of thought. 'Already at the level of existence thought-less nothingness becomes a limiting factor.' *Logic*, Vol. III, p. 94.

[6] See also Aristotle's *Analytica Posteriora*, Bk. II, c. 7, §2, and Bk. I, §10.

could be an object for thought, which could be called a ground; what I say is as much as nothing. Hence all I express is my own ignorance, my own arbitrariness. Nothingness is an absolute self-deception, *proton pseudos*, the absolute lie in itself. The thought of nothingness is thought contradicting itself. He who thinks nothingness thinks precisely nothing. Nothingness is the negation of thought; it can therefore only be thought at all in so far as it is made into *something*. In the moment nothingness is thought of, it is also not thought of, for I also think the opposite of nothingness. 'Nothingness is simple sameness with itself.' Oh really? But are simplicity and sameness then not *real* determinations? Do I really think nothingness when I think simple sameness? Do I therefore not deny nothingness the moment I posit it? 'Nothingness is complete vacuity, complete absence of determination and content, complete undifferentiatedness in itself.' What? Is nothingness undifferentiated in itself? Do I then not posit something in nothingness in exactly the same way in which nothingness in *creatio ex nihilo* is posited as quasi-matter in so far as the world is supposed to be created out of nothingness? Can I then speak of nothingness without contradicting myself? Nothingness is complete vacuity. But what is vacuity? Vacuity is where there is nothing, but at the same time where there should be or can be something. In other words, vacuity is the expression for capacity. Now this would make nothingness into an entity, and an entity whose capacity to contain is the greatest. But you say that it is absolutely without determination and content. However, I cannot think of something that lacks all determination and content, for it is impossible to have a notion of something that lacks all determination. By using the word 'lack', I give expression to the fact that something is missing, that a default is involved. This means that I think of content and determination as primary because they are positive, or, in other words, I think nothingness through something which is not nothingness. I set nothingness in relation to that which is full of content. But this also means that where I set things in relation to one another I at the same time posit determinations. Thought is a determinate, i.e., an affirmative activity to such a degree that that which is absolutely indeterminate becomes something determinate the moment it is thought; that through the very act of thought the idea of nothingness reveals itself directly as thoughtlessness, as an untrue thought, as something that just simply cannot be thought. If it were really possible to think nothingness, the distinction between reason and unreason, thought and thoughtlessness would disappear. In that case it would be possible to think and justify any and everything, even the greatest impossibility and nonsense. This also explains why the most senseless fantasies and the most preposterous miracle-mongering could flourish as long as the idea of a *creatio ex nihilo* was held to be true, for they naturally followed from the idea of nothingness which, as a sanctified authority, stood at the head of creation. Nothingness is the *limit* of reason. A follower of Kant would of course interpret this limit – as all other limits – in the sense of the limitation of reason. Nothingness, however, is a rational limit, a limit which reason itself imposes upon itself and which is an expression of its essence and reality because nothingness is simply the absence of all reason. If it were possible for reason to think nothingness, it would in that case have taken leave of itself.

And yet 'there does exist a difference in whether something or nothing is intuited or thought. Therefore, to intuit or think nothingness does have a meaning; it is there in our intuition or thought, or rather it is vacuous thought or intuition itself.' However, vacuous thought is no thought at all. Vacuous thought is nonsense, thought only imagined, but which does not really exist. If to think nothingness should have a meaning – and a meaning it surely has; namely, that of being no thought at all – and, indeed, one such that it confers objectivity on nothingness, then knowledge of nothingness must also mean knowledge. And hence, if I were to say of an unknowing person that he knew *nothing*, I would be open to the retort that I am nevertheless attributing knowledge to him: that the person concerned *knows* nothing means that he is not unknowing. Nothingness is here a short and telling expression for want of thoroughness, competence, rationality, vagueness, etc. It has the same semantic level as in the following proposition: that which contradicts itself is nothing. Nothing has only a tautological sense here. What I am saying is that the subject of the proposition is self-contradictory, self-refuting, irrational. Here nothing has only a linguistic meaning. However, one could further object that 'in spite of everything, nothingness has its existence in the medium of thought and imagination. Hence the assertion that nothingness, although existing in thought and imagination, has no real existence; what it is, is found only in thought and imagination.' Admittedly, it occurs in our thought and imagination, but must it for that reason have a place in Logic? A ghost, too, can be imagined by us, but does it for that reason figure as a real being in psychology? Of course, it has a place in philosophical discussion, but only because philosophy has to inquire into the origin of the belief in ghosts. And what after all is nothingness if not a ghost haunting the speculative imagination? It is an idea that is no idea, a thought that is no thought, just as a ghost is a being that is no being, a body that is no body. And, after all, does nothingness not owe its existence to darkness, like a ghost? Is not the idea of darkness the same thing for sensuous consciousness as the idea of nothingness for abstract consciousness? Hegel himself says: 'Nothingness is here the pure absence of Being – *nihil privativum* – as darkness is the absence of light.' That is, an affinity between darkness and nothingness is conceded here, an affinity which manifests itself in the fact that the eye is just as little able to perceive darkness as the intellect is able to think nothingness. But it is precisely this unmistakable affinity between the two that leads us to the recognition of their common origin. Nothingness, as the opposite of being, is a product of the oriental imagination which conceives of that which has no being as having being; which opposes death to life as an autonomous rational principle; which opposes darkness to light as if it were not just the pure absence of light but something positive in itself. Thus, darkness as an entity opposed to light has as much or as little reality as nothingness has opposed to being – indeed, there is a much less rational basis for its reality. But darkness is substantialized only where man is not yet able to make the distinction between what is subjective and what is objective; where he makes his subjective impressions and feelings into objective qualities, where the horizon of his ideational power is highly limited, where his own local standpoint appears to him as the standpoint of the world or the universe itself, and where, therefore, the disappearance of light appears to him as a real movement and darkness as the going down of the source of the light itself – i.e., the sun – and, finally, where he can, therefore, explain to himself the phenomenon of 'darkening' by assuming the existence of a particular being that is hostile to light and which he also believes to be involved, in the form of a dragon or a snake, in a struggle with the being of light as at the occurrence of a solar eclipse. However, the idea of darkness as a definite being that is hostile to light has its source only in the darkness of the intellect: this darkness exists only in imagination. In nature, there is no real antithesis of light. Matter in itself is not darkness, but rather that which is illuminable, or that which is unilluminated only for itself. The light, to use scholastic terms, is only the reality (*actus*) of a possibility (*potentia*) that lies in matter itself. Hence, all darkness is only relative. Even density is not antithetical to light. Quite apart from the density of transparent diamonds and crystals, there are bodies that, even when made dense – oil-besmeared paper, for example – become transparent. Even the densest and the darkest bodies become transparent if cut into thin laminae. Of course, there does not exist an absolutely transparent body, but this rests – not considering the accompanying empirical circumstances – on the 'itselfness' of a body and is just as natural as the fact that one and the same thought becomes changed in the minds of the different people who take it up. This change rests on their independence and self-activity. However, this self-activity does not, for that matter, express an opposition to the activity of the being who is communicating and revealing his thoughts. It is the same thing with the idea of nothingness as with the Zoroastrian conception of night. Nothingness is only the limit imposed upon human thought; it does not emanate from thought, but rather from non-thought. Nothingness is just nothing; that is all that can be said of it. Hence nothingness constitutes its own refutation. Fantasy alone is responsible for making a substance out of nothingness, but only by way of metamorphosing nothingness into a ghost-like, being-less being. It can, therefore, be said that Hegel did not inquire into the genesis of nothingness, thus accepting it at its face value. In view of the analysis of the meaning of nothingness just given, the opposition between being and nothingness as such is by no means – let it be said in passing – a universal and metaphysical opposition.[7] Rather it falls into a definite area – the relationship of individual to general being – of the imagining and reflecting individual to the species. The species is *indifferent* to the individual. The reflecting individual carries the consciousness of the species within himself, which means that he can transcend his 'now-being', regard it as of no consequence, and anticipate by imagination a 'not-being' in opposition to his 'now-being' – 'not-being' has meaning only as an imagined opposite of 'now-being'. A man can say to himself: 'What am I worth? What meaning is there in life? What in death? Who is going to bother whether I exist or not? And, once I am dead, I am without pain and consciousness anyway.' Not-being is here taken, and given independent existence, as a state of pure apathy and non-sentience. The unity of being and nothingness has its positive meaning only as the *indifference* of the species or of the consciousness of the species towards the particular individual. However, the opposition itself between being and nothingness exists only in the imagination, for being, of course, exists in reality – or rather it is the real itself – but nothingness, not-being, exists only in imagination and reflection.

However, just as it is with nothingness in the *Logic*, so it also is with

[7] In Greek philosophy, the opposition between being and not-being is obviously an abstract expression of the opposition between affirmation and negation, between reality and unreality in the sense of truth and untruth. At least in Plato's *Sophist* this opposition has obviously no other meaning than the opposition between truth and untruth. Hence, the central concept, around which the whole dialogue revolves, is the concept of difference; for where there is no difference, there is also no truth; where everything can be true without distinction, as with the Sophists, nothing is true.

other matters in the philosophy of Hegel. Hegel disregarded – and not accidentally, but rather as a consequence of the spirit of German speculative philosophy since Kant and Fichte – the secondary causes (which are, however, very often the primary causes and are truly grasped only when they are grasped not only empirically, but also metaphysically; i.e., philosophically) together with the *natural* grounds and causes of things which form the fundamental principles of the genetico-critical philosophy. From the extremes of a hyper-critical subjectivism, we are, in Hegel's philosophy, hurled into the extremes of an uncritical objectivism. Of course, the natural and psychological ways of explaining things in the early days of philosophy were superficial, but only because one did not see logic in psychology, metaphysics in physics, and reason in nature. If, on the other hand, nature is understood as it should be understood – as objective reason – then it is the only canon equally as true of philosophy as of art. The *summum bonum* of art is human form (taken not only in the narrowest sense, but also in the sense of poetry); the *summum bonum* of philosophy is human *being*. Human form cannot be regarded as limited and finite, because even if it were so the artistic-creative spirit could easily remove the limits and conjure up a higher form from it. The human form is rather the genus of the manifold animal species; it no longer exists as species in man, but as genus. The being of man is no longer a particular and subjective, but a universal being, for man has the whole universe as the object of his drive for knowledge. And only a cosmopolitan being can have the cosmos as its object. It is true that the stars are not the objects of an immediate sensuous perception, but they obey the same laws as we do. All speculation that would rather go beyond nature and man is therefore futile – as futile as the kind of art that would like to give us something higher than human form, but gives us only distortions. Futile, too, is the speculative philosophy that has risen against Hegel and is in vogue now – the speculative philosophy of the positivists. For intead of going beyond Hegel, it has actually retrogressed far behind Hegel in so far as it has failed to grasp precisely the most significant directions suggested by Hegel and his predecesors, Kant and Fichte, in their own characteristic ways. Philosophy is the science of reality in its truth and totality. However, the all-inclusive and all-encompassing reality is nature (taken in the most universal sense of the word). The deepest secrets are to be found in the simplest natural things, but, pining away for the Beyond, the speculative fantast treads them under his feet. The only source of salvation lies in a return to nature. It is wrong to look upon nature as contradicting ethical freedom. Nature has built not only the mean workshop of the stomach, but also the temple of the brain. It has not only given us a tongue whose *papillae* correspond to intestinal *villi*, but also ears that are enchanted by the harmony of sounds and eyes that only the heavenly and generous being of light ravishes. Nature opposes only fantastic, not rational, freedom. Each glass of wine that we drink one too many of is a very pathetic and even peripatetic proof that the servilism of passions enrages the blood; a proof that the Greek *sophrosyne* is completely in conformity with nature. As we know, the maxim of the Stoics – and I mean the rigorous Stoics, those scarecrows of the Christian moralists – was: live in conformity with nature.

The Essence of Christianity

CHAPTER ONE
INTRODUCTION

§ 1. *The essential nature of man*

Religion has its basis in the essential difference between man and the brute – the brutes have no religion. It is true that the old uncritical writers on natural history attributed to the elephant, among other laudable qualities, the virtue of religiousness; but the religion of elephants belongs to the realm of fable. Cuvier, one of the greatest authorities on the animal kingdom, assigns, on the strength of his personal observations, no higher grade of intelligence to the elephant than to the dog.

But what is this essential difference between man and the brute? The most simple, general, and also the most popular answer to this question is – consciousness: – but consciousness in the strict sense; for the consciousness implied in the feeling of self as an individual, in discrimination by the senses, in the perception and even judgment of outward things according to definite sensible signs, cannot be denied to the brutes. Consciousness in the strictest sense is present only in a being to whom his species, his essential nature, is an object of thought. The brute is indeed conscious of himself as an individual – and he has accordingly the feeling of self as the common centre of successive sensations – but not as a species: hence, he is without that consciousness which in its nature, as in its name, is akin to science. Where there is this higher consciousness there is a capability of science. Science is the cognizance of species. In practical life we have to do with individuals; in science, with species. But only a being to whom his own species, his own nature, is an object of thought, can make the essential nature of other things or beings an object of thought.

Hence the brute has only a simple, man a twofold life: in the brute, the inner life is one with the outer; man has both an inner and an outer life. The inner life of man is the life which has relation to his species, to his general, as distinguished from his individual, nature. Man thinks – that is, he converses with himself. The brute can exercise no function which has relation to its species without another individual external to itself; but man can perform the functions of thought and speech, which strictly imply such a relation, apart from another individual. Man is himself at once I and thou; he can put himself in the place of another, for this reason, that to him his species, his essential nature, and not merely his individuality, is an object of thought.

Religion being identical with the distinctive characteristic of man, is then identical with self-consciousness – with the consciousness which man has of his nature. But religion, expressed generally, is consciousness of the infinite; thus it is and can be nothing else than the consciousness which man has of his own – not finite and limited, but infinite nature. A really finite being has not even the faintest adumbration, still less consciousness, of an infinite being, for the limit of the nature is also the limit of the consciousness. The consciouness of the caterpillar, whose life is confined to a particular species of plant, does not extend itself beyond this narrow domain. It does, indeed, discriminate between this plant and other plants, but more it knows not. A consciousness so limited, but on account of that very limitation so infallible, we do not call consciousness, but instinct. Consciousness, in the strict or proper sense, is identical with consciousness of the infinite; a limited consciousness is no consciousness; consciousness is essentially infinite in its nature.[1] The consciousness of the infinite is nothing else than the consciousness of the infinity of the consciousness; or, in the consciousness of the infinite, the conscious subject has for his object the infinity of his own nature.

What, then, *is* the nature of man, of which he is conscious, or what constitutes the specific distinction, the proper humanity of man?[2] Reason, Will, Affection. To a complete man belong the power of thought, the power of will, the power of affection. The power of thought is the light of the intellect, the power of will is energy of character, the power of affection is love. Reason, love, force of will, are perfections – the perfections of the human being – nay, more, they are absolute perfections of being. To will, to love, to think, are the highest powers, are the absolute nature of man as man, and the

[1] 'Objectum intellectus esse illimitatum sive omne verum ac, ut loquuntur, omne ens ut ens, ex eo constat, quod ad nullum non genus rerum extenditur, nullumque est, cujus cognoscendi capax non sit, licet ob varia obstacula multa sint, quae re ipsa non norit.' [That the object of the intellect is unlimited or all truth, and, as they say, all being as being, is clear from the fact that it is extended to the genus of things, and there is nothing which it is not capable to understand, although because of various obstacles, there may be many things which in reality it does not know. (Gassendi, *Op. Omn. Phys.*)]

basis of his existence. Man exists to think, to love, to will. Now that which is the end, the ultimate aim, is also the true basis and principle of a being. But what is the end of reason? Reason. Of love? Love. Of will? Freedom of the will. We think for the sake of thinking; love for the sake of loving; will for the sake of willing – i.e., that we may be free. True existence is thinking, loving, willing existence. That alone is true, perfect, divine, which exists for its own sake. But such is love, such is reason, such is will. The divine trinity in man, above the individual man, is the unity of reason, love, will. Reason, Will, Love, are not powers which man possesses, for he is nothing without them, he is what he is only by them; they are the constituent elements of his nature, which he neither has nor makes, the animating, determining, governing powers – divine, absolute powers – to which he can oppose no resistance.[3]

How can the feeling man resist feeling, the loving one love, the rational one reason? Who has not experienced the overwhelming power of melody? And what else is the power of melody but the power of feeling? Music is the language of feeling; melody is audible feeling – feeling communicating itself. Who has not experienced the power of love, or at least heard of it? Which is the stronger – love or the individual man? Is it man that possesses love, or is it not much rather love that possesses man? When love impels a man to suffer death even joyfully for the beloved one, is this death-conquering power his own individual power, or is it not rather the power of love? And who that ever truly thought has not experienced that quiet, subtle power – the power of thought? When thou sinkest into deep reflection, forgetting thyself and what is around thee, dost thou govern reason, or is it not reason which governs and absorbs thee? Scientific enthusiasm – is it not the most glorious triumph of intellect over thee? The desire of knowledge – is it not a simply irresistible, and all-conquering power? And when thou suppressest a passion, renouncest a habit, in short, achievest a victory over thyself, is this victorious power thy own personal power, or is it not rather the energy or will, the force of morality, which seizes the mastery of thee, and fills thee with indignation against thyself and thy individual weaknesses?

Man is nothing without an object. The great models of humanity,

[2] The obtuse Materialist says: 'Man is distinguished from the brute *only* by consciousness – he is an animal with consciousness superadded'; not reflecting, that in a being which awakes to consciousness, there takes place a qualitative change, a differentiation of the entire nature. For the rest, our words are by no means intended to depreciate the nature of the lower animals. This is not the place to enter further into that question.

[3] 'Toute opinion est assez forte pour se faire exposer au prix de la vie.' – Montaigne.

such men as reveal to us what man is capable of, have attested the truth of this proposition by their lives. They had only one dominant passion – the realization of the aim which was the essential object of their activity. But the object to which a subject essentially, necessarily relates, is nothing else than this subject's own, but objective, nature. If it be an object common to several individuals of the same species, but under various conditions, it is still, at least as to the form under which it presents itself to each of them according to their respective modifications, their own, but objective, nature.

Thus the Sun is the common object of the planets, but it is an object to Mercury, to Venus, to Saturn, to Uranus, under other conditions than to the Earth. Each planet has its own sun. The Sun which lights and warms Uranus has no physical (only an astronomical, scientific) existence for the Earth; and not only does the Sun appear different, but it really is *another* sun on Uranus than on the Earth. The relation of the Sun to the Earth is therefore at the same time a relation of the Earth to itself, or to its own nature, for the measure of the size and of the intensity of light which the Sun possesses as the object of the Earth is the measure of the distance which determines the peculiar nature of the Earth. Hence each planet has in its sun the mirror of its own nature.

In the object which he contemplates, therefore, man becomes acquainted with himself; consciousness of the objective is the self-consciousness of man. We know the man by the object, by his conception of what is external to himself; in it his nature becomes evident; this object is his manifested nature, his true objective *ego*. And this is true not merely of spiritual, but also of sensuous objects. Even the objects which are the most remote from man, *because* they are objects to him, and to the extent to which they are so, are revelations of human nature. Even the moon, the sun, the stars, call to man *Γνῶθι σεαυτόν*. That he sees them, and so sees them, is an evidence of his own nature. The animal is sensible only of the beam which immediately affects life; while man perceives the ray, to him physically indifferent, of the remotest star. Man alone has purely intellectual, disinterested joys and passions; the eye of man alone keeps theoretic festivals. The eye which looks into the starry heavens, which gazes at that light, alike useless and harmless, having nothing in common with the earth and its necessities – this eye sees in that light its own nature, its own origin. The eye is heavenly in its nature. Hence man elevates himself above the earth only with the eye; hence theory begins with the contemplation of the heavens. The first philosophers were astronomers. It is the heavens that admonish man of his destination, and remind him that he is destined not merely to action, but also to contemplation.

The *absolute* to man is his own nature. The power of the object over him is therefore the power of his own nature. Thus the power of the object of feeling is the power of feeling itself; the power of the object of the intellect is the power of the intellect itself; the power of the object of the will is the power of the will itself. The man who is affected by musical sounds is governed by feeling; by the feeling, that is, which finds its corresponding element in musical sounds. But it is not melody as such, it is only melody pregnant with meaning and emotion, which has power over feeling. Feeling is only acted on by that which conveys feeling, i.e., by itself, its own nature. Thus also the will; thus, and infinitely more, the intellect. Whatever kind of object, therefore, we are at any time conscious of, we are always at the same time conscious of our own nature; we can affirm nothing without affirming ourselves. And since to will, to feel, to think, are perfections, essences, realities, it is impossible that intellect, feeling, and will should feel or perceive themselves as limited, finite powers, i.e., as worthless, as nothing. For finiteness and nothingness are identical; finiteness is only a euphemism for nothingness. Finiteness is the metaphysical, the theoretical – nothingness the pathological, practical expression. What is finite to the understanding is nothing to the heart. But it is impossible that we should be conscious of will, feeling, and intellect, as finite powers, because every perfect existence, every original power and essence, is the immediate verification and affirmation of itself. It is impossible to love, will, or think, without perceiving these activities to be perfections – impossible to feel that one is a loving, willing, thinking being, without experiencing an infinite joy therein. Consciousness consists in a being becoming objective to itself; hence it is nothing apart, nothing distinct from the being which is conscious of itself. How could it otherwise become conscious of itself? It is therefore impossible to be conscious of a perfection as an imperfection, impossible to feel feeling limited, to think thought limited.

Consciousness is self-verification, self-affirmation, self-love, joy in one's own perfection. Consciousness is the characteristic mark of a perfect nature; it exists only in a self-sufficing, complete being. Even human vanity attests this truth. A man looks in the glass; he has complacency in his appearance. This complacency is a necessary, involuntary consequence of the completeness, the beauty of his form. A beautiful form is satisfied in itself; it has necessarily joy in itself – in self-contemplation. This complacency becomes vanity only when a man piques himself on his form as being his individual form, not when he admires it as a specimen of human beauty in general. It is fitting that he should admire it thus: he can conceive no form more beautiful, more sublime than the human.[4] Assuredly every being loves itself, its existence – and fitly so. To exist is a good. *Quidquid essentia dignum est, scientia dignum est.* Everything that exists has value, is a being of distinction – at least this is true of the species: hence it asserts, maintains itself. But the highest form of self-assertion, the form which is itself a superiority, a perfection, a bliss, a good, is consciousness.

Every limitation of the reason, or in general of the nature of man rests on a delusion, an error. It is true that the human being, as an individual, can and must – herein consists his distinction from the brute – feel and recognize himself to be limited; but he can become conscious of his limits, his finiteness, only because the perfection, the infinitude of his species, is perceived by him, whether as an object of feeling, of conscience, or of the thinking consciousness. If he makes his own limitations the limitations of the species, this arises from the mistake that he identifies himself immediately with the species – a mistake which is intimately connected with the individual's love of ease, sloth, vanity, and egoism. For a limitation which I know to be merely mine humiliates, shames, and perturbs me. Hence to free myself from this feeling of shame, from this state of dissatisfaction, I convert the limits of my individuality into the limits of human nature in general. What is incomprehensible to me is incomprehensible to others; why should I trouble myself further? It is no fault of mine; my understanding is not to blame, but the understanding of the race. But it is a ludicrous and even culpable error to define as finite and limited what constitutes the essence of man, the nature of the species, which is the absolute nature of the individual. Every being is sufficient to itself. No being can deny itself, i.e., its own nature; no being is a limited one to itself. Rather, every being is in and by itself infinite – has its God, its highest conceivable being, in itself. Every limit of a being is cognizable only by another being out of and above him. The life of the ephemera is extraordinarily short in comparison with that of longer-lived creatures; but nevertheless, for the ephemera this short life is as long as a life of years to others. The leaf on which the caterpillar lives is for it a world, an infinite space.

4 Homini homine nihil pulchrius. [To man nothing is more beautiful than man. (Cic. *de Nat.* D. l. i.).] And this is no sign of limitation, for he regards other beings as beautiful besides himself; he delights in the beautiful forms of animals, in the beautiful forms of plants, in the beauty of nature in general. But only the absolute, the perfect form, can delight without envy in the forms of other beings.

That which makes a being what it is, is its talent, its power, its wealth, its adornment. How can it possibly hold its existence non-existence, its wealth poverty, its talent incapacity? If the plants had eyes, taste, and judgment, each plant would declare its own flower the most beautiful; for its comprehension, its taste, would reach no farther than its natural power of production. What the productive power of its nature has brought forth as the highest, that must also its taste, its judgment, recognize and affirm as the highest. What the nature affirms, the understanding, the taste, the judgment, cannot deny; otherwise the understanding, the judgment, would no longer be the understanding and judgment of this particular being, but of some other. The measure of the nature is also the measure of the understanding. If the nature is limited, so also is the feeling, so also is the understanding. But to a limited being its limited understanding is not felt to be a limitation; on the contrary, it is perfectly happy and contented with this understanding; it regards it, praises and values it, as a glorious, divine power; and the limited understanding, on its part, values the limited nature whose understanding it is. Each is exactly adapted to the other; how should they be at issue with each other? A being's understanding is its sphere of vision. As far as thou seest, so far extends thy nature; and conversely. The eye of the brute reaches no farther than its needs, and its nature no farther than its needs. And so far as thy nature reaches, so far reaches thy unlimited self-consciousness, so far art thou God. The discrepancy between the understanding and the nature, between the power of conception and the power of production in the human consciousness, on the one hand, is merely of individual significance and has not a universal application; and, on the other hand, it is only apparent. He who, having written a bad poem, knows it to be bad, is in his intelligence, and therefore in his nature, not so limited as he who, having written a bad poem, admires it and thinks it good.

It follows that if thou thinkest the infinite, thou perceivest and affirmest the infinitude of the power of thought; if thou feelest the infinite, thou feelest and affirmest the infinitude of the power of feeling. The object of the intellect is intellect objective to itself; the object of feeling is feeling objective to itself. If thou hast no sensibility, no feeling for music, thou perceivest in the finest music nothing more than in the wind that whistles by thy ear, or than in the brook which rushes past thy feet. What, then, is it which acts on thee when thou art affected by melody? What dost thou perceive in it? What else than the voice of thy own heart? Feeling speaks only to feeling; feeling is comprehensible only by feeling, that is, by itself – for this reason, that the object of feeling is nothing else than feeling. Music is a monologue of emotion. But the dialogue of philosophy also is in truth only a monologue of the intellect; thought speaks only to thought. The splendours of the crystal charm the sense, but the intellect is interested only in the laws of crystallization. The intellectual only is the object of the intellect.[5]

All therefore which, in the point of view of metaphysical, transcendental speculation and religion, has the significance only of the secondary, the subjective, the medium, the organ – has in truth the significance of the primary, of the essence, of the object itself. If, for example, feeling is the essential organ of religion, the nature of God is nothing else than an expression of the nature of feeling. The true but latent sense of the phrase, 'Feeling is the organ of the divine', is, feeling is the noblest, the most excellent, i.e., the divine, in man. How couldst thou perceive the divine by feeling, if feeling were not itself divine in its nature? The divine assuredly is known only by means of the divine – God is known only by himself. The divine nature which is discerned by feeling is in truth nothing else than feeling enraptured, in ecstasy with itself – feeling intoxicated with joy, blissful in its own plenitude.

It is already clear from this that where feeling is held to be the organ of the infinite, the subjective essence of religion – the external data of religion lose their objective value. And thus, since feeling has been held the cardinal principle in religion, the doctrines of Christianity, formerly so sacred, have lost their importance. If, from this point of view, some value is still conceded to Christian ideas, it is a value springing entirely from the relation they bear to feeling; if another object would excite the same emotions, it would be just as welcome. But the object of religious feeling is become a matter of indifference, only because when once feeling has been pronounced to be the subjective essence of religion, it in fact is also the objective essence of religion, though it may not be declared, at least directly, to be such. I say directly; for indirectly this is certainly admitted, when it is declared that feeling, as such, is religious, and thus the distinction between specifically religious and irreligious, or at least non-religious, feelings is abolished – a necessary consequence of the point of view in which feeling only is regarded as the organ of the divine. For on what other ground than that of its essence, its nature, dost thou hold feeling to be the organ of the infinite, the divine being? And is not the nature of feeling in general also the nature of every special feeling, be its object what it may? What, then, makes this feeling religious? A given object? Not at all; for this object is itself a religious one only when it is not an object of the cold understanding or memory, but

[5] 'The understanding is percipient only of understanding, and what proceeds thence.' – Reimarus (*Wahrh. der Natürl. Religion*, iv, Abth. §8).

of feeling. What then? The nature of feeling – a nature of which every special feeling, without distinction of objects, partakes. Thus, feeling is pronounced to be religious, simply because it is feeling; the ground of its religiousness is its own nature – lies in itself. But is not feeling thereby declared to be itself the absolute, the divine? If feeling in itself is good, religious, i.e., holy, divine, has not feeling its God in itself?

But if, notwithstanding, thou wilt posit an object of feeling, but at the same time seekest to express thy feeling truly, without introducing by thy reflection any foreign element, what remains to thee but to distinguish between thy individual feeling and the general nature of feeling; to separate the universal in feeling from the disturbing, adulterating influences with which feeling is bound up in thee, under thy individual conditions? Hence what thou canst alone contemplate, declare to be the infinite, and define as its essence, is merely the nature of feeling. Thou hast thus no other definition of God than this: God is pure, unlimited, free Feeling. Every other God, whom thou supposest, is a God thrust upon thy feeling from without. Feeling is atheistic in the sense of the orthodox belief, which attaches religion to an external object; it denies an objective God – it is itself God. In this point of view only the negation of feeling is the negation of God. Thou art simply too cowardly or too narrow to confess in words what thy feeling tacitly affirms. Fettered by outward considerations, still in bondage to vulgar empiricism, incapable of comprehending the spiritual grandeur of feeling, thou art terrified before the religious atheism of thy heart. By this fear thou destroyest the unity of thy feeling with itself, in imagining to thyself an objective being distinct from thy feeling, and thus necessarily sinking back into the old questions and doubts – is there a God or not? – questions and doubts which vanish, nay, are impossible, where feeling is defined as the essence of religion. Feeling is thy own inward power, but at the same time a power distinct from thee, and independent of thee; it is in thee, above thee; it is itself that which constitutes the objective in thee – thy own being which impresses thee as another being; in short, thy God. How wilt thou, then, distinguish from this objective being within thee another objective being? how wilt thou get beyond thy feeling?

But feeling has here been adduced only as an example. It is the same with every other power, faculty, potentiality, reality, activity – the name is indifferent – which is defined as the essential organ of any object. Whatever is a subjective expression of a nature is simultaneously also its objective expression. Man cannot get beyond his true nature. He may indeed by means of the imagination conceive individuals of another so-called higher kind, but he can never get loose from his species, his nature; the conditions of being, the positive final predicates which he gives to these other individuals, are always determinations or qualities drawn from his own nature – qualities in which he in truth only images and projects himself. There may certainly be thinking beings besides men on the other planets of our solar system. But by the supposition of such beings we do not change our standing point – we extend our conceptions *quantitatively* not *qualitatively*. For as surely as on the other planets there are the same laws of motion, so surely are there the same laws of perception and thought as here. In fact, we people the other planets, not that we may place there different beings from ourselves, but *more* beings of our own or of a similar nature.[6]

§2. *The essence of religion considered generally*

What we have hitherto been maintaining generally, even with regard to sensational impressions, of the relation between subject and object, applies especially to the relation between the subject and the religious object.

In the perceptions of the senses consciousness of the object is distinguishable from consciousness of self; but in religion, consciousness of the object and self-consciousness coincide. The object of the senses is out of man, the religious object is within him, and therefore as little forsakes him as his self-consciousness or his conscience; it is the intimate, the closest object. 'God', says Augustine, for example, 'is nearer, more related to us, and therefore more easily known by us, than sensible, corporeal things.'[7] The object of the senses is in itself indifferent – independent of the disposition or of the judgment; but the object of religion is a selected object; the most excellent, the first, the supreme being; it essentially presupposes a critical judgment, a discrimination between the divine and the non-divine, between that which is worthy of adoration and that which is not worthy.[8] And here

[6] 'Verisimile est, non minus quam geometriae, etiam musicae oblectationem ad plures quam ad nos pertinere. Positis enim aliis terris atque animalibus ratione et auditu pollentibus, cur tantum his nostris contigisset ea voluptas, quae sola ex sono percipi potest?' [It is probable that the pleasure of music also, no less than of geometry pertains to more beings than just to us. For if other bodies and animals endowed with reason and hearing be posited, why would that pleasure, which is only able to be perceived by sound, only touch our senses? (Christ. Hugenius, *Cosrmotheor.*, I, i).]

[7] *De Genesi ad litteram*, l. v. c. 16.

[8] 'Unusquisque vestrum non cogitat, *prius* se debere Deum *nosse*, quam *colere*.' [Not one of you thinks that he ought to have known God before he worships God. (M. Minucii Felicis Octavianus, c. 24)].

may be applied, without any limitation, the proposition: the object of any subject is nothing else than the subject's own nature taken objectively. Such as are a man's thoughts and dispositions, such is his God; so much worth as a man has, so much and no more has his God. Consciousness of God is self-consciousness, knowledge of God is self-knowledge. By his God thou knowest the man, and by the man his God; the two are identical. Whatever is God to a man, that is his heart and soul; and conversely, God is the manifested inward nature, the expressed self of a man – religion the solemn unveiling of a man's hidden treasures, the revelation of his intimate thoughts, the open confession of his love-secrets.

But when religion – consciousness of God – is designated as the self-consciousness of man, this is not to be understood as affirming that the religious man is directly aware of this identity; for, on the contrary, ignorance of it is fundamental to the peculiar nature of religion. To preclude this misconception, it is better to say, religion is man's earliest and also indirect form of self-knowledge. Hence religion everywhere precedes philosophy, as in the history of the race, so also in that of the individual. Man first of all sees his nature as if *out of* himself, before he finds it in himself. His own nature is in the first instance contemplated by him as that of another being. Religion is the childlike condition of humanity; but the child sees his nature – man – out of himself; in childhood a man is an object to himself, under the form of another man. Hence the historical progress of religion consists in this: that what by an earlier religion was regarded as objective, is now recognized as subjective; that is, what was formerly contemplated and worshipped as God is now perceived to be something *human*. What was at first religion becomes at a later period idolatry; man is seen to have adored his own nature. Man has given objectivity to himself, but has not recognized the object as his own nature: a later religion takes this forward step; every advance in religion is therefore a deeper self-knowledge. But every particular religion, while it pronounces its predecessors idolatrous, excepts itself – and necessarily so, otherwise it would no longer be religion – from the fate, the common nature of all religions: it imputes only to other religions what is the fault, if fault it be, of religion in general. Because it has a different object, a different tenor, because it has transcended the ideas of preceding religions, it erroneously supposes itself exalted above the necessary eternal laws which constitute the essence of religion – it fancies its object, its ideas, to be superhuman. But the essence of religion, thus hidden from the religious, is evident to the thinker, by whom religion is viewed objectively, which it cannot be by its votaries. And it is our task to show that the antithesis of divine and human is altogether illusory, that it is nothing else than the antithesis between the human nature in general and the human individual; that, consequently, the object and contents of the Christian religion are altogether human.

Religion, at least the Christian, is the relation of man to himself, or more correctly to his own nature (i.e., his subjective nature);[9] but a relation to it, viewed as a nature apart from his own. The divine being is nothing else than the human being, or, rather, the human nature purified, freed from the limits of the individual man, made objective – i.e., contemplated and revered as another, a distinct being. All the attributes of the divine nature are, therefore, attributes of the human nature.[10]

In relation to the attributes, the predicates, of the Divine Being, this is admitted without hesitation, but by no means in relation to the subject of these predicates. The negation of the subject is held to be irreligion, nay, atheism; though not so the negation of the predicates. But that which has no predicates or qualities, has no effect upon me; that which has no effect upon me has no existence for me. To deny all the qualities of a being is equivalent to denying the being himself. A being without qualities is one which cannot become an object to the mind, and such a being is virtually non-existent. Where man deprives God of all qualities, God is no longer anything more to him than a negative being. To the truly religious man, God is not a being without qualities, because to him he is a positive, real being. The theory that God cannot be defined, and consequently cannot be known by man, is therefore the offspring of recent times, a product of modern unbelief.

As reason is and can be pronounced finite only where man regards sensual enjoyment, or religious emotion, or aesthetic contemplation, or moral sentiment, as the absolute, the true; so the proposition that God is unknowable or undefinable, can only be enunciated and

[9] The meaning of this parenthetic limitation will be clear in the sequel.

[10] 'Les perfections de Dieu sont celles de nos âmes, mais il les possède sans bornes – il y a en nous quelque puissance, quelque connaissance, quelque bonté, mais elles sont toutes entières en Dieu.' – Leibniz (*Théod.* Preface). 'Nihil in anima esse putemus eximium, quod non etiam divinae naturae proprium sit – Quidquid a Deo alienum extra definitionem animae.' – St. Gregorius Nyss. 'Est ergo, ut videtur, disciplinarum omnium pulcherrima et maxima se ipsum nosse; si quis enim se ipsum norit, Deum cognoscet.' [We should think that there is nothing extraordinary in the soul which is not proper also to the divine nature. Whatever is foreign to God is outside the definition of the soul. – Greg. Nyssa. The most beautiful of all disciplines and the greatest, as it seems, therefore, is to have known oneself; for if anyone had known himself, he will know God. (Clement of Alexandria, *Paedagogia*, lec. 3, ch. 1.)]

become fixed as a dogma, where this object has no longer any interest for the intellect; where the real, the positive, alone has any hold on man, where the real alone has for him the significance of the essential, of the absolute, divine object, but where at the same time, in contradiction with this purely worldly tendency, there yet exist some old remains of religiousness. On the ground that God is unknowable, man excuses himself to what is yet remaining of his religious conscience for his forgetfulness of God, his absorption in the world: he denies God practically by his conduct – the world has possession of all his thoughts and inclinations – but he does not deny him theoretically, he does not attack his existence; he lets that rest. But this existence does not affect or incommode him; it is a merely negative existence, an existence without existence, a self-contradictory existence – a state of being which, as to its effects, is not distinguishable from non-being. The denial of determinate, positive predicates concerning the divine nature is nothing else than a denial of religion, with, however, an appearance of religion in its favour, so that it is not recognized as a denial; it is simply a subtle, disguised atheism. The alleged religious horror of limiting God by positive predicates is only the irreligious wish to know nothing more of God, to banish God from the mind. Dread of limitation is dread of existence. All real existence, i.e., all existence which is truly such, is qualitative, determinative existence. He who earnestly believes in the Divine existence is not shocked at the attributing even of gross sensuous qualities to God. He who dreads an existence that may give offence, who shrinks from the grossness of a positive predicate, may as well renounce existence altogether. A God who is injured by determinate qualities has not the courage and the strength to exist. Qualities are the fire, the vital breath, the oxygen, the salt of existence. An existence in general, an existence without qualities, is an insipidity, an absurdity. But there can be no more in God than is supplied by religion. Only where man loses his taste for religion, and thus religion itself becomes insipid, does the existence of God become an insipid existence – an existence without qualities.

There is, however, a still milder way of denying the divine predicates than the direct one just described. It is admitted that the predicates of the divine nature are finite, and, more particularly, human qualities, but their rejection is rejected; they are even taken under protection, because it is necessary to man to have a definite conception of God, and since he is man he can form no other than a human conception of him. In relation to God, it is said, these predicates are certainly without any objective validity; but to me, if he is to exist for me, he cannot appear otherwise than as he does appear to me, namely, as a being with attributes analogous to the human. But this distinction between what God is in himself, and what he is for me destroys the peace of religion, and is besides in itself an unfounded and untenable distinction. I cannot know whether God is something else in himself or for himself than he is for me; what he is to me is to me all that he is. For me, there lies in these predicates under which he exists for me, what he is in himself, his very nature; he is for me what he can alone ever be for me. The religious man finds perfect satisfaction in that which God is in relation to himself; of any other relation he knows nothing, for God is to him what he can alone be to man. In the distinction above stated, man takes a point of view above himself, i.e., above his nature, the absolute measure of his being; but this transcendentalism is only an illusion; for I can make the distinction between the object as it is in itself, and the object as it is for me, only where an object can really appear otherwise to me, not where it appears to me such as the absolute measure of my nature determines it to appear – such as it must appear to me. It is true that I may have a merely subjective conception, i.e., one which does not arise out of the general constitution of my species; but if my conception is determined by the constitution of my species, the distinction between what an object is in itself, and what it is for me ceases; for this conception is itself an absolute one. The measure of the species is the absolute measure, law, and criterion of man. And, indeed, religion has the conviction that its conceptions, its predicates of God, are such as every man ought to have, and must have, if he would have the true ones – that they are the conceptions necessary to human nature; nay, further, that they are objectively true, representing God as he is. To every religion the gods of *other* religions are only notions concerning God, but its own conception of God is to it God himself, the true God – God such as he is in himself. Religion is satisfied only with a complete Deity, a God without reservation; it will not have a mere phantasm of God; it demands God himself. Religion gives up its own existence when it gives up the nature of God; it is no longer a truth when it renounces the possession of the true God. Scepticism is the arch-enemy of religion; but the distinction between object and conception – between God as he is in himself, and God as he is for me – is a sceptical distinction, and therefore an irreligious one.

That which is to man the self-existent, the highest being, to which he can conceive nothing higher – that is to him the Divine Being. How then should he inquire concerning this being, what he is in himself? If God were an object to the bird, he would be a winged being: the bird knows nothing higher, nothing more blissful, than the winged condition. How ludicrous would it be if this bird pronounced: to me God appears as a bird, but what he is in himself I know not. To the bird the highest nature is the bird-nature; take from him the conception of this, and you take from him the conception of the highest being. How, then, could he ask whether God in himself were winged? To ask whether God is in himself what he is for me, is to ask whether God is God, is to lift oneself above one's God, to rise up against him.

Wherever, therefore, this idea, that the religious predicates are only anthropomorphisms, has taken possession of a man, there has doubt, has unbelief, obtained the mastery of faith. And it is only the inconsequence of faint-heartedness and intellectual imbecility which does not proceed from this idea to the formal negation of the predicates, and from thence to the negation of the subject to which they relate. If thou doubtest the objective truth of the predicates, thou must also doubt the objective truth of the subject whose predicates they are. If thy predicates are anthropomorphisms, the subject of them is an anthropomorphism too. If love, goodness, personality, &c., are human attributes, so also is the subject which thou presupposest, the existence of God, the belief that there is a God, an anthropomorphism – a presupposition purely human. Whence knowest thou that the belief in a God at all is not a limitation of man's mode of conception? Higher beings – and thou supposest such – are perhaps so blest in themselves, so at unity with themselves, that they are not hung in suspense between themselves and a yet higher being. To know God and not oneself to be God, to know blessedness and not oneself to enjoy it, is a state of disunity, of unhappiness. Higher beings know nothing of this unhappiness; they have no conception of that which they are not.

Thou believest in love as a divine attribute because thou thyself lovest; thou believest that God is a wise, benevolent being because thou knowest nothing better in thyself than benevolence and wisdom; and thou believest that God exists, that therefore he is a subject – whatever exists is a subject, whether it be defined as substance, person, essence, or otherwise – because thou thyself existest, art thyself a subject. Thou knowest no higher human good than to love, than to be good and wise; and even so thou knowest no higher happiness than to exist, to be a subject; for the consciousness of all reality, of all bliss, is for thee bound up in the consciousness of being a subject, of existing. God is an existence, a subject to thee, for the same reason that he is to thee a wise, a blessed, a personal being. The distinction between the divine predicates and the divine subject is only this, that to thee the subject, the existence, does not appear an anthropomorphism, because the conception of it is necessarily involved in thy own existence as a subject, whereas the predicates do appear anthropomorphisms, because their necessity – the necessity that God should be conscious, wise, good, &c. – is not an immediate necessity, identical with the being of man, but is evolved by his self-consciousness, by the activity of his thought. I am a subject, I exist, whether I be wise or unwise, good or bad. To exist is to man the first datum; it constitutes the very idea of the subject; it is presupposed by the predicates. Hence man relinquishes the predicates, but the existence of God is to him a settled, irrefragable, absolutely certain, objective truth. But, nevertheless, this distinction is merely an apparent one. The necessity of the subject lies only in the necessity of the predicate. Thou art a subject only in so far as thou art a human subject; the certainty and reality of thy existence lie only in the certainty and reality of thy human attributes. What the subject is lies only in the predicate; the predicate is the *truth* of the subject – the subject only the personified, existing predicate, the predicate conceived as existing. Subject and predicate are distinguished only as existence and essence. The negation of the predicates is therefore the negation of the subject. What remains of the human subject when abstracted from the human attributes? Even in the language of common life the divine predicates – Providence, Omniscience, Omnipotence – are put for the divine subject.

The certainty of the existence of God, of which it has been said that it is as certain, nay, more certain to man than his own existence, depends only on the certainty of the qualities of God – it is in itself no immediate certainty. To the Christian the existence of the Christian God only is a certainty; to the heathen that of the heathen God only. The heathen did not doubt the existence of Jupiter, because he took no offence at the nature of Jupiter, because he could conceive of God under no other qualities, because to him these qualities were a certainty, a divine reality. The reality of the predicate is the sole guarantee of existence.

Whatever man conceives to be true, he immediately conceives to be real (that is, to have an objective existence), because, originally, only the real is true to him – true in opposition to what is merely conceived, dreamed, imagined. The idea of being, of existence, is the original idea of truth; or, originally, man makes truth dependent on existence, subsequently, existence dependent on truth. Now God is the nature of man regarded as absolute truth, – the truth of man; but God, or, what is the same thing, religion, is as various as are the conditions under which man conceives this his nature, regards it as the highest being. These conditions, then, under which man conceives

God, are to him the truth, and for that reason they are also the highest existence, or rather they are existence itself; for only the emphatic, the highest existence, is existence, and deserves this name. Therefore, God is an existent, real being, on the very same ground that he is a particular, definite being; for the qualities of God are nothing else than the essential qualities of man himself, and a particular man is what he is, has his existence, his reality, only in his particular conditions. Take away from the Greek the quality of being Greek, and you take away his existence. On this ground it is true that for a definite positive religion – that is, relatively – the certainty of the existence of God is *immediate*; for just as involuntarily, as necessarily, as the Greek was a Greek, so necessarily were his gods Greek beings, so necessarily were they real, existent beings. Religion is that conception of the nature of the world and of man which is essential to, i.e., identical with, a man's nature. But man does not stand above this his necessary conception; on the contrary, it stands above him; it animates, determines, governs him. The necessity of a proof, of a middle term to unite qualities with existence, the possibility of a doubt, is abolished. Only that which is apart from my own being is capable of being doubted by me. How then can I doubt of God, who is my being? To doubt of God is to doubt of myself. Only when God is thought of abstractly, when his predicates are the result of philosophic abstraction, arises the distinction or separation between subject and predicate, existence and nature – arises the fiction that the existence or the subject is something else than the predicate, something immediate, indubitable, in distinction from the predicate, which is held to be doubtful. But this is only a fiction. A God who has abstract predicates has also an abstract existence. Existence, being, varies with varying qualities.

The identity of the subject and predicate is clearly evidenced by the progressive development of religion, which is identical with the progressive development of human culture. So long as man is in a mere state of nature, so long is his god a mere nature-god – a personification of some natural force. Where man inhabits houses, he also encloses his gods in temples. The temple is only a manifestation of the value which man attaches to beautiful buildings. Temples in honour of religion are in truth temples in honour of architecture. With the emerging of man from a state of savagery and wildness to one of culture, with the distinction between what is fitting for man and what is not fitting, arises simultaneously the distinction between that which is fitting and that which is not fitting for God. God is the idea of majesty, of the highest dignity: the religious sentiment is the sentiment of supreme fitness. The later more cultured artists of Greece were the first to embody in the statues of the gods the ideas of dignity, of spiritual grandeur, of imperturbable repose and serenity. But why were these qualities in their view attributes, predicates of God? Because they were in themselves regarded by the Greeks as divinities. Why did those artists exclude all disgusting and low passions? Because they perceived them to be unbecoming, unworthy, unhuman, and consequently ungodlike. The Homeric gods eat and drink – that implies eating and drinking is a divine pleasure. Physical strength is an attribute of the Homeric gods: Zeus is the strongest of the gods. Why? Because physical strength, in and by itself, was regarded as something glorious, divine. To the ancient Germans the highest virtues were those of the warrior; therefore their supreme god was the god of war, Odin – war, 'the original or oldest law'. Not the attribute of the divinity, but the divineness or deity of the attribute, is the first true Divine Being. Thus what theology and philosophy have held to be God, the Absolute, the Infinite, is not God; but that which they have held not to be God is God: namely, the attribute, the quality, whatever has reality. Hence he alone is the true atheist to whom the predicates of the Divine Being – for example, love, wisdom, justice – are nothing; not he to whom merely the subject of these predicates is nothing. And in no wise is the negation of the subject necessarily also a negation of the predicates considered in themselves. These have an intrinsic, independent reality; they force their recognition upon man by their very nature; they are self-evident truths to him; they prove, they attest themselves. It does not follow that goodness, justice, wisdom, are chimæras because the existence of God is a chimæra, nor truths because this is a truth. The idea of God is dependent on the idea of justice, of benevolence; a God who is not benevolent, not just, not wise, is no God; but the converse does not hold. The fact is not that a quality is divine because God has it, but that God has it because it is in itself divine: because without it God would be a defective being. Justice, wisdom, in general every quality which constitutes the divinity of God, is determined and known by itself independently, but the idea of God is determined by the qualities which have thus been previously judged to be worthy of the divine nature; only in the case in which I identify God and justice, in which I think of God immediately as the reality of the idea of justice, is the idea of God self-determined. But if God as a subject is the determined, while the quality, the predicate, is the determining, then in truth the rank of the godhead is due not to the subject, but to the predicate.

Not until several, and those contradictory, attributes are united in one being, and this being is conceived as personal – the personality being thus brought into especial prominence – not until then is the origin of religion lost sight of, is it forgotten that what the activity of the reflective power has converted into a predicate distinguishable or separable from the subject, was originally the true subject. Thus the Greeks and Romans deified accidents as substances; virtues, states of mind, passions, as independent beings. Man, especially the religious man, is to himself the measure of all things, of all reality. Whatever strongly impresses a man, whatever produces an unusual effect on his mind, if it be only a peculiar, inexplicable sound or note, he personifies as a divine being. Religion embraces all the objects of the world: everything existing has been an object of religious reverence; in the nature and consciousness of religion there is nothing else than what lies in the nature of man in his consciousness of himself and of the world. Religion has no material exclusively its own. In Rome even the passions of fear and terror had their temples. The Christians also made mental phenomena into independent beings, their own feelings into qualities of things, the passions which governed them into powers which governed the world, in short, predicates of their own nature, whether recognized as such or not, into independent subjective existences. Devils, kobolds, witches, ghosts, angels, were sacred truths as long as the religious spirit held undivided sway over mankind.

In order to banish from the mind the identity of the divine and human predicates, and the consequent identity of the divine and human nature, recourse is had to the idea that God, as the absolute, real Being, has an infinite fullness of various predicates, of which we here know only a part, and those such as are analogous to our own; while the rest, by virtue of which God must thus have quite a different nature from the human or that which is analogous to the human, we shall only know in the future – that is, after death. But an infinite plenitude or multitude of predicates which are really different, so different that the one does not immediately involve the other, is realized only in an infinite plenitude or multitude of different beings or individuals. Thus the human nature presents an infinite abundance of different predicates, and for that very reason it presents an infinite abundance of different individuals. Each new man is a new predicate, a new phasis of humanity. As many as are the men, so many are the powers, the properties of humanity. It is true that there are the same elements in every individual, but under such various conditions and modifications that they appear new and peculiar. The mystery of the inexhaustible fullness of the divine predicates is therefore nothing else than the mystery of human nature considered as an infinitely varied, infinitely modifiable, but, consequently, phenomenal being. Only in the realm of the senses, only in space and time, does there exist a being of really infinite qualities or predicates. Where there are really different predicates there are different times. One man is a distinguished musician, a distinguished author, a distinguished physician; but he cannot compose music, write books, and perform cures in the same moment of time. Time, and not the Hegelian dialectic, is the medium of uniting opposites, contradictories, in one and the same subject. But distinguished and detached from the nature of man, and combined with the idea of God, the infinite fulness of various predicates is a conception without reality, a mere phantasy, a conception derived from the sensible world, but without the essential conditions, without the truth of sensible existence, a conception which stands in direct contradiction with the Divine Being considered as a spiritual, i.e., an abstract, simple, single being; for the predicates of God are precisely of this character, that one involves all the others, because there is no real difference between them. If, therefore, in the present predicates I have not the future, in the present God not the future God, then the future God is not the present, but they are two distinct beings.[11] But this distinction is in contradiction with the unity and simplicity of the theological God. Why is a given predicate a predicate of God? Because it is divine in its nature, i.e., because it expresses no limitation, no defect. Why are other predicates applied to him? Because, however various in themselves, they agree in this, that they all alike express perfection, unlimitedness. Hence I can conceive innumerable predicates of God, because they must all agree with the abstract idea of the Godhead, and must have in common that which constitutes every single predicate a divine attribute. Thus it is in the system of Spinoza. He speaks of an infinite number of attributes of the divine substance, but he specifies none except Thought and Extension. Why? Because it is a matter of indifference to know them; nay, because they are in themselves indifferent, superfluous; for with all these innumerable predicates, I yet always mean to say the same thing as when I speak of Thought and Extension. Why is Thought an attribute of substance? Because, according to Spinoza, it is capable of being conceived by itself, because it expresses something indivisible, perfect, infinite. Why Extension or Matter? For the same reason. Thus, substance can have an indefinite number of predicates, because it is not their specific

[11] For religious faith there is no other distinction between the present and future God than that the former is an object of faith, of conception, of imagination, while the latter is to be an object of immediate, that is, personal, sensible perception. In this life and in the next he is the same God; but in the one he is incomprehensible, in the other comprehensible.

definition, their difference, but their identity, their equivalence, which makes them attributes of substance. Or rather, substance has innumerable predicates only because (how strange!) it has properly no predicate; that is, no definite, real predicate. The indefinite unity which is the product of thought, completes itself by the indefinite multiplicity which is the product of the imagination. Because the predicate is not *multum*, it is *multa*. In truth, the positive predicates are Thought and Extension. In these two infinitely more is said than in the nameless innumerable predicates; for they express something definite – in them I have something. But substance is too indifferent, too apathetic to be *something*; that is, to have qualities and passions; that it may not be something, it is rather nothing.

Now, when it is shown that what the subject is lies entirely in the attributes of the subject; that is, that the predicate is the true subject; it is also proved that if the divine predicates are attributes of the human nature, the subject of those predicates is also of the human nature. But the divine predicates are partly general, partly personal. The general predicates are the metaphysical, but these serve only as external points of support to religion; they are not the characteristic definitions of religion. It is the personal predicates alone which constitute the essence of religion – in which the Divine Being is the object of religion. Such are, for example, that God is a Person, that he is the moral Lawgiver, the Father of mankind, the Holy One, the Just, the Good, the Merciful. It is, however, at once clear, or it will at least be clear in the sequel, with regard to these and other definitions, that, especially as applied to a personality, they are purely human definitions, and that consequently man in religion – in his relation to God – is in relation to his own nature; for to the religious sentiment these predicates are not mere conceptions, mere images, which man forms of God, to be distinguished from that which God is in himself, but truths, facts, realities. Religion knows nothing of anthropomorphisms; to it they are not anthropomorphisms. It is the very essence of religion, that to it these definitions express the nature of God. They are pronounced to be images only by the understanding, which reflects on religion, and which while defending them yet before its own tribunal denies them. But to the religious sentiment God is a real Father, real Love and Mercy; for to it he is a real, living, personal being, and therefore his attributes are also living and personal. Nay, the definitions which are the most sufficing to the religious sentiment are precisely those which give the most offence to the understanding, and which in the process of reflection on religion it denies. Religion is essentially emotion; hence, objectively also, emotion is to it necessarily of a divine nature. Even anger appears to it an emotion not unworthy of God, provided only there be a religious motive at the foundation of this anger.

But here it is also essential to observe, and this phenomenon is an extremely remarkable one, characterizing the very core of religion, that in proportion as the divine subject is in reality human, the greater is the apparent difference between God and man; that is, the more, by reflection on religion, by theology, is the identity of the divine and human denied, and the human, considered as such, is depreciated.[12] The reason of this is, that as what is positive in the conception of the divine being can only be human, the conception of man, as an object of consciousness, can only be negative. To enrich God, man must become poor; that God may be all, man must be nothing. But he desires to be nothing in himself, because what he takes from himself is not lost to him, since it is preserved in God. Man has his being in God; why then should he have it in himself? Where is the necessity of positing the same thing twice, of having it twice? What man withdraws from himself, what he renounces in himself, he only enjoys in an incomparably higher and fuller measure in God.

The monks made a vow of chastity to God; they mortified the sexual passion in themselves, but therefore they had in heaven, in the Virgin Mary, the image of woman – an image of love. They could the more easily dispense with real woman in proportion as an ideal woman was an object of love to them. The greater the importance they attached to the denial of sensuality, the greater the importance of the heavenly virgin for them: she was to them in the place of Christ, in the stead of God. The more the sensual tendencies are renounced, the more sensual is the God to whom they are sacrificed. For whatever is made an offering to God has an especial value attached to it; in it God is supposed to have especial pleasure. That which is the highest in the estimation of man is naturally the highest in the estimation of his God; what pleases man pleases God also. The Hebrews did not offer to Jehovah unclean, ill-conditioned animals; on the contrary, those which they most highly prized, which they themselves ate, were also the food of God (*Dibus Dei*, Lev. iii. 2). Wherever, therefore, the denial of the sensual delights is made a special offering, a sacrifice well-pleasing to God, there the highest

[12] Inter creatorem et creaturam non potest tanta similitudo notari, quin inter eos major sit dissimilitudo notanda. [Between the Creator and the creature such great similarity cannot be noted that a greater difference between them would not be noted. Lateran Council, Canon 2. (*Summa Omn. Conc.*,, Carranza, Antw. 1559, p. 326.)] The last distinction between man and God, between the finite and infinite nature, to which the religious speculative imagination soars, is the distinction between Something and Nothing, Ens and Non Ens; for only in Nothing is all community with other beings abolished.

value is attached to the senses, and the sensuality which has been renounced is unconsciously restored, in the fact that God takes the place of the material delights which have been renounced. The nun weds herself to God; she has a heavenly bridegroom, the monk a heavenly bride. But the heavenly virgin is only a sensible presentation of a general truth, having relation to the essence of religion. Man denies as to himself only what he attributes to God. Religion abstracts from man, from the world; but it can only abstract from the limitations, from the phenomena; in short, from the negative, not from the essence, the positive, of the world and humanity: hence, in the very abstraction and negation it must recover that from which it abstracts, or believes itself to abstract. And thus, in reality, whatever religion consciously denies – always supposing that what is denied by it is something essential, true, and consequently incapable of being ultimately denied – it unconsciously restores in God. Thus, in religion man denies his reason; of himself he knows nothing of God, his thoughts are only worldly, earthly; he can only believe what God reveals to him. But on this account the thoughts of God are human, earthly thoughts: like man, he has plans in his mind, he accommodates himself to circumstances and grades of intelligence, like a tutor with his pupils; he calculates closely the effect of his gifts and revelations; he observes man in all his doings; he knows all things, even the most earthly, the commonest, the most trivial. In brief, man in relation to God denies his own knowledge, his own thoughts, that he may place them in God. Man gives up his personality; but in return, God, the Almighty, infinite, unlimited being is a person; he denies human dignity, the human *ego*; but in return God is to him a selfish, egoistical being, who in all things seeks only himself, his own honour, his own ends; he represents God as simply seeking the satisfaction of his own selfishness, while yet he frowns on that of every other being; his God is the very luxury of egoism.[13] Religion further denies goodness as a quality of human nature; man is wicked, corrupt, incapable of good; but, on the other hand, God is only good – the Good Being. Man's nature demands as an object goodness, personified as God; but is it not hereby declared that goodness is an essential tendency of man? If my heart is wicked, my understanding perverted, how can I perceive and feel the holy to be holy, the good to be good? Could I perceive the beauty of a fine picture if my mind were aesthetically

[13] Gloriam suam plus amat Deus quam omnes creaturas. [God loves his own glory more than all creatures.] 'God can only love himself, can only think of himself, can only work for himself. In creating man, God seeks his own ends, his own glory', &c. – Vide P. Bayle, *Ein Beitrag zur Geschichte der Philos. u. Menschh.*, pp. 104–7.

an absolute piece of perversion? Though I may not be a painter, though I may not have the power of producing what is beautiful myself, I must yet have aesthetic feeling, aesthetic comprehension, since I perceive the beauty that is presented to me externally. Either goodness does not exist at all for man, or, if it does exist, therein is revealed to the individual man the holiness and goodness of human nature. That which is absolutely opposed to my nature, to which I am united by no bond of sympathy, is not even conceivable or perceptible by me. The holy is in opposition to me only as regards the modifications of my personality, but as regards my fundamental nature it is in unity with me. The holy is a reproach to my sinfulness; in it I recognize myself as a sinner; but in so doing, while I blame myself, I acknowledge what I am not, but ought to be, and what, for that very reason, I, according to my destination, can be; for an 'ought' which has no corresponding capability does not affect me, is a ludicrous chimaera without any true relation to my mental constitution. But when I acknowledge goodness as my destination, as my law, I acknowledge it, whether consciously or unconsciously, as my own nature. Another nature than my own, one different in quality, cannot touch me. I can perceive sin as sin, only when I perceive it to be a contradiction of myself with myself – that is, of my personality with my fundamental nature. As a contradiction of the absolute, considered as another being, the feeling of sin is inexplicable, unmeaning.

The distinction between Augustinianism and Pelagianism consists only in this, that the former expresses after the manner of religion what the latter expresses after the manner of Rationalism. Both say the same thing, both vindicate the goodness of man; but Pelagianism does it directly, in a rationalistic and moral form; Augustinianism indirectly, in a mystical, that is, a religious form.[14] For that which is given to man's God is in truth given to man himself; what a man

[14] Pelagianism denies God, religion – isti tantam tribuunt potestatem voluntati, ut pietati auferant orationem. (*Augustin de Nat. et Grat. cont. Pelagium*, c. 58). [They attribute such great power to the will that they take away prayer from piety. (Augustine, *Concerning Nature and Grace against Pelagius*, Ch. 58.)] It has only the Creator, i.e., Nature, as a basis, not the Saviour, the true God of the religious sentiment – in a word, it denies God; but, as a consequence of this, it elevates man into a God, since it makes him a being not needing God, self-sufficing, independent. (See on this subject Luther against Erasmus and Augustine, l. c. c. 33.) Augustinianism denies man; but, as a consequence of this, it reduces God to the level of man, even to the ignominy of the cross, for the sake of man. The former puts man in the place of God, the latter puts God in the place of man; both lead to the same result – the distinction is only apparent, a pious illusion. Augustinianism is only an inverted Pelagianism; what to the latter is a subject, is to the former an object.

declares concerning God, he in truth declares concerning himself. Augustinianism would be a truth, and a truth opposed to Pelagianism, only if man had the devil for his God, and, with the consciousness that he was the devil, honoured, reverenced, and worshipped him as the highest being. But so long as man adores a good being as his God, so long does he contemplate in God the goodness of his own nature.

As with the doctrine of the radical corruption of human nature, so is it with the identical doctrine, that man can do nothing good, i.e., in truth, nothing of himself – by his own strength. For the denial of human strength and spontaneous moral activity to be true, the moral activity of God must also be denied; and we must say, with the Oriental nihilist or pantheist: the Divine being is absolutely without will or action, indifferent, knowing nothing of the discrimination between evil and good. But he who defines God as an active being, and not only so, but as morally active and morally critical – as a being who loves, works, and rewards good, punishes, rejects, and condemns evil – he who thus defines God only in appearance denies human activity, in fact, making it the highest, the most real activity. He who makes God act humanly, declares human activity to be divine; he says: a god who is not active, and not morally or humanly active, is no god; and thus he makes the idea of the Godhead dependent on the idea of activity, that is, of human activity, for a higher he knows not.

Man – this is the mystery of religion – projects his being into objectivity,[15] and then again makes himself an object to this projected image of himself thus converted into a subject; he thinks of himself is an object to himself, but as the object of an object, of another being than himself. Thus here. Man is an object to God. That man is good or evil is not indifferent to God; no! He has a lively, profound interest in man's being good; he wills that man should be good, happy – for without goodness there is no happiness. Thus the religious man virtually retracts the nothingness of human activity, by making his dispositions and actions an object to God, by making man the end of God – for that which is an object to the mind is an end in action; by making the divine activity a means of human salvation. God acts, that man may be good and happy. Thus man, while he is apparently humiliated to the lowest degree, is in truth exalted to the highest.

[15] The religious, the original mode in which man becomes objective to himself, is (as is clearly enough explained in this work) to be distinguished from the mode in which this occurs in reflection and speculation; the latter is voluntary, the former involuntary, necessary – as necessary as art, as speech. With the progress of time, it is true, theology coincides with religion.

Thus, in and through God, man has in view himself alone. It is true that man places the aim of his action in God, but God has no other aim of action than the moral and eternal salvation of man: thus man has in fact no other aim than himself. The divine activity is not distinct from the human.

How could the divine activity work on me as its object, nay, work in me, if it were essentially different from me; how could it have a human aim, the aim of ameliorating and blessing man, if it were not itself human? Does not the purpose determine the nature of the act? When man makes his moral improvement an aim to himself, he has divine resolutions, divine projects; but also, when God seeks the salvation of man, he has human ends and a human mode of activity corresponding to these ends. Thus in God man has only his own activity as an object. But for the very reason that he regards his own activity as objective, goodness only as an object, he necessarily receives the impulse, the motive not from himself, but from this object. He contemplates his nature as external to himself, and this nature as goodness; thus it is self-evident, it is mere tautology to say that the impulse to good comes only from thence where he places the good.

God is the highest subjectivity of man abstracted from himself; hence man can do nothing of himself, all goodness comes from God. The more subjective God is, the more completely does man divest himself of his subjectivity, because God is, *per se*, his relinquished self, the possession of which he however again vindicates to himself. As the action of the arteries drives the blood into the extremities, and the action of the veins brings it back again, as life in general consists in a perpetual systole and diastole; so is it in religion. In the religious systole man propels his own nature from himself, he throws himself outward; in the religious diastole he receives the rejected nature into his heart again. God alone is the being who acts of himself – this is the force of repulsion in religion; God is the being who acts in me, with me, through me, upon me, for me, is the principle of my salvation, of my good dispositions and actions, consequently my own good principle and nature – this is the force of attraction in religion.

The course of religious development which has been generally indicated consists specifically in this, that man abstracts more and more from God, and attributes more and more to himself. This is especially apparent in the belief in revelation. That which to a later age or a cultured people is given by nature or reason, is to an earlier age, or to a yet uncultured people, given by God. Every tendency of man, however natural – even the impulse to cleanliness, was conceived by the Israelites as a positive divine ordinance. From this example we again see that God is lowered, is conceived more entirely on the type of ordinary humanity, in proportion as man detracts from himself. How can the self-humiliation of man go further than when he disclaims the capability of fulfilling spontaneously the requirements of common decency?[16] The Christian religion, on the other hand, distinguished the impulses and passions of man according to their quality, their character; it represented only good emotions, good dispositions, good thoughts, as revelations, operations – that is, as dispositions, feelings, thoughts, – of God; for what God reveals is a quality of God himself: that of which the heart is full overflows the lips; as is the effect such is the cause; as the revelation, such the being who reveals himself. A God who reveals himself in good dispositions is a God whose essential attribute is only moral perfection. The Christian religion distinguishes inward moral purity from external physical purity; the Israelites identified the two.[17] In relation to the Israelitish religion, the Christian religion is one of criticism and freedom. The Israelite trusted himself to do nothing except what was commanded by God; he was without will even in external things; the authority of religion extended itself even to his food. The Christian religion, on the other hand, in all these external things made man dependent on himself, i.e., placed in man what the Israelite placed out of himself in God. Israel is the most complete presentation of Positivism in religion. In relation to the Israelite, the Christian is an *esprit fort*, a free-thinker. Thus do things change. What yesterday was still religion is no longer such today; and what today is atheism, tomorrow will be religion.

[16] Deut. xxiii. 12, 13.

[17] See, for example, Gen. xxxv. 2; Levit. xi. 44; xx. 26; and the Commentary of Le Clerc on these passages.

Provisional Theses for the Reformation of Philosophy

The secret of *theology* is *anthropology*, but the secret of *speculative philosophy* is *theology*, the *speculative* theology. Speculative theology distinguishes itself from *ordinary* theology by the fact that it transfers the divine essence into this world. That is, speculative theology *envisions*, *determines*, and *realizes* in this world the divine essence transported by ordinary theology out of fear and ignorance into another world.

Spinoza is the originator of speculative philosophy, *Schelling* its restorer, *Hegel* its perfecter.

Pantheism is the *necessary consequence* of theology (or of theism). It is *consistent* theology. *Atheism* is the *necessary consequence* of pantheism. It is *consistent* pantheism.[1]

Christianity is the *contradiction* of *polytheism* and *monotheism*. Pantheism is monotheism with the predicate of polytheism. That is, pantheism makes the independent entities of polytheism into predicates or attributes of one independent entity. Thus Spinoza makes thinking, as the quintessence of thinking things, and matter, as the quintessence of extended things, into attributes of the substance, i.e., of God. God is a thinking thing and God is an extended thing.

The philosophy of identity differed from the Spinozist philosophy only by the fact that it animated the dead, phlegmatic thing that is Spinoza's substance with the spirit of idealism. Hegel in particular made the activity of the self, the power of distinguishing itself, and

[1] These theological characterizations are used here only in the sense of trivial *nicknames*. [What follows this sentence is deleted from this footnote in the second edition. (Tr.)] In themselves they are false. As little as Spinoza's and Hegel's philosophy is pantheism (pantheism is an orientalism) is the new philosophy atheism. Concerning the transition from the *half-way* to the *complete* theology, i.e., to pantheism, see § 112 of my *History of Philosophy from Bacon to Spinoza*.

the consciousness of the self into the attribute of the substance. Hegel's paradoxical assertion: 'the consciousness of God is God's self-consciousness' rests upon *the same foundation* as Spinoza's paradoxical assertion: 'extension or matter is an attribute of substance'. Hegel's assertion only means that self-consciousness is an attribute of the substance or of God: God is I. The consciousness, which the theist attributes to God in distinction from *actual* consciousness, is only a representation without reality. However, Spinoza's assertion, 'matter is an *attribute* of substance', expresses only that matter is a substantial and divine essentiality; must as Hegel's assertion expresses only that consciousness is a divine essence.

The method of the reformatory critique of *speculative philosophy in general* does not differ from the critique already applied in the *philosophy of religion*. We only need always make the *predicate* into the *subject* and thus, as the subject, into the *object* and *principle*. Hence we need only *invert* speculative philosophy and then have the unmasked, pure, bare truth.

Atheism is the inverted pantheism.

Pantheism is the *negation of theology from the standpoint of theology*.

Just as for Spinoza (*Ethics*, Part I, Definition 3 and Proposition 10) the attribute or predicate of the substance is the substance itself, so also for Hegel the *predicate* of the absolute, of the subject in general, is the *subject itself*. The absolute is for Hegel being, essence and concept (spirit, self-consciousness). However, the absolute, thought only as being, is *nothing other* than being. The absolute, insofar as it is thought under this or that determinacy or category, is *completely* absorbed into this category or determinacy, so that *apart* from that determinacy it is a mere name. Yet in spite of this, the absolute *as the subject* still lies at the basis. The *true* subject, the *determination* by means of which the absolute is not a mere name but *something*, still has the significance of a mere predicate, just like the attribute for Spinoza.

The absolute or infinite of speculative philosophy is, psychologically considered, nothing other than something not determined, the indeterminate – the abstraction from everything determined, supposed as an essence distinguished from this abstraction but at the same time re-identified with it. Historically considered, however, it is nothing other than the old theological-metaphysical entity or non-entity which is *not* finite, *not* human, *not* material, not determined and *not* created – the pre-worldly nothing, supposed *as act*.

The Hegelian logic is the *theology* brought to *reason* and brought *up to date*, *theology* rendered as *logic. As the divine essence of theology is the ideal or abstract embodiment of all realities, i.e. of all determinations, of all finitudes, so is the Logic.* Everything on earth rediscovers itself in theology's heaven. So also *everything in nature* rediscovers itself *in the heaven of the divine logic*: quality, quantity, measure, essence, chemism, mechanism, organism. We have everything *twice* in theology, the one time *in abstracto*, the other time *in concreto*. We also have everything *twice* in the Hegelian philosophy, as an object of the logic and then again as an object of the philosophy of nature and the philosophy of spirit.

The essence of theology is the *transcendent* essence of the human being, placed outside human beings. The essence of Hegel's *Logic* is *transcendent* thinking, the thinking of the human being *supposed outside human beings*.

Just as theology *divides* and *alienates* the human being in order then to re-identify the alienated essence with the human being, so Hegel *multiplies* and *splits up* the *simple*, *self-identical essence* of nature and the human being in order, then, to mediate forcibly what was forcibly separated.

Metaphysics or logic is then a *real*, *immanent* science only when it is *not detached* from the so-called *subjective spirit*. Metaphysics is esoteric *psychology*. What arbitrariness, what brutality to consider quality for itself or sensation for itself, to rip them apart into particular sciences as if quality were something without sensation or sensation something without quality.

Hegel's absolute spirit is nothing but the *abstract*, the so-called *finite* spirit separated from itself, just as the infinite essence of theology is nothing but the *abstract*, finite essence.

According to Hegel the absolute spirit reveals or realizes itself in art, in religion, and in philosophy. In German that means the *spirit of art*, of *religion*, *and of philosophy is the absolute spirit*. But one cannot separate art from human feeling and intuition, nor religion from the heart and fantasy, nor philosophy from thinking. In short, one cannot separate the absolute spirit from the subjective spirit or essence of the human being without placing us back in the old perspective of theology and deluding us that the absolute spirit is an *other* spirit, distinguished from the human essence, a ghost of ourselves existing outside us.

The 'absolute spirit' is the 'departed spirit' of theology, a *ghost* still haunting the Hegelian philosophy.

Theology is *belief in ghosts. Ordinary* theology, however, has its ghosts in sensory imagination, *speculative* theology in non-sensory abstraction.

'To abstract' means to suppose the *essence* of nature *outside nature*, the *essence* of the human being *outside the human being*, the *essence* of thinking *outside the act of thinking*. In that its entire system rests upon these acts of abstraction, Hegelian philosophy has *estranged* the human being *from its very self*. It of course re-identifies what it separates, but only in a manner which is itself in turn *separable* and *intermediate*. Hegelian philosophy lacks *immediate unity*, *immediate certainty*, *immediate truth*.

The immediate, evident, undeceptive identification of the human essence with the human being, an essence alienated from the human being by an abstraction, cannot be derived in any positive manner but only by the *negation* in the Hegelian philosophy. In general, this identification can be *conceived* and *understood* only if it is conceived *as the total negation* of speculative philosophy, even though it is *truth* of the same. Everything, of course, is in the Hegelian philosophy, but at the same time always with its *negation*, its *opposite*.

The *obvious* proof that the absolute spirit is the so-called finite, subjective spirit and thus that the former cannot and may not be separated from the latter, is *art*. Art arises from the feeling that the life of this world is true life, that the *finite* is the *infinite*. It arises from the enthusiasm for a *determined*, *actual* essence as the *highest*, the *divine* essence. Christian *monotheism* has no *principle* of *artistic* and *scientific culture in itself*. Only *polytheism*, the so-called *idolatry*, is the *source of art and science*. The Greeks elevated themselves to the perfection of plastic arts only because for them the human form was *unconditionally* and *unreservedly* the highest form, the form of divinity. The Christians first came to poetry when they *negated Christian theology in practice* and venerated the *female* essence as a *divine* essence. Christians *contradicted* the essence of their religion, as they imagined it and as it was an *object* of their consciousness, as artists and poets. On the basis of his religion Petrarch *regretted* the poems in which he had made his Laura divine. Why do the Christians not have, as do the heathens, works of art adequate to their religious images? Why do they not have a perfectly satisfactory picture of Christ? Because the religious art of Christians flounders on the pernicious *contradiction* between their *consciousness* and the *truth*. The essence of the Christian religion is, in truth, the human essence. Yet in the consciousness of Christians it is *something else*, a *non*-human essence. Christ is supposed to be a human being and yet not a human being. He is an equivocation. Art, however, can only present what is true, the *unequivocal*.

Consciousness become flesh and blood, the resolute consciousness that the human is the divine and the finite the infinite, is the source of a new poetry and art which will surpass all its predecessors in energy, depth, and fire. The belief in an other world is an absolutely unpoetic belief. Pain is the source of poetry. Only someone who feels the loss of a finite entity as an infinite loss possesses the power of lyrical fire. Only the painful charm of the memory of what is no more is the first artist, the first idealist in the human being. But the belief in another world makes every pain an illusion, an untruth.

Philosophy which derives the finite from the infinite or the determined from the undetermined *never arrives at a true position of the finite and determined.* The finite is derived from the infinite – that means, the undetermined is determined, is *negated.* It is admitted that the infinite is *nothing without* determination, *i.e. without finitude,* that thus as the *reality* of the infinite the finite is supposed. Yet the negative non-entity of the absolute remains at the basis. The supposed finitude is thus suspended again and again. The *finite* is the *negation* of the *infinite* and the *infinite* in turn the *negation* of the *finite.* The philosophy of the absolute is a contradiction.

All predicates which make God as God real and which make God an *actual entity,* predicates like power, wisdom, goodness, love, even infinity and personality which have as a condition the *distinction* from what is finite, these predicates are first supposed *in* and *with* human beings. Just as in theology the *human* being is the *truth* and *reality* of God, so in speculative philosophy the *truth* of the *infinite* is the finite.

The truth of the finite is articulated by the absolute philosophy only in an *indirect* and *inverted* manner. If the infinite only is and only has *truth* and *actuality* when it is supposed *determined,* i.e. when it is supposed not as something infinite but rather as *something finite,* then indeed the *finite* is in truth the *infinite.*

The task of true philosophy is not to know the infinite as the finite but rather the finite as *not* finite, as the infinite. Or, the task is not to suppose the finite in the infinite but rather the infinite in the finite.

The beginning of philosophy is not God and the beginnings of the absolute is not the absolute, not being as a *predicate* of the idea. The beginning of philosophy is the finite,[2] the determined, the actual. The

[2] I use the word 'finite' always and only in the sense of the 'absolute' philosophy. From the standpoint of the absolute what is real and actual appears to this philosophy to be something not actual and something insignificant. For what is not actual and not determined is valued by this philosophy as something real.

infinite cannot even be thought *without* the finite. Can you think or determine quality in general without thinking of a *determined quality*? Is not, therefore, the determined, rather than the undetermined, what is primary? For the *determined* quality is nothing but the *actual* quality and the actual quality precedes the thought of the quality.

The *subjective* origin and course of philosophy is also its *objective* course and origin. Before you think the quality, you *feel* the quality. The *suffering* precedes the thinking.

The infinite is the finite's *true* essence – the *true* finite. Speculation is nothing but the truth and *universal empiricism*. One of Hegel's deepest and truest thoughts is expressed by him in his history of philosophy, although only accidentally, in the section on Aristotle: 'The *empirical*, in its *totality*, is the *speculative*.'[3]

The infinite of religion and philosophy is and was never anything other than something *finite*, something determined, yet *mystified*, i.e., a finite and determined something *with the postulate* of being *not* finite and *not* determined. Speculative philosophy has rendered itself guilty of *the same mistake* as did theology. The determinations of actuality or finitude are made determinations and predicates of the infinite only through the *negation* of the determinacy in which they are *what they are*.

Honor and honesty are useful in all things – even philosophy. However, philosophy is honorable and honest only if it admits the finiteness of its speculative infinity – admits, therefore, that the mystery of the nature in God, for example, is nothing other than the mystery of human nature, that the *night* which it supposes in God in order to produce from it the light of consciousness is nothing but its own *dark*, *instinctive* feeling for the reality and indispensability of matter.

Speculative philosophy's procedure up to now, of going from the abstract to the concrete and from the ideal to the real, is a distorted procedure. People never come in this way to the *true*, *objective* reality but rather only to the *realization of their own abstractions*. Precisely for this reason people in this way never arrive at true *freedom* of spirit. *For only intuition of things and essences in their objective actuality makes the*

Yet, on the other hand, from the *standpoint of nothingness*, what is finite and insignificant appears to be something real – a contradiction which emerges especially in the earlier philosophy of Schelling, but also still lies *at the bottom* of Hegelian philosophy.

[3] [This last sentence beginning with the words 'One of Hegel's...' is not in the second edition. (Tr.)]

human being free and devoid of all prejudices. The transition from the ideal to the real has its place only in practical philosophy.

Philosophy is the knowledge of *what is*. Things and essences are to be thought and to be known *just* as *they are* – this is the highest law, the foremost task of philosophy.

To have articulated what is *such as it is*, in other words, to have *truthfully* articulated what truly is, *appears superficial*. To have articulated what is *such as it is not*, in other words, to have *falsely* and *distortedly* articulated what truly is, *appears profound*.

Truthfulness, *simplicity*, and *determinacy* are the formal marks of the *real* philosophy.

The being with which philosophy begins cannot be separated from consciousness nor can consciousness be separated from being. As the reality of the sensation is the quality and, in turn, the sensation is the reality of the quality, so also is being the reality of the consciousness. But likewise in turn the consciousness is the reality of the being. Consciousness is alone the *actual* being. The *real* unity of spirit and nature is simply consciousness.

All the determinations, forms, categories, or however one wishes to refer to it, which speculative philosophy has stripped of the absolute and expelled to the region of the finite and empirical, precisely contain the *true essence* of the finite, the *true infinite*, the *true and ultimate mysteries* of philosophy.

Space and *time* are the forms of existence of every entity. Only the existence in space and time is *existence*. The negation of space and time is always only the *negation of their limits*, *not of their essence*. A timeless feeling, a timeless will, a timeless thought, a timeless entity are non-things. Whoever has not time in general, also has no time and no urge to want and to think.

The negation of space and time in metaphysics, in the essence of things, has the most deleterious practical consequences. Only someone who *everywhere* takes a stand in space and time has also *tact* and *practical understanding* in life. Space and time are the first criteria of praxis. A people which excludes time from its metaphysics and sanctifies the eternal, i.e. *abstract*, existence detached from time, as a consequence excludes time also from its politics and sanctifies the anti-historical principle of stability, a principle contrary to right and reason.

Speculative philosophy has made the *development* separated from *time* into a form and attribute of the absolute. Yet this separation of development from time is a true masterpiece of *speculative arbitrariness* and the resounding proof that speculative philosophers have dealt with their absolute just as have theologians with their God who has all the emotions of the human being *without emotion*, who loves *without love*, and rages *without rage*. Development without time is as much as development *without development*. The assertion: 'the absolute entity develops itself out of itself' moreover, is a true and rational assertion only *in reverse*. In other words, it must mean: 'only a self-developing entity, temporally unfolding, is a *true*, an *actual*, an *absolute* entity'.

Where there is no limitation, no time and no need, there is also no quality, no energy, no spirit, no fire and no love. Only the *needy* entity is a *necessary* entity. Existence *without need* is unnecessary existence. What is generally free of needs also has no need of existence. Whether it is or is not is one thing for it and another thing for someone else. An entity with no need is an entity with no basis. Only what can *suffer* deserves to exist. Only the *entity rich in pain is a divine entity*. An essence without suffering is an essence *without an essence*. An entity *devoid of sensibility, devoid of matter*.[4]

A philosophy which has no *passive principle* within itself, a philosophy which speculates about existence *without time*, about determinate being *without duration*, about quality *without sensation*, about the essence *without an essence* and about the life *without a life*, devoid of flesh and blood – such a philosophy, like that of the absolute in general, as a thoroughly *one-sided* philosophy, *necessarily* has empiricism as its opposite. Spinoza, of course, made matter an attribute of his substance but not as a principle of suffering. Rather matter is a substantial attribute precisely because it does *not* suffer, because it is singular, indivisible, and infinite. For then it has the *same* determinations as the attribute *contrasted with* it, viz. thinking. In short, matter is one of Spinoza's substantial attributes because it is an *abstract* matter, a matter *without matter*, just as the essence of the Hegelian *Logic* is the essence of nature and of the human being, but is itself *without an essence, without a nature, and without a human being*.

The philosopher must consider what in the human being does *not* philosophize, but rather is *at odds with* philosophy and *opposed* to abstract thinking. Thus the philosopher must bring into the *text* of philosophy what Hegel relegated to mere *remarks*. Only in this way

[4] ['Essence' and 'entity' in this paragraph are both translations of *Wesen*. (Tr.)]

will philosophy be *irrefutable* and *uncontested*, a *universal* and irresistible power. Genuine philosophy thus has to begin not *with itself*, but with its *antithesis*, with *what is not philosophy*.[5] This unphilosophical, absolutely antischolastic essence in us, distinguished from thinking, is the principle of sensualism.

The essential tools or organs of philosophy are the *head*, the source of activity, of freedom, of metaphysical infinity, and of idealism, and the *heart*, the source of suffering, of finitude, of need, of sensualism. Theoretically expressed, these philosophical tools are *thinking* and *intuition*. For *thinking* is the *need* of the *head*, *intuition* or *sense* the *need* of the *heart*. Thinking is the principle of the school, of the system; intuition, the *principle of life*. In intuition I am *determined* by an object, in thinking I *determine* the object. In thinking I am an *I*, in intuition a *not-I*. True, objective thought, the true and objective philosophy, is generated only from thinking's *negation*, from *being determined* by an object, from *passion*, the source of all desire and need. The intuition yields simply the essence *immediately identical with existence*. Thinking yields the essence *mediated* by its *distinction* and its *separation* from existence. Therefore, only where the existence unites with the essence, the intuition with the thinking, the passivity with the activity, where the *anti-scholastic*, *sanguine principle of French sensualism* and *materialism* unite with the *scholastic stodginess of German metaphysics*, is there alone *life* and *truth*.

As is the philosophy, so is the philosopher and vice versa. The properties of the philosopher, i.e., the *subjective conditions* and *elements* of the philosophy, are also the latter's *objective* conditions. The true philosopher, the philosopher *identical with life* and *human being* must be of *Franco-German* descent. Don't be frightened by this mixture, you German purists! Already in the year 1716 the *Acta Philosophorum* declared such thoughts. 'If we compare the *Germans* and *French*, then, of course, the latter's mentality is quicker, the former's more solid. One could rightly say that the Franco-German temperament is the most fitting for a philosopher. Or a child who has a Frenchman for a father and a German for a mother, must have (*caeteribus paribus*)[6] a good *ingenium philosophicum*.'[7] Completely correct, only we must make the mother French and the father German. The *heart* – the

[5] Concerning this point, as in general concerning the philosophy of Schelling and Hegel, see my 'Critique of the Hegelian Philosophy' which appeared in the *Hallischen Jahrbüchern* (Sept. 1839), and was glossed over in the most flippant manner, which of course at that time was not to have been expected otherwise. [This footnote is missing in the second edition. (Tr.)]

[6] ['Other things being equal' (Tr.)]

[7] 'Philosophical mentality' (Tr.)]

feminine principle, the *sense* for the finite, the seat of materialism – is a *French disposition*, whereas the *head* – the masculine principle, the seat of idealism – is German. The heart revolutionizes, the head reforms. The head brings things to completion, the heart sets them in *motion*. But only where there is movement, agitation, passion, blood, sensibility is there also *spirit*. It was Leibniz's *Esprit* alone, his sanguine, *materialistically*-idealistic principle that first tore the Germans away from their philosophical pedantry and scholasticism.

Hitherto in philosophy the heart was considered the parapet of theology. Yet precisely the heart is the unreservedly *antitheological* principle in the human being. In the sense of thology the heart is the unbelieving, atheistic principle. For it believes in *nothing* other than *its own self*, the irrefutable, divine, and absolute reality of *its* essence. However, since separating and distinguishing into subject and object is the mind's affair, *the* head which does *not* understand the heart transforms the heart's very essence into an *objective* and *external* entity, *distinguished* from the heart. Of course, to the heart an *other* entity is a need, but only an entity like itself, which is *neither* distinguished from the heart *nor* contradicting it. Theology denies the *truth of the heart*, the *truth of religious emotion*. Religious affection, the heart, says, for example, 'God *suffers*'. Theology, on the other hand, says, 'God does *not* suffer'. That is, the heart *denies* the distinction of God from the human being and theology *maintains* it.

Theism rests upon the *discord* between *head* and *heart*. Pantheism is this discord's suspension *in a discord* since it makes the divine essence immanent only *as some thing transcendent*. Anthropotheism is this discord's suspension *without discord*. Anthropotheism is the heart brought to *understanding*. It articulates inside the head, only in the manner of the understanding, what the heart says in its own way. It supposes as an absolute essence *the* essence which the heart knows as an essential part of itself.[8] Religion is only emotion, feeling, heart, love, i.e., the negation and *dissolution* of God in the human being. Thus, as the *negation of the theology* which denies the truth of religious emotion, the new philosophy is the *position of religion*. Anthropotheism is the *self-conscious religion*, the religion *which understands itself*. In contrast to it, theology negates religion under the illusion of *positing* it.

Schelling and *Hegel* are opposites. Hegel represents the masculine principle of self-sufficience and of self-activity, in short, the idealistic principle. Schelling represents the feminine principle of receptivity

[8] [This sentence is not in the second edition. (Tr.)]

and of impressionability, in short, the materialist principle. (First he accepted Fichte, then Plato and Spinoza, finally Jacob Boehme.) Hegel lacks *intuition*, *Schelling the power of thought and determination*. Schelling is a thinker only in *general*, but when it comes to a thing in particular, to something determined, he lapses into the somnambulism of the imagination. For Schelling rationalism is only a *disguise*, irrationalism the *truth*. Whereas Hegel arrives at only an *abstract* existence, contradicting the irrational principle, Schelling arrives at only a *mystical*, *imaginary* existence and reality contradicting the rational principle. Hegel makes up for the lack in realism with *bluntly sensuous* words, Schelling with *beautiful* words. Hegel expresses the uncommon in a common way, Schelling the common in an uncommon way. Hegel makes *things* into *mere thoughts*, Schelling makes mere *thoughts*, e.g., the aseity[9] in God, into *things*. Hegel deceives the thinking heads, Schelling the *un*thinking. Hegel makes unreason into reason. Schelling, on the other hand, makes reason into unreason. Schelling's is the real philosophy in a *dream*, Hegel's is the real philosophy in a *concept*. While Schelling negates abstract thinking *in fantasy*, Hegel does so in *abstract thinking*. As the *self-negation* of negative thinking and as the completion of the old philosophy, Hegel's philosophy is the negative beginning of the new philosophy. Schelling's is the old philosophy *with the presumption and the illusion* of being the new real philosophy.

Hegelian philosophy is the suspension of the contradiction of thinking and being, as in particular Kant had articulated it. But, note well, the suspension of this contradiction is only *within contradiction*, i.e., within the *one* element, *within thinking*. For Hegel *thought* is *being*, *thought* the *subject*, *being* the predicate. The *Logic* is thinking in the element of thinking or the thought thinking itself, the thought as a *predicate-less subject* or the thought as *a subject and predicate of itself at the same time*. Yet the thinking in the element of thinking is still abstract. Hence, it realizes and expresses itself. This realized and expressed thought is nature or, in general, the real or being. Yet what is truly real in this reality? The thought, which for this reason immediately strips itself of the predicate of reality once again, in order to restore its predicatelessness as its true essence. But this is precisely why Hegel has not come to *being as being*, to free and self-sufficient being, satisfied with itself. Hegel has thought of the object only as a *predicate* of the thought thinking itself. The very contradiction

[9] [The word 'aseity' is simply a transliteration of the German 'Aseität', a derivative of the Latin 'a se' or 'from itself'. The term's origin is scholastic philosophy where it signified God's utter self-sufficiency. (Tr.)]

between the *existing* religion and religion in *thought*, admitted in the Hegelian *philosophy of religion*, simply comes to this, that even here, as everywhere else, the thought is made into the subject, but the object, the religion, is made into a mere *predicate* of the thought.

Whoever fails to give up the Hegelian philosophy, fails to give up theology. The Hegelian doctrine, that nature or reality is *posited* by the idea, is merely the *rational* expression of the theological doctrine that nature is created by God, that the material essence is created by an immaterial, i.e., abstract, essence. At the end of the *Logic* the absolute even comes to a nebulous 'resolution',[10] in order to document with its own hand its descent from the theological heaven.

The Hegelian philosophy is the last place of refuge and the last rational support of theology. As once Catholic theologians became *de facto* Aristotelians in order to be able to combat Protestantism, so must Protestant theologians now become *de jure Hegelians* in order to be able to combat atheism.

The true relation of thinking and being is simply this. *Being* is *subject* and *thinking* a *predicate* but a predicate such as contains the *essence* of its subject.[11] Thinking comes from being but being does not come from thinking. Being comes from itself and through itself.

Being is given only through being. Being has its ground in itself, because only being is sense, reason, necessity, truth, in short, everything in everything. Being *is*, because not-being is not-being, i.e., nothing, *nonsense*.

The essence of being *as being* is the essence of nature. The temporal genesis extends only to the forms, not to the essence of nature.

Being is derived from thinking only where the *true unity* of thinking and being is *severed*, where one has already taken from being its *soul* and *essence* through abstraction and then afterwards again finds in the essence distilled from being the *sense* and *ground* to this, of itself empty being. In a similar way the world is and must be derived from God where one arbitrarily separates the essence of the world from the world.

Whoever speculates according to some *particular* real principle of philosophy as do the so-called positive philosophers

[10] [Cf. Hegel, *Wissenschaft der Logik*, II, herausgegeben von Georg Lasson (Hamburg: Meiner, 1969), S. 506; *Hegel's Science of Logic*, translated by A. V. Miller (New York: Humanities, 1969), p. 843. (Tr.)]

[11] [The phrase 'but a predicate such as contains the *essence* of its subject' is deleted from the second edition. (Tr.)]

Is like an animal in a *field that is fallow*
Led around in a *circle* by an *evil spirit*
While all around it lies a *beautiful green meadow*.

This beautiful green meadow is nature and the human being, for both belong together. Look upon nature, look upon the human being! Here right before your eyes you have the mysteries of philosophy.

Nature is the essence *not distinguished* from *existence*, the human being the *essence distinguishing* itself from existence. The essence not distinguishing itself is the ground of the distinguishing essence. Nature, therefore, is the ground of the human being.

The new and only positive philosophy is the *negation of academic philosophy*, although it contains in itself what is true in the latter. The positive philosophy is the negation of philosophy *as an abstract*, *particular*, *i.e.*, *scholastic*, quality. It has no particular and no abstract principle. It has no *Shibboleth*, no *particular* language, no *particular* name, no *particular* principle. The new philosophy is no longer an abstract *quality* and *particular faculty*. It is the *thinking human being* itself, the human being who *is* and *knows itself* to be the self-conscious essence of nature, the essence of history, the essence of states, and the essence of religion. This is the human being who *is* and *knows itself* to be the *actual* (not imaginary) *absolute identity* of all contraries and contradictions, of all active and passive, spiritual and sensuous, political and social qualities; the human being who *knows* that the *pantheistic* essence, which speculative philosophers or much more theologians have *separated* from the human being and objectified as an *abstract* essence, is nothing else but its *own* essence undetermined, but capable of *infinite determinations*.

The new philosophy is the *negation* as much of *rationalism* as of *mysticism*, as much of *pantheism* as of *personalism*, and as much of *atheism* as of *theism*. It is the *unity of all these antithetical truths* as an *absolutely self-sufficient* and *explicit truth*.

The new philosophy has already articulated itself as a philosophy of religion in a manner as *negative* as it is *positive*. People may simply construct the *conclusions* of its analysis into *premises* in order to recognize the principles of a positive philosophy. But the new philosophy is not interested in public approval. Certain of itself, it disdains *appearing* to be what it is. Instead, precisely for our time, a time in which the appearance is taken for the essence, the illusion for the reality, and the name for the thing, it must *be* what it is *not*. Thus do opposites complement each other! Where *nothing* is taken for *something* and the *lie* for *a truth*, *something* must consequently be taken for nothing and the truth for a lie. It is ironic that at the very moment philosophy is involved in a decisive and universal *act of self-deception*, and people are making the unheard-of attempt to ground philosophy solely on the *approval* and *opinion* of the *newspaper public*, they have to try, in honorable and Christian fashion, to *refute* philosophical works merely by slandering them publicly in the *Augsburg General News*.[12] Oh, how honorable, how moral are the public conditions of Germany?

A new principle always makes its appearance with a *new name*. That is, it elevates its name from a humble and lowly position to the princely rank, making its name the mark of the highest distinction. If people *translate* the name of the new philosophy, i.e., the name 'human being', with 'self-consciousness', then people would interpret the new philosophy in the sense of the old, placing it in the old perspective once again. For the self-consciousness of the old philosophy, *separated from the human being*, is an *abstraction without reality*. The human being *is* the self-consciousness.

In terms of language, the name 'human being' is indeed a particular name, but in terms of truth it is the name of all names. The predicate '*πολυώνυμος*'[13] is proper to the human being. Whatever the human being names and articulates, it always articulates its own essence. Language is thus the criterion of how high or low humanity's degree of cultivation is. The name of God is but the name for what the human being regards as the highest power and the highest essence, i.e., the highest feeling and the highest thought.

The name 'human being' commonly signifies simply the human being with its needs, feelings, sentiments, the human being as a person, in distinction from its spirit, its universal, public qualities, i.e.,

[12] [A reference to a review of Bruno Bauer's *Die Posaune des jüngsten Gerichts über Hegel den Atheisten und Antichristen* in the *Augsburger Allgemeine Zeitung* in December 1841. While Feuerbach viewed his own philosophy of religion as the result of opposition to Hegel's philosophy, Bauer viewed his work as an explication of Hegel. Bauer's work was published anonymously and after the publication of Feuerbach's *The Essence of Christianity*. At this time some people considered Feuerbach the author or at least the inspiration for Bauer's work. Thus a correspondent of the Augsburg newspaper writes about *Die Posaune*: 'One needs only to have read a few pages in order to be convinced that this work in no way is *opposed* to Hegel... One needs then only read a few pages in the work by L. Feuerbach, *The Essence of Christianity*, in order to be convinced that one has encountered, if not Mr. Feuerbach, nevertheless a spiritual brother, scarcely to be distinguished from him.' Angered, Feuerbach responded with 'Zur Beurteilung der Schrift "Das Wesen des Christentums"' in *Deutschen Jahrbüchern*, February 1842. Cf. Ludwig Feuerbach, *Werke in sechs Bänden*, Band 3; Kritiken und Abhandlungen II (1839–1843), herausgegeben von Erich Thies (Frankfurt am Main: Suhrkamp, 1975), S. 351–2. (Tr.)]

[13] ['Many-named' or 'worshipped under many names' (Tr.)]

in distinction, for example, from the artist, thinker, writer, judge, as if it were not a *characteristic* and *essential property of the human being* to be a thinker, an artist, a judge, and so forth, or as if the human being in art, in science, and so forth were *outside itself*. Speculative philosophy has theoretically fixed this separation of the human being's essential qualities from the human being and thereby deified purely abstract qualities as self-sufficient essences. So, for example, in Hegel's *Natural Law*, § 190, it reads: 'In law the object is the *person*, in the moral sphere the *subject*, in the family the family member, in the civil society in general the citizen (as bourgeois). Here, on the standpoint of needs, the concrete entity of the *representation* is what people call a "human being". It is therefore first here, and also properly only here, that the discussion concerns the human being in this sense.' 'In *this* sense', that is, even if the discussion concerns the citizen, the subject, the family member, or the person, in truth it is always a matter solely of *one* and the *same* essence, the human being, only in a different sense and in a different quality.

All speculation about right, willing, freedom, personality without the human being, i.e., outside of or even beyond the human being, is speculation *without unity*, *without necessity*, *without substance*, *without foundation*, and *without reality*. The human being is the existence of freedom, the existence of personality, and the existence of right. Only the human being is the *foundation* and *basis* of the Fichtean I, of the Leibnizian monad, and of the absolute.

All sciences must ground themselves in *nature*. A doctrine is only an *hypothesis* as long as its *natural basis* is not uncovered. This holds particularly for the *doctrine of freedom*. Only the new philosophy will succeed in *naturalizing* freedom, which formerly was an *unnatural* and *supernatural hypothesis*.

Philosophy must again combine itself with natural science and natural science with philosophy. This combining, based on mutual need and inner necessity, will be more lasting, more successful, and more fruitful than the *previous mésalliance* between philosophy and theology.

The human being is the *Εν κâι πâν*[14] of the state. The state is the realized, cultivated, explicit totality of the human essence. In the state the essential qualities or activities of the human being are realized in particular classes, but brought back to an identity in the person of the head of state.

[14] ['One and all' (Tr.)]

The head of state has to represent all classes without distinction. Before the head of state they are all equally necessary and equally justified. The head of state is the representative of the universal human being.

The Christian religion has combined the name of the human being with the name of God in the one name: 'the God-Man'. Thus it has extolled the name of the human being as an attribute of the highest essence. In keeping with this truth, the new philosophy has made this attribute the substance, i.e., it has made the predicate the subject. The new philosophy is the *realized idea*, the *truth* of Christianity. But precisely by having the *essence* of Christianity in itself, it abandons the *name* of Christianity. Christianity has articulated the truth only in *contradiction with the truth*. The pure, unfalsified truth without contradiction is a *new truth* – a *new*, *autonomous deed* of humanity.

IV

Bruno Bauer

1809–1882

Bruno Bauer

In 1853, almost two decades after the emergence – and shortly after the collapse – of Young Hegelianism, Karl Rosenkranz, a leading figure among the 'center' Hegelians, recalled that 'Among the so-called "Free-Ones" in Berlin, Bruno Bauer was undoubtedly the most important, in character as well as in culture and talent.' And indeed, during the late 1830s and early 1840s, Bauer was recognized as the leader of the Berlin circle. His powerful effect upon the course of the Young Hegelian movement was grounded not only in his intelligent grasp of Hegelianism, but in his extraordinarily attractive personality. Unlike Strauss, or Cieszkowski – or later, Feuerbach – who could influence others only through their writing – Bauer faced his audience directly. Among the many and noisy groups that gathered in *Weinstuben* and cafés, Bauer was a popular source of a new Hegelianism which questioned both Church and State, a critical Hegelianism which obsessed the minds of many transient and obscure publicists and ideologues who then peopled the subterranean liberal world of pre-revolutionary Berlin. He not only exercised a personal and powerful influence upon such now well-known revolutionaries as Marx, Engels, and Stirner – but upon such lesser figures as Adolph Rutenberg, or his brother Edgar, and that last Young Hegelian, Karl Schmidt. But by 1853, Bauer was little more than a memory.

Few of the Young Hegelians, if any, can claim a longer or more distinguished relationship to Hegelian thought than Bauer. Bauer, along with Stirner and Feuerbach, were among the very few who had heard Hegel lecture, and only Bauer was invited to be the first champion of orthodox Hegelianism against Strauss' *Life of Jesus*. This invitation was soon followed by another: to contribute his edited class-notes toward the publication of Hegel's *Collected Works*. Marheineke, in his *preface* to the 1842 edition of Hegel's *Lectures on the Philosophy of Religion*, praised Bauer, his 'young friend' for his 'insight, learning, speculative talent, and tact'. Certainly – with the possible exception of Feuerbach – no Young Hegelian had a firmer understanding of Hegel's philosophy of religion than Bauer and it was his interpretation of this important side of Hegelian philosophy that he communicated to his followers.

As the following selections from his writings illustrate, Bauer interpreted Hegel's religious thought as but an exaltation of human self-consciousness, an apotheosis of self-reflection, in which the individual self-consciousness discovered itself to be infinite in nature and completely uninhibited in its critical reflections. In short, the 'Critic' was God.

The following three selections from the writings of Bauer are set forth in the order of their publication. The first is taken from Bauer's 1841 extravagant study of Hegelianism, *The Trumpet of the Last Judgement over Hegel the Atheist and Antichrist: An Ultimatum* (*Die Posaune des jüngsten Gerichts über Hegel den Atheisten und Antichristen: ein Ultimatum*). It appeared anonymously, but as if written by a violently anti-Hegelian Pietist. This short work, whose authorship was soon revealed, cast Hegel into the form of a covert revolutionary and atheist – the exact opposite of what had been generally held concerning him at that time. It attempted to prove, by an expert employment of citations taken from the works of Hegel, that the Young Hegelians were not heretical Hegelians, but the true disciples of Hegel – and that what had long been suspected by the reactionary aristocracy and orthodox Pietists that surrounded the throne of Friedrich Wilhelm IV was true: Hegelianism was a deep well of dangerous doctrine. Those who yet fear Marxism might well agree. The *introduction* and Fourth Chapter, 'Hatred of the Established Order' are here, annotated, and, for the first time, translated into English by the editor of this anthology.

The second selection is taken from Bauer's 1843 monograph, *The Jewish Problem* [*Die Judenfrage*]. Sections from the Introduction and the Conclusion of this work not only indicate that Bauer's 'spiritual homeland' was more in the age of the Enlightenment than in that of the Romantic, but provide the reader with the basis for a fuller understanding of Marx's famous review of this work. It also marks how this 'problem' irritated these early German liberals, for all wished it somehow to quietly vanish – along with the Jews – but their evident anti-semitism only prepared the ground for a terrible and violent solution. This work has been translated by Helen Lederer, and appears here by permission of Hebrew Union College.

The final selection, 'The Genus and the Crowd' appeared as an article in Bruno Bauer's own journal, the *Allgemeine Literaturzeitung*, in September of 1844. It clearly indicates the latent conservatism of Bauer's Hegelianism, for in one whose divinity found a source in their own critical self-consciousness, there could be little concern for the docile consciousness of the masses – proletarian or otherwise. It is here translated by Michael Malloy, who notes that although translations of Feuerbach's writings have caused the term '*Gattung*' to enter the literature as 'species', it has been taken in its primary meaning as 'genus' in this translation of 'Die Gattung und die Masse'. The term 'die Masse' could also be rendered as 'the mob', or 'the mass'.

The Trumpet of the Last Judgement

INTRODUCTION

Though thou exalt thyself as the eagle, and though thou set thy nest among the stars, thence will I bring thee down, saith the Lord (Obadiah I. 4).[1]

So saith the Lord! So has He spoken, so will He speak, and so speaks He to all who will not recognize His Majesty, to those who would raise themselves up and not mark that they are but men. So He speaketh and so pulls He down from their imagined heights those who would be like unto Him, those who say – in their hearts or in their books – it is not He, He does not exist, but only we who are Lords and Masters of all, only Man is God, I am the Lord, the Almighty, the Omnipotent and Only Great One. So saith the Lord: 'I will bring thee down.'

The hour has now struck in which the last, the worst, and the proudest enemy of the Lord will be brought to earth. This last enemy is also the most dangerous, for these 'Wild Men' – these people of the Antichrist – have dared to declare the non-existence of the Eternal Lord, and this in the full light of day, in the market, before all Christian Europe, in the light of the sun which has never shone upon such wickedness. They have practiced an idolatrous adultery with the Whore of Reason while they have murdered the Anointed of God. But Europe, once filled with Holy Zeal, strangled the Whore, and then bound itself into a Holy Alliance so as to cast the Antichrist into chains and to once again set up the eternal altars of the True Lord.

But then came – No! – but then was scented, nursed, protected, sheltered, indeed honored and paid, a man who was stronger than the French, that enemy from without which had been conquered, and he gave new foundation to the principles of Hell, and raised them into the power of a law. Hegel was called forth and fixed at the center of the University of Berlin! He had, with the attractive power of Philosophy over German youth, secured his introduction. This

[1] [Bauer's citations from both the scriptures and Hegel will be retained in the text. Translator's notes will be footnoted. (Ed./Tr.)]

man – if we are still allowed to give him human title – filled with hate against everything Godly and Consecrated – now turned perversely under the shield of philosophy to attack everything which men should hold as exalted and honorable. A mob of disciples closed about him, and never – in the whole of history, never – had anyone such obedience, dependency, such blind trust given to him as he was given by his disciples and hangers-on. Wherever he led, they followed him, and they followed him in the war against the One.

Oh that my head were waters, and mine eyes a fountain of tears, that I might weep day and night for the slain of the daughter of my people (Jeremiah 9.1).

Oh how many has he slaughtered! He has cut down the power and bloom of our youth and has robbed us of the last strength of our cause. And even now, his work reaches out from his grave, and it even seems that in his death his power yet grows. In the beginning, he and his school seemed innocent, particularly when we compare its workings with the monstrously matured mob of disciples and their doings today, their leveling of everything high and valuable, and their efforts to set self-consciousness – as they call it – on the throne of the All-Highest.[2] The government wishes but to protect Christianity, Love, Trust, Patience, and Holy Faith against this danger, the danger of that hideous mob freeing the bonds of dishonorable reason, and once again set up the Abomination of Desolation within the Holy Kingdom. Church and State would be shaken to the core by such a hellish discharge.

One cannot believe that this mob, with which the Christian state in our times is compelled to struggle against, is fixed upon any other principle or other teaching than that set out by the Master of Deceit. It is certainly true that the younger school of Hegelians is quite different from that first which gathered itself about its master, for this younger school have openly cast away all godliness and modesty, and struggle openly against Church and State. They have inverted the cross and threaten to upset the throne itself – such opinions and hellish deeds of which the old school might appear incapable. But if the older school did not rise up to these things, to this devilish energy, it was only the result of chance circumstances, for fundamentally and in principle, if we go back to the actual teaching of the master, the latest disciples have added nothing new – they have only

[2] [This is Bauer's viewpoint, for as he later notes in the *Trumpet* 'God is dead for philosophy and only the self as self-consciousness lives, creates, acts and is everything.' See also Rosen, *Bruno Bauer and Karl Marx* (Boston, 1977), 85ff. (Ed./Tr.)]

torn away the thin veil which briefly concealed the thought of the master and have revealed – shamelessly enough! – the system in its nakedness.[3] It was only the cunning of the old serpent, the same which brought our forebears to the Fall, which by devilish fabrication gave that thought the appearance of Christianity, Churchliness, and piety. The early followers were deceived by this appearance, it so enticed them that they were soon fixed upon the deadly web of the system and then infected by the insinuous poison of principles. This philosophic acid entered ever more deeply into them until all was corroded, sense, heart, soul, thought, and conscience. Words and ambition soured, and the appearance of sweetness and heavenly mildness fell away! Everything is acid!

> Whose mouth is full of cursing and bitterness (Romans 3.14).

Ha! Here is the sword of the Lord and Gideon! We now smite you so that that mask which has led so many to a fall will itself fall, and to let all know, for their good, what is the true shape of this worldly-wisdom.

Away with the mask! No one should deceive themselves! The day of judgement is coming in which that which is now concealed will be revealed. Have courage! Arm yourself strongly, so that you will be able to bear the sight of the Concealed One and view the mystery of its iniquity. It is the mystery of the Serpent.

We can proceed directly to the center point of this philosophy, its destruction of religion – for we affirm that this is the core which, after the husk has been removed, is that from which every consequence of this system can be brought into the light.

Oh! those poor and miserable creatures who let themselves be deceived when it was whispered to them that 'The Object of religion as of philosophy is the Eternal Truth in its Objectivity Itself, God and nothing but God and the explication of God' (*Phil. of Relig.* I, 21 – we cite from the second, 'improved' edition). Oh, those poor souls who were pleased to hear that 'Religion and philosophy coincide' (*Ibid.*), and who still thought to have their God when they heard, and accepted, the statement that religion was 'the self-consciousness of the Absolute Spirit' (*Ibid.*, I, 200) – namely that self-consciousness in which the Divine Spirit itself in its holiness and belief is present and knows itself to be in God and from God, and is to be honored as such. The poor souls! They have not rightly heard nor rightly seen, nor have they recalled the saying 'He that hath ears

[3] [This theme of 'exposure' is a dominant one throughout Young Hegelianism, particularly with Marx and Bauer. See Stanley E. Hyman's *The Tangled Bank: Darwin, Marx, Frazer and Freud as Imaginative Writers* (New York, 1962). (Ed./Tr.)]

to hear, let him hear' (Mark. 4.9, 12). They have eyes yet do not see, hear and do not understand.

Hegel, for himself and his disciples, has cast aside and destroyed religion. In itself it is inaccessible to his fiery darts, and the True Believers are protected by 'the shield of faith, wherewith ye shall be able to quench all the fiery darts of the wicked' (*Ephesians* 6.16) – but he has prepared for the destruction of religion. He has drawn a double cover over his work of destruction, which only the critical knife of belief can cut away. We will now proceed.

Very often, countless times, on almost every page of his work on the philosophy of religion, Hegel speaks about God, and it always appears that he understands the term 'God' to mean that living God Who was before the world was, and to whom alone reality belongs, Who 'the One True Reality is' (*Phil. of Relig.* I, 92), He Who existed as the 'Trinity' before the creation of the world and who revealed his love to man in Christ.

The older Hegelians (Göschel at their head),[4] moved by Christian piety, stayed at this viewpoint, and so were hindered from going on to the more dangerous points of the dialectic in which it would be killed. Now we certainly recognize the residual piety of the older Hegelians, as it is proper to do so, but we would only make ourselves ridiculous if we took this first superficial appearance of piety as a matter of particular significance, as it will vanish of itself when the second hull, which covers the kernel of the system, is drawn away. This first appearance of piety will be denied by the negative dialectic of the central principle of Hegelianism itself, and even if piety is wanted in itself, or the appearance of it, it will in principle be entirely excluded.

Strauss and some of the more clever of the older disciples have dressed themselves up in large measure with this piety, so that only here and there is the kernel of the system glimpsed through the two hulls. The second appearance is given when religion is to be taken as a dialectical *substance-relationship*, in which the individual spirit is related to the universal, which as substance, or – as it is still said – *Absolute Idea* as to that which has power over it. The individual spirit will abandon its particular uniqueness and set itself in unity with the *Absolute Idea*.

This second appearance is a dangerous appearance, and many powerful intellects have been captured by it. It is the appearance of *Pantheism*. But more dangerous than this appearance is the thing itself,

[4] [Karl Friedrich Göschel (1784–1861). Hegel's very favorable review of Göschel's 1829 work, *Aphorismen über Nichtwissen und absolutes Wissen*, insured that Göschel would be considered among the orthodox followers of Hegel. (Ed./Tr.)]

which is immediately present to every open and expert eye when it but exerts itself to a certain extent: this is presented as the understanding of religion as being nothing more than an inward relationship of self-consciousness to itself, and that all powers, which exist as substance or *Absolute Idea* are but appearance differentiated from self-consciousness, merely religious images objectified out of self-consciousness.

This is the terrible, dreadful, religiously mortifying kernel of the system. Who partakes of this kernel is dead to God, for he holds God dead. Who eats of this kernel is deeper fallen than Eve, for she ate of the apple and Adam was seduced by her, and Adam hoped to be as God. But the disciple of this system, with sinful pride, has no wish to be as God, but only to be Ego = Ego, to be the blasphemous infinity, to win and to enjoy but the freedom and self-pleasure of self-consciousness. This philosophy wants no God, nor Gods as the heathen, it wants but man and his self-conscious and everything set towards its vain self-consciousness.

As a warning to all right-minded, we will now present how the appearance of religion as a substance-relationship is dissolved by Hegel himself to leave but a residue of infinite self-consciousness.

CHAPTER IV
HATRED OF THE ESTABLISHED ORDER

Pride is the only feeling which Hegel can instill into his disciples. That meekness and humility which alone can give honor to the Lord and modesty to man is foreign to him.

The first thing to which he calls forth his disciples is a profane travesty of the *sursum corda*: 'Man cannot think highly enough of the greatness and power of his mind' (*G.P.* 1, 6; *H.* 1, xiii).[5] But one must be a philosopher to think in such an unlimited manner concerning oneself. To Hegel, all men other than philosophers are oxen, and the

[5] [Bauer's footnoting is to Michelet's 1840 edition of Hegel's *Vorlesungen über die Geschichte der Philosophie*, which appeared in volumes 17 through 19 in the collected works (hereafter refered to as *G.P.*). It is evident that Bauer was using a variant text, for although most of his citations can be located in *G.P.*, some cannot. However, in no instance does Bauer's citation run counter to the general context. For the convenience of the English reader, references in the *G.P.* have been correlated to the translated material found in the three volume E. S. Haldane translation, *Hegel's Lectures on the History of Philosophy* (London, 1955). Haldane's translation is not, in all cases, in as direct accord with the original text as might be desired, and has, in some unimportant instances, been altered by the present translator. The Haldane translation is referred to as *H.* in the footnoting citation. (Ed./Tr.)]

philosopher among those who have knowledge, are in opposition to the oxen: 'It was a celebration, a festival of knowledge – *at the cost of the oxen*' (*G.P.* I, 279; *H.* I, 238). The ordinary folk, the decent citizens are said to lie once and for all 'in the ditch' – in the trench of finiteness (*G.P.* I, 196; *H.* I, 172). Hegel speaks, with inward satisfaction, of the boundless contempt which Heraclitus had against the people, and for this calls him a 'noble character' (*G.P.* I, 329; *H.* I, 279). He lacks all love for the common and honest man.

Philosophy is, for him, the '*Temple* of self-conscious reason', a temple which is quite other than the temple of the 'Jews' in which the Living God resides (*G.P.* I, 49; *H.* I, 35). The philosophers are the architects of this temple, in which the cult of self-consciousness is celebrated, that unity of God, Priest and Community. Philosophers are the Lords of this World, and create the destiny of mankind, and their acts are the acts of destiny. They 'write the executive orders of World History as originally received', and people must obey them, and the King, by acting in accord with these directives, is but as a secretary *copying* the directives written originally by philosophers. What pride! What a basis for revolution if a royal decree would not have the good fortune to please the philosophers. The philosophers are always 'obligated to begin' if an 'advance' in history is to occur. They direct the whole, and have always the whole in sight, while 'others have their *particular* interests – this dominion, these riches, this girl' (*G.P.* III, 96; *H.* II, 453).

But not only when an advance is to occur do philosophers have hands in the affair, but whenever the established order is to be disturbed, and here the positive forms, the institutions, the constitution, and religious statues are to collapse and fall. The philosophers are truly of a singular danger, for they are the most consistent and unrestrained[6] revolutionaries. 'Philosophy begins with the decline of the actual world.' That has a somewhat ambiguous ring about it, and might in any case be yet so understood that Philosophy requires the actual world to be put into confusion for it to exist. The same ambiguity is yet also present when it is said

> that Philosophy first commences when...a gulf has arisen *between inward strivings and external reality*, and the old forms of Religion, etc., are no longer satisfying; when Mind manifests indifference to its living existence or rest unsatisfied therein, and moral life becomes dissolved. Then it is that Mind takes refuge in the clear space of thought to create for itself a kingdom of thought in *opposition* to the actual world (*G.P.* I, 66; *H.* I, 52).

[6] [The German term here is '*rücksichtslos*'. It is used frequently by both Bauer and Marx, e.g., in Marx's letter to Ruge found in this collection. (Ed./Tr.)]

But then Hegel goes on to say that the Mind

> *lays hold of and troubles* this real, substantial kind of existence, this morality and faith, and thus the period of destruction commences (*G.P.* I, 66; *H.* I, 51–2).

Furthermore,

> The definite character of the standpoint of *thought* is the *same* character which permeates all the other historical sides of the spirit of the people, which is most intimately related to them, and which constitutes their *foundation* (*G.P.* I, 68; *H.* I, 53).

Now then, is it not evident that Philosophy insidiously removes the foundations of real life, of the State, of the religious community whenever it withdraws the soul, pure and simple, which infuses all forms of life? Whenever the Idea is seized and raised to self-consciousness, and so develops 'as the thought and knowledge of that which is the substantial spirit of its time'?

Now once Hegel has placed knowledge and theory so infinitely high, so must he then assert that Philosophy, as the knowledge of the substantial, 'in form stands *above its time*' (*G.P.* I, 69; *H.* 54).

The mob of Young Hegelians would like to convince us that Hegel has sunk himself within the folds of theory, and has not thought to lead this *theory to praxis*. As though Hegel had not attacked religion with a hellish rage, as if he had not set forth upon the destruction of the established world. But his *theory* is *praxis*, and for that very reason most dangerous, far-reaching and destructive. It is the revolution itself. Why then are these dissolute disciples acting so foolishly concerning their Master? It cannot be believed that they have not recognized the destructive rage of this system, for they have taken their principle only from their Master. It is possible that they so act – even to reviling Hegel himself – so as to insure that these extensive and most dangerous writings are quietly left to circulate undisturbed in all hands, so that the government would not finally detect their criminality and so forbid these writings, teachings and preachings. The devil is clever! He certainly is! But these tactics can no longer help him! It must be openly and publicly declared: Hegel was a greater revolutionary than the total of all his disciples. The ax must be laid to him, he must be uprooted!

Of that wisdom which has been set over time and place,[7] Hegel says 'it is what a new form of development has brought forth. Philosophy is the inner birthplace of the Spirit, which will later step forth into real form' (*G.P.* I, 70; cf. *H.* I, 55). This then is the crucial

[7] [Hegel is discussing the emergence of Christianity. (Ed./Tr.)]

point to which Philosophy has led; that every knowledge not only develops a new form, but a new content as well. At one time substance, self-affirming, lay at the foundation of reality, directly dominating it, and expressing itself in outward laws. Hence, the mind was not radically free. But now, knowledge has been freed, and the mind and its related determinations have taken upon a new form – the form of freedom and self-consciousness. And so, Philosophy becomes the critic of the established order: 'Through knowledge the spirit posits a difference between what is *known* and that which *is*' (*Ibid.*). 'Through knowledge, Mind makes manifest a distinction between *knowledge* and that which *is*' (*Ibid.*). That which is and that which should be are now distinguished. However, only the *should* is true and justified, and must be brought to authority, domination and power. It must pass through to 'its opposite'. – 'Whenever a principle is set forth which is determined upon giving birth to a new and higher actuality, so it appears in a direct and even hostile and destructive relation to reality, and not merely as opinion and doctrine.' (Cf. *G.P.* II, 118; *H.* I, 445). And so, a theoretical principle must not merely play a supportive role, but must come to the act, to practical opposition, to turn itself directly into praxis and action. 'This practical relationship lies even in the principle; that it contains this is its true status' (*Ibid.*). Hence it is not enough that the incitement to general revolt and 'excitation is the highest service and highest activity of a teacher', but the opposition must be serious, sharp, thoroughgoing, unrestrained, and must see its highest goal in the overthrow of the established order.

And so philosophy must be active in politics, and whenever the established order contradicts the self-consciousness of philosophy, it must be directly attacked and shaken. Servitude, tutelage, is unbearable to the free spirit:

To sleep, to live, to have a certain office, is not our real Being, and certainly to be no slave is such (*G.P.* I, 118; *H.* I, 100).

Every nation in course of time makes such alterations in its existing constitution as will bring it nearer to the true constitution. The nation's mind itself shakes off its leading-strings (its childhood shoes), and the constitution expresses the consciousness of what it is in itself – the form of truth, of self-knowledge. If a nation can no longer accept as implicitly true what its constitution expresses to it as the truth, if its consciousness or Notion and its actuality are not at one, then the nation's mind is torn asunder (*G.P.* II, 276; *H.* II, 97).

A government must, however, recognize that the time for this has come; should it, on the contrary, knowing not the truth, cling to temporary institutions, taking what – though recognized – is unessential, to be a bulwark guarding it from the essential (and the essential is what is contained in the Ideal), that government will fall, along with its institutions, before the force of the mind (*G.P.* II, 277; *H.* II, 98).

[Bauer continues this with a sentence not found in the passage he cites] It lies in the Idea of a constitution that a temporal institution, which has lost its truth, and is as *impudent* as to want itself to continue, must be dissolved.

And who should it be who is to declare when a temporal institution, a regulation, is no longer to be allowed validity? To whom is it given to pass final judgment upon the 'impudence' of the established and positive order? Who is to give the signal for the ruin of the actual state of affairs? Now, you know that well enough yourself! Only the philosopher! 'This insight (into the emptiness of the given state) can be reached through Philosophy alone' (*Ibid.*).

Hear! Hear this self-recognition of the philosopher! Have the Young Hegelians proclaimed anything more criminal, or more treasonable? As yet they have not gone so far – as shameless as they are, as insolent, yet they have not spoken out. It is time that we, the elders, fasten our eyes once again upon their father and turn ourselves against him!

Hegel not only is set against the state, the Church and religion, but opposes everything firm and established, for – as he asserts – the philosophical principle has in recent times become general, all-encompassing and without limit.

In this new period the universal principle...the independently existent thought, this culminating point of inwardness, is now set forth and firmly grasped as such, the dead externality of authority is set aside and regarded as out of place (*G.P.* III, 328; *H.* III, 217).

Indeed, we can no longer be amazed when Hegel envisions the French Revolution, this work of an atheistic Philosophy, to be the greatest event in history, when he envisions it as the salvation of Mankind, and considers it to be the deed in which the calling of Philosophy to world-domination has been perfectly proven. He says:

The conception, the idea of Right asserted its authority *all at once*, and the old framework of injustice could offer no resistance to its onslaught. A constitution, therefore, was established in harmony with the conception of Right, and on this foundation all future legislation was to be based. Never since the sun had stood in the firmament and the planets revolved around him had it been perceived that man's existence centres in his head, i.e., in Thought, inspired by which he builds up the world of reality. Anaxagoras had been the first to say that νοῦς governs the world; but not until now had man advanced to the recognition of the principle that Thought ought to govern spiritual reality. This was accordingly a glorious mental dawn. All thinking beings shared in the jubilation of this epoch. Emotions of a lofty character stirred men's minds at that time; a spiritual enthusiasm thrilled through the world, as if the reconciliation between the Divine and the Secular was now first accomplished.[8]

Again, Hegel's atheism reveals itself even more clearly and displays itself in its full nakedness,[9] when we observe how this Antichrist extols the French – since they have made an insurrection against God – and scorns the Germans, since even in the time of Godlessness, in the time of the *Aufklärung*, they lacked the brashness to deny God, and could not totally set aside God and religion. The French are to him the true men, the Germans but beasts of burden; the former are spirited people, the latter but lazy drones; the former true philosophers, the latter but mere complainers; the former are the discoverers of the true Kingdom of the Spirit, the latter but weaklings who first ask their guardians and beg permission from their bureaucrats so that they might be allowed to enjoy the fruits of knowledge; the former are the heroes of freedom, the latter but slaves, who tremble should they become free. In sum, the French are everything for him, the Germans less than nothing.[10]

[8] [Refers to Hegel's *Vorlesungen über die Philosophie der Weltgeschichte*, p. 441; for English translation see *Hegel's Philosophy of History*, translated by J. Sibree (New York, 1956), p. 447. (Ed./Tr.)]

[9] [Again the 'exposure' theme. (Ed./Tr.)]

[10] [A particularly damning charge. As Treitschke, the historian of the period observed, a 'war fever' directed against the French gripped all of Germany in 1840, a fever first occasioned by Prussia's support of English Mediterranean interest against the French. The wide appeal of such vehemently patriotic poetry as Becker's 1840 *Sie sollen ihn nicht haben*, or Schneckenburger's *Die Wacht am Rhein*, which appeared in the same year, was a sign of the popular resentment over stubborn French territorial claims in the Rhineland. (Ed./Tr.)]

The Jewish Problem

INTRODUCTION

'Freedom, human rights, emancipation, expiation of a thousand-year-old wrong' – these are such great rights and obligations that the heart of every honest man is certain to respond to their appeal. The mere words are often sufficient to make the cause which is defended by their use popular.

All to often, however, one thinks victory of a cause has been won, if one only uses words which serve, so to say, as a holy symbol which nobody would dare deny lest he be looked upon as a monster, a scoffer, or a friend of tyranny. Momentary success can be won in this manner, but real victories can not be won this way, nor can real difficulties be overcome.

In the course of the present negotiations regarding the Jewish question the great words 'liberty, human rights, emancipation' were often heard and applauded; but they did not contribute much to progress in the matter itself, and it will perhaps be useful to abstain for once from using them continuously and instead to give serious thought to the subject under discussion.

The popular interest in the Jewish problem cannot be explained by the merits of its advocates, but only by the fact that the public feels that the emancipation of the Jews is connected with the development of our general conditions.

The advocates of emancipation did not seek out and explain this connection. In a period when not a single power that ruled the world till now was safe from criticism, Jews and Judaism were left alone. One did not even ask the question as: what are they and whether or not their essence is compatible with freedom were freedom to be granted to them?

There is an outcry as if it were treason against humanity if a critic starts to investigate the particular character of the Jew. The very same people who look on with pleasure when criticism is aimed at Christianity, or who consider such criticism necessary and desirable, are ready to condemn the man who subjects Judaism too to criticism.

So Judaism is privileged: now, when privileges come tumbling down under the blows of criticism; and subsequently after they have fallen?

The advocates of emancipation are therefore in the strange position that they fight against privilege and at the same time grant to Judaism the privilege of unchangeability, immunity, and irresponsibility. They fight for the Jews with the best of intentions, but lack true enthusiasm, for they treat the Jewish problem as a matter foreign to them. If they are partisans of progress and the higher development of humanity, the Jews are excluded from their party. They demand that the Christians and the Christian state give up prejudices which not only have grown into their hearts but which are an essential part of their heart and being, and yet they demand no such thing from the Jews. The heart of Judaism must not be touched.

The birth of the new epoch which is now emerging will cost the Christian world great pains: are the Jews to suffer no pain, are they to have equal rights with those who fought and suffered for the new world? As if that could be! As if they could feel at home in a world which they did not make, did not help to make, which is contrary to their unchanged nature!

Those people who want to spare them the pains of criticism are the worst enemies of the Jews. Nobody who has not gone through the flames of criticism will be able to enter the new world which will soon come.

Besides, you have not brought the Jewish problem to the general public. You have talked about the injustices of the Christian states, but have not asked whether these injustices and hardships did not have their basis in the nature of the old state organizations.

If the treatment of the Jews in the Christian state has its basis in its nature, then the emancipation of the Jews only under the condition that they change that nature – i.e., as far as the Jews themselves change their nature – means that the Jewish problem is only a part of the general problem, the solution of which our age is seeking.

Until now the enemies of emancipation had much the advantage over its advocates, because they considered the contrast between the Jew as such to the Christian state. Their only mistake was that they presupposed the Christian state as the only true state and did not subject it to the same criticism that they applied to Judaism. Their opinion of Judaism seemed harsh and unjust only because they did not at the same time look critically at the state which denied and had to deny liberty to the Jews.

Our criticism will be aimed at both sides: only in this way will we be able to find a solution. Perhaps our understanding of Judaism will appear even harsher than that which used to be expressed by the enemies of emancipation. Perhaps it is harsher: but my only concern can be whether it is correct. The only problem will be whether an evil is thoroughly abolished if it is not torn out by the roots. Whoever insists upon complaining, may accuse Liberty, because it demands not only from other nations but from the Jews as well, that they sacrifice antiquated traditions before they win liberty. If the criticism seems, or really is, harsh, it will still lead to Liberty and nothing else will.

At the outset, we want to pose the problem correctly and remove the wrong formulations it was given before.

The problem posed correctly

What advocates usually do at the end of a trial, namely, appeal to the emotions of the judge and the public, be it only that they explain how their clients were driven by dire necessity to go astray, the advocates of the Jews do right at the start. They either complain about the oppression under which the Jews lived in the Christian world, or, if they admit that some of the reproaches regarding the attitude, the character, and the condition of the Jews are in part justified, they make that oppression appear even more hateful by asserting that it alone was the cause of those characteristics.

The innocence of the Jews

To defend the Jews in this manner is really to do them a great disservice and it is detrimental to their cause.

One usually says of martyrs that they were killed, though innocent – this is really the greatest insult. Was what they did and for what they died nothing? Was it not contrary to the way of life and the ideas of their adversaries? The greater, the more important they are as martyrs, the greater must have been their deed, which was against the existing laws; therefore, the greater their guilt against the powers that ruled in their time.

Of the Jews it will at least be admitted that they suffered for their Law, for their way of life and for their nationality, that they were martyrs. They were thus themselves to blame for the oppression they suffered, because they provoked it by their adherence to their law, their language, to their whole way of life. A nothing cannot be oppressed. Wherever there is pressure something must have caused it by its existence, by its nature.

In history nothing stands outside the law of causality, least of all the Jews. With a stubbornness which their advocates themselves praise and admire they have clung to their nationality and resisted the movements and changes of history. The will of history is evolution, new forms, progress, change; the Jews want to stay forever what they are, therefore they fought against the first law of history – does this not prove that by pressing against this mighty spring they provoked counter-pressure? They were oppressed because they first pressed by placing themselves against the wheel of history.

Had the Jews been outside this action of the law of causality, had they been entirely passive, had they not from their side strained against the Christian world, there would not be any tie to connect them with history. They could never have entered into the new development of history and have influenced it. Then their cause would be quite lost.

Therefore, give the Jews the honor that they were to blame for the oppression which they suffered, that the hardening of their character caused by this oppression was their own fault. Then you admit them to a place in a two-thousand-year-old history, although a subordinate one; then you make them a member which is capable, and finally had the duty to take part in history's progress.

Sometimes the advocates of Judaism forget that they ascribe to it the purely passive role of the sufferer and boast that it has a very beneficial influence on the life of the states. An example!

Spain

Look, they say, what became of Spain after the Most Catholic Majesties condemned the industrious, enlightened and active Jewish population to exile!

Spain, however, did not decline because of the absence of the Jewish population. The reasons for its decline were the intolerance, oppression and persecution practiced by its government. It sank deeper and deeper under the pressure of these principles and the same would have happened, had the Jews remained. Did the condition of France become desperate because the repeal of the Edict of Nantes sent thousands of Huguenots into exile? No! It was the tyranny of the government, the privileges of the aristocracy and the clergy, the strict police regime, which brought France to the point where only revolution could bring relief. Who knows whether the stubborn Huguenots would have contributed a great deal to the liberation of their country. Enough, France did manage without them.

Spain, too, liberated itself without the Jews from the oppression of the Most Catholic government, and it is very questionable whether the Jews, had they remained in Spain, would have made an important contribution to this liberation.

This proves that the Christian states are alone responsible for the rise and decline of their power, and even if the Jews play some role, it is prescribed by the principle of the Christian state. On the other hand, we can clear the Jews from the accusation that they were responsible for the ruin of a state, for instance, Poland.

Poland

The constitution of Poland was such that there was an immense gap between the ruling aristocracy and the masses of the serfs, a gap which enabled the Jews to settle there in greater numbers than anywhere else. This constitution, which by failing to provide an element equivalent to that in Western Europe developed into the third estate, instead utilized a foreign element which led Poland to its doom.

Poland is itself to blame for its misfortune. It is also itself to blame for permitting a foreign population to settle there and contribute to making more dangerous and fatal the sore in its national existence.

Although Poland is itself to blame for its fate, it does not, on the other hand, speak favorably for the Jews that they could settle in numbers which about equal their number in all other European countries together, only in the most imperfect state of Europe and gain a position which can almost be called indispensable and a necessary complement. That they could thus make a home for themselves only in a state which to a great extent is no state, speaks against their ability to become members of a real state; what speaks even more against them is the fact that they utilized the defects in the Polish constitution for their private profit, that they enlarged the gap instead of forming the material to fill it in an organic and politically useful manner.

An enemy of Jewish emancipation remarks and complains that 'all distilleries in Galicia are exclusively in the possession of the Jews, and thereby the moral strength of the inhabitants is given in their hands'. As if it were the fault of the Jews that the moral strength of a nation is in a glass of brandy or can be lost in a glass of brandy! That enemy of the Jews has to admit himself that the Pole 'sees in brandy his only consolation for all his toils and for the oppressions of his landlord'. It is therefore the oppression of the regime which drives the peasant to the Jew. It is the mindless materialism of his life which makes the peasant reach for the glass of brandy, so that the minds of the people are in the hands of the Jew if the Jew is in possession of the distilleries.

The constitution has given the Jew his important position and it put the minds of the people in his hands – but is it an honor for the Jew that he utilizes this position to distill the last consequences out of this condition? Does it speak for him that he is ready, that he makes it his only business to oppress the victims of the regime once more? The constitution is to blame for oppressing the peasant, for putting him in the hands of the Jew, but the Jew is culpable if he draws only the worst consequences from the constitution.

This situation repeats itself in civil society in general.

Civil society

Demand is the mighty spring which puts civil society in motion. Everyone utilizes everyone else to satisfy his own needs, and he in turn is utilized by others for the same purpose. The tailor utilizes my need to support his family. I utilize him to supply my need.

This egotistic activity of civil society has been restricted in the Christian state by forms which take some of its ugliness away and which connect it with the interests of honor. The special ways of supplying certain needs have been brought together in estates; and that class in which the need of the moment had the greatest power, in which, therefore, greed is most rampant, the tradesmen, were organized in the Christian state in the form of corporations. The member of the corporation has as such the obligation to pursue not only his personal interests but the interests of his guild. In this manner certain limits are set to his own interests, and he feels honored because he feels now that he cares not only for the needs of individuals but for the needs of society in general.

But where demand with its accidental caprices and moods rules absolutely, where the satisfaction of the demand is again dependent on accidents of nature, there the individual can personally remain honest, but cannot protect himself against sudden, unexpected changes which are beyond his calculation. Demand, the basis of civil society, which secures its existence and guarantees its necessity, exposes it at the same time to continuous dangers, gives it an element of insecurity, and causes that ever changing mixture of poverty and wealth, misery and prosperity to change.

This element of insecurity was not created by the Jews; it belongs to society; they are not to be blamed for its existence. But is is another question whether it should perhaps be counted as a merit that they – by means of usury – have exploited it and have made this their domain to the exclusion of all other activities in the circles of civil society.

Like the gods of Epicurus who live in interstellar spaces and are freed from specific labors, so the Jews have struck roots outside the corporate interests in the gaps and crevices of society, and have caught the victims of the element of insecurity in civil society.

But, their advocates reply, they were denied admittance to these estates and corporations. But the question is this, would they, who regard themselves as a nation, have been able to assume a real and sincere position in those circles, did they not exclude themselves? As they, as a nation, stand outside the interests of the peoples, were they not forced to assume a position outside the interests of estates and corporations?

What? they will reply again, you will not acknowledge the industry of the Jews, their frugality, their perseverance in their work, their inventiveness in seeking new sources of profit, their indefatigable endurance? We have acknowledged all this. Now we allow ourselves two more questions.

The industry of the Jews

Who worked for eighteen hundred years to educate Europe? Who fought the battles in which a hierarchy which wanted to rule beyond its time was defeated? Who created Christian and modern art and filled the cities of Europe with enduring monuments? Who developed the sciences? Who developed the theory of state constitutions?

There is not one Jewish name. Spinoza was no longer a Jew when he created his system. Moses Mendelssohn died of grief when he heard that Lessing, his deceased friend, had been an adherent of Spinoza.

Now the second question! True, the European nations excluded the Jews from their general affairs. But could they have done it, if the Jews had not excluded themselves? Can the Jew as such, that is without ceasing to be a Jew, work for the progress of art and science, for freedom from the hierarchy? Can he take interest in the state and give thought to the general principles of government? On the other hand: Are art and science subjects which can be made inaccessible by the accidental situation somebody finds himself in by birth? Are they not free goods that cannot be denied to anybody? How many men who had great influence in art and science have come from the lowest classes and had to surmount extraordinary obstacles to gain entry into the realm of art and science? Why did not Jews do this? The reason is probably that their particular national spirit is opposed to the general interests of art and science.

The industry of the Jews is of such a kind that it has nothing to do with the interests of history.

The same is true of the tenacity of the Jewish spirit which is frequently praised.

The tenacity of the Jewish spirit

It would not be cruel, it would only be just and fair to tell our adversaries the names of all those tribes that also survived all the storms of history and maintained their identity in the dispersion among civilized peoples. But even without doing this we will be able to put the matter in its true position.

Is it a dishonor for the tribes which were melted together into the French nation to have given up and lost their identity? Certainly not! That they dissolved into the new whole proves their malleability and their ability to make a contribution to the formation of this particular historical national genius.

Have the tribes which formed the population of the great new republic in North America kept their former identities? No! Even now, German immigrants for instance, assume in a short time the character of the whole, and this is certainly not a dishonor. It only proves their ability to adjust to the general direction of national life and to make themselves at home.

Do the European nations in general keep their identity with the tenacity which is praised in the Jews? On the contrary, they change their character and these changes are according to the will of History.

Instead of praising the tenacity of the Jewish national spirit and regarding it as an advantage, one should ask what its basis is and where it comes from.

Its base is lack of ability to develop with history, it is the reason of the quite unhistorical character of that nation, and this again is due to its oriental nature. Such stationary nations exist in the Orient, because there human liberty and the possibility of progress are still limited. In the Orient and in India, we still find Parsees living in dispersion and worshipping the holy fire of Ormuzd.

The individual as well as the nation which in its thought and deeds follows universal laws will progress with history; for universal laws have their base in reason and liberty, they develop with the progress of Reason. This progress is to be expected and it is effected with certainty and ease, because Reason in its laws has to do with its own products, and does not have to ask permission from a foreign, supernatural power.

In the Orient, man does not yet know that he is free and gifted with reason. He does not recognize freedom and reason as his real nature. He sees his highest task in the performance of mindless, baseless ceremonies. The original man likewise, has as yet no history if only that which is a development of general human liberty deserves to be called history. To sit under his vine and his fig tree, is for the oriental the highest boon man can achieve. He performs his religious ceremonies again and again, he considers their unchanged performance his highest duty, and he is content that they are just so and must be so because he knows of no reason other than this is so and has to be so according to the will of a higher, inscrutable being.

True, a character, a law such as this must impart a peculiar tenacity to a nation, but at the same time such a character will rob it of the possibility of historic development.

The Jews are right if they talk of a fence around the Law. The Law has fenced them off from the influences of history, the more so, as their Law commanded from the start seclusion from the other nations.

They have survived; but the question is whether the content of the Law is so exalted that they are to be praised because they survived with it without change.

Are the mountains of Greece greater and more worthy of our admiration than the Greek nation because these mountains stand today, unchanged, while the Greeks of Homer, Sophocles, Pericles and Aristotle are gone?

Moses Mendelssohn said the advantage of the Jewish religion is that it does not teach universal truths, but gives only positive commandments for which no universal reason can be given. He declared therefore – and he is right, for if something is beyond my horizon and I can give no account of it to myself, then I have no power over it – that the Law keeps its validity for the Jew until Jehovah abolishes it expressly and unmistakably, as He revealed it on Sinai.

Is this tenacity an honor? Does it make the nation, whose existence is due to it, an historical nation? It only keeps it alive against History.

Life under oppression

If a nation does not progress with History, if it is never caught up in the enthusiasm which is necessary for the fight for new historical ideas, if it keeps aloof from political passions, then it lacks one of the most important incentives to exalted and pure morality. At the end it will lose interest in general human affairs. One's only care will be his private profit, and the feeling for true honor will be lost.

One will reply that because of the oppression under which the Jews lived this could not be otherwise, that it was natural that the nobler sentiments be suppressed. Shall we reproach them for a lack of morality when they were excluded from the affairs and interests which gave ever new incentives to the spirit of the European nations?

• • •

CONCLUSION

In a manner tried by the Sanhedrin the servants of the Mosaic Law will not be helped to freedom. The distinction between religious and political commands in the revealed law, the declaration that only the former are absolutely binding while the latter lose their power in changed social conditions, is in itself an outrage against the Old Testament Law and an admission that it contains commands and regulations which are contrary to our concept of human society. This admission is, however, withdrawn by the assertion that all objections made in the past against the Law are based on prejudices and are an outrage against the most holy. Sophistry and Jesuitism and a clumsy exegesis have brought out now, for instance, that the Law did not intend to distinguish between the Israelite and the stranger in the way asserted until now by the 'enemies' of Judaism.

The same lie appears in the distinction between religious and political commands. This distinction is an admission that the adherent of a law like the Mosaic law can not live in the real world and participate in its interests. It would be fine if the Jew openly declared: 'I want – since I wish to remain a Jew – to keep only that much of the Law which seems to be a purely religious element; everything else which I recognize as anti-social I shall weed out and sacrifice.' But instead he pretends to himself, and he wants to make others believe that in this distinction between religious and political commands he remains in accord with the Law, that the Law itself recognizes and establishes this distinction. Instead of breaking with a part of the Law he remains a servant of the whole, and as such he must give up that distinction again and alienate himself through his religious consciousness from the real world.

Judaism cannot be helped, the Jews cannot be reconciled with the world, by the lie.

But neither can force liberate the Jew from his chimerical tyrant, the Law, and restore him to the world; especially not if that force is used by slaves who obey the same tyrant. So, how can he be helped?

We have to be free ourselves before we can think of inviting others to freedom. We have to remove the beam from our own eye before we have the right to call the attention of our brother to the mote in his eye. Only a free world can liberate the slaves of prejudice.

The lie in the sophistry of the Jews is a sure sign that Judaism, too, is near its disintegration. It is, however, a dishonest state of affairs if in theory political rights are withheld from the Jew, while in practice he wields great power and exerts political influence wholesale while he cannot assert it in small things. For instance, while the Jew in Vienna is only tolerated, his financial power decides the fate of the whole monarchy. The Jew who may have no political rights in the smallest German state rules the fate of Europe. While corporations and guilds close their doors to him or are still unfriendly, the inventiveness of industry scoffs at the stubbornness of the medieval institutions. The new movement has long broken through the barriers of the old; their existence can now be called theoretical only. The power of the old is a sophistic theory, opposed to the theory of sincerity and the immense superiority of a practice, the importance of which can be seen in our daily life.

Judaism has followed Christianity on its path of conquest around the world. It has always reminded it of its origin and of its true nature. It is the incarnate doubt in the heavenly origin of Christianity, the religious adversary of the religion which announced itself as the perfect, the only true religion, and could not even overcome the small number of those in the midst of whom it had been born. Judaism was the proofstone of which Christianity proved most clearly that its nature is the nature of privilege.

Both religions could torture each other, scoff at each other, embitter each other's life, but none could overcome the other. The crude religious criticism voiced by Judaism, and Judaism itself, is at least made superfluous by the free, human critique which has demonstrated that Christianity and revealed Judaism were a medieval luxury. Judaism was a mere appendix to the history of Christianity, and its critique of Christianity was unjustified because it needed Christian scholarship to make the critique possible.

Theory has now completed its task, it has dissolved the old contradiction between Judaism and Christianity and can look confidently to History, which pronounces the final judgment on principles which have lost their validity.

The Genus and the Crowd

To partake of greatness, some people have recently taken to emblazoning 'The Crowd' on their shields.

They want the crowd to raise itself up; one wonders how high! As if then somehow the crowd would be raised up out of its element, its massiveness, the dead form of the multitude! It is the same case as with the Jews two years ago. There it had been maintained that they could take in hand the gift of freedom without further ado, since they still cherished, jointly with them, the same prejudices.

They withdrew the crowd from the critique, as they would have liked to withdraw themselves from it. They now make use of the crowd as a remedy against the Spirit. The crowd is now made a cult-object, so as to be a new palliative against the old egoism.

The crowd, it is said, has no prejudices – but, its prejudices are merely the most hollow, since those atoms which belong to it do not have that large orbit of motion in which the atomistic points of that higher, leading multitude are driven about. There above they would obtain the general view, the power of comparison, the capability to correct their errors and so attain the consciousness of their egoism.

The crowd, determined as proletariat, is but the image and the result of the decay of that opposition which confronts it – its inorganic mass is now only possible when common class interests have dissolved into a pure interest, into an infinity of competing interests. And so, here and there, above and below, solitariness prevails. But if it must submit to the higher and wider sphere of the social movement itself, against its will and in combinations which connect solitary labor to a sort of system which gives it the appearance of thought and speculation, so below it is yet restricted materially to a particular, fixed occupation and operation, and the possibility of any sort of spirituality is taken from it. The slave of purely manual labor has no notion at all of the spiritual slavery of general competition. He only has an elementary feeling of its pressure, without being able to interpret and explain it, and what he cannot have a presentiment of, what cannot be brought to his consciousness, he is also unable to oppose.

Well then, Spirit, which developed itself in the struggle of the higher interests, might finally yet find the scheme of an order in which all interests are satisfied, in which casualties to a cause of egotistical solitariness are no longer demanded. But the Spirit must first convince the multitude of the truth of its idea. (The Spirit must save it the trouble.) It will raise the multitude, calmly and certainly, to the standpoint of universal labor. It will let it free itself easily and gladly from the fetters of restricted, eternally repetitious labor.

So? but if that idea – whatever it may be – is from the first not possible without struggle, if it can only result from the friction of great and spiritual masses of interests, from a friction which must bring about an enormous collision, then would the crowd allow itself to be convinced of this truth without opposition? Should struggle only occur above, and will peace sincerely exist only below? Only above, where the consciousness of disunion keep the spirits strained and indeed where it can also only truly be fought, only there is the cause to be settled. But will it from the first be viewed as agreed upon and be bid welcome from below? Rather a struggle is but hard to introduce below, but not unnecessary, not impossible. But they have not thought about a struggle with the crowd, since they do not and cannot know the new turn of the struggle initiated after the decline of the parties – in short, they have fallen from the 'Height of the Party' itself into the crowd. Yet it may not be conceded that the truth would not be accepted if it were offered.

Meanwhile the struggle is long since introduced. One has long since accepted it, almost without notice. Even the multitude, which one might bring to confession like a congregation of unprejudiced martyrs to virtue, must occupy the position which is due it. But as a result of the spiritless condition which it reflects in faint and confused form, this spiritlessness will be leveled against development. Slave to its puzzlement, indolence, fear and restriction to a point which impedes its need and its work, it is – for the present – hardly accessible to a Universal Idea. But those allies which it will win after the decay of parties will give its fear a greater power, will help its indolence to its legs, and set its hate in motion against the spirit.

The crowd, as such, is but an appearance which could only make its entrance after the specific differences in which the genus had so far expressed itself had grown vague and pale. The crowd is the decay of the genus into a mass of individual atoms, a dissolution of specific barriers which, although yet separating individuals, nevertheless united them and set them in a manifold relation. The crowd is mere elementary stuff, the sediment of a decomposed organic form.

How would it be then, if you made an attempt to bring the genus again to recognition and thereby to strengthen again and thus to unite these slackened individuals now unsteadied and unbridled in their exhaustion? If you showed to them the genus of higher, universal power? Should not the crowd again abolish the genus, and not restore it?

At the time, when in France systems are created for the organization of the crowd, that attempt to restore the genus to all its honor was undertaken in Germany from the direction of criticism – from the direction which Feuerbach had taken.

This criticism starts from the fact that religion, whose 'essence' he wants to explain, had disrupted the idea of the human genus, while it merely made individual happiness the purpose of that ultimate order which was already set forth in an eternal decree before the creation of the world. To Feuerbach, men would have to submit to a 'measure, law and criterion', and this 'absolute measure' is the measure of human genus. 'What I think of the measure of the genus, I think in general only as a man can think and so must consequently think of individuals, if he wants to think normally, legitimately and consequently in truth.' What corresponds to the essence of the genus is true. 'Man can and should rise only above the bounds of his individuality, but not above the laws, the positive essential determinations of his genus. Man cannot think of, represent, feel, believe, want, love and revere any other essence than the absolute essence as the essence of human nature.' What then is the essence, the 'true Mankind in man'? 'The reason, the will, the heart.' 'Reason, love, will-power are the perfections of the human essence, indeed the essential perfections, the highest powers, the absolute essence of man as such, the foundations of his being. They are divine, absolute powers, the powers constituting his essence, which he neither has nor makes.'

But then they are rather his weakness. That essence which he does not make – that essence which withdraws itself from his creative power, or rather which presupposes that he has no productive power for his highest, indeed for his only human concerns – is but the expression of his weakness. The truly human in him would thereby become a barrier which is unattainable for him. His perfections, which confront him as fixed ideas or as dogmas, could, at most, be only the object of a cult or a faith which absolute imperfection – to which he is condemned from their otherworldly throne – is made necessary.

Feuerbach has let stand in essence the very relation which he wanted to criticize. It has become, in the form of the substance, still more fixed. For although he has converted it into the relation of the human essence he yet has only made it more difficult for the man.

If, namely, as Feuerbach sets down as an axiom: 'every essence is sufficient in itself, no essence can negate itself, that is, its essentiality, no essence is itself a restricted one, but rather every essence is in and for itself infinite', then the human essence is for man a power which he may not nor cannot submit at all to the critique. He is therefore infinite and self-sufficient like the caterpillar, which is self-sufficient and infinite, in the same sense since he cannot attain his barrier, or, since his barrier so firmly encircles him, that it has destroyed his thought and will both here and beyond.

This narcissism of man, who views his infinity in his essence, which is but an infinite that has been simply withdrawn from his influence and his activity, is an infinity which he does not possess and which possesses him. This narcissism must lead to resignation, apathy, and surrender to that fixed restriction which is allotted to every individual.

The human genus is thereby restored only so that the pains of its dissolution are silenced. The brutal impulses of the crowd are externally fettered and the contradictions into which history has gone astray are silenced.

The essence has not been able to heal the damages – but for compensation it spreads its mantle out over the wounds.

It is in vain. Despair thrusts the veil away. Selfishness does not want to satisfy itself, and the healing power, still at hand, does not want to let itself suffocate under this death-mantle.

What Feuerbach promotes is a work of art, an appearance, which can persevere for a moment and appear at one time as personal talent, but which vanishes before the ardor of the passions which move reality.

Does it not lie within the meaning of the human genus to bring itself in appearance into specific differences? Is it not the power of the genus which begets that gradation of power and gifts out of which finally the universal struggle of all individuals results? And is it not the weakness of the genus that numberless seeds are suffocated at birth and multitudes of individuals obtain only a stunted existence? Is the awakening consciousness of the enfeebled and the crippled not already a doubt against the genus, and the expiration of specific differences not a sign of the creation of the genus? Is not history, which is finally considered critically, the proof, insofar as it considers the genus as such? Is not criticism the proof that the essence which has represented itself in this history is a determination which by no means so encloses man as would the essence of a caterpillar make a leaf for this crawling thing into its only and highest world?

On the contrary, says Feuerbach – 'Surrender! Resign!' – even if in other words.

He says: 'whoever is somewhat proficient in his class, in his art, whoever, as one says in life, fills his post, and is devoted to his vocation body and soul, so he also imagines his vocation as the highest and most beautiful. How can he renounce his spirit, and humble in his thought what he celebrates through action, while he consecrates his powers with the same joy? Still I must, and so is my activity an unhappy one, for I am at variance with myself. Labor in service. But how can I serve an object if it does not stand above me in spirit?' But committed labor must dominate, continues Feuerbach, since it is at the same time labor and being for the genus. 'Whoever therefore lives in the consciousness of the genus as a reality so takes his being to be Other, and takes his public, socially useful being to be the being which is at one with the being of his essence.'

But the fixed and limited vocation which the laborer already takes to be as such the highest and most beautiful is a barrier which bars him the view of the remaining collective labor of the genus, and aggravates a comparison with the achievements of others. If, furthermore, labor is service, and common labor loses its character of struggle and command, then can it not become slavery, slavery under material and particular needs and the dullest of mechanical slavery? The idea of the genus should be a comfort to this base mechanism but is it not just the genus which makes labor necessary, and which suffocates the idea of a further unity and a higher universality? On the other hand, does not this comparison of the restricted sphere of labor – in which the slave is banished with his best power to a higher sphere of life – does not this comparison, if it is correctly pursued, lead to a critique of that human genus-essence, which has brought about this disunion?

Should the feeling of misfortune and of disintegration be removed and obliviated in the fire of labor?

As is well known, there are insects which are so similar in color and shape to the leaf which nourishes them and shapes their world, that they are scarcely distinguished from it.

With such leaf insects, which – according to Feuerbach – the laborers had to become in order to overcome their feeling of disunion, Fourier has wanted to populate the world.

It is not denied, as elsewhere said that the actions of the genus has claimed many victims in its course, as it was not correctly and consciously directed. Labor is necessary, but so far it has alienated itself and has worn itself out in isolation. The equalization of need and production has not been achieved, for it was abandoned to the same chance which in nature, for example, determined how many seeds for the maintenance of a species should escape from a thousand sorts of destruction. And so, one parliamentary group who speak for the 'Organization of Labor' declare that the government must behave as the highest steward of production. It would be granted a greater authority, so that by virtue of its wisdom and general view it would prevent the future from having the evil which results from the elementary struggle of the various species of the genus. It would be given the means to annihilate the competition of small and isolated wealth through one capital which could devour all others.

This proposition results from a disbelief – which credits the genus with no power at all in the present crisis – that freely breathing humans could result from the struggle of competing powers. This view wants this last remnant of independence to collaborate in a manner in which only one thought, will, and arranging power has its place henceforth, and which should thus form a singular rising over the enormous plane of laboring society.

According to this view, reason, will and character remain the opposite from which they are from Feuerbach's standpoint. They will shape the essence of a society which neither has nor makes this essence, but rather, is purely and solely constituted by it. The genus relation has remained, but has become more narrow, for the collective power of the genus has organized itself into an authority which must punish in the most severe manner any attempt of the laborer-slaves to concern themselves with anything other than the tasks assigned to them.

This standpoint knows nothing of spirit and self-consciousness – nothing in the least – for it is unconcerned in assigning as a prerogative to that industrial authority all the directed cleverness and cunning which is necessary for the annihilation of competition.

But then is this collaboration the single and solely remaining task given to the infinite majority, to entire Mankind – the industrial authorities excepted – as they remain occupied only with the collection and distribution of the particular work? Does it not matter to abolish the depressing and withering power of labor? Is competition only between capital and labor? Has not the spirit power to compete? And if it has fallen asleep in this struggle of the genus, will not the increased pressure of labor all the more awaken it?

The exhaustion following upon the illusions of the Enlightenment very likely makes certain the training of an unrestricted commanding industrial authority which will embrace every thought and will.

Criticism has brought forth bright and rigid men into an illusory self-reliance, and they already claim to know the whole of the world and are quite ready to rule it. But it also calls forth a reaction which also grows to become universal and all-encompassing, for it strengthens itself through these bright figures who have now become puzzled by the criticisms thrown at them.

The Competition leads to one-sided accumulation of wealth which must at least submit to become a single capital. Would a crowd which knows nothing higher than its material existence hesitate to subordinate itself to a capital assuring its occupation and life?

The Competition is then simplified, and self-consciousness will set itself specifically against privilege, the pure form of completed reaction. The affair will then take upon a clearly new form.

Another hypothesis – that of French communism – will lead to the same end. The constitution of the industrial authority starts from the presupposition that the crowd now opposing itself in exhausting competition no longer has the power to help itself. This communist view starts from a dogma which is more exclusive than any dogma that has ever guided man – from the dogma that 'the laborers produce everything, and so have a right to everything'. According to this view, only a part of the organism suffers but the whole remaining system is – this one part excepted – in the most perfect health. Hence, the medical treatment corresponding to this strange pathological view: the suffering part should be amputated, and the whole remaining organism separated from it. This radical remedy consists in negating everyone besides the crowd of useful laborers, and replacing them through their opposites. In place of the state the non-state abruptly enters, in place of government, anarchy, and in place of the amputated distinctions, unity, brotherly love, freedom and equality enter. But this occurs only for a moment, only as a chimera, for this crude negation is compelled once again to abolish itself just as crudely and thus to reveal this method of healing as a failure. The crowd of free brothers can only assure its freedom and equality through a state which will 'determine the principle for all questions concerning the nourishment, clothing, lodging, marriage, family, work' – in short, through a state which also abolishes freedom in the smallest things. Therefore only in this society will there be 'no crimes and lawsuits', for its essence no longer has a will. The unity of the society is troubled no more, since in it there will be but *one* dogma, and this dogma as the expression of the entire truth – rules all brothers in the same way. For 'the truth is indivisible. It alone may direct the reason of men, and therefore one must proclaim it entirely and everywhere in a suitable way.' And so, through the idea of contradiction, which lives in the notion of the genus, the happiness of this new brotherly community is finally abolished altogether. This vast working union and its exclusive dogma, this despotic condition of subdued atoms, would take vain comfort in the proposition: 'for man nothing is innate, neither idea, nor taste, nor inclinations, nor skill – as otherwise one must accept that there are different human genera'. Its existence is only possible through the exclusion of the spirit and so it presupposes the distinctions of the genus and must recognize these even against its will. The contradictions of the genus – the interruptions of unity through the specific differences – is thus preserved in this kingdom of the indiscriminate crowd, into which the genus has fallen. It preserves itself as a threatening force, as a necessary perfection, as a determination of that crowd which is unable to deny the essence of the human genus.

Hence, all these attempts end in an inevitable war of the multitude against spirit and self-consciousness, and the significance of this war is found in nothing less than the fact that in it the cause of criticism is set against the genus.

V
Arnold Ruge
1802–1880

Arnold Ruge

Arnold Ruge was, in effect, the devoted publicity manager of Young Hegelianism. From the time he was a student within the notoriously liberal *Burschenschaften* until his death in exile, Ruge remained the brave and tireless champion of humanism – a humanism which he conceived could only take root in the rich philosophical soil of German culture. Unlike so many of the other Young Hegelians – such as Stirner or Schmidt, who looked upon their roles with some irony, or Bauer and Strauss, who finally gave up the ghost of liberalism – Ruge remained serious about advancing the grand causes of reason and freedom, causes which he understood to be the true content of Hegelianism.

As befitting the magnitude of his task, Ruge exhausted his every talent to its advancement. In the words of William Brazill, Ruge 'wrote on religion, art, literature, philosophy, and politics; he was a journalist and essayist; he was a teacher; he was the leader of a philosophical party; he was a politician. He could not be described as a specialist, he did not believe in professionalism. He believed, rather, that his *Weltanschauung* provided the key to understanding all phases of life.' This 'Weltanschauung' rested directly upon his conviction that Hegelianism had insured that the advance of history was also the advance of truth and freedom. In Heine's words, Ruge was 'the grim doorkeeper of Hegelian philosophy', for to him being a philosopher meant not only to know the good, but to will it.

His first test came early in his life, for in 1824 he was imprisoned for five years for having engaged in forbidden political activity while yet a student at Jena. The five years were spent in an intensive study of Hegel.

In 1837, he joined with another Young Hegelian, Theodor Echtermeyer to establish the *Hallische Jahrbücher*. It soon became the central organ of Young Hegelian propaganda, and for a generation of German liberals it served as the only bridge between philosophical theory and political and social activism. In 1841, the journal was suppressed in Prussia, but Ruge took its editorial offices to the more liberal climate of Dresden, where it re-appeared under a new title, the *Deutsche Jahrbücher*. It lost none of its humanistic fire, and continued to provide a platform for Young Hegelian themes and writers, themes which continually provoked the authorities of both Church and state, and writers whose unrestrained atheistic and revolutionary sentiments could not be ignored. Within two years even

Dresden had had enough, and Ruge sought another home for his journal. In 1843, Ruge joined with the ex-editor of the suppressed *Rheinische Zeitung*, Karl Marx, to establish a new journal, the *Deutsch-Französische*, *Jahrbücher*. Paris, the home of the new journal, proved liberal enough, but the journal attracted little attention, and Marx and Ruge parted in anger after it had made its first and final appearance in February of 1844.

With this final blow – the collapse of his optimistic plans to form an 'alliance of German and French liberals', Ruge retreated despondently to Switzerland. But the 1848 revolutions revived his political optimism, and he returned to Germany to establish yet one more liberal journal, *Die Reform*. But the sorry collapse of the German revolution, and the subsequent suppression of *Die Reform* finally ended his active career. He joined the ranks of exiles, both liberal and conservative, who found some cold refuge in London, far from Bismarck's 'realpolitik'. There, until his death, Ruge's voice was heard only in muted and ignored writings which passively followed the course of European political history.

The following two selections are articles by Ruge taken from his *Deutsche Jahrbücher*; the first, 'Hegel's "Philosophy of Right" and the Politics of Our Times' appeared in issues 189 and 190 (August, 1842). In 1867, Ruge recalled the article, and noted that he still subscribed to the same principles, principles which in 1842 had 'theoretically anticipated' the revolution of 1848. The second article, 'A Self-Critique of Liberalism' appeared in the first issue of 1843. These articles are here translated into English for the first time, as well as annotated, by Professor James A. Massey.

Column references to the original text appear in square brackets in the translation, with the bracketed word following the column reference being the first word of the new column.

Hegel's 'Philosophy of Right' and the Politics of our Times

[755b] Our times are political, and our politics intend the freedom of this world. No longer do we lay the ground for the ecclesiastical state, but for the secular state, and the interest in the public issue of freedom in the state grows with every breath that humans take. So-called materialistic interests only appear to contradict the idea of this century. As a child with every breath also inhales the spiritual atmosphere of reason and self-consciousness, so every material increase in our contemporary world is directly a spiritual increase. But we need not pursue this further; our political lineaments need not be conjured forth under a mask of material well-being, but lie open for every eye to see. Even we Germans no longer live in total devotion to nature – the idyllic life has only a momentary charm – and no longer exclusively in the family – the patriarchal life would be boring, not to say ridiculous – and just as rarely only in the city and in trade, i.e., as petty burghers. Indeed, we are no longer satisfied to let history play itself out 'way over there in Turkey'; we are really beginning to expand our interest for the 'domestic' in our daily papers, to get a feel for the state, its governing and inner self-regulation. Very soon our scholarship on foreign relations and foreign affairs will be complemented, maybe even diminished, by scholarship on domestic affairs, as in the case of politically free peoples. The English, American, and French writers present us a unified example of this, and they all must have the same basis to be able to produce such a common effect. One may be so bold as to assume that the condition of the public consciousness among free peoples, and not pure ignorance, raises domestic affairs to the almost exclusive matter for discussion, even if this assumption may well run the danger of offending the *Augsburg News* and the Austrian politicians.[1] For to find

[1] [The reference is to the prestigious *Augsberger Allgemeine Zeitung*, which, in the name of an editorial policy of assessing international politics, followed French affairs almost to the exclusion of German affairs, and which echoed the politics of the ministers under Metternich, i.e., of Austrian hegemony and restoration against Prussian modernization. (Tr.)]

history, matters of interest, matters that one ought to know, the praiseworthy and blameworthy merely in other countries is an absence of Spirit, a taking-leave of consciousness (a romanticism), which may be politely called unfreedom, but impolitely spiritual and political degeneracy, because it is moral degeneracy to feel at home more in foreign lands than in one's own family (this latter being the true form of the patriarchal Spirit) and to find one's satisfaction more in gossiping on foreign affairs than in the proper conduct of one's own affairs. [756a] [To] see abroad only the foreign is a mistake that we long ago put aside – the Revolution and the ensuing wars made the continuity of Europe extremely visible – but to recover in foreign affairs only the domestic, and to understand in all foreign events the possible *hic tua res agitur*[2] is a virtue in which we have been weak for far too long; finally, to have more understanding and interest for 'boring' domestic affairs than for the 'curiosities' of foreign events – this is totally new, this happened only yesterday, and this 'yesterday' remains extremely clear in the memory of the common man. But what event caused domestic affairs to cease to be boring?

There has been what we shall call a heightened political feeling of life, the beginning of a sense for citizenship in the state, whose essential development, in our opinion, is tied to the history of Prussia.

But if the bright daylight of a real political life were finally to grow out of this first dawn, would all the splendor of the old art and science disappear? Would we become philosophically uncouth and hypocritically bigoted like the English, metaphysically superficial like the French, and only practical, prosaic men like the North Americans? A horrible prospect! – but not to be feared.

The Greeks, those utterly political humans, were neither prosaic nor unphilosophical; they were more free than the English and just as free as the North Americans without being as uncouth or as bigoted as these two nations. But if anyone is worried about the gloominess, or, more accurately, the brutishness of feeling of the German Spirit, and if he should deem it an honor to set his anxious heart on the worst relics of a very lackluster spiritual development in religion and politics, he might console himself with England and North America. And yet it is not right to help oneself with foreign examples when one is present to one's own consciousness. We have come to a certain kind of conclusion with our limitless naiveté in science and art with the life of theoretical Spirit totally in our own private hands. This is not to say that our good German science and art, of which we are so proud, in which alone we put such total trust,

[2] [*Hic tua res agitur*: 'this matter concerns you'. (Tr.)]

would cease and disappear right away – though it will be necessary to burn up our Alexandrine time and much of its dead wood[3] – this is not to say that, along with the old legalism and, I am sorry to say, theology, even the natural sciences would have to be disbanded immediately. By no means! It is necessary only that those historical sciences that can change their objects [756b] [undertake] this radical reform when the time is fulfilled, and it is easy to see that the fulfillment of our time will be the death of the *present* legalism and theology, while it is impossible for the natural sciences to change their objects. In a word: jurisprudence and theology have as their objects historic existences of Spirit; thus history, which allows these existences to consume one another, from time to time deprives both of these esteemed faculties of their object. Greek theology died with the Greek gods; Greek jurisprudence died with the Greek state; a monstrous juridical world, a true paradise of the great suffering grandchildren of legal scholarship, went under with the Holy Roman Empire. Yet even now with the luck of ecclesiastical law, which the papacy has reestablished, the entire Cologne mixup[4] might have almost engulfed our profane law and our Napoleonic Code – we won't even speak of the Eldorado of Catholic and Jewish theology lest we stimulate our leaders to reestablish these glories, under which they could plunge ten generations of unhappy people. Only the knowledge of facts which, like those of nature, lie behind us or under us is natural; as soon as jurisprudence and theology must contemplate facts that they now no longer can prevent, they and their naiveté are at an end. Thus a new political world, a real public life, and a real freedom in the state will deprive a large wasteland of knowledge of its present importance. This will already have happened in poetry and other art. The poetry of nature, of the Spirit of the family, the poetry of the family or of love – this is a *genre* that is as everlasting as the nature on which it is founded, but it is clear enough how things stand presently with it. The *historic*, i.e., the political movement of feeling, the life of the human Spirit in its most proper element, in freedom

[3] [Ruge is probably referring to Germany's 'classical' period during the late eighteenth century, in which especially poetic style was influenced by Greek aesthetic philosophy and poetic models. (Tr.)]

[4] [In 1837, the Prussian government incarcerated the newly appointed archbishop of Cologne, Clemens August Droste-Vischerung, principally because, in contravention of a previous papal Concordat, he had refused to give the Catholic blessing to mixed marriages unless all offspring were to be brought up to be Catholics. The ensuing pamphlet war resuscitated the question of the relation between ecclesiastical and secular law. The upheaval gave focus to increasing Catholic unrest in the Rhineland principalities that had been annexed to Prussia as a result of the Congress of Vienna. (Tr.)]

and its historical construction, the interest in helping to shape this world – these are what now arrest the most capable minds and fill the most passionate hearts, and an individualistic spinning away at poetic scenes of nature, love, family, and the bourgeoisie would please no one. The absurdities of the caprices of love, from Wertherlike suicides to those stolen from the ancient examples, and the demand which lies behind these inferior interests, i.e., that humanity never gets beyond possessions and enjoyment (which always remain the bottom line, even if they both are represented in the most beautiful and brilliant woman), that the place of birth, the nest of Spirit and mores, the family, should never be abandoned – lately, this demand has appeared to us to be an insult. We do not feel that we are Negroes who have to work as the *proles* for the plantation of the state, but that we are lords of equal birth with anyone, whoever he may be, existing in the *realm* of ethics and freedom, which, though it certainly develops out of the family, exists only for the sake of a community of free humans.

[757a] [This] feeling of indignation at being a proletariat, as it is exposed in our history and literature in such harsh colors, is engendered by our awakened interest in the state and our sense for politics, and it everywhere produces new life; we will now be able to detect among ourselves a new form of virtue, the *public*, a new form of art, the *historical* (the *historical lyric* and the *historical* comedy); we will now be able to detect among ourselves the comedy that, as opposed to the *genre* comedy, does not destroy the shapes of the common or natural and bourgeois Spirit, but that destroys Spirit's actual historical stages, as *Don Quixote* chivalry – we mention Herwegh, Hoffman von Fallersleben,[5] further, the *Trumpet of the Last Judgment*,[6] then, the little tracts, *Schelling, the Philosopher in Christo* and *The Critique of a Believer of Hegel's Doctrine of Art and Religion*,[7] books

[5] [Georg Herwegh (1817–1875) and August Heinrich Hoffman (1798–1874) – pen name, von Fallersleben – were lyric poets whose writings championed the cause of modernizing political progress; they reached the height of their popularity in the 1840s, when their songs were sung in mass movements of those groups who were beginning to feel political oppression. The major theme of their poetry: the German 'philistine' as a major hindrance to intellectual development and political progress. (Tr.)]

[6] [*Die Posaune der jüngsten gerichts über Hegel, den Atheisten und Antichristen* (Leipzig: Otto Wigand, 1841) was written, and published anonymously, by Bruno Bauer (1809–1882), a leading member of the Berlin wing of the Young Hegelians. In the voice of a fundamentalist pietist who fulminates against the Hegelian doctrines, it gave a brilliant interpretation of the implications for religion of Hegel's philosophy. (Tr.)]

[7] [*Schelling, der Philosoph in Christo, oder die Verklärung der Weltweisheit zur Gottesweisheit. Für gläubige Christen, denen der philosophische Sprachgebrauch unbekannt ist. Ein Tractätchen* (Berlin: A. Eyssenhardt, 1842) by F. Engels and *Hegel's Lehre von der*

which are *historical comedies* when taken as artistic endeavors; finally, we recall the historical and political dramas and novels and that which, recently in these pages, Vischer has stated concerning the subject matter of the new painting,[8] and we will speak in greater detail in another place, because of 'circumstances out of our control', concerning the significance of the emergence of *historical comedy* in our times),[9] and a new form of philosophy, the free form, or the form totally freeing itself from scholasticism.[10]

These new forms are extremely visible in philosophy and art, but less so in politics, where the element of public virtue, the state, still has to be created. Meanwhile, it would not be difficult to point to a series of illustrious names from Prussia, Hanover, and Baden, whose political deeds have earned them the sympathy of their fellow citizens and the recognition of posterity.

All these taken together – public virtue, historical art, and free philosophy – express the very jolt of consciousness by which we [757b] [have] been raised out of a narrow domesticity and have become capable of a new life, the political life.

It is easy to see that a work like Hegel's *Philosophy of Right* must be essentially threatened by this movement of Spirit, for it is a child of its time and takes its stand from a totally different consciousness than ours.

Hegel's time was not very favorable for politics; it totally lacked public discussion and public life (that is, in Germany); it retreated into the wisdom of theory, and humans caught for years in indolence forget that their theory is dead when they bury themselves in it

Religion und Kunst, vom Standpunkte des Glaubens aus beurtheilt (Leipzig: Otto Wigand, 1842) by B. Bauer were published anonymously. The former compares Schelling's return to Christianity to Paul's conversion on the road to Damascus and considers it providential that a philosopher should deny that reason unaided by grace is a proper tool for understanding God. The latter brings to bear on Hegel's doctrines the criteria of strict dogmatic orthodoxy in order to satirize so-called liberal attempts to compromise between Hegel and Christianity. (Tr.)]

8 ['Die Aquarell-Copien von Ramboux in der Gallerie zu Düsseldorf', *Deutsche Jahrbücher*, v, Nos. 138–40 (June 11–14, 1842), cols. 550a–559a, Nos. 211–16 (September 5–10, 1842), cols. 841a–846b, 849a–851a, 853a–855a, 857a–863b argues that the lack of any unified theme in the great variety of subjects chosen for the latest German paintings presages the beginning of a new artistic age. The main contribution of Friedrich Theodor Vischer (1807–1887) to the Young Hegelian body of thought was *Ueber das Erhabene und Komische, ein Beitrag zu der Philosophie des Schönen* (Stuttgart: Imle & Krauss, 1837), which refuted Hegel's identification of the ultimate ideal of art with classical Greek forms. (Tr.)]

9 ['Circumstances out of our control' refers to the censorship, which Ruge must have believed would have prohibited such a discussion in the journal; to my knowledge, Ruge never completed such a project. (Tr.)]

10 [In Ruge's mind, Feuerbach's *Vorläufige Thesen zur Reformation der Philosophie* was the primary example of this mode of philosophizing. (Tr.)]

instead of reshaping the world from it. Hegel intentionally depreciated this arrogance, which every theory must possess. And yet no one felt more deeply than he that we Germans had not yet achieved the state in the form of the state. Hegel read the Greeks with too much intelligence and lived through his times, the age of the Revolution, with too clear a consciousness not to attain, beyond the familial state (of dynastic possession) and the state of bourgeois society (police state[11] and bureaucracy), the demand for the state in the form of a public, self-determining structure. And he actually did this implicitly, theoretically, or, as is said, *in abstracto*, when he expressly distinguished the 'needy state of bourgeois society' from the free state or its actuality and asserted the most profound concept of the state that humanity had thus far attained. He says, 'The state is the actuality of the ethical idea; it is the ethical Spirit as the *manifest* (*offenbare*), clear-to-itself, substantial will, which thinks and knows itself and brings into reality what it knows to the extent that it knows it. The state has its immediate existence in *public mores* and its mediated existence in the *self-consciousness* of the individual, its knowledge and activity, just as the self-consciousness of the individual has its substantial freedom by conviction – in the state, as the essence, the goal, and the product of its activity.'[12]

Therefore the public (*öffentliche*) Spirit and the process of public (*öffentlichen*) thinking and achievement is the state; the state is the essence, and the self-conscious subject is its [758a] [existence;] yet the essence is not only the goal, but also the *product* of the activity of the self-conscious subject, and thus freedom is the *self-producing* and *self-ruling thinking* and *willing*, which exists immediately as *mores*, but mediately by self-conscious *subjects*.

Thus, in order to have the state in the form of the state, it is necessary to have all those great institutions, national representation, juries, and freedom of the press – institutions that we Germans still

[11] [This term, *Polizeistaat*, is used in opposition to *Rechtstaat* to denote the difference between a state in which a public system of rights and responsibilities is the foundation of governance and a state in which the vast majority of domestic organization is delegated to government appointed civil servants, therefore, by 'secret' appointments of the royal authority. At this point in nineteenth-century political discussion the term means 'authoritarian government' much more than 'government by police surveillance'. (Tr.)]

[12] [Hegel first published this work as *Grundlinien der Philosophie des Rechts* (Berlin: Nicolaischen Buchhandlung, 1821); the citation can be found in vol. VI of the edition of Georg Lasson, *Grundlinien der Philosophie des Rechts* (Leipzig: Felix Meiner, 1911), p. 195. While the translation of this, and of all other cited passages, is mine, readers may wish to consult the classic English version, *Hegel's Philosophy of Right*, trans., with notes, by T. M. Knox (London: Oxford University Press, 1967), p. 155. (Tr.)]

almost totally lack – that raise humans in their total worth and in the full light of public consciousness to creators of their own freedom. At any rate, even if they were somewhat tainted and faded, Hegel assumed all these institutions into his theory of the state; at any rate, he showed that he knew very well, in his 1817 critique of the processes of the Würtemberg Provincial Diet, that, since the Freedom War and the destruction of the Old Empire, the old estates had been transported into a totally new element, the *political* (*Werke* XVI, 246).[13] There he says: 'Out of the *political nothingness* to which the German people had sunk through its system of government, out of the incapacity to have a proper resolve and will of the many small totalities that constituted the greater part of the Estates of the Empire, there had to come forth a Spirit of getting bogged down in private interests and of indifference, even of enmity, against the idea of having a national doctrine and of making sacrifices for it. When, for example, in the English nation, the feeling for a national doctrine had generally penetrated the various classes of the people, the right of the Parliament to approve the annual taxes had a totally different meaning than the same right would have among people who had been educated in the *sense for privacy*, and who, because they *had been placed outside the political point of view*, were kept in the Spirit of narrowness and seeking for private gain. To maintain the *state* against such a Spirit, the governments needed new guarantees.' With sovereignty and state unity in place of the unending parcelling into different divisions of land, there now came for the first time the possibility of *promising* the people free constitutions, the state in the form of the state. Hegel lays the total accent on *this* form and distinguishes very well the old provincial estates, those models of political nothingness, from that which was the true meaning of this promise of a constitution. He says (p. 23): 'The promise was capable of being fulfilled in a manner that could be considered to be the most shrewd, that even could be passed off as the most just, but that would have been the *most treacherous counsel* that the ministers could have

[13] [The essay to which Ruge refers is 'Beurteilung der im Druck erschienen Verhandlung in der Versammlung der Landstände des Königreichs Würtemberg im Jahre 1815 und 1816', which first appeared in the *Heidelbergische Jahrbücher der Literatur*, Nos. 66–8, 73–7 (1817). Ruge's citation is to the first edition of Hegel's collected works. G. W. F. Hegel, *Werke: Vollständige Ausgabe durch einen Verein von Freunden des Verewigten*, 18 vols. (Berlin: Duncker and Humblot, 1832–1845). The following citation can be found in vol. VII of the Lasson edition, *Hegels Schriften zur Politik und Rechtsphilosophie* (Leipzig: Felix Meiner, 1913), p. 192; the emphasized words are Ruge's. Part of this essay has been translated into English, in *Hegel's Political Writings*, trans. by T. M. Knox (Oxford: Clarendon Press, 1964); this passage is found on pp. 267–8. (Tr.)]

given. If the princes of the new realms [758b] [had] wanted totally to deceive their people and to gain honor, so to speak, before God and humanity, they would have given back to their people the so-called old constitutions. Honor before God and the world – for, according to so many public voices and especially in line with previous history, one could think that the people would have streamed into the churches to sing a heartfelt *Te Deum*. In the name of Machiavelli, the princes could have earned the fame of the delicate politics of *Augustus* and *Tiberius*, both of whom let stand the forms of the previous government, at that time a republic, while the reality no longer existed and incontestably could no longer exist – a *status quo* (conservative) and a deception into which the Romans entered, because of which the erection of a rational monarchical condition, the concept of which the Romans had not yet discovered, became impossible...King Frederick of Würtemberg showed himself to be above the temptation to this deception.'[14] At any rate, therefore, Hegel knew very well where our German shoe pinched. Nonetheless, he wrote in 1831 in the *Prussian State Journal* that famous article that took it to be its most proper task to reject the *political form* of the English state in favor of the police state,[15] 'whose forms have not hindered the avoidance of an unending confusion of privileges and injustices, and which so rationally bases the choice of its officials on examinations, and which, moreover, has in prospect this *profound content* of the scientific foundation of all relations'.[16] The profound wisdom of our Muftis or Mandarins is the consolation for the fact that we have no sense for the state and no political life – the same old story! To get beyond the abstractions, you comfort yourself with abstractions! The rhetorical talent of this article is marvelous; one can still feel its calming effect today. Let one forget for one second that everything depends on the state, that the state must exist in the *form* of the state and that its content is the sense for *politics*, and one will grant that England is far behind us; all her weaknesses are uncovered, and the total superiority of our state system, although we see and hear nothing about it – yes, not even Hegel himself 'could get an experience of how the Town-Councillor-Elect is getting on' – is proven on its own grounds. The article contains much truth

[14] [Lasson, VII, 161–2; in this passage, all the emphases are Hegel's; Knox, *Hegel's Political Writings*, pp. 250–1. (Tr.)]

[15] [See above, n. 11. (Tr.)]

[16] ['Über die englische Reformbill', *Allgemeine Preussische Staatszeitung*, Nos. 115–16, 118 (1831); I cannot find the precise citation in the version of the essay appearing in Lasson, VII, 283–326, or in Knox, *Hegel's Political Writings*, which follows Lasson (pp. 295–330). The version of the *Werke* that Ruge was using (see above, n. 13) is unavailable to me. (Tr.)]

and is very instructive on England; indeed, it treats only of England – how could it speak of domestic affairs in those times? – but it is to be regretted that Hegel in Berlin in 1831 was no longer in the mood to come to terms with the other side of the subject, with 'the political nothingness' of the states, which wanted only the 'sense for privacy' and did not want the state in the form of the state. And when Hegel, in his comparisons, [759a] [mentioned] now Germany, now the continent, it did not become clear that he basically preferred only the products of the French revolution to the English feudal abuses. For he didn't state this. Hegel is an enemy of 'dissatisfaction that knows better about everything'; otherwise he could have easily concluded his article with the solution to the dilemma, i.e., that, because of its more profound content, the historic continent, *as soon as it attained for this content the free forms of the actual state*, would have far surpassed England. But clearly that would have meant to gain a different soul, and to cite such a soul in the state periodical in 1831 – that wouldn't have helped. Rather, Hegel rebuked the idealists of his times, especially the demagogues, their ideals, and their demands.[17] But he did them an injustice when he accused them of ignorance concerning the state because they demanded nothing more zealously than the possibility of making an end to this ignorance and because, whether or not he intended to, he himself asserted an ideal and a demand with his concept of the state, an ideal and a demand that could not be more fundamentally thought out. Either he did this unconsciously or he sought to conceal it from himself and the world, and, as he came out against the dogmatic idealists who returned from the War of Liberation [the *Befreiungskriege* of 1813–1815], he also did not neglect to cover over as much as possible the liberal consequences that, for example, Gans drew while he was still alive.[18] In this respect, it is known that death interrupted the preparation of lectures on the philosophy of right directed against Gans.

[17] [Many of the students and some of the younger professors returned to the universities from the War of Liberation with nationalistic and democratic ideals and formed student societies, called *Burschenschäften*, to foster these ideals. They responded to government pressure to disband by forming secret societies, the leaders of which became called 'demagogues' in government communications concerned to repress them; Ruge himself had been one of the leaders of the most radical student group. (Tr.)]

[18] [Eduard Gans (1798–1839) was a student of Hegel who took it to be his task to apply the philosophical conclusion of his mentor to the realm of jurisprudence. He began teaching at the University of Berlin in 1820, and was appointed ordinary professor of law there in 1828. He was one of the founders of the Hegelian *Jahrbücher für wissenschaftliche Kritik* (1827), and in 1833 edited the *Philosophy of Right* for Hegel's collected works, expanding the edition of 1821 with the 'additions' of students' lecture notes. (Tr.)]

It is not to be denied that contradictions that lie in such applications in favor of the 'rationality' of an 'unreality' such as a state that is still no state and does not wish to become one are betrayals of principle. And when these are a product of calculation, they do not particularly jibe with wisdom or with the concept.

Well then, even Hegel was a diplomat! We Germans are not as awkward as we seem; even Kant, this *anima candida*, was a diplomat. Neither of these men *came out* in opposition; they were satisfied to *be* in opposition. Their systems are systems of reason and freedom in the midst of irrationality and lack of freedom. Yet it would be extremely unfair to mistake how deeply both Kant and Hegel fit into the consciousness of their own times and the limits of its standpoint or to deny that they are to be understood as having different ethical positions when they did not wish to *represent* the opposition that they really *were*.

We should be very careful to observe the difference in political stance between these two. Kant's famous statement is: 'Certainly I think with the most clear [759b] [conviction] of much that I would never have the courage to say, but I would never say something that I did not think' (*Werke*, Th. 11, 1. 7).[19] In this day and age there is no longer any doubt that even this form of honesty is diplomatic and not philosophical. It will be granted that Kant's position even under Frederick II (the letter to Mendelssohn that contains this statement is dated 1778) was extremely restricted by the condition of the public spirit of those times, and one will not demand that those times should have put up with a fully open philosophy if one reflects that even the present times have not yet attained this ability. Kant, despite his reticence, and Frederick the Great, even though he had been king, very soon became objects of public condemnation and slander. Only a free people are capable of bearing a free philosophy, and, if one wants to keep in mind respect towards one's contemporaries, one will have to admit that no people are so free that at some time its philosophers do not become too free for it. And yet, there inevitably accompanies the loss of candor the feeling of living among barbarians. And yet, nothing is philosophical unless it is the total, full, unrestricted expression of thought. Whoever loves wisdom follows it. But now Kant is the truest and purest character imaginable; how did this man arrive at the maxim of circumspection? The split between theory and praxis, between thinking and saying, that he

[19] [This statement can be found in Immanuel Kant, *Briefe*, ed., with an intro., by Jürgen Zehbe (Göttingen: Vanderhoeck & Ruprecht, 1970), p. 30. The letter to Moses Mendelssohn in which it is contained is dated 1786, and not 1778, as Ruge states below. (Tr.)]

expresses in these famous words still belongs even to the German Spirit in general. Kant could not undertake to raise this split out of his proper medium, so he enveloped himself in his consciousness. He speaks in this letter of *self-approbation* as the principle of morality; he says, 'You will never have cause to change your opinion of me because, throughout the greater part of my life, I have learned to scorn and dispense with most of that which usually corrupts the character, and therefore the loss of a self-approbation that springs from the awareness of an honest intention would be the greatest evil that could ever befall me, though I am certain it never will. Certainly I think',[20] etc. This is almost the same position that Goethe, Kant's contemporary expresses thus: 'But you shouldn't say before humans/ The best that you can know.' But as a philosopher, Kant had the obligation to say the best; therefore, in connection with the conflict that all enlightened men of these times had to face, he reflected on his conscience. It is clear that *this* morality, *this* fidelity to conviction and self-approbation is the concern of the human who is *still oppressed under a foreign power*, and who [760a] [is] not yet appointed to pursue nothing but reason without conditions. Such a foreign power is the state, when it does not correspond to its concept as we have seen Hegel define it. Thus, later, in 1794, under Frederick Wilhelm II, because of the Wöllner Rescript, which censured in his writings 'the misrepresentation and degradation of some leading and principle doctrines of the Holy Scripture and of Christianity', and which strictly enjoined him 'no longer to allow these kinds of writings and teachings to come out',[21] Kant was really placed in the proper situation for making use of his maxim and thus, in his answer to this Christian Minister, actually pledged 'totally to refrain from all public statements relating to religion, whether natural or revealed, both in my lectures and writings'. He had also written almost word for word, only in a more practical sense, the former moral maxim in one of the outlines for his answer (*Werke*, II, 2. 138). There it reads, 'Contradiction or denial of one's inner conviction is *base*, but keeping silent in a situation such as the present is the *duty of a subject* and if everything

[20] [*Ibid.* (Tr.)]

[21] [Johann Christoph von Wöllner (1732–1800) was a pietist and a member of the Rosicrucians who gained influence over Frederick Wilhelm II of Prussia and was appointed Minister of Domestic Affairs. His first edict on religion in 1788 began an attempt to roll back the incursions of rationalism among Protestant ministers and professors; the 'Rescript' of 1794, which Ruge quotes, was an attempt at sterner measures when it became clear that the first attempts had failed. The Cabinet Order that contains these quotations can be found in vol. XI of the edition of the Royal Prussian Academy of Sciences, *Kant's Briefwechsel: Band II, 1789–1794* (Berlin and Leipzig: Walter de Gruyter & Co., 1922), pp. 525–6. (Tr.)]

that one says must be true, that does not also mean the duty *to say the full truth publicly*.'[22] The maxim is negative; but, if one also accords to morality the positive obligation to duty, then it might well happen that a philosopher might consider it precisely to be the highest *philosophical duty to say publicly all of the truth or the whole truth*. And, in fact, what is the philosophical duty if not this? But then in the case of Kant there would have to be a conflict between the duty of a subject and the duty of the philosopher, which is the same as the conflict between the written and the unwritten laws in *Antigone*. In a word: The *subject* in Wöllner's state was not permitted to be a *philosopher*. The 'subject' is a diplomat; he does nothing absolutely, but only what is to be done under 'circumstances beyond one's control'.[23]

Thus Kant's action in accord with his famous maxim is by no means ethical in the highest sense (his most proper and highest ethical stance would have been the philosophical one, and philosophy is outspokenness), even though he does not deserve to be accused of lack of character. He did not raise himself to the concept of opposition that derives from the right of the unwritten law. But without a doubt he felt in his subjection the self-approbation by which morality is conditioned. The standpoint is limited; it is Protestant narrowness to claim freedom only as freedom of conscience, but the lack in his standpoint is the lack of the then German Spirit and still of the present German Spirit, which [760b] [recognizes] no other virtue than this *private virtue* of inward self-congratulation, and which considers to be immoral *political virtue*, not only to say publicly the whole truth, but also to demand it. In such a people there are only moralistic, self-directed subjects, not state citizens, and the conscience itself is not certain, for it will require one to obey even those orders that do not recognize its total content, its reason. Kant is an example of this.

Where does Hegel stand in relation to this question? Should the man who asserted against Kantian morality the point of view of the higher ethics of the state citizen still be permitted to remain with the Kantian self-approbation? Rather, must he not be expected, by his own example, to develop the *political virtue* that in his philosophy he opposed to *private virtue*?

[22] [For Kant's pledge, see Zehbe, *Briefe*, p. 232. The edition of Kant's outlines for this letter that is available to me is vol. XIII of the Royal Prussian Academy edition: *Kant's Briefwechsel: Band IV, Anmerkungen und Register* (Berlin and Leipzig: Walter de Gruyter & Co., 1922), pp. 372–87; however, it does not contain this statement. (Tr.)]

[23] [This is an ironical reference to censorship repression, which Ruge has used above in regard to his own 'circumstances'; see above, n. 9. (Tr.)]

The abstract inwardness of Protestantism did not free even Hegel from the illusion that one could be theoretically free without being politically free. His standpoint is essentially *theoretical*, and his time attained the German state just as little as the time of Kant. His unique position in Prussia contributed to this. Hegel did not experience the practical battle of philosophy, and the difference between his philosophy and the police state[24] must have been concealed from his consciousness because he never, as did Kant, experienced hostility to his principles, but rather, as long as he taught, under the charge of the state itself, he did so with freedom that was complete in every respect. It is therefore easy to see that, just as little as the state, did he notice the contradiction in his position and that both Hegel and the authorities attempted to conceal whatever they did notice in order, following good old Protestant custom, to avoid conflict and to let the contradictions die out rather then to let them live out their lives in battle. Only the resoluteness of the Catholic principle, which does not tolerate even contradictory inwardness and which makes war on theory, also forces theory to declare war on the Catholic state. Hegel 'neither contradicted nor denied his convictions' because it was in no way demanded of him, but his terms were ready to tolerate appearances, as if theoretical contradictions were not important or even no contradictions at all. So Hegel could make his abstract assertions on the side of theory, and this is what he did.

[761a] [If] Kant treated thinking as a private matter, so to speak, and the philosopher as a private person, but not as the man whose duty it also is to promote the political Spirit and to throw into the world the ferment of the whole truth without remainder (whether Kant suppressed anything essential or what he did suppress does not belong here, but might not be too difficult to answer), then at least Hegel knew enough to say that philosophy grasps the time in thought, that valid philosophy expresses the word of the times, but he understood this word to be a word directed *merely at insight*, not at human wills. *This is the theoretical standpoint.* From his Olympian repose, he looked at everything that reason had made, and *he saw it was good*, for reason can be demonstrated in all of its products or existences. And, amazingly, as long as one sticks with the rational side of the subject, *there is nothing left to do with it*; reason composes itself with reason, and Hegel lay down next to an absolutism that was just rational enough to recognize the rationality of the Hegelian system. The rational side is the rosy and comfortable side, as difficult as it is, occasionally, to vindicate reason in existing things – even

[24] [See above, n. 11. (Tr.)]

Hegel, in the *Philosophy of Religion*, declared this to be the most difficult of all tasks! But as soon as the view is shifted to the other side, to the irrationality of existing things, there enters unrest, dissatisfaction, the demand, and the nasty 'should' of praxis. *Now something must be done*! Reason must have its rights even in this existence; it must again come to itself; the theoretical standpoint is abandoned; the word of criticism turns itself to the wills of humans, and, although pure insight into the subject is the starting point, yet the decision to subjugate the subject to insight is the end point of this thinking. The standpoint of thinking is therefore now no longer abstract or onesidedly theoretical, but is the correct unity of thinking and willing. *Only* [761b] [*willing*] (that is to say, on this basis of rational insight) *is real thinking*.

In the case of Hegel, what must be called a matter of conscious decision is the very choice of the standpoint. He wanted to carry through his theory *as such*; he was interested in asserting it as abstract theory or as the word of pure insight in itself. But thereby it appeared to be a matter once again of raising philosophy from a praxis for everybody to an exact science, to an existence that was disciplined and that presupposed discipline, to a subject that every fool didn't have in his possession by nature. Theory, science as such, science purely and simply, this was the principal task – a gigantic work – and Hegel made it so difficult for himself and others that people noticed right away how very serious a task it was to obtain the scientific method and to do philosophy, for whoever did not study with industry and consistency had his state of lay ignorance made clear to him with every Hegelian word, even clearer than this had been the case with the words of Kant. On his own ground, Hegel was no enemy of political praxis and of the effective thinking that comes forth as will and applied itself to the will – his earlier activity proves this – but his life calling, to ground and carry through the system of pure insight, throws him to the *onesided theoretical standpoint*.

But now this standpoint, just because it is and should be onesided, must develop the most crying contradictions; it even presses beyond itself against its own will: as soon as pure insight is really achieved and has confronted reality as living critique, practical pathos can no longer be bound. We have shown that critique engenders decision, and that therefore it does not repulse practical application, as does 'speculation', but rather grasps it into itself. 'Speculation' is satisfied in itself and compares spiritual reality, not according to its difference, but according to its identity with external reality. The opinion of Hegel, that the reconciliation of both of these was presently at hand, because the distinction was covered over and only the identity, that both were reason, was brought forward, corresponded to the opinion of the state, that it did not need to change its forms for the sake of theory, [762a] [especially] since the theory recognized the reason in it. This is the consciousness of his times, beyond which Hegel could not go, in which both sides could avoid conflict without losing self-approbation.

If Hegel had been presented with the opportunity to stand up for his theory, his times would have had to turn against him, as happened with Kant. Only under these conditions could he have become more than moral: only then could he have attained a *political character*. Indeed, he would have *had* to become so. For it is now no longer thinkable that someone like Kant could lock the demands of a Wöllner in his desk and merely salve his conscience. But the *public* defense of a philosophy under attack would have been a *political deed*. This conflict that Hegel was spared was prepared for later philosophers. The minute philosophy comes forward critically (Strauss broke the ground),[25] the conflict is here. And whoever is still satisfied with self-approbation and does not dare to come out for his cause is no longer a philosopher. Thus it is clear that the times, or the standpoint of consciousness, have been essentially altered. Development is no longer abstract, but the *times are political*, even though there is much to do before they are political enough.

The failure in the turn of the entire Hegelian philosophy to place itself apart from living history at the onesided theoretical standpoint and to establish this standpoint as the absolute is also the failure in his *Philosophy of Right*, and it is precisely here that the general failure must be experienced most painfully.

It is impossible to grasp the state absolutely and to detach it from history because every concept of it, as every determinate philosophy, is itself already a product of history. But it is also impossible to grasp a *system of state government*, i.e., a determinate state, as an eternal form because the determinate state is nothing but an existence of Spirit in which Spirit is realized *historically*.

In any case, the universal *essence* of the state is just as conceivable as the essence of Spirit in general; indeed, the essence of the state is nothing but Spirit itself in the form of its public (manifest) self-realizing. But the *actual* state and the *existence* of its governing system

[25] [Ruge is referring to Strauss' *Das Leben Jesu, kritisch bearbeitet*, 2 vols. (Tübingen: Osiander, 1835), which he sees as the first attempt to apply Hegel's philosophy to practical affairs, in this case, the presuppositions of contemporary piety. The Young Hegelians themselves, as well as twentieth-century historians, saw this work as inaugurating their publishing activity to change German culture. (Tr.)]

have the same interest as the *actual* philosophy, the historical philosophy. Therefore, as soon as philosophy steps onto the ground of the state and thereby of the *historical* Spirit, its relation to that which *exists* is changed.

In logic, or the investigation of the eternal process and the determinations and forms of the dialectic of thinking, *there are no existences*. Here that which exists, the thinker and his Spirit, are unimportant [762b] [factors] because this individual should do nothing but the universal deed, or rather the universal act, of thinking itself. In a word, it is here a matter of the universal essence as such, not of its existence. In natural science, the *existences* of the things of nature are *irrelevant*. Although the things of nature and their actual processes are the objects of research, they are only the *ever identically recurring examples* of the eternal laws and of the eternal behavior of nature in the cycle of its self-reproduction. Only with the entrance of history into the realm of science *does existence itself assume relevance*. The movement of history is no longer the cycle of ever-recurring development, as is the movement of nature, but, in the self-production of Spirit, it presses forth ever *new* shapes. The *governing system* of a state, of Spirit at various times, as this existing reality, has a scientific relevance. The conditions of development are no longer recurring examples, but are *stages* of a process, and the knowledge of these historical existences has to do essentially with their uniqueness; it is a matter of *this* existent as such.

Therefore, as soon as the Hegelian system stepped into the sphere of actual Spirit, it had to take up the form of historical development, for here historical development is the form of the object. As is well known, critique has already been leveled at the *Philosophy of Religion*, which has thus been pressed into a historical form – thus Strauss and Stuhr[26] – and if it must also be granted that history is engendered only by the battle of Spirit with interior and external nature, that therefore religions attain historical development only when their content is altered by world-development, only when they cease to have as their objects phantasies that are neither art nor science, neither beautiful nor true, still, the religion of Hellenism already had a history, and Christianity became no less historical by its entangle-

[26] [Ruge is referring to Strauss' *Die christliche Glaubenslehre in ihrer geschichtliches Entwicklung und in Kampfe mit der modernen Wissenschaft*, 2 vols. (Tübingen: Osiander, 1840–1). Peter Feddersen Stuhr (1787–1851), who lectured on German history, Nordic mythology, and the philosophy of mythology at the University of Berlin from 1826 until his death, was a frequent contributor of articles for the liberal cause in the journal. The book to which Ruge refers is *Das Verhältnis der christlichen Theologie zur Philosophie und Mythologie nach dem heutigen Standpunkte der Wissenschaft* (Berlin: 1842). (Tr.)]

ment both with art and science, as well as with the state and its government. In fact, it entered history as its own state, in the hierarchical system. These entanglements are its history. In general, the relation of Christianity to these other phenomena is presented in Strauss' *Dogmatics*.[27] But, because he ascribes the development to dogmatics itself, his standpoint is still theological and abstract, it is more an avoiding of the entanglements than their express indication. But that Strauss had to bring in world-development – he treats Spinoza and the most recent philosophy – lay in the nature of the subject, for the historical development of Christian belief cannot [763a] [be] established in abstraction from secular history. In the *Aesthetics*, Hegel already effectively brought in the historical moment, although he did not carry it through consistently; thus, many artistic forms that could only be explained historically remain unexplained. But, in his philosophy of right and of the state, Hegel brought in the historical process least of all, and yet this has become the most lively and pressing demand on him because of the tension of the times in which we live and the nature of his subject.

The historical process is the relating of theory to the historical existences of Spirit; this relating is *critique*. Indeed, historical development itself is *objective critique* (see the Foreword to Strauss' *Dogmatics*).[28] This application of theory to existence is lacking in Hegel's political thought. The application was not totally expunged, but it is intentionally avoided, and the result is something like the *Phenomenology*: the book somewhat nebulous, has the character of a painting of clouds, which one cannot grab and hold. Hegel's state (his doctrine of government) is no more real than Plato's, and it will never become so, for he recovers the present state like Plato recovered the Greek state; he even calls it by name, but he never lets its implications flow out of the historical process, and thus he has no direct effect on the development of political life and consciousness. The French already have done this; they are thoroughly historical. In the French thinkers, Spirit is living and develops the world in its image. This is why their relevant critiques of the present have such a deep effect and discover a sensibility of which we Germans have hardly a dream.

Theory can abstract from the critical process of history only when it has in mind eternal determinations, such as personhood, family, society, state, or their principles, will, love, right, the concept of

[27] [See above, n. 26. (Tr.)]

[28] [Most probably, Ruge is referring to Strauss' statement, 'The true critique of dogma is its history', which, however, does not appear in the Foreword, but on I, 71, of *Die christliche Glaubenslehre*. (Tr.)]

freedom. These determinations can be grasped in *the form of universality* – Hegel would say, 'in their concept'. Thus they are logical or metaphysical determintions; their delineation leads to a metaphysics of the ethical realm, and in such a metaphysics there can be no talk of the governmental system of a state or generally of the *historical* forms of freedom without relating the concept of the forms of freedom to their *existence*, i.e., without the business of *critique*. Moreover, any contemporary metaphysics is itself an historical existent; it can be developed as a metaphysics only by allowing its concepts to spring from historical critique; it must make its own dissolution the task of the future. Thus it is immaterial whether in its development metaphysics precedes critique or vice versa because, in the consciousness of the one doing the philosophizing, [763b] [the] one always exists only through the other; without critique there is no concept, and without the concept there is no relating of the concept to actual existence, there is no critique.

But theory has the task of clearly distinguishing where it proceeds as metaphysics from where it proceeds as critique, where it intends a *logical* category from where it intends *historical* category, or where it explains the determination in the form of universality from where it explains it in the form of existence. The Hegelian *Philosophy of Right*, in order to proceed as 'speculation' or as absolute theory, therefore, in order not to let 'critique' out in the open, raises *existences* or *historical* determinations to *logical* determinations. Thus, for example, in Hegel the *governmental system* of the state, its historical form, this historical position of Spirit, is not a product of historical critique or of the development of humanity, and, while it could not fail that the then present position of Spirit was starkly brought out in the presentation, yet there was a total lack of conscious distinguishing between the historical and the metaphysical. Thus Hegel undertook to present the hereditary monarch, the majority, the bicameral system, etc., as *logical necessities*, whereas it had to be a matter of establishing all these as products of history and of explaining and criticizing them as *historical existences*. The nature of government in general and its purpose can be discussed in abstraction from the development of Spirit, but it is clear that an *actual government* is a historical category and that only the critique of this existent is the pulse of development. This explains the minimal effect of Hegel's metaphysics of politics. The Reason that retreats from this present life of Spirit becomes pale and impotent; the Reason that would offer us the passing realities of history as eternal figures collapses into a foolish juggling act. Precisely because they are not eternal or necessary, are not representatives of a cycle, but are free and singular determinations, are, so to speak, spiritual individualities, historical existences are of a rather exalted nature; they have a relevance *as existences*, and, in this relevance, disclose to Spirit new depths of its essence.

This interest in the existence of the historical stages of existence and their corresponding political shapes, so lacking in Hegel's politics, will not allow the politics of the future to escape; it is already present in every critical word that becomes loud and clear, and, with even more intensity, it burrows into every heart in which it is held back. For the true union between the concept and reality is not the apotheosis of existence in the concept, but the [764a] [incarnating] of the divine concept in existence. The dissolution of this union comes next.

But this relation between essence and actuality, between idea and reality, gives us a new point of view on what Hegel calls the relationship between absolute Spirit and the state. Hegel speaks of this relationship under the rubric, religion and state, a subject that has lately become a much-discussed concern. He treats this question on page 332 in a long remark, which, however, contributes more confusion than clarity to the matter.[29] And why the confusion? It is again the same problem that runs through the entire work, that, for the most part, *existing religion* is substituted for the concept of religion, but in several instances, the presupposed concept of religion is substituted for existing religion, so that the reader never is sure of his ground. In this book, Hegel did not attain the popular reading audience that he apears to have aimed for by his presupposing of actual conditions, and he probably did not intend a sharp determination of concepts in order to spare himself the difficulty of an extensive treatment. He 'recalls the concept'; occasionally, he says 'that in religion *all content* has the form of *subjectivity*', that 'piety, when it takes the place of the state, cannot bear the determinate, and thus destroys it',[30] but again, he takes religion to be the determinate, as a determinate 'doctrine' and 'representation'. This confuses the issue. How is religion supposed to be capable of bearing the determinacy of doctrine in itself when it cannot bear anything determinate?

To get to the root of this problem, we need to take a step back. The state is for Hegel the objectivity and actuality of Spirit, the self-realization of freedom. Good. But now why are the forms of the realization of Spirit, represented as religion, art, and science placed

[29] [Lasson, VI, 207–19; Knox, *Hegel's Philosophy of Right*, pp. 165–74. (Tr.)]

[30] [Lasson, VI, 356; Knox, *Hegel's Philosophy of Right*, p. 284; the citation is from the student lecture notes added by Gans in the edition of 1833. (Tr.)]

beyond the spheres of the state and history? Can there be something more exalted than the self-realization of freedom, and can this self-realization proceed through time without religion, science, and art? Rather, do not all three of these constantly engage in history? Isn't it precisely these that create history?

This problem is also explained by Hegel's turn to abstract theory. As he wrenches the state out of history and considers all of its historical forms only under logical categories (thus, [764b] [right] from the start the categories of universality, specificity, and singularity are employed again and again), so, too, he takes the practical side from religion, art, and science. Certainly, for him, they are the self-realization of freedom, but only in the element of the (theoretical) Spirit itself. He maintains them on the side of the purely theoretical Spirit. The experiencing, the perceiving, and the knowing of truth are *ends in themselves*, surely, but the truth is itself an historical determinancy; the world contradicts its latest forms. The end in itself is not to be attained *abstractly*, but only in relation to what external reality has already attained, therefore as a *determinate*, *finite* goal and as a product of finite actuality. And freedom in the element of theoretical Spirit is not *absolute*, *emancipated*, and *perfect freedom*, but only the *liberation* of Spirit from one determinate externality or existence. Spirit must ever turn against these, even if they are nothing but its proper forms of thought and development. This is criticism and praxis. And Hegel avoids this turn. For him, science is not also critique, art is not also elaboration and clarification of the present, religion is essentially representation and doctrine, but not also practical pathos.

[765a] [All] this is not to deny that art and science are theoretical forms; nor do we intend to teach Hegel what we have learned from him alone, i.e., that the moment is the totality, that there is no willing without thinking and no thinking without willing, that all theory is itself praxis and the distinction between them is nothing but the inward or outward turning of Spirit. But we are asserting something that gradually has become accepted as fact by the public consciousness: both Hegel's philosophy and the German Spirit in general have hidden and covered over the practical relation and meaning of theory, to say nothing at all about the essence of religion.

Science does not go back into logic, but into history, and logic itself is drawn into history; it must allow itself to be grasped as existence, because it belongs to the developmental position of *this* philosophy. That is to say, science, which is itself an historical form of Spirit, does not grasp truth in an absolute form; it casts *the entire content of the idea* (or of the truth) into *its* form; but, insofar as it is grasped as existence and is therefore subjected to critique, history transcends it. Critique is movement, the process of secretion that at the same time is a process of engendering.

This movement proceeds both within theory and against the entire material of theory and especially against objective Spirit or life. It is by means of critique that science disposes of its content. Critique is the understanding of the world that grasps and digests this content; it is the presupposition of art and religion, and works through both of these. If this sounds paradoxical, perhaps we can clarify. Art is the presentation of the idea; it presupposes the understanding, or the appreciation of the content that the scientific Spirit has attained; it is *praxis*, but it is *joyful* praxis, 'the play (*Schein*) of the idea in its opposite'. It is wit, and wit is critique in the aesthetic form. Wit is the presupposition of all [765b] [art;] its element is *cheerfulness*, the ability to deal with all reality, a reality taken not as *appearance* (*Erscheinung*) but basically as *show* (*Schein*). Because art does not intend appearance, or the idea in its spatial and temporal (external) reality, but simply objectivizing in the inner subjective reality of Spirit, objectivizing only for perception, not for the finite goals, it takes its shapes out of all times and lets past times reappear in the present. But because art has for its presupposition the moment of critique and imprints the liberation that is wit, the stamp of cheerfulness, on all of its developments, it is nothing less than impractical. *It liberates the entire contemporary Spirit from its old form because it gives it a new form* and shows it this new form in its mirror. However, the highest form of art is that which also breaks out expressly into self-critique of Spirit; it is *comedy*, the pure enjoyment of the lordship of creative Spirit over all its shapes, enjoyment, however, that is itself a shaping. The relationship of knowing and art is that of *idea* and *ideal*. The relationship of science and religion is that of *idea* and *realizing of the idea*, not as ideal, but as *reality*. As the Hegelian system neglects critique, so also in the *Aesthetics*, it neglects that which corresponds to critique, e.g., *wit* and the *comical*, although, on the other hand, in relation to *comedy*, the positioning of Aristophanes in relation to the Greek Spirit brings about the most profound and most beautiful discussion of this great philosopher.

Religion can have no content other than that which science and art give it. The development of Spirit as science and as ideal self-formation is all content. It never has had another content, and thus, as Hegel very correctly felt, is not to be distinguished in content from religion. But when Hegel grants religion its own theory of the 'Absolute', he thereby reflects on an empirical existent which emerges with this pretension, not on the pure essence of religion.

Religion in its concept is nothing but the practical pathos for the ideal, for the truth. It compresses the idea into feeling; it turns pure insight into the substance of character, [776a] [and,] in this concentration of the content, it directs itself toward its realization. Its essence is this praxis, which by no means is brought to an end by the subject taking up the idea into feeling for the sake of its own empty daydreams – which would be abstraction – but by the self-revelation of praxis as *real critique*, insofar as it negates the old existences and founds the new.

Thus religion is no everyday affair and not for everyone. The abstract, half-hearted assumption of truth (the idea, the Spirit of the times, substance, the divine) into feeling that could probably be demanded of everyone would be no real affair of passion. If the heart is really filled, it immediately spills over, and it cannot fail that any religious reality existing in every heart must become a great world celebration, a last judgment, and a 'destruction of something determinate'.[31] Those who now cry out so much for religion have nothing to fear more than the reawakening of religion and nothing to extol as much as the rarity of the universal reality of religion. In any case, concentration into the feeling abstracts from the determinate delineation of the content; practical pathos breaks off contemplation at some stage and then throws the subject, as it then exists, into battle. However, there is always a determinate content presupposed in the totality, and the determinateness of the theoretical expansion that religion momentarily cancels immediately returns again out of the praxis of religion. It is a matter of honor for the religious person to be true to the idea in its totality and personally to stand up for a new form of the idea even to the point of indeterminacy. Thus, with the theoretical determination of the public situation, and with the development in detail of the appropriated reality that follows religious praxis, the task is to continue to effect that religiosity and to let all new determinations be penetrated by fidelity to the principle. Recall the War of Liberation, or the July Revolution,[32] or the first French Revolution. Religion asserted itself as pathos and as devotion for the determinate idea, but at first totally as a movement of feeling for it. The later determinations were true and authoritative as long as they still recalled the religiosity of the times. The fall from the idea, or the irreligiosity, when, in the transitional times, humans ceased to be filled with the Spirit and with the truth, laid itself as a great burden on human hearts, and concentrated their feelings to

[31] [See above, n. 30. (Tr.)]

[32] [The Paris revolution of 1830 which deposed the Bourbon Charles X in favor of the 'Citizen-King' Louis Philippe. (Tr.)]

new manifestations of the divine which was silently and inwardly working in them. Thus religion even at that time never lacked objects either for historical anger or for historical longing. We have seen Hegel state, [766b] ['When] religion takes the place of the state, it destroys the determinate.'[33]

When, then, does religion take the place of the state?

Clearly, only when the state has become so spiritless that idealistic praxis, pathos for the idea, has totally alienated it and has become its enemy. The pathos of the Reformation just in this way took the place of the hierarchy; the pathos of the Revolution just in this way took the place of the old state abuses.

Then how are religion and the state related?

Very simply, as *essence* and *existence*, for true religion concentrates in itself all the content of the Spirit of the times – the content is the essence – and, as subjective power or movement of feeling, aims to establish it in the world. This world is *the state and its existence*; the content of the Spirit of the times is its essence, and the task is to raise the essence and its movement, not to the status of an *enemy*, but to the *soul* of the state's existence. This is to say that practical pathos, enthusiasm for the idea, the drive of critique, which seek to bring the attained stages of the theoretical Spirit together with what exists, must themselves be taken into the state. A state that has science, art, and religion *outside* of it, or even is capable of having them as *enemies*, must experience a *sudden* downfall into the movement of the essence that it rejects. An *ordered destruction* of the existent into essence is the only protection from the tragedy of this *sudden* destruction; that is, the articulation of the real Spirit, the articulation that is the state, should not compromise the concentration of the newly attained idea in feeling, religion, to the breaking point, but rather must so organize itself that the new striving, this swelling or budding development, works to the good of the state's own inner life.

Therefore, in very general terms, on the side of the *state*, the teaching of history is to erect state government on the basis of the essential movement of the human Spirit, to recognize, to organize, and then to allow to be actualized self-ruling reason. On the other hand, it is the task of religion to seek its positive reality and its content, its existence, and its element, only in state, art, and science, but not to lay claim to a positive doctrine that lies beyond either reason or the state and reality.

People will not agree that this is really the true state of affairs; rather, people will appeal to history and assert that religion has

[33] [See above, n. 30. (Tr.)]

always possessed its own content. But these people will only strike themselves down with history. Religion [767a] [is] much more practical than these, its impractical and truly incompetent defenders, think. As soon as it ceased to be worship of nature, religion struck out on the two roads of praxis that lay open to it, the way of idealistic praxis, that of artistic development, and of real praxis, that of the development of states. It is superfluous to speak further of the Greek, Judaic, or Muhammadan religions in this respect, for the artistic creations of the one and the state-building energy of the other two are self-evident. But now Christianity comes along, which seems to be propitious neither for the state nor for art, because it wants to found only the kingdom of *heaven*. 'Only the kingdom of heaven?' 'No, the kingdom of heaven *on earth*.' Indeed, it would have been possible really to live only in feeling, only in the inwardness of Spirit, and actually to escape the earth, if Christianity had not become practical pathos, had it not ceased to wish for this escape, and it would have ceased to hope for the founding of a kingdom, even if only a heavenly kingdom. In any case, it would not have taken steps to engender an earthly state. But it did, and there remained for it nothing but the *kingdom of heaven on earth*, and ever has there been founded a more thoroughly developed, consistent kingdom than the kingdom of the *hierarchy*, a holy but not any less earthly political reality, as purely developed out of theory as any other state, and certainly not without the concentration of the theory of that time into practical pathos. Against this admirable, world-ruling state of priests, there now arose science; and when science again concentrated itself into religion and asserted the true essence against the existence that had become spiritless and then put the stress on religion *as such* and on *the movement of essence in the inwardness of feeling*, the political reality of the hierarchy was broken. But the Reformation, just as little as original Christianity, was in a position to refrain from state construction. It destroyed the political sensibility of Catholicism, but it had to see a state develop out of itself, even if only as a 'needy state' and as external protection for humans with superterrestrial interests. There thus arose the states without *political sensibility*, the Protestant development of states, which was not actually *wanted*, but only *extorted* by necessity, because this was the only way to obtain *interior* freedom, the freedom of belief and Spirit. This, then, is the source of the theoretical advancement, but also the theoretical abstractness, of the German world. Abstract religion as *purely theoretical movement of feeling*, in the way that we have it in the Protestant cultus, soon became weak and took the form of *indifferentism*; [767b] [practical] religiosity, the practical pathos, can come forth among true Protestants only in times of need and danger, for the state is merely the state out of necessity; it has no relation to the citizens, except insofar as it protects them. Humans are concerned only with their private affairs, and religion cares only for the needs of private feelings, for the blessedness of individual souls, for the salvation of the private subject in that other world. Religion no longer is related to a community that it has created and has to further; the communality is lost to it; the Church has become the *invisible* Church, and the state has become the *clandestine* state. In fact this situation is extremely abstract and, despite all theoretical development, is fully to be compared to a devastation of Spirit in its most noble relation.

Political sensibility, the state-developing pathos, which true Protestantism (in England, one can only speak of Catholic Protestantism) has stifled in the breasts of the Germans, was thus taken up again by the Catholic nations. At least, they have not allowed theoretical abstraction to become a fixed idea, and have first gone to work to raise the new content that the Protestant cultivation of Spirit brought into the world to practical pathos and to political development. The present time seems now to be engaged in the mutual development of 'the abstract theoreticians' and 'the onesided politicians', the *Germans* and the *French*. If Catholicism hinders spiritual freedom, then, Protestant abstraction, whose extremely upsetting heights appear in Hegel, hinders political freedom. It is not to be denied that, without political freedom, only an abstract spiritual freedom can occur, and no real development can take place out of our own inward power, but only if it is forced on us by external emergencies. Thus Germany has just as much sought to appropriate what is necessary from the practical pathos of the French as France makes use of the theoretical consequences of the Reformation. But both must go much farther than has happened till now in this exchange of goods. Perchance one may urge the Old Germans to recognize that, because of their private mores and egoistic religiosity against political ethics and the religious onset of political sensibility – since both of these latter have come forth in French history in a truly world-shaking manner – they are infinitely behind the French, and that if the Germans wish to have something over the French, they might well appeal with Hegel to their science rather than with Germanic pedants to their ethical life.

To such a great extent does the history of all the centuries, [768a] [no] less the present world situation, come to the aid of our perspective on the relation of religion to the state. To hold them apart from one another means to cut the life-nerves of both.

Therefore, when someone frightened by the movement of these

powerful forces, which, however, the world cannot defend itself against, wants to retreat, does not want to face history, thus thinks and feels mainly in the mode of weakened Protestantism, indifferent narrowmindedness, he will call out: '*This* religion is only fanaticism and, what is worst of all, in this manner of thinking religious and political fanaticism are united into one bomb in order all the more surely to smash the shelter of everything positive. The French development is therefore "insane".' Although the concept of fanaticism is not easy to grasp, still it must be granted that the powerful outbreak of this smashing is always intended by it. The fanatic pays attention to no hindrance, either moral or external; he plunges relentlessly in pursuit of his religious pressure (that of practical pathos); he blows himself into the air when he has only his opponent on his mind; he says, with Goetz: 'It doesn't matter to me one bit that I will die / If only all the dogs are choked with me!'[34] In fanaticism, the practical pathos raises the feeling of self to such *passion* that the human is totally consumed in it, and, as in the case of van Spyk, when there is something to explode, one goes up in smoke with it, so that ultimately, while not sparing oneself, one also sacrifices others *horribly* to one's purposes. Fanaticism is *intensified religion*, its tragic shape, and, if religion is experienced as *desire* (*Lust*) for liberation, fanaticism is experienced as *passion* (*Wollust*) arising from the compromised breakthrough. If religion raises the unjustified existence to a true existence, fanaticism blows into the air everything, even itself, if it cannot in any other way carry through its project. If, therefore, religion is *without respect* towards the hindrances to its movement, fanaticism is *horrible* towards them. Thus religion and fanaticism are different; but whether and how fanaticism is to be avoided is easy to understand. As long as there are batteries to man and positions to be defended with one's life, we will have no history without fanaticism. But we have already established that it is the purpose of state government to assume the movement of religion into itself and to let it work in ordered circulation.

[768b] [Thus] in its strict sense, how the state is to be ordered means how its domestic history is to be ordered, since we have finally recognized that the entire content of our theoretical attainment must be put into practical circulation again and again and that, therefore, the reformatory practical pathos of religion must be legalized.

[34] [This is a quotation from Goethe's play, published in 1773, *Goetz von Berlichingen*, which contrasted lofty ideals of right and wrong and an enthusiasm for freedom to the artificial conventions and philistinism of the existing order. (Tr.)]

A Self-critique of Liberalism

The previous year

[1a] A philosopher recently explained that he would not write under censorship and that he refused to permit a state bureaucrat to mutilate his ideas. How right he was: all that is needed is for everyone to think the same way; indeed, this has to happen if slaves are ever to grow into free men. It is easy to be free; people need only to want it. Who gives us censorship? Those who put up with it as least as much as those who impose it. But we, too, have we shown the will for freedom in this journal? Was the move from Halle to Dresden a radical one?[1] No, it was no move at all; we could not get any closer to freedom by it, but only remained stuck in the old bondage. Who would not have the thought go through his head for once and for all to give up this degrading position and of continuing to print only in free lands, perhaps in France or Switzerland? 'But the individual does not exist merely for himself', one says to oneself, and, with Odysseus: 'Bear this patiently my heart, or you will soon bear much worse!' one takes the servitude of one's brothers upon himself. One must believe in a general raising of consciousness, and one should never abandon one's trust in the terrorism of reason, if one doesn't want to shake the dust from one's shoes. And this trust has been rewarded in the previous months. At the beginning of last year we had a difficult fight. People saw in this journal, not the stimulus to a heightened spiritual life, but simply the source of all evil, and thought seriously of putting a stop to it. It was especially the critique of theology that seemed to be unbearable. The negation of the entire sphere of the fantastical thinking of theology, which Feuerbach's *The Essence of Christianity* hurled with such unstoppable force into the old confused machinery, aroused the theological censorship against us. To be sure, theological censorship is grounded letter for letter in the

[1] [In 1841, Ruge moved the editorial offices from Halle to Dresden in Saxony to escape the Prussian censorship; the ploy failed because Prussia was able to exert pressure on the Saxon authorities to be just as strict. (Tr.)]

Censorship Ordinances. But the problem was that the question of whether theological oversight of thinking was still feasible [1b] [was] not discussed, but simply the question of whether it was decreed, and even the Saxon rationalists, these until recently so brave defenders of freedom of thought, now only remembered the blessed efficacy of their orthodox forebears and did not contradict the godless critique, but blotted it out – *ad maiorem Dei gloriam*. From this, there came a momentary restriction and tension of the most painful kind. The progress of the theoretical Spirit, this dearly won fruit of the Peace of Westphalia, was destroyed in our organ, and nothing remained for the repressed critiques but to 'emigrate', in order, in their time, to re-establish their regular course by a detour and to make up for the great gaps of the previous year.[2]

Meanwhile, principally in Prussia, there has occurred an expansion of consciousness, which promises to engender out of itself a whole new world and which stands very close to the idea, or rather to the decision, to be free. The outstanding *Rhineland News*, the leading articles of the *Königsberg News*, and, from the side of the lawgivers, the fully and honestly intended freedom from censorship for books in excess of twenty printed sheets [Bogen], are evidences of a totally new mode of thinking.[3] In connection with this movement, the censorship of this journal has now returned to a praxis that no longer simply negates the heretics among our writers and philosophers, but again recognizes in them human beings, to cut off whose intellectual noses and ears without further ado would be, to say the least, Turkish. If the vast majority of the Old Saxon scholars considered the newest philosophy to be a mad impudence, or rather, an impudent madness, yet a secret intelligence found its way to them, to the effect that the madness of thinking and of freedom deserves some attention, even if not the least imitation. But, lest I become bitter towards these paupers – 'The sword of tyranny / Will still be smashed'[4] – a free

[2] [Ruge means that he edited articles prohibited by the censor and had them published in Switzerland; for the title of this work, see n. 10 to the previous essay. (Tr.)]

[3] [Soon after Frederick Wilhelm IV assumed the Prussian throne in 1840, he relaxed the censorship laws, thus permitting a voice for the two liberal camps, in the Rhineland and East Prussia, in the two mentioned papers; by the time of this article, Marx was editor of the *Rheinische Zeitung*. The total relaxation of surveillance of books over a specified length – a printed 'sheet' might, for example, consist of 8, 16 or 32 pages – occasioned the ironic title of another famous book of articles that had already been censored, also published out of Switzerland: Georg Herwegh, ed., *Einundzwangzig Bogen aus der Schweiz*, 336 pages, 21 Bogen; 'Bogen' here = 16 pp. (Zürich and Winterthur: Literarische Comptoir, 1843). (Tr.)]

[4] [I do not know the source of this quotation. (Tr.)]

man might well assume the burden of subjecting himself to the arbitrariness of another because the destruction of this arbitrariness is itself the prize.

But no prisoner loves his chains, even if they are covered with velvet, and it would be no sight of great presence of mind if one now [2a] [thought] to have attained something special and, because of a mere easing of the censorship, mistook the general enervation and political hopelessness of our times. The procrastination of the Germans is enormous; any working together for great practical purposes – even if it is only in the theoretical realm, for example, for freedom of the press – the entire world of the praxis of citizens of a state, is as good as unknown to us. How are the people to get out of the dreaming and effeminacy of private life to attain the existence of ideal interests in a common life and the really free daily life of political humans; that is, how are they to attain their concept? For this, the people would have to take the enormous step of concentrating all the splendors of interior freedom, all the treasures of the Protestant world of thought, into matters of feeling and will, into religion and world-shaking passion. Can critique help to this end? But rather is it not the concept of critique that it only splits, never binds, that it only dissolves, never concentrates? Yes, this is its concept, and yet nothing but critique remains to us for making a beginning of praxis. If it splits, it also purifies; every growth in self-knowledge is progress in consciousness and the onset of action. Now, therefore, if we turn critique thoroughly and inexorably towards ourselves, could it not happen that we will really get free of ourselves and grow out of the stale self-satisfaction of knowledge towards surrender to great common purposes? At any rate, this step would be a transition into a totally new territory and therefore much more difficult than anything that we have attained thus far. But it is worth the trouble to try it. Therefore let us turn our attention to the entire phenomenon of liberalism. Perhaps better than its opponents, we will discover what is lacking in it and advise as to what it needs, keeping in mind, of course, the condition that there still can be talk of helping it.

1. *The liberal party*

The complaints about the confusion of liberalism are widespread, and it is confused, it appears, because everybody has had enough of the beautiful speeches and the ready formulas of complaint, and because everybody now longs for the deeds of the liberal party. The most profound wisdom, without energy of character and without the surrender to a single cause which has become a religion for us, has already descended to foolishness. The demand is justified. But then, is there really a *liberal party*; can there ever be one among us? Clearly our good fortune consists in the fact that we have no parties, and, even if this were really not good fortune, still, it is our condition – but, remember, our political condition. For in science, where we lead a public life, the most outspoken opponents continually fight against one another and make no secret of the fact that they are parties. [2b] [How] did we come to be without political parties?

A party that destroys its opposition party destroys itself; recall the party of Sulla, of St Bartholomew's Night, of the Mountain.[5] The entire question is then placed on a new basis. Upon this death there follows the disintegration and decay out of which, however, the centuries often call forth a new life. And yet, when history goes forward by this very destruction, this does not happen in the direction of the victorious party. The present time in Germany is still such a time of death and decay; to date, so little has taken place towards a real rebirth that, in the sovereign sphere of our politics, we do not even have before us one open question the answer to which holds us in suspense. In the War of Liberation, there was one bud of the new Germany, the radical democrats, whose greatest effectiveness lay in the regeneration of Prussia and in the total popular rising against Napoleon.[6] The bud was nipped – we must admit it to ourselves – the old Gracchi of the Freedom War have disappeared from the earth; their ferment did not develop; in peacetime, when their progress really would have had an effect, they never made a serious beginning. The reconstruction was carried out, not by representatives of the people, but by diplomats. Thus the reconstruction still carried on all the problems of the time; for every one of them, there is a paragraph in the Act of Federation, but no one will deny that not one single problem was really solved.[7] On the contrary, all of them, the problems of unity as well as those of all modes of freedom, freedom of the press not excluded, are still problems. The task was to found

[5] [Ruge is referring to three attempts to eliminate opposition by terrorism: Lucius Cornelius Sulla (138–78 B.C.), Roman general and dictator, in 81 B.C. published in the Forum a list of his enemies, declaring them to be outlaws; St Bartholomew's Night, August 24, 1572, was the night of the slaughter of Huguenots, instigated by Catherine de Medici; the Mountain was the party of Danton and Robespierre, who began the Reign of Terror during the French Revolution. (Tr.)]

[6] [The reference is to the party of modernizing reform within the Prussian ministry during the Napoleonic occupation, led by Heinrich Friedrich Karl vom und zum Stein (1757–1831) and Karl August von Hardenberg (1750–1822). (Tr.)]

[7] [The Act of Federation was the charter document of the new German Federation, itself the product of diplomatic maneuvering at the Congress of Vienna, especially of Metternich's attempts to gain a 'balance of power' in favor of Austria among the reorganized German States. (Tr.)]

a new Germany, and what happened? What actually was founded was a picture of the old Germany, the German Federation. If there had been popular parties, if the democratic saviors of Germany had wanted to save democracy, they would have had to oppose this result of Vienna. These men, in whose name Stein[8] had said that the dynasties were immaterial to him, were now to see raised to the principles of the new time the dynasties and the old German private states in all their old splendors, the landed classes, the bishops, even the Holy Father. With the first breath of life of the German Federation, the bud of the democratic party in Germany was nipped; the demagogic intrigues were nonsense without anything but fantastical reality; the old territorial lords once again had all the ground of the real world in their possession, and whatever wasn't attached to their residences hung in the air as revolutionary fantasies. This was the necessary fate of the so-called demagoguery.[9] Therefore there are no political parties; the good fortune of political death has become our lot. We [3a] [putrefy] in privacy; we are politically a joyful cadaver, if not totally, then as much as possible according to the model of the German nation of the Holy Roman Empire, it goes without saying, the model from the time when there wasn't any nation.

Therefore, who has actually been victorious? The restoration of the historic private rights. And who has been conquered? Democracy and the human rights of the Revolution. Moreover, the democratic party is destroyed.

Now if, in accord with our theory, these facts are no joyful tidings for the victors – the future gapes before them like a black, barbaric abyss; no one is able to plumb it because what we are to be is totally hidden, and only the events that test will bring it to the light of day – they are also truly no compliment to *liberalism*, this theoretical son of the prematurely dead democratic party. For, what is liberalism, if it is not a party, but the blue haze of an unproductive theory? Or should we say that a *liberal party* exists in Germany when political Germany doesn't exist, but only, if we are not mistaken (and who could be wrong on this point?), thirty-seven territories? And even if there could be any talk of a liberal party in any of these territories, perhaps in Baden, or even right in front of the gates of the Federation, in East Prussia, to what political effect do their existence and discussions serve when their existence is a luxury and their discussions are written on the wind? Is there in fact a more telling proof of the non-existence of the liberal party in the German Federation than the

[8] [See above, n. 6. (Tr.)]

[9] [See n. 17 to the previous article. (Tr.)]

powerless realities in Baden and East Prussia? If their writings and speeches find approval and real political value, then something that is now only a matter of talk will really get done, and then liberalism will cancel itself. Right at the time when the realization of democracy in Germany was made impossible by the German Federation, there arose liberalism, i.e., this good German intention, this pious wish for freedom, this '*free-thinking mood*', or this sympathy with democracy – 'in intention'. A sympathizer does not want to or cannot do something himself; whoever is sympathetic watches the battle going on out the window and wishes good luck and blessings on all the heroes of freedom. This disposition is very commendable, but it is colorless theory. Yet, it is true; this 'good intention' has such an indeterminacy and breadth that anything can fit into it, every God and every state. Thus, at the beginning, liberalism was brought along to the Federal Diet,[10] where it could have become a German party if a 'purification from these elements' had not been immediately undertaken. But, in fact, a liberal party of the present can never come to real existence [3b] [because] it never knows what it wants and does not will what it does know, but only wants to let other people want. People have gradually come to understand this, and thus the time has come when the German Trajan and the Count von Blittersdorf can concede the *rara temporum felicitas*[11] whereby people think what they want and speak what they think. To take action against the purely theoretical speeches of the liberals would be superfluous; to take action for them is unnecessary. In the polemicist Börne,[12] we

[10] [The Federal Diet was the assembly of diplomats at Frankfurt am Main who set policy and adjudicated disputes of the member-states of the German Federation. (Tr.)]

[11] [*Rara temporum felicitate, ubi sentire quae velis, et quae sentias dicere licet* [Such was the uncommon happiness of the times, that you might think what you would and speak what you thought]. From Tacitus, *Histories* I, i. A description of the freedom and happiness enjoyed by the Roman empire in the reigns of Nerva and Trajan. Ruge's reference to the 'German Trajan' is evidently an allusion to Friedrich Wilhelm IV, who had become King of Prussia in 1840. Friedrich Landolin Karl Freiherr von Blittersdorf (1792–1861) was a Baden statesman who held an ambassadorial post at the Diet (1821–35, 1843–8) and who was Baden's Minister of Foreign Affairs (1835–43). He was a constant opponent of the relatively liberal Baden Constitution of 1818, and belonged to the party of nobles who worked to strengthen the German Federation in the service of individual state sovereignty and monarchicalism. Ruge's point is that liberalism is so weak that paternalistic authoritarians such as these can actually *grant* short periods of freedom of speech. Friedrich Wilhelm IV had actually lightened censorship regulations for the first two years of his reign, but then returned to the more rigid policies of his father, Friedrich Wilhelm III. (Tr.)]

[12] [Ludwig Börne (1786–1837), along with Heinrich Heine (1799–1837), was one of the most effective political journalists of the 1820s and 1830s. Both had emigrated to Paris; their reports back to the homeland pointed up the contrast

have already had our Tacitus, and he was clearer, he could point forward better than the Roman Tacitus, but we could wear out ten more of these without getting a liberal party.

What could a German liberal party want? Perhaps to solve just one problem of political freedom in our time in a sovereign state? Can it therefore want provinces, or can it have them as objects of its political goals? No! For in provinces it can have no free will and still less carry one through. But now if it encounters only provinces, what can it want at that point? It is clear that it cannot know this and if it did, it could not will it, for liberalism is not revolutionary. In clear words: the political development of Germany broke off when the democracy of the period of regeneration was destroyed.

For a long time, any development was feared. But the fear that development would come about had no foundation. Thus the present, which has become convinced of this, has come to almost the same charming tolerance in respect to revolutionaries as it had towards liberals. We can write the most beautiful battle-songs and accompany them with rousing melodies; no human takes them seriously, and were it to happen that the poet put under each verse the assurance, 'and this is my opinion!' no one would consider him to be so very bad. Thus, how perverse that people at first were shocked with a *Herwegh*, how absurd that we promised ourselves from the just dismissal of the philistine by such a revolutionary a political enlivening of the sleeping Fatherland![13] Why should we continue to pretend; rather, should we not let all the people find the explanation in their own awareness, that this is just theory? We already have the proof. In all of Germany, especially in spirited Berlin, one finds everything excellently put and powerfully expressed; people are enthused at the fiery poet, but people think, 'Poetry is poetry; there is no bridge from the heaven of its visions to our earth?' The liberals sympathize with the republicans; what else is new? Didn't they already do that? [4a] [Aren't] all schoolchildren encouraged to do this? All this produces no change of the political consciousness; all this does not free us from theory, from the condition of the spectator, from the mere sympathizing of a powerless, spineless, and insubstantial liberalism.

Liberalism is the freedom of a people who remain stuck in theory. Liberalism, which is no freedom, but only sympathy for a foreign freedom, and which is at most only occasional longing for one's own

between French and German political conditions, often with great satire; their informal and unstilted literary style inspired the writers of the group known as Young Germany. Börne had much more radical and democratic political sympathies than Heine. (Tr.)]

[13] [See n. 5 to the previous essay. (Tr.)]

freedom, which is something to be imported by some kind of chance, is so little a party that in fact it is the entirety of our present freedom itself.

2. *Liberalism – our freedom*

Because liberalism is not a party, it is a non-political, that is, a purely theoretical and passive attitude in politics. Political freedom consists in the free movement of opponents on practical ground; liberalism cannot attain such a freedom for the simple reason that its opponent is overpowering and appears to it as overpowering. We must grant that the opposition between the *sovereign* and the 'Freethinkers' is not on an equal footing even if the sovereign himself might be freethinking. The good intentions of liberalism let the rulers get away with murder only to be able to take the fantasy of freedom for its reality. Our freedom is a freedom that exists in fantasy because it is a freedom that is *granted from above*. The entire Act of Federation has the character of a *gift*, first, towards the *mediatized sovereigns*,[14] whose lot aroused such great sympathy that, in the Sixth Article, there is serious discussion of whether they should not obtain a plural vote in the Diet (to say nothing of the many privileges of the Fourteenth Article), second, towards the *subjects* who were again to be provided with *provincial* governments. Clearly the Congress of Vienna had sympathy for rights and freedom, only, just as clearly the *rights* were the *princely rights* and the *privileges* of the mediatized and of whoever else had suffered injustices at the hands of the French, and the freedom was the freedom of *subjects*. At any rate, these sympathies were liberal, and they were experienced as such; indeed, they were even discussed by non-liberal writers as imprudent ecstasies of freedom. But people deceive themselves concerning this freedom; it was *granted*, and very soon merely became *tolerated*. Four-and-twenty small states obtained *bestowed* constitutions, which, to be sure, did not leave the estates totally in place, [4b] [but] whose principles of publication of governmental affairs, of freedom of the press, of consent to taxation, were to develop only as far as these were to be *tolerated* by the large states and the Assembly of the Diet. The history of constitutional life in Baden proves this most clearly. But the freedom of not only the small states is bound to these external factors; in every land freedom is a product of the theories and calculations of the territorial governments and not of a universal and sovereign

[14] [For the Act of Federation, see above, n. 7. The mediatized sovereigns were the landowning royalty who were stripped of their domains by the Napoleonic reorganization of much of central Germany into the Confederation of the Rhine. (Tr.)]

popular Spirit, even though it should not be denied that the governments generally created their new laws under the influence of this Spirit. The freedom of the small states, as *granted*, is a self-limitation of the sovereign that is distinguished from the freedom of subjects in an absolute monarchy only by the fact that the laws of the absolute monarchy relate to the political sphere, while every law of the personal sovereign on the ground of civil, criminal, police, and military legislation is equally a self-restriction. Thus, with every law, the subjects receive a right and, insofar as the laws come from above, they are granted. 'Whoever does not think, to him it shall be granted.' In 1813 and 1815, the Germans didn't think at all, and we will still have to pay for our thoughtlessness.

Clearly, this freedom of *small states* and the freedom of *subjects*, as we Germans presently enjoy it, could produce no other Spirit than that of liberalism, the *good will* for freedom, but not the *effective will* for freedom. Perhaps *subjects* obey only their *laws*, but these are granted to them. Subjects are not really autonomous; they have no concept of the fact that the laws of a freer life must be their own product. The *small states* have in their constitutions the 'most well-intentioned and most freethinking' paragraphs, but the conditions do not permit their realization; they are not autonomous, i.e., they have no sovereignty in respect to external forces. And, conversely, the sovereigns of the large states, to whom the state is given dynastically and properly by God, have only the good wills, not the effective wills, for inner autonomy. Their relation to freedom is therefore also totally that of liberalism, an inclination, perhaps even a burning love for freedom. But this love for freedom totally deceives itself concerning the concept of freedom, and, because it lacks its entire sphere for freedom, that is, the true autonomy and sovereignty of the state (domestic and foreign), it seeks to make up for this lack by good intention and by so-called freedom-loving speeches.

[5a] [The] liberal sovereign wishes that his subjects be free, but that, naturally, they leave him his sovereignty; the liberal subjects wish that the king would have them free, but that, naturally, he retains his sovereignty. Everything is pure love and goodness, and the earth would be a paradise that is, if wood were iron, or, still better, if all iron wanted to turn itself into cotton. Whenever there is serious talk of freedom, the liberal says what that Frenchman answered when he was supposed to pay his debts, 'Just believe that I am these two words: I am noble and good!'

Once again we have returned to the old lack of opposition, to the German uniqueness, that they have no political parties, i.e., that they are politically dead. Political liberalism has as its presupposition the old petty burgher-consciousness; its new Spirit is only apparent. The ghost of the old Holy Roman Empire still haunts it. It has not even extricated itself from Roman law, the inquisition, the popes, and the privileges of the high, middle, and lower nobility; on the contrary, public, therefore really secured rights and freedom of the press, actual freedom, at least in the realm of theory – what exalted, completely unattainable things! And the idea of the sovereignty of the people, which would have been the basis of all of this, is now seen as totally French. But it would be very superficial to want to derive all of the perversity of our political consciousness from the ghost of the old German Empire; on the contrary, this ghost is to be derived from our perverse, deeply and unspeakably confused Germanness, from the Germanness that wants to have everything different from the 'Franks', and that, with its powerful originality, has derived from them nothing but the pure appearance of everything that they have attained, for the simple reason that there is always only one freedom and, by chance, the French, and not the good Germans, have discovered the freedom of our times. But enough said, enough complaining. We should complain no more in these pages, but only, from these facts, draw the conclusion that our freedom is nothing but our consciousness and its products. [5b] [Thus] we will continue to critique liberalism by discussing the liberal consciousness itself.

3. *The liberal consciousness*

Because the Germans have forgotten politics for the sake of thinking, praxis for theory, the external world for the inner world, since the Reformation they have been without ideas in political matters. Their entire life is filled by the fact that all politics are the regal prerogative. Therefore their politicizing is not their most essential business, but a robbery that they commit, an audacity that they should not have, a neglect of their most essential business, namely, their private affairs. Now, indeed, they refer to politics, but only in the way that they refer to the weather, which they also do not produce; and when they wish for good politics, as they wish for good weather, they gaze trustfully, indeed, dumbly, to the heavens. Despite all this, it has happened that the fundament of the old consciousness has endured no longer. The highest affair of humanity is no longer its concern for its eternal blessedness; the highest is the free Spirit as science and poetry develop it; the state is no longer the old iron uncouth knight who protects the spiritual, conscience-free men who research the Scriptures; rather, the state is freedom itself, and the Spirit of freedom constantly has to engender the state out of itself; the state is the product of Spirit, not its lord. Now, therefore, the relation between the lord and the theoretical Spirit is reversed, and the theoretical or free Spirit would immediately become practical if it actually succeeded in producing the state with full consciousness (it still does this without consciousness of its action); it would become its lord, and it is clear that the lord of chivalry does not let the spiritual lord come forward as long as he is able to hinder him.

This opposition is sharp and relentless, and, for this very reason, its clash is unavoidable. It has already flamed up; every day and every hour battles are fought, lost, and won. But the broad and well-tread consciousness of humans will not get rid of the old conditions and hopes; everything is still to be peacefully negotiated and no one to be injured in property, body, or life. In order to be able to fulfill this pious wish, [6a] [liberalism] pretends that spiritual property is no real property, that it can be erased, repressed, confiscated, and pulverized, even when it is represented by a substantial sum of money, that the spiritual life can be killed without being injured. Liberalism does not notice that only in this way does it maintain unviolated its body and its pious wishes. It cannot save that property, which is the life of Spirit that will be freedom itself and which does not want to have freedom granted. It cannot save freedom because it knows only a *granted* freedom. But freedom cannot be granted, for it is no thing but a being, a condition of Spirit, a position of consciousness that can only be fought for and won. If your son has any character, he will free himself from your authority; if he has none, and you set him free, he will only become one of many other servants. The Freedom War proves this. It was the violent shaking of a total servitude, and, for a moment it meant: 'Now, you Germans, dear brothers and brave men, you are free; what will you do with yourselves?' And what did they do? They knew how to do nothing more speedily than to fall back into the old Protestant consciousness of theoretical freedom and under the many chivalrous lords of the many states which Protestantism brought into the world. To prove this, one need only cite the Act of Federation; every statement in it is dictated by this consciousness. And perhaps we shouldn't blame the Lords in Vienna for all of this; it would be too much to say that they had created this consciousness; they would have been happy to create a new one had they the power. And let no one think that the noblest and best men there could have done this and didn't only because they were not included in the counsels; no indeed, they were of one mind with the others. We have only to cite Hegel's inaugural speech at Heidelberg,[15] in which he rejoices that now the loud cry of political intrigues is again laid to rest and the kingdom of the God of pure theory can once again come to expression. What does this mean? Nothing less than this: we continue on, my friends, where we stood before the Revolution and the War, that is, in the development of inner freedom, the feeedom of the Protestant Spirit or of abstract theory, whose fulfillment is philosophy. Hegel fulfilled this form of freedom and pushed it to its pinnacle, where it was to be overthrown. This has happened, and it had to happen. If philosophy was really the theoretical freeing of Spirit, by now philosophy should have become free enough to recognize that merely theoretical freedom is still no freedom. This was in fact recognized, and there was practical proof of it, for the supposed theoretical freedom has experienced that it stands under the claws of those for whom [6b] [it] did not care and who did not care for it, indeed, who negate and condemn it. Therefore philosophical liberation is no liberation because it merely runs along next to the private state, indeed, because it is nothing but the proper presentation of the private state within its boundaries, a private being-for-itself of freedom, not in a public communal existence, but in the separate, categorically trained self-consciousness of the subject. This excellent philosophy, which fancies itself to be raised so high above poor liberalism, has, however, an essential share in it; the *new consciousness* is as absent from it as it is from liberalism. It recognizes the new consciousness only theoretically; it despises its praxis. It is lacking the awareness that the public Spirit must have the dialectical life of the scientific Spirit and the scientific Spirit must have the content of the public Spirit. The problems of the times must be in possession of the people and for the people in order that we can lead a real life in this world. The concept of the people is the negation of caste and of the restrictions of class, not only of the illusory boundaries between nobles and peasants, between high-born and bourgeois (it is only narrowness to continue to give weight to these boundaries after the crudeness of their rights have been broken), but also of the real boundaries between the knowers and the ignorant, in which much more can be accomplished than at first appears. I do not want to cite here Sancho Panza's rule over his island to prove that the Spirit is not commandeered by the scholars; it is a matter of a far deeper problem, that only the unity or self-consciousness and of world-consciousness is Spirit and freedom. Why do you honor the power of the poet? Because he knows how to expand his self-

[15] [An English translation of this address, delivered October 28, 1816, is in *Hegel's Lectures on the History of Philosophy*, trans. by E. S. Haldane and Frances H. Simson; 3 vols. (New York: Humanities Press, 1968), I, xi–xiii. (Tr.)]

consciousness to world-consciousness, because he knows how to use the form that injects the highest and deepest of which he is aware and feels into your heart, your soul, your sensible experience. The excluding form is the untrue form. As wisdom comes forth only out of all history and out of the real consciousness of the people, it must mortify itself with its form until it is capable of again returning among the people. If the philosophers neglect this, the poets do it – but it must be done. The true form is the Archimedian lever, which raises the world out of its axis. But to this form belongs more than knowledge, talent, or material; there belong to it courage and character. Only Spirit is the unity of all these, the Spirit that is not frightened of its own audacity and puts its all into its brave word.

The discovery of the true form is an infringement of the theoretical Spirit and thereby of liberalism in its most noble shape, the philosophical. Every form, even the most extreme, of the theoretical Spirit will soon be completely legitimate, but the true form that [7a] [kindles] the fire of the new consciousness will be greeted by the old with fear and horror, much more in its prose than in its verse, but most of all in the first speech in which it appears at the right place. For it will be a *religion*, and will move and reshape the world with irresistible power. Many spirits, even those who do not know or will it, now work for this progress from the love for freedom (as one could translate liberalism) to real freedom. Our times are barren and evil; they can be moved only superficially, but it is still enjoyable to feel this struggling and growth of the seed of a not too distant free future. A foreigner, whose people still have to struggle with the beginnings of civilization, once heard a discussion on these matters, including the complaints that were connected with the inertia of the times. But he did not agree with the complaints; on the contrary, he broke out in the cry: 'What lucky people you are to have such questions move your lives!' He was right, for this combat is the highest good, and whoever wants to experience what it means to go without it, let him try to live his life among barbarians, even if it be in the most beautiful stretch of heaven in the south. This battle is the purification of consciousness in all spheres, therefore the battle of the true religion with religious illusion, the battle of living philosophy with abstract philosophy, or equally with its illusions, and of the practical problems of political life with pretended and fantastical problems, which in no way are or are intended to be real, but are discovered only to shove the real problems aside. It is always the simplest operation possible to grasp the real matter instead of its semblance and to have a totally conscientious seriousness (religion) in the highest interests instead of frivolous and empty play with them. The love of freedom will be married with these interests. Liberalism, with its good intentions, is to be taken at and held to its word, finally, and in all seriousness, to engender offspring with its long-venerated and long-desired bride.

4. *The religious illusion of the liberal consciousness*

Liberalism (in the narrow sense) never attacks the root of consciousness. It always presupposes that the whole world must think as it does and that the only thing lacking is good will, that is, liberalism. Therefore it thinks that popularity is an uncommonly trifling thing and wonders, for example, just as much about the strange confusions of the Cologne affair[16] as it did previously about the savor of people for the infinitely abstruse Hegelian philosophy, which, according to Fries,[17] discovered its jargonistic terminology only to [7b] [cover] over the emptiness of its ideas. Liberalism believes that it can let the consciousness of humans stand where it is, and yet that it is in a position to bring them freedom; it wants to give people freedom in the way that it obtained it, so to speak, bestowed from above. Therefore it simply does not grasp how people could be concerned with religious questions and could not let other people believe what they want to. It escapes liberalism that it itself is a product of religion and is nothing but the old moralistic Spirit of Protestantism, the empty good will, which, indeed, is very precious, but which is also very powerless because it extends no further than to demand of everybody that they should also have this good will. Clearly this form of religiosity is already an abstraction from religiosity itself because it is no longer interested in the glory of the old consciousness, eternal blessedness, and has not yet attained the new consciousness, which puts the earth in place of the heavens, the reign of freedom in place of the heavenly realm, the state and the public Spirit in place of the visible and invisible Church. For even if its actions had no other goals than these, *it still would not consider itself* to be radical. It wants to obtain surreptitiously all the glories of freedom, and imagines that the private state, which could arise on earth simply because humans with their interests had already emigrated to the heavenly kingdom, could be destroyed by humans who live in the heavenly kingdom as before. Not only does the old religious consciousness do the same thing, even

[16] [See n. 4 to the previous essay. (Tr.)]

[17] [Jakob Friedrich Fries (1773–1843) was professor of philosophy, first at Heidelberg (1805–16), where he was Hegel's predecessor, and thereafter at Jena; he was an object of government suspicion because of his leadership of the radical student movements and for his liberal political views (see n. 17 to the previous essay). (Tr.)]

the philosophically freed private person does it, in a word, all those who place science, religion, and art beyond the state into an abstract heaven of self-consciousness and think to find the ideal interests, in which they can satisfy their Spirit, in the theory of belief, of knowledge, and of writing outside of the state, as if all this were not a public affair and an organized reality of the freedom of political nature. Only the incarnation of religion, the secularization of science, and the descent of art and poetry into the real world, which all of us have only to create and win every day, move the point of gravity of the spiritual interest into the state, and this, my friends, is the religious question.

Yet this is not the cancellation of religion, but its rebirth, for it is a matter of nothing less than a new idealism, a new spiritualization of our petrified life, or a changing of the semblance of religion into real religion.

You may think that religion is irrelevant; every confession, even the Jews, could become politically happy. If this were true, what would it prove? The same thing that your false view of the matter proves, religious [8a] [indifferentism] or the dissolution of the old consciousness. (Real Christians and Jews in no way want to be *politically* happy, but only *privately* happy.) Why do you create for yourself the illusion that indifference is still respectable and that your cause would be embarrassed if men come forward who want again to pour religion into the empty hearts of Christians and Jews? Without religion, you move no stone from another; without religion, the centuries, as the decades after 1815, would pass without a trace over Germany, and all the wisdom of its wise men would bring no freedom. Freedom itself is now becoming a religion, and there never has been any religion besides freedom. But now freedom's form and content are becoming nobler than ever before. The entire world of humanistic ideals, the entire Spirit of our times, must enter the crucible of feeling, out of which it must again come forth as a glowing stream and build a new world. And yet, whatever my main subject must be, I know that, although it agrees very well with your *wishes*, you only find it dangerous for your cause. But your cause is lost if it itself does not pass through this fire. Theory in itself is an impotent shade which abandons the living spring of Spirit and presents only its caricature.

The liberals say, and everybody knows that 'confessing' or *established* religion has come to be a matter of indifference; and since it hardly matters any longer whether one is labeled a Jew, a Protestant or a Catholic, as long as one is a reasonable, cultured human being, since these oppositions no longer have any practical meaning or the weight of a party denomination behind them, so it comes about that people find themselves faced with the expedient of stubbornly taking their stand on this indifference and inscribing the universal as such – Christianity – on the banner of the times; it is as if someone who can no longer use any determinate expression or avail themself of any substantial utterance, had attained to speech in general rather than having lost, along with particular language, any possibility of speech whatever. We have termed this the religious illusion, and we have even seen that it is essentially nothing other than the ephemeral fad of the times – to remain with the general and not to put the actual, true content of one's most cherished wishes to the test by bringing it to consciousness. The test of theory is praxis. A cause still has life in it and a future as long as it stirs men's hearts, so long as they struggle about it and attach themselves to it with a partisanship resounding in hatred and love. When the struggle ceases to occupy the hearts and minds of men, so too the cause ceases [8b] to occupy their hearts and minds. Such is the case with the old religious realm. In contrast with this our contemporaries will know at once what they must struggle for or against when political liberty and any declaration of it is made the object of partisanship.

Thus we have made great progress over 1837 and 1838. At that time, the religious nuances, pietists, rationalists, even Catholics – if this latter only in extreme form, as in the case of Görres[18] – had partisan followings so that it was necessary to use these at least as a front, if only to obtain a practical return to the absolutely unavoidable politics. But all these religious oppositions are not really religious. They had already become impractical; they were not in a position to put the masses into motion and to fill them with sustained enthusiasm (even in Zürich this was attained only in the name of politics).[19] These are theoretical oppositions and thus were resolved very quickly and were absorbed into the indefinite universality of Christianity in general, a form that now can be called a party only insofar as there might be a party that wants nothing definite and thus again is the expression of our dead, oppositionless life. The pietists, who for the most part evaporated into 'Christians

[18] [Joseph Görres (1776–1848) was a leading Catholic political writer during the late 1830s, who polemicized for a return to the medieval Germany of the papacy; his most famous tract, *Athanasius*, (Regensburg: G. J. Manz, 1838) inaugurated the literary battle concerning church–state relations that was triggered by the Cologne affair (see n. 4 to the previous essay). (Tr.)]

[19] [Ruge is referring to the attempts, in early spring of 1839, of the political reformers in Zürich to appoint Strauss to a university chair, which galvanized the conservative opposition and led to a collapse of the reform government that summer. (Tr.)]

in general' and who trusted themselves to will or carry out nothing definite, nothing bitingly pietistic, have lost all relevance. To pursue the indefinite means to create self-illusions. Even this illusion is a liberal illusion. The pietists have only the *good* will to be Christians in general; they do not have the *real* will to be definite Christians and to make the rest of us so with all their power. They are so blasé they mock themselves and all the world; they write elegant and infinitely superclever articles in Hengstenberg's *Ecclesiastical News*,[20] hatch on all sides imposing little plots and are always surprised when these suffer miserable shipwreck. Now, when they could amount to something, they are nothing, and even the former zeal and wrath that they used to produce as *ecclesia pressa*[21] has petered out. We are joyful that they have gained experience, and we grant them time fully to bring it about that no one talks about them any more. It was already almost too late even to grant them this little time. So, sleep well, my dear Christians, and let yourselves dream of a great law with which you draw us all together in one great fishnet once again into the land of the old consciousness. You are blasé theoreticians; you have no religion.

The religion of these folks is no religion because it abstracts from the life and ideas of our times; it is *abstract* theory, doctrine, and not life. Religion cannot be taught, but *true* theory is religion and will be experienced and exercised as religion. Doctrine that is not present as a power in the life of feeling engenders the blasé consciousness of our day and appears not only in forced piety but also in worldly culture and its highest form, philosophy.

5. *Blasé theoreticians and the illusion of abstract philosophy*

[9a] Self-satisfied and therefore abstract knowing despises even the highest ends of the idea and of the Spirit of freedom, the end of self-realization and of existing in battle with the world, which are precisely the highest practical pathos and religion. This falsely construed self-satisfaction, which has penetrated philosophy and all the science of our times, corrupts character; even more, it cancels it and engenders the lack of character and cowardice that is found so

[20] [Ernst Wilhelm Hengstenberg (1802–69) was a pietistic and strictly confessionalist theologian at the University of Berlin who belonged to the powerful and reactionary circle of the crown prince, who reigned as Frederick Wilhelm IV from 1840 to 1861. He founded and edited the *Evangelische Kirchenzeitung* (1827–69), which was to become the most effective organ in swaying public opinion against the religious thought of the Young Hegelians. (Tr.)]

[21] [*Ecclesia pressa*: 'church under siege'. (Tr.)]

commonly among scholars that already they have become common objects of contemporary comedy. Only the philosophy that wants to raise itself to world-consciousness is relevant to philosophers, but if the philosopher himself no longer has this interest, why should his philosophy interest the world? Great heaps of philosophical books glut the market; not one of them arouses interest. Why? Because they contain nothing but the egoism, the vanity, the perversity of their authors, who ever and again prepare themselves to say something new, and yet never notice that they do not escape the old magic circle of abstract theory which pays no attention to the cares of any human because they themselves have no other care than whether Fischer or Schmidt[22] have now solved the problems of the present – yes, the problems of the present! But one single book appears by a human who has heart and fire in his body, a book that pierces the times with full seriousness and cutting energy to the point of life itself – I don't need to name it[23] – and the whole world is put into motion to new writing and new deeds.

Do our wise men draw any conclusions out of this? No, to them, this human is only a person like themselves. The vanity of the abstract theoretician is incapable of grasping the qualitative distinction between itself and a total human no matter whether this theoretician relates himself to history as a grim or a genial egoist, whether angry or frivolous.

[9b] [Here] it is not a matter of morality; it is a matter of the religion of philosophy; it is not a matter of the dedication of the philosopher to philosophy as a craft, a business, as to *his* domain, but as to the highest form of the life of Spirit, in which all life is moved. The philosophy that forgets its radical intention, just as the general worldly cultivation of the purely private person, always runs the danger of destroying itself in narcissism and in vain movement inside one's own subjectivity. The wit and the stale humor of great cities, which are always on the lookout for momentary stars and leaders, the idolization of every genius and of every bit of fame, the hollow enthusiasm for dancing girls, gladiators, musicians, athletes – what does all this demonstrate? Nothing but the blasé culture that lacks real work for great goals, nothing but the infinite self-satisfaction of theoretical idleness, nothing but the frivolity of purely formal intelligence and talent, and one must have made the decision to

[22] [I do not think that Ruge has any particular philosophers in mind here; the names are as common as Smith and Jones in English. The date of this article would preclude reference to the 1847 debate between Kuno Fischer and Johann C. Schmidt (Max Stirner). (Tr.)]

[23] [Ruge is clearly referring to one of Feuerbach's major works, either *The Essence of Christianity* (1841) or *Preliminary Theses for the Reform in Philosophy* (1843). (Tr.)]

despise all these gifts and all this cleverness in order to escape being pulled into the same hollow, insipid, and powerless mélange. Play with your supercleverness and bore yourself to death, if you have decided that you too can play along and shine; then reflect on this dandelion-consciousness in which you have attained everything, along with the insight that you cannot do any better than this super-satiation and blaséness, but do not think that you are a total human, even if you could shoot yourself out of sheer boredom.

The same phenomena that the over-refined life of the Capital produces also arise from self-satisfied philosophy. Its illusion is the same as that of worldly culture, i.e., that a formal theoretizing is already Spirit and an end in itself. The purpose of worldly culture, only to want to be clever, and of philosophism, only to want to be knowledgeable, is an *indeterminate* purpose and is related to real, effective, determinate purposes exactly as Christianity in general is related to a real confession of Christianity. Thus, in the case of a philosophy which does not have the goal of penetrating this determinate reality to its roots and of realizing its concept in it – which is a matter of passion – nothing [10a] [can] issue but the joy of the philosopher in his own wisdom. The most frightening example of philosophical self-seeking, of self-praise, of bitterness about someone else's conclusions, and of total hollowness and depravity in egoistic attempts at brilliance is so famous that I would be superfluous in making a celebrity still more renowned.[24]

That truth is its own purpose means that its purpose is to exist in the consciousness of the world and as living, moving principle; that is, the purpose of theory is the praxis of theory.

Thus we should dissolve any philosophy that is an otherworldly weaving of thought without will or passion. Even logic is a polemic against the world-consciousness of the past, and every thought, even the most abstract, expends boiling blood and wrath against its boundaries, or it is capable of no effect and worthy of no life. But this means nothing else than that we must destroy in principle the blasé consciousness of our times.

The blasé consciousness is the theoretical Spirit that has completed its work or has developed it to over-refinement and now does not know what to do with itself. It is the condition of the sot or the idler who cannot liberate himself from himself, no matter how much he is a burden to himself. If the individual human has to contend with normal troubles, this enemy does not approach him, but the spiritual life of a people can escape this enemy only by a political agitation

[24] [It was extremely discouraging for the Young Hegelians to watch a 'born again' Schelling take the chair of philosophy at Berlin that Hegel had once held. For one of their literary attacks, see n. 7 to the previous essay. (Tr.)]

in great practical problems that can grasp every individual by the hair and tear him out of his super-satiation with himself. Thus the dissolution of the abstract theoretical Spirit, even in the form of philosophy, is to be brought about by involving it in political life and by giving it the tasks of the radical reform of consciousness and of igniting the religion of freedom.

6. *The reform of consciousness and practical problems*

[10b] It is self-evident that the reform of consciousness is a reform of philosophy itself. If one leaves the state, religion, and the arts go where they want to, all three will degenerate, and if the philosopher is proud of his thoughts, they too will take pride in their thoughtlessness. But if one takes an interest in them, if one attaches oneself where they stand, then there results a totally new science, as Feuerbach, Strauss, and Bruno Bauer have clearly demonstrated in theology. This is a reform of consciousness, for it grasps the actually existing consciousness by the roots and thereby also reforms philosophy and science, i.e., creates a totally new, effective, and powerful science. In political affairs, the French have set the example, especially Rousseau among the forefathers and Lamennais[25] in most recent times; the publicistic power of Lamennais is truly overwhelming. Those Germans who can read and sympathize with him must immediately understand that all our little attempts are bloodless shadows in comparison to these words that are themselves deeds. And now, I am sure you will say that his shades have drunk from the bloody ditch of the revolution, of political freedom, and freedom of the press. But who engendered for the French the new, world-shaking consciousness; who breathed into them this greatness of soul so that they dared to be free? Their philosophers, their immortal writers. To expect the salvation of the world from the reform of political structures is the old mistake of liberalism; it all depends on the reform of consciousness. The reform of consciousness is the reform of the world, and no God can prevent it.

Liberalism is presently the consciousness of the people, and we have seen that it is also our freedom, the freedom of a people who have remained stuck fast in theory. Thus, where abstract theory is abandoned and we move to a reform of consciousness, for example,

[25] [Félicité de Lamennais (1782–1854) was a leader of the liberal and ultramontane movements of the French Catholic Church and co-editor of the liberal journal *Avenir* (1830–1); at the time of this essay, discouraged in his belief that Catholicism could ever be an agent for the regeneration of society, he was writing as a democrat and a socialist. (Tr.)]

in religious matters, liberalism would immediately feel itself transcended, for, as we have said, it wants to let humans think what they want, but, beyond this they should be free in the way that simpletons or thoughtless people are free. The reform of consciousness – and from the religious reform, the total reform follows of itself – is therefore in fact the dissolution of liberalism and the conquering of a new, real freedom. Its essential difference from the bestowed freedom of liberalism is that it will be its own product and a new condition of Spirit that has been gained in battle, a possession that rests totally in itself and that is secured without any external guarantees.

[11a] [Praxis] can be miserable only if the consciousness of the people places no value in it. When the scholars think: 'We have nothing to say that our colleagues, the censors, will not pass; we have more exalted things to think and do than concern ourselves with such trifles as this practical quarreling', and when, as a result of this, the people think, 'It doesn't matter to us what the scholars are about; they and their lot have nothing to do with us; it is enough for us if our life and property are secure; it is more than enough if our welfare is secure; the purpose of everything, anyway, is nothing but our dear life' – if people think and act this way, if they are dumb enough to do this, it is no wonder at all that their press is not free and that the only political life at hand is merely semblance and shadow. If you do not want to learn to despise this consciousness in its total baseness, it will indeed be doubtful what kind of lords you will always have at a given time, but that you will always have lords and will certainly remain total slaves is again nothing but your own will.

At any rate, the cause must be grasped by the roots; that is, only philosophy can attain and grasp freedom. But, as we have already said, the philosopher as much as the poet has the task of grasping the general consciousness and of pulling it into his power. Thus the transcendence of liberalism is possible only by the dissolution of the old sense of superiority and powerless self-seclusion of philosophy, only insofar as all minds with talent and fire are directed to the one, great, infinitely profitable purpose of causing the breakup of boneheaded philistine consciousness and the engendering of a living, sensitive, political Spirit. As long as everyone is still convinced that the most rational and exalted task is to write for others from one's study or to bury one's most beautiful powers in the dust of never-read *acta*, as long as people only stand near our poets and admire them and do not recognize that their power lies in their letting themselves down into the consciousness of the people, as long as people do not grasp that it is nothing but crudeness and impoverished impotence when all that one knows to accomplish is to let the highest affairs of humanity fall victim to death and decay – so long will enormous powers be dissipated, suffocated, and decayed, and the world will be betrayed of its most sacred right, the participation in a free life of Spirit. This is the world in which we live, the world of Indian penitents and Syrian self-castrators. How many powers are dissipated in the service of a world-view whose core is caste and flight from the world itself? How many people lose their lives and all their powers in the service of a system whose principle is the fear of [11b] [humanity] itself? Is not the direct way of developing all state citizens into humans and then of allowing each one to be free to cherish others infinitely more simple and secure than to undertake to import this police order that is presently the ideal, whereby it is pretended that these servants of order are reason itself, but that all the rest of the human material without remainder is irrationality? And with just hope classify the entire standing army under the police state,[26] and do not forget that the education and arming of the people, if one wanted only to understand and love them, and not to fear them, would be a much more imposing power, the only invincible power. All armies are standing; they are a standing swamp that, for years, puts into practice the play of many previous years, and their officers suffer the most, for they have to be serious about this play all their lives. Only the public life and the combination of school and the military can heal these wounds, out of which a mortal sickness once again threatens to arise.

Out of the illusions of consciousness on which our present political and religious life rest, i.e., the *transcendent* spiritual world, the police order that stands *over* life, the secret judicial process that is suspended *over* the people, and a military that is *isolated*, set up as an end, and even in part to a life-goal, the following simple practical problems arise:

(1) of turning the churches into schools and of organizing them for an effective popular education that draws in all the masses,

(2) of thereby totally fusing military training with this new system,

(3) of letting the educated and organized people rule themselves and of letting them administrate justice in public life and public courts. Let no one retort that these are a chimera; they are only the world of our antipodes turned on its head and brought to all its consequences. And, whoever takes offense at the fact that our world stands on its head, let him ask himself whether perhaps among us Germans the world does not stand on the extremely headless illusion

[26] [See n. 11 to the previous essay. (Tr.)]

that reason is to be sought *beyond* the people and is to be given to them from above.

Besides, without doubt, the fearful question of communism has penetrated to the ears of our wise men, if not to their hearts. People are horrified *that* the masses philosophize and are even more horrified *how* they philosophize. Therefore, destroy [*aufheben*] them, or better, consider how they can be raised [*aufheben*]; this is one of the practical problems whose solution teaches avoidance of the violent overthrow of the old system by willingly developing a system out of the new consciousness. Or would you rather rub out the masses as soon as it [12a] [occurs] to them to return the blows that they now peacefully suffer? Certainly not. And it would never succeed. Humanity is immortal, and just as immortal is its right in itself and in its concept. There is no more real question of freedom than of raising all humans to the dignity of humanity, and the world must concern itself with this problem until it is solved.

In confrontation with the real questions of freedom, the illusory questions, which everyone with understanding already sees through, will soon totally disappear. Or what further can be accomplished by the provincial freedom of the estates and their old German splendor, by the empty talk about nationality, or, indeed, about the unity of Germany, by the symbols, the city ardor, the collecting of money, the monuments, the splendid architecture, and the alliances by which these are to be manifested, or placed in prospect, or even finally to be attained? Nothing in the world. The insight that these are illusions no longer needs to be engendered. But for the question of freedom, the unity of Germany, this old imperial dogma of an indefinite liberalism, has now no more significance than the question of sovereignty. A city like Athens, which was sovereign and could beat the Persians, was enough on its own and really bore a world in its bosom, a world that was capable of fructifying and liberating the following centuries. But in a time in which such a territory cannot be sovereign, it also will not be free. Whoever wants freedom must want the sovereign state, and whoever wants the sovereign state must want its conditions. There is nothing further to do with the unity of the people, since otherwise North America and England are one and the Germans on the Ohio must belong to the Holy German Empire.

The German world, in order to tear its present from death and to secure its future, needs nothing but the new consciousness that raises free humanity in all spheres to its principle and the people to its goal; in a word, the Germans need *the dissolution of liberalism into democratism.*

VI
Edgar Bauer
1820–1886

Edgar Bauer

In their mock-epic poem of 1842, *The Triumph of Belief* [*Der Triumph des Glaubens*], the young Engels and Edgar Bauer drew a hyperbolic picture of some of the personalities and issues which then occupied Berlin's 'Free Ones'. Much of the exaggerated poetics was directed to the praise and defense of Bruno Bauer, who had just been discharged from his teaching post at the University of Bonn. His younger brother, then as always, had little chance to gain the notoriety of his brother. Still, as the mock-epic indicates, it was not from lack of trying:

> Who sits near Engels, solid as a Brewer?
> Why there, the thirst for blood itself, Edgar Bauer.
> His brown face set within a sprouting beard,
> Young in years, old in cunning.

Among the Young Hegelians, Edgar was the most anarchistic politically, with proposals for violence based on his view of Hegelianism which often exceeded those of his Berlin contemporary, Michael Bakunin. Indeed, it is possible to discern, in the early writings of Edgar Bauer, the theoretical justification of political terrorism.

Just as his brother, Edgar began his academic career as a theology student. However, he soon turned to the study of history, and left the university to become a political writer who also supplemented his small income acting as a proof-reader in the small publishing house of his brother Egbert.

The widely-argued dismissal of Bruno from his Professorship at Bonn in March of 1842 – a governmentally provoked dismissal bearing heavily upon the relationship of academic freedom to political and religious criticism – caused Edgar to come into immediate conflict with the Prussian authorities. His first essay on the matter, *Bruno Bauer and his Enemies* [*Bruno Bauer und seine Gegner*] which appeared late in 1842, insured that he would become a particular object of suspicion among the conservatives who gathered about the throne of Friedrich Wilhelm III. The work was filled with imprudently revolutionary sentiments, as the Berlin intelligentsia were of the opinion that Bauer's dismissal from Bonn would mark the onset of a general revolution. With such rhetorical questions as: 'What is our time? It is a revolutionary one', and assertions such as 'Only fanaticism for the cause of Reason can bear fruit', and for espousing the principle that 'the Cause can only be brought to its end by a violent and destructive struggle', Edgar became a marked man.

In 1844, Edgar Bauer published his most audacious work, *Critique's Quarrel with Church and State* [*Der Streit der Kritik mit Kirche und Staat*]. It not only detailed the embarrassing history of his brother's dismissal from Bonn, but went on to propose revolution. The work was immediately confiscated, and Edgar was rightly accused of violating Prussian censorship laws. The reactionary government moved inexorably to convict him. In 1846 he began a four-year sentence at Magdeburg Prison, one specially prepared for the imprisonment of dissidents. Reasons for the severity of the sentence were summed up by the court. The author was sentenced 'for insulting the religious community and the Royal Majesty, for empty and groundless slander and mockery of the civil law and state directives with the intent to excite discontent against the government'.

After the imprisonment, Edgar's life was spent in much the same way as the lives of most Young Hegelians after 1848 – in disillusioned liberalism, a cynical conservatism, and poverty.

The following selection, 'The Political Revolution' is taken from *Critique's Quarrel*. It serves as a conclusion to that work, and is here translated into English for the first time, as well as annotated, by Eric von der Luft.

Critique's Quarrel with Church and State

THE POLITICAL REVOLUTION

We are reproached often enough that our most ambitious fantasies really go no further than to a restoration of the French Revolution: Here, among the anarchists of 1793, we sought our ideals and the Jacobins are our heroes. Indeed those who say so are mistaken: Our business then would be indeed nothing but a reaction; and a reaction has never in history brought any good with it. Are we, then, held to be blind? Are we believed to be unable to see the consequences of the Revolution? The consequence of the Revolution was the empire of Napoleon and [the Bourbon restoration with] the installation of Louis XVIII. An alert historian will perceive that even a new, purely political revolution will only arrive at the restoration of legitimacy.

Generally, there is nothing to gain from such a returning toward the so-called original good. Yet the Reformation once affirmed that it only wanted to return to the pure Christianity which had been deformed by tradition and human institution. But what resulted from this reaction? They arrived at a new religious tyranny, a Lutheran papacy which was equally zealous in its accusations against heretics. The Reformation has given us the great precept that we cannot radically heal any evil within an organism unless we submit the entire organism to new laws of life. The Reformation wanted to undertake a transformation within religion; however, it did not know that religion will always continue in the same evil, in papacy and force. Therefore the Reformation was only fulfilled when it was preserved, cancelled, and raised to a higher level according to its essence, and when the struggle was directed against religion itself.

Similar is the case of the Revolution. As it returned toward the so-called original human rights, it wanted to bring these rights to recognition *within the state*; it was nothing but the attempt – as if it were possible – to make man free in the state, and its result proved that this is not possible. If revolution is to be fulfilled, then freedom must become more widely apprehended and it must slough off its exclusively *political* character.

We substantiate this through a scrupulous consideration of the Revolution.

The Revolution was a result of the life of the state. Revolution will never desist from uniting within itself two contradictory sides: on the one hand, privilege, law sanctified by tradition, the claim of trust and obedience – the religious side; on the other hand, the striving for freedom, which, of course, will always remain an illusion in the life of the state, the consciousness of self-reliant action, the insight into my rights as a man, which the state patronizes because it above all is that which absorbs me into a societal life of the species. These two sides were in conflict as they entered the Revolution, and the beginning of the Revolution was – as always – an attempt at mediation. The freedom party proceeded from the opinion that everyone must take part in the life of the state; it made the word 'people' into its pretentious display and declared the people to be the sole legitimate power in the state. Let the individual not be tolerated, calling himself to a higher traditional right, to claim title to all state power, to have exclusively the enjoyment of freedom, but then to make the living conditions of the people dependent upon his mere grace. Let there be no law to which the people's reason has not assented. Let there be no right which does not find its confirmation in the advantage of the state and in the demand of universal equality. The freedom party was in the right. But the other party was in the right too, for itself, on its own terms. It demonstrated that state power has its natural representative in the king, that the king's *right* to mastery could not be allowed, and that the *law* would be shaken if the inherited rights of many citizens no longer found support in him.

The beginning of the Revolution was, as said above, the constitutional mediation between both parties, a truce in which the rights of each were pared somewhat, i.e., each was done an injustice. Kingship retained the privilege of its hereditary succession; however it was no longer appointed by God but by the people. Kingship was to be concluded, but only in accordance with the laws which had been debated by the so-called people's representatives. But then the people only half perceived their power over kingship; and to the contrary, they reduced this power of theirs to a mere illusion, since they pronounced kingship to be hereditary. The people were supposed to give themselves their laws through their representatives, but they withheld the negative vote from kingship. Kingship was weakened, for the glorious halo of its divine legitimacy had been taken from it. The people's right was ridiculed, for an exclusive, untouchable power still was to persist against it. The constitutional truce was nothing but the beginning of the dispute; it was a pause in which the people's right sought to recover from its first exertion, as kingship sought to recover from its first defeat. It was only the prospect of greater struggles: Should the stability of the state be preserved, or should the striving for freedom, which of course was still in the dark as to how it would be completely satisfied, proceed toward an ever more vigorous abrogation of what existed? These were the questions which the constitution raised. In it, the essence of the state was already halfway infringed – and that is generally the sole good of a constitution – for there still indeed remained a sort of stability in kingship, but at the same time, according to the principle, the laws had been made dependent upon the developing reason of the people. The demand of freedom, without itself being clear about it, pointed beyond the state. Yet even if the people did, through their representatives, raise themselves above the 'rights' of private property, still for all that they annulled the inherited rights of life, spiritual and worldly privileges. Where was the security of the life of the state when I was endangered in what had become sacred to me by the right of possession?

The Revolution went further. The contradiction which lies in constitutional organization made itself felt. The cause of freedom was victorious and the tenth of August[1] demonstrated the power of the people to tear down what was legitimate, stable, and, moreover, what insisted upon being maintained in the state. Kingship was abolished. The execution of Louis XVI should have taught all nations that it is a crime to be called king in a free state, and that nothing holy and inviolable may be permitted to stand before the people. Now, they believed, the free state, the true republic, had been won.

Anarchy, which is the beginning of all good things, was there at least: Events moved toward a hopeful demolition; religion was cancelled, preserved, and raised to a higher level. But that anarchy was an anarchy within the state. Could the state endure without stability, without police supervision, without stern military command? Certainly not! And that was the mistake, the only mistake, of the revolutionaries. They believed that true freedom is to be realized in the state, and they did not see that all of the endeavors of freedom since the beginning of the Revolution had proceeded, according to their nature, against the state. Robespierre surely

[1] [On August 10, 1792, a mob sacked the Tuileries and the Assembly imprisoned the royal family, thus initiating the brief rule of Danton, which included, on September 21, 1792, the formal abolition of the monarchy and, on January 21, 1793, the execution of the king. (Tr.)]

wanted a universal equality and wanted even the *sans-culotte*, the have-not, to be taken into the life of the state and to have his voice in it. But could this equality have been accomplished as long as the differences in position and possession still evoked a difference in thinking and knowing? A communal education is required for a social life of equality, as is an equal opportunity to satisfy the higher demands of the spirit. But, considering the inequality of possessions, this opportunity was not to be made common; thus the Revolution, because it did not go far enough, because it could not go far enough, had to go very quickly backwards. No doubt Robespierre saw himself forced in that direction. He decreed the existence of God, the reintroduction of a supreme being; and the village dwellers lit bonfires to celebrate the returned God; through all France rang the cry, 'Vive l'Éternel!' Even the desperate and magnificently striving terrorists soon had to reach their end in order to maintain equality through the guillotine. The people disentangled themselves from politics, which, after all, had not brought them any freedom; they turned back to their humdrum, everyday interests – and every door was opened to reaction, i.e., to the attempt to form a state and to make it sacred again.

Therefore Napoleon's tyrannical empire was a necessary result of the inconsistent Revolution. If ever someone wanted to live in a state, then, by all means, he also had to get accustomed to its differences, its domineering police, its surveillance, its stability, its medals, and its privileges. Terrorists willingly accepted their medals from the emperor, inveterate republicans gladly allowed themselves to be made counts and dukes – and almost without becoming inconsistent; at least it was the state and the circumstances which made them inconsistent. Indeed the reaction was not satisfied even with the empire; for had it not been the Revolution which created this empire?

In 1791 a woman from a village near Paris gave birth to triplets. At their baptism she named the first People, the second Freedom, and the third King. People and Freedom died after a few days; King remained vigorous and healthy. In this little incident the course of the whole Revolution was indicated – at its end stood legitimate kingship.

And you want to assert that the political revolution is our exemplar? No; it is not our exemplar because nothing old, nothing settled, may be the goal of our efforts. If the political revolution does not know how to overcome itself, then it does not understand how to order the abstraction of the state to depart, and how to proceed to the understanding of full, communal freedom – hence it will forever arrive at legitimacy and at the tyranny of stability. What exists will always place itself above the freedom of the spirit – and with perfect right, for freedom is dangerous to it.

The political revolution serves us as nothing further than as a proof that it alone does not finish the project – it is an instructive example, and that may be enough. It is a historical phenomenon, complete in itself; it cannot and may not recur *as it once was*.

No, says the radical; the Revolution was not complete in itself: Do you not see that the July Revolution[2] was the beginning of the repetition of the French Revolution in an improved way, the beginning of the now historical elaboration of that which, in its swift run, was almost a celestial apparition? We are now in the era of the constructive assembly. Everyone knows that another tenth of August will be a long time coming.

All right, we do not deny that the eternal strivings of revolution – in search of freedom – will work continuously in history; we do not deny that the course of these strivings will be similar to the course of the Revolution; but we do deny that the lessons of the Revolution will pass away in history without a trace, and we deny that the development of modern history will arrive at the same abstract goal at which the Revolution remained stationary in order to go downhill.

We believe that the new experiments with political freedom which the people of many nations perform are useful just precisely to show mankind that there is nothing of value in political freedom or in the exalted constitutional and republican forms of the state. The attempts at a state, for which these various peoples now toil, will finally lead them beyond the state. The very word, 'freedom', is repugnant to the state – so history will teach.

What jubilation there was in 1830 when France again received its 'freedom', when the people became aware of their own 'sovereignty', when they deposed the king who ruled by divine right and chose *their own* king! And what arose from that freedom? The state has asserted more and more its power to stagnate; the majority of property owners, who profit from no alteration, rule; ideas are suppressed; trials in the press persecute free expression; and the free spirit who loves the fresh air of agitation sighs under the burden of a dull, bourgeois, egoistic administration. Thereto leads a constitution, and thereto must it lead: Only give it enough time and it will become just as oppressive as any other form of the state; its laws will generally invest themselves with the tyranny of law.

[2] [The July Revolution was the armed revolt in Paris from July 27 to July 30, 1830, which overthrew the last Bourbon king of France, Charles X, and thus established, on August 7, 1830, the 'bourgeois monarchy' of Louis Philippe, the 'citizen king', who was on the throne at the time of this polemic. (Tr.)]

Certainly time is not lacking for freedom, grown smart through experience, to rebel against these laws. Constitutional organization, however, will not sign its own death warrant; it will not voluntarily surrender its laws to the progress which criticizes them.

It is therefore clear that there can never be anything but struggle, specifically, the life-and-death struggle through which those laws will be destroyed. But supposing that freedom begins this devastating struggle, will it itself contradict itself and will it consecrate new laws? Or will it finally tear down everything completely?

The free community

You ask: 'But then what do you want? Can you proclaim for us a form of life which will be more suitable to freedom after the perishing of the institutions of the state? Can you construct for us a society in which private property will be cancelled, preserved, and raised to a higher level? Which gangs are to hold humanity together if the laws of Christian ethical life are despised, if every sense is relaxed and left merely to its arbitrary comfort, if the institution of marriage does not protect chastity, if genial family life neither makes a person's first years happy nor makes him receptive to delicate feelings, if it is not obedience to the authority of the state which checks passions? Do you offer us any other prospect besides anarchy, murder, and robbery? Show us a free, safe form of life and we would gladly agree with you.'

To this I respond quite simply that it is not our business to construct. Indeed, can any new crop sprout up as long as the old weeds thrive luxuriantly? Thus you must first exterminate the old weeds. And surely no new thoughts can come into the world before the old ones have been overcome, can they? Do you know that you are like a group of Ph.D.s who believe that we want to give the people a philosophy with propositions, conclusions, and concepts? Nonsense! In any case, our philosophy exists only for the purpose of clearing away the traditional ideas of belief from human heads; thus, just at first, we can do nothing further than to criticize political forms, political concepts, and the religio-political trust, and to be satisfied if our critique is accurate and if it has proven that it is a contradiction to want to win freedom within the context of existing forms. Then in spite of all that, everyone and his brother may come and say: 'But my God, there must be religion, there must be a state, there must be righteousness, there must be law.' This outcry does not bother us, since it proceeds against critique out of fear, out of the presuppositions of faithfulness; there is no other way to refute it than by referring to history. Now those people are just naturally deaf to deductive arguments for a rational freedom.

'No private property, no privilege, no difference in status, no usurpatory regime.' So reads our pronunciamento; it is negative, but history will write its affirmation.

Therefore you ask me what 'the free community' is, what it looks like, how it is possible. To that I can give you no answer, for who is permitted to think beyond his own time? Our time, though, is only critical and destructive.

You question further: 'But then what do you want to do? Nothing depends on forms, everything depends only on people. You want to make people free and rational – very well, existing institutions are oppressive only because of the wickedness of mankind, but surely good people will live freely within them. Imagine, for example, a wise, good king: Will anyone experience any tyranny under him? Imagine an administration composed of rational men: Will it restrict the freedom of the spirit in any way, and will it fail to know how to insure that no-one starves in physical or emotional need? Imagine that all men are good; then can their marriages be unhappy? Will they educate their children to be narrow-minded and commonplace fellows? Forms are of no importance; people are the main thing and those forms are only necessary in order to check the human propensity to commit crimes.'

That sounds very convincing, except that it is only sentimental chatter. Forms are not at all accidental; they are creations of the human spirit and therefore they are only suitable to this or that determined content of spirit. If people change, then the forms of life must also change. We set ourselves directly against our determined institutions, because the spirit of non-freedom (*Unfreiheit*) manifests itself in them. We do not bear ill will toward kings, but toward kingship; strip this man of the glitter of the throne, and he will be harmless. We do not accuse wicked married couples, but marriage, the vulgar exclusivity, the religious control of the form, the reciprocal constraint, the dominion which one sex exercises over the other, the aristocratic use which one intends to make of the other. You say that a wise administration will rule wisely. Very smart! But we say that it lies in the nature of administration to assume police supervision and to resist critique.

Obviously, for you, forms are only something external, because you consider them superficial. But we seek to fathom their character and to prove that they are not harmonious with the demand of freedom. Forms which have arisen out of egoism will create, in their turn, as long as they exist, egoistic people. Therefore they are not of no importance.

The human propensity to commit crimes! You must know that crimes are always a result, a product, of these determined conditions;

crimes are the complements of institutions, their reverse image. Robbery and murder are a result of private property, because this possession itself is a kind of robbery; and the egoism of privilege commits, not daily, but hourly, the murder of the soul of a poor, oppressed person, deprived of cultural sophistication. So-called immorality is nothing but a reaction which natural freedom instigates against the artful and supernatural pretensions of Christian ethical life. Prostitution is a result of marriage, because...

If this determined possession is for one, then the necessary complement of that is that it is for all who feel themselves wronged by it, who hold it to be usurpation, and who seek to appropriate it. If this woman is for one, then there will be other women who are for all.

Here you interrupt me and say: 'Then your whole plan for the improvement of the world thus amounts to you wanting to make us all into thieves, and all women into prostitutes; you want to abolish robbery while you make it universal, and abolish prostitution while you transform it from the exception into the rule.'

Now, now, I have already told you truly that the existing relationships themselves generate the crimes which correspond to them. Whether these relationships will now perish through these so-called crimes; whether, for example, private property in a general theft, marriage in a general prostitution, will find their ends – who can say? But the one will cease to be only with the other.

'Do you therefore want', you say further, 'to remedy by general murder the aristocrat's murder of the poor person's soul?'

Favete linguis.[3] When kings lead entire nations into war, are murder and manslaughter then contained in their plan? Have they not rather higher aims; are there not principles in the service of which the peoples' blood is shed? You are much too willing to make us into preachers of the universal bloodbath. And we are indeed nothing but the servants of thought who, as honestly and as truthfully as possible, seek to articulate what critique says to them. Do you want to hold kings accountable for every drop of blood which has flowed from their slaughters? No, here you are not sentimental, here you unfeelingly tally up the thousands who have fallen in battle. Indeed you celebrate properly your lord's great military glory. But if blood flows in the service of freedom, or in the struggle of principles, then do you want to hold these things accountable? The crowns of your kings always radiate beams of pure splendor, and their wars may have cost just

[3] [Horace, *Odes*, Book III, Ode 1, line 2. Literally, 'Favor your tongues', a call for the laymen or the uninitiated in a religious order to use their silence to avoid saying anything foolish, blasphemous, or ill-omened. (Tr.)]

as many human lives; but freedom and its axioms are to be stained forthwith if egoism and human obstinacy force them to do battle! If it is true that no great cause can succeed without thoroughly vigorous strife, without blood, then, by all means, history accuses any such cause of moving forward according to these laws, or, better, history complains to you about the human half-deafness which is insensitive to the voice of freedom and reason.

'And then here we stand again', you say, 'and we still do not know what you understand by your free community.'

But I want to tell you of something distinct from the life of the state. Only with revolution, which begins the destruction of the forms of the state, does genuine history commence, because here it becomes *conscious*. Although peoples have hitherto comported themselves religiously, even over against history, and, because they did not understand history, have seen in it the governance of a divine spirit; although they were unconsciously driven forward, and were at one time the plaything of kings, then of priests, then of a blind religious fanaticism; we know now that it is human beings alone who make history. The modern pressure to busy themselves with politics – what is it other than the consciousness that history is something human, communal, and that nothing higher drives them except the spirit of society?

From now on history is a *self-conscious* history, because mankind knows the principles by which it moves forward, because mankind has history's goal – freedom – in sight.

Mere political curiosity is already properly hostile to the state, since a person signifies thereby that he no longer is fully confident to let only the holy power of the state conduct business, and that he wants, in spite of all that may happen, to be present at hand with his insight.

And that is the characteristic of the free community. *It knows what it is doing.*

On this account the designation 'people' really no longer fits it; 'people' is a political concept, a word of the heart; 'the people' is the trusting flock which allows itself to be led. What prevents a tyrant from perpetrating his deeds in the name of the people? What prevents a people from standing up for and shedding blood for a determined reigning family? Thus, the concept of freedom is not yet included in the political concept of people. Indeed, the people is merely this external union, this messy bundle of conditions and individuals, begotten on this determined ground, grown up in this climate, according to these laws. Indeed, for the most part, the people finds its representation outwardly only in a certain national pride, in national fads.

In our discussion we have had to accommodate ourselves to the use of language; we have used the word 'people' when we had in mind a higher and freer society; we have spoken of 'people' as the conceptual content (*Inbegriff*) of spiritually gifted human beings, who, as such, are together the conceptual content of all rights of spirit. Only if we grasp this signification of 'people', only then can we show that the people must be free. But then we no longer have the political concept of people. We repeat once again: In a free community there is no longer any exclusive people.

The simple result of our critique of the Christian state is:

All institutions of this state are contrivances of non-freedom, creations of a consciousness which is still, in itself, weak, dull, and bourgeois. But even the liberal idea of a state falls far short of satisfying the claims of freedom. On the contrary, free thought, critique, is always above and beyond the state.

VII
Friedrich Engels
1820–1895

Friedrich Engels

In September of 1841, the young volunteer Lieutenant, Friedrich Engels, reported for his year of duty at the artillery garrison in Berlin.

In the next month, Bauer's *Trumpet of the Last Judgment* would appear, and in the next, Friedrich Schelling would begin his series of lectures proposing an alternative to Hegelianism. It would not be long before the drab and meticulous duties of garrison life would provoke the precocious Engels to seek out what intellectual life could be found in colorful cafes and *Weinstuben* near Berlin's famous university.

As Engels had entered upon a career of political journalism when he was but 18 – his 'Letters Out of Wuppertal' were published in Karl Gutzkow's liberal *Telegraph für Deutschland* – and as he was a Hegelian for at least as long – having read and approved of Strauss' *Life of Jesus* that same year – it seems only natural that he would soon find, and be found by, the 'Free Ones'. Within a short time he became a member of their inner circle, being particularly close to both Edgar Bauer and Max Stirner. He soon displayed his willingness to enter into the political and philosophical fray by writing a series of three critical and daring articles against the newly-arrived Schelling. During this exciting year in Berlin, the young Engels contributed to both major publications of the Young Hegelians, the *Rheinischen Zeitung* – soon to be edited by Karl Marx – and Ruge's *Deutsche Jahrbücher*. In the course of this year, his interest in literature and philosophy are seen to slowly give way to a concern with liberal politics.

In late 1843, his writing of the *Outlines of a Critique of Political Economy* [*Umrisse zu einer Kritik der Nationalökonomie*] signaled a decisive turn in his thought. It was his first essay into political economy, and henceforth, literature, philosophy, and pure politics would be subordinated to his interests in economic and social reform. Nevertheless, this essay, which appeared in Marx and Ruge's *Deutsch-Französische Jahrbücher*, cannot conceal those earlier interests, and terms such as 'self-alienation' and references to Feuerbach could not but evoke a sympathetic response in Marx. In short, by 1843, Engels was already a reform-minded economist, whereas Marx had yet to find his way out of philosophy.

The first English-language translation of the *Outlines of a Critique of Political Economy* is here reprinted in full by permission of Progress Publishers, of Moscow. It is taken from Marx–Engels, *Collected Works*, vol. 2, pp. 418–43.

Outlines of a Critique of Political Economy

Political economy came into being as a natural result of the expansion of trade, and with its appearance elementary, unscientific huckstering was replaced by a developed system of licensed fraud, an entire science of enrichment.

This political economy or science of enrichment born of the merchants' mutual envy and greed, bears on its brow the mark of the most detestable selfishness. People still lived in the naive belief that gold and silver were wealth, and therefore considered nothing more urgent than the prohibition everywhere of the export of the 'precious' metals. The nations faced each other like misers, each clasping to himself with both arms his precious money-bag, eyeing his neighbours with envy and distrust. Every conceivable means was employed to lure from the nations with whom one had commerce as much ready cash as possible, and to retain snugly within the customs-boundary all which had happily been gathered in.

If this principle had been rigorously carried through trade would have been killed. People therefore began to go beyond this first stage. They came to appreciate that capital locked up in a chest was dead capital, while capital in circulation increased continuously. They then became more sociable, sent off their ducats as call-birds to bring others back with them, and realized that there is no harm in paying A too much for his commodity so long as it can be disposed of to B at a higher price.

On this basis the *mercantile system* was built. The avaricious character of trade was to some extent already beginning to be hidden. The nations drew slightly nearer to one another, concluded trade and friendship agreements, did business with one another and, for the sake of larger profits, treated one another with all possible love and kindness. But in fact there was still the old avarice and selfishness and from time to time this erupted in wars, which in that day were all based on trade jealousy. In these wars it also became evident that trade, like robbery, is based on the law of the strong hand. No scruples whatever were felt about exacting by cunning or violence such treaties as were held to be the most advantageous.

The cardinal point in the whole mercantile system is the theory of the balance of trade. For as it still subscribed to the dictum that gold and silver constitute wealth, only such transactions as would finally bring ready cash into the country were considered profitable. To ascertain this, exports were compared with imports. When more had been exported than imported, it was believed that the difference had come into the country in ready cash, and that the country was richer by that difference. The art of the economists, therefore, consisted in ensuring that at the end of each year exports should show a favourable balance over imports; and for the sake of this ridiculous illusion thousands of men have been slaughtered! Trade, too, has had its crusades and inquisitions.

The eighteenth century, the century of revolution, also revolutionized economics. But just as all the revolutions of this century were one-sided and bogged down in antitheses – just as abstract materialism was set in opposition to abstract spiritualism, the republic to monarchy, the social contract to divine right – likewise the economic revolution did not get beyond antithesis. The premises remained everywhere in force: materialism did not attack the Christian contempt for and humiliation of Man, and merely posited Nature instead of the Christian God as the Absolute confronting Man. In politics no one dreamt of examining the premises of the state as such. It did not occur to economics to question the *validity of private property*. Therefore, the new economics was only half an advance. It was obliged to betray and to disavow its own premises, to have recourse to sophistry and hypocrisy so as to cover up the contradictions in which it became entangled, so as to reach the conclusions to which it was driven not by its premises but by the humane spirit of the century. Thus economics took on a philanthropic character. It withdrew its favour from the producers and bestowed it on the consumers. It affected a solemn abhorrence of the bloody terror of the mercantile system, and proclaimed trade to be a bond of friendship and union among nations as among individuals. All was pure splendour and magnificence – yet the premises reasserted themselves soon enough, and in contrast to this sham philanthropy produced the Malthusian population theory – the crudest, most barbarous theory that ever existed, a system of despair which struck down all those beautiful phrases about philanthropy and world citizenship. The premises begot and reared the factory system and modern slavery, which yields nothing in inhumanity and cruelty to ancient slavery. Modern economics – the system of free trade based on Adam Smith's *Wealth of Nations* – reveals itself to be that same hypocrisy, inconsistency and immorality which now confront free humanity in every sphere.

But was Smith's system, then, not an advance? Of course it was, and a necessary advance at that. It was necessary to overthrow the mercantile system with its monopolies and hindrances to trade, so that the true consequences of private property could come to light. It was necessary for all these petty, local and national considerations to recede into the background, so that the struggle of our time could become a universal human struggle. It was necessary for the theory of private property to leave the purely empirical path of merely objective inquiry and to acquire a more scientific character which would also make it responsible for the consequences, and thus transfer the matter to a universally human sphere. It was necessary to carry the immorality contained in the old economics to its highest pitch, by attempting to deny it and by the hypocrisy introduced (a necessary result of that attempt). All this lay in the nature of the case. We gladly concede that it is only the justification and accomplishment of free trade that has enabled us to go beyond the economics of private property; but we must at the same time have the right to expose the utter theoretical and practical nullity of this free trade.

The nearer to our time the economists whom we have to judge, the more severe must our judgment become. For while Smith and Malthus found only scattered fragments, the modern economists had the whole system complete before them: the consequences had all been drawn; the contradictions came clearly enough to light; yet they did not come to examining the premises, and still accepted the responsibility for the whole system. The nearer the economists come to the present time, the further they depart from honesty. With every advance of time, sophistry necessarily increases, so as to prevent economics from lagging behind the times. This is why *Ricardo*, for instance is more guilty than *Adam Smith*, and *McCulloch* and *Mill* more guilty than *Ricardo*.

Even the mercantile system cannot be correctly judged by modern economics since the latter is itself one-sided and as yet burdened with that very system's premises. Only that view which rises above the opposition of the two systems, which criticizes the premises common to both and proceeds from a purely human, universal basis, can assign to both their proper position. It will become evident that the protagonists of free trade are more inveterate monopolists than the old mercantilists themselves. It will become evident that the sham humanity of the modern economists hides a barbarism of which their predecessors knew nothing; that the older economists' conceptual confusion is simple and consistent compared with the double-tongued logic of their attackers, and that neither of the two factions can reproach the other with anything which would not recoil upon themselves.

This is why modern liberal economics cannot comprehend the restoration of the mercantile system by List, whilst for us the matter is quite simple. The inconsistency and ambiguity of liberal economics must of necessity dissolve again into its basic components. Just as theology must either regress to blind faith or progress towards free philosophy, free trade must produce the restoration of monopolies on the one hand and the abolition of private property on the other.

The only *positive* advance which liberal economics has made is the elaboration of the laws of private property. These are contained in it, at any rate, although not yet fully elaborated and clearly expressed. It follows that on all points where it is a question of deciding which is the shortest road to wealth – i.e., all strictly economic controversies – the protagonists of free trade have right on their side. That is, needless to say, in controversies with the monopolists – not with the opponents of private property, for the English Socialists have long since proved both practically and theoretically that the latter are in a position to settle economic questions more correctly even from an economic point of view.

In the critique of political economy, therefore, we shall examine the basic categories, uncover the contradiction introduced by the free-trade system, and bring out the consequences of both sides of the contradiction.

The term national wealth has only arisen as a result of the liberal economists' passion for generalization. As long as private property exists, this term has no meaning. The 'national wealth' of the English is very great and yet they are the poorest people under the sun. One must either discard this term completely, or accept such premises as give it meaning. Similarly with the terms national economy and political or public economy. In the present circumstances that science ought to be called *private* economy, for its public connections exist only for the sake of private property.

The immediate consequence of private property is *trade* – exchange of reciprocal requirements – buying and selling. This trade, like every activity, must under the dominion of private property become a direct source of gain for the trader; i.e., each must seek to sell as dear as possible and buy as cheap as possible. In every purchase and sale, therefore, two men with diametrically opposed interests confront each other. The confrontation is decidedly antagonistic, for each knows the intentions of the other – knows that they are opposed to his own. Therefore, the first consequence is mutual mistrust, on the one hand, and the justification of this mistrust – the application of immoral means to attain an immoral end – on the other. Thus, the first maxim in trade is secretiveness – the concealment of everything which might reduce the value of the article in question. The result is that in trade it is permitted to take the utmost advantage of the ignorance, the trust, of the opposing party, and likewise to impute qualities to one's commodity which it does not possess. In a word, trade is legalized fraud. Any merchant who wants to give truth its due can bear me witness that actual practice conforms with this theory.

The mercantile system still had a certain artless Catholic candour and did not in the least conceal the immoral nature of trade. We have seen how it openly paraded its mean avarice. The mutually hostile attitude of the nations in the eighteenth century, loathsome envy and trade jealousy, were the logical consequences of trade as such. Public opinion had not yet become humanized. Why, therefore, conceal things which resulted from the inhuman, hostile nature of trade itself?

But when the *economic Luther*,[1] Adam Smith, criticized past economics things had changed considerably. The century had been humanized; reason had asserted itself; morality began to claim its eternal right. The extorted trade treaties, the commercial wars, the strict isolation of the nations, offended too greatly against advanced consciousness. Protestant hypocrisy took the place of Catholic candour. Smith proved that humanity, too, was rooted in the nature of commerce; that commerce must become 'among nations, as among individuals, a bond of union and friendship' instead of being 'the most fertile source of discord and animosity' (cf. *Wealth of Nations*, Bk. 4, Ch. 3, § 2); that after all it lay in the nature of things for trade, taken overall, to be advantageous to *all* parties concerned.

Smith was right to eulogize trade as humane. There is nothing absolutely immoral in the world. Trade, too, has an aspect wherein it pays homage to morality and humanity. But what homage! The law of the strong hand, the open highway robbery of the Middle Ages, became humanized when it passed over into trade; and trade became humanized when its first stage characterized by the prohibition of the export of money passed over into the mercantile system. Then the mercantile system itself was humanized. Naturally, it is in the interest of the trader to be on good terms with the one from whom

[1] [Cf. Karl Marx, *Economic and Philosophic Manuscripts of 1844*. (Tr.)]

he buys cheap as well as with the other to whom he sells dear. A nation therefore acts very imprudently if it fosters feelings of animosity in its suppliers and customers. The more friendly, the more advantageous. Such is the humanity of trade. And this hypocritical way of misusing morality for immoral purposes is the pride of the free-trade system. 'Have we not overthrown the barbarism of the monopolies?' exclaim the hypocrites. 'Have we not carried civilization to distant parts of the world? Have we not brought about the fraternization of the peoples, and reduced the number of wars?' Yes, all this you have done – but *how*! You have destroyed the small monopolies so that the *one* great basic monopoly, property, may function the more freely and unrestrictedly. You have civilized the ends of the earth to win new terrain for the development of your vile avarice. You have brought about the fraternization of the peoples – but the fraternity is the fraternity of thieves. You have reduced the number of wars – to earn all the bigger profits in peace, to intensify to the utmost the enmity between individuals, the ignominious war of competition! When have you done anything 'out of pure humanity, from consciousness of the futility of the opposition between the general and the individual interest? When have you been moral without being interested, without harbouring at the back of your mind immoral, egoistical motives?

By dissolving nationalities, the liberal economic system had done its best to universalize enmity, to transform mankind into a horde of ravenous beasts (for what else are competitors?) who devour one another just *because* each has identical interests with all the others – after this preparatory work there remained but one step to take before the goal was reached, the dissolution of the family. To accomplish this, economy's own beautiful invention, the factory system, came to its aid. The last vestige of common interests, the community of goods in the possession of the family, has been undermined by the factory system and – at least here in England – is already in the process of dissolution. It is a common practice for children, as soon as they are capable of work (i.e., as soon as they reach the age of nine), to spend their wages themselves, to look upon their parental home as a mere boarding-house, and hand over to their parents a fixed amount for food and lodging. How can it be otherwise? What else can result from the separation of interests, such as forms the basis of the free-trade system? Once a principle is set in motion, it works by its own impetus through all its consequences, whether the economists like it or not.

But the economist does not know himself what cause he serves. He does not know that with all his egoistical reasoning he nevertheless forms but a link in the chain of mankind's universal progress. He does not know that by his dissolution of all sectional interests he merely paves the way for the great transformation to which the century is moving – the reconciliation of mankind with nature and with itself.

The next category established by trade is *value*. There is no dispute between the old and the modern economists over this category, just as there is none over all the others, since the monopolists in their obsessive mania for getting rich had no time left to concern themselves with categories. All controversies over such points stem from the modern economists.

The economist who lives by antitheses has also of course a *double* value – abstract or real value and exchange-value. There was a protracted quarrel over the nature of real value between the English, who defined the costs of production as the expression of real value, and the Frenchman Say, who claimed to measure this value by the utility of an object. The quarrel hung in doubt from the beginning of the century, then became dormant without a decision having been reached. The economists cannot decide anything.

The English – McCulloch and Ricardo in particular – thus assert that the abstract value of a thing is determined by the costs of production. *Nota bene* the abstract value, not the exchange-value, the *exchangeable value*,[2] value in exchange – that, they say, is something quite different. Why are the costs of production the measure of value? Because – listen to this! – because no one in ordinary conditions and leaving aside the circumstance of competition would sell an object for less than it costs him to produce it. Would sell? What have we to do with 'selling' here, where it is not a question of value in *exchange*? So we find trade again, which we are specifically supposed to leave aside – and what trade! A trade in which the cardinal factor, the circumstance of competition, is not to be taken into account! First, an abstract value; now also an abstract trade – a trade without competition, i.e., a man without a body, a thought without a brain to produce thoughts. And does the economist never stop to think that as soon as competition is left out of account there is no guarantee at all that the producer will sell his commodity just at the cost of production? What confusion!

Furthermore: let us concede for a moment that everything is as the economist says. Supposing someone were to make with tremendous exertion and at enormous cost something utterly useless, something which no one desires – is that also worth its production costs? Certainly not, says the economist: who will want to buy it?

[2] [English term quoted by Engels. (Tr.)]

So we suddenly have not only Say's much decried utility but alongside it – with 'buying' – the circumstance of competition. It can't be done – the economist cannot for one moment hold on to his abstraction. Not only what he painfully seeks to remove – competition – but also what he attacks – utility – crops up at every moment. Abstract value and its determination by the costs of production are, after all, only abstractions, nonentities.

But let us suppose once more for a moment that the economist is correct – how then will he determine the costs of production without taking account of competition? When examining the costs of production we shall see that this category too is based on competition, and here once more it becomes evident how little the economist is able to substantiate his claims.

If we turn to Say, we find the same abstraction. The utility of an object is something purely subjective, something which cannot be decided absolutely, and certainly something which cannot be decided at least as long as one still roams about in antitheses. According to this theory, the necessities of life ought to possess more value than luxury articles. The only possible way to arrive at a more or less objective, *apparently* general decision on the greater or lesser utility of an object is, under the dominion of private property, by competition; and yet it is precisely that circumstance which is to be left aside. But if competition is admitted production costs come in as well; for no one will sell for less than what he has himself invested in production. Thus, here, too, the one side of the opposition passes over involuntarily into the other.

Let us try to introduce clarity into this confusion. The value of an object includes both factors, which the contending parties arbitrarily separate – and, as we have seen, unsuccessfully. Value is the relation of production costs to utility. The first application of value is the decision as to whether a thing ought to be produced at all; i.e., as to whether utility counterbalances production costs. Only then can one talk of the application of value to exchange. The production costs of two objects being equal, the deciding factor determining their comparative value will be utility.

This basis is the only just basis of exchange. But if one proceeds from this basis, who is to decide the utility of the object? The mere opinion of the parties concerned? Then in any event *one* will be cheated. Or are we to assume a determination grounded in the inherent utility of the object independent of the parties concerned, and not apparent to them? If so, the exchange can only be effected by *coercion*, and each party considers itself cheated. The contradiction between the real inherent utility of the thing and the determination of that utility, between the determination of utility and the freedom of those who exchange, cannot be superseded without superseding private property; and once this is superseded, there can no longer be any question of exchange as it exists at present. The practical application of the concept of value will then be increasingly confined to the decision about production, and that is its proper sphere.

But how do matters stand at present? We have seen that the concept of value is violently torn asunder, and that each of the separate sides is declared to be the whole. Production costs, distorted from the outset by competition, are supposed to be value itself. So is mere subjective utility – since no other kind of utility can exist at present. To help these lame definitions on to their feet, it is in both cases necessary to have recourse to competition; and the best of it is that with the English competition represents utility, in contrast to the costs of production, whilst inversely with Say it introduces the costs of production in contrast to utility. But what kind of utility, what kind of production costs, does it introduce? Its utility depends on chance, on fashion, on the whim of the rich; its production costs fluctuate with the fortuitous relationship of demand and supply.

The difference between real value and exchange-value is based on a fact – namely, that the value of a thing differs from the so-called equivalent given for it in trade; i.e., that this equivalent is not an equivalent. This so-called equivalent is the *price* of the thing, and if the economist were honest, he would employ this term for 'value in exchange'. But he has still to keep up some sort of pretence that price is somehow bound up with value, lest the immorality of trade become too obvious. It is, however, quite correct, and a fundamental law of private property, that *price* is determined by the reciprocal action of production costs and competition. This purely empirical law was the first to be discovered by the economist; and from this law he then abstracted his 'real value', i.e., the price at the time when competition is in a state of equilibrium, when demand and supply cover each other. Then, of course, what remains over are the costs of production and it is these which the economist proceeds to call ' real value', whereas it is merely a definite aspect of price. Thus everything in economics stands on its head. Value, the primary factor, the source of price, is made dependent on price, its own product. As is well known, this inversion is the essence of abstraction; on which see Feuerbach.

According to the economists, the production costs of a commodity consist of three elements: the rent for the piece of land required to produce the raw material; the capital with its profit and the wages for the labour required for production and manufacture. But it becomes immediately evident that capital and labour are identical, since the economists themselves confess that capital is 'stored-up labour'. We are therefore left with only two sides – the natural, objective side, land; and the human subjective side, labour, which includes capital and, besides capital, a third factor which the economist does not think about – I mean the mental element of invention, of thought, alongside the physical element of sheer labour. What has the economist to do with inventiveness? Have not all inventions fallen into his lap without any effort on his part? Has *one* of them cost him anything? Why then should he bother about them in the calculation of production costs? Land, capital and labour are for him the conditions of wealth, and he requires nothing else. Science is no concern of his. What does it matter to him that he has received its gifts through Berthollet, Davy, Liebig, Watt, Cartwright, etc. – gifts which have benefited him and his production immeasurably? He does not know how to calculate such things; the advances of science go beyond his figures. But in a rational order which has gone beyond the division of interests as it is found with the economist, the mental element certainly belongs among the elements of production and will find its place, too, in economics among the costs of production. And here it is certainly gratifying to know that the promotion of science also brings its material reward, to know that a single achievement of science like James Watt's steam-engine has brought in more for the world in the first fifty years of its existence than the world has spent on the promotion of science since the beginning of time.

We have, then, two elements of production in operation – nature and man, with man again active physically and mentally, and can now return to the economist and his production costs.

What cannot be monopolized has no value, says the economist – a proposition which we shall examine more closely later on. If we say 'has no *price*', then the proposition is valid for the order which rests on private property. If land could be had as easily as air, no one would pay rent. Since this is not the case, but since, rather, the extent of a piece of land to be appropriated is limited in any particular case, one pays rent for the appropriated, i.e., the monopolized land, or one pays down a purchase price for it. After this enlightenment about the origin of the value of land it is, however, very strange to have to hear from the economist that the rent of land is the difference between the yield from the land for which rent is paid and from the worst land worth cultivating at all. As is well known, this is the definition of rent fully developed for the first time by Ricardo. This definition is indeed correct in practice if one presupposes that a fall in demand reacts *instantaneously* on rent, and at once puts a corresponding amount of the worst cultivated land out of cultivation. This, however, is not the case, and the definition is therefore inadequate. Moreover, it does not cover the causation of rent, and is therefore even for that reason untenable. In opposition to this definition, Col. T. P. Thompson, the champion of the Anti-Corn Law League, revived Adam Smith's definition, and substantiated it. According to him, rent is the relation between the competition of those striving for the use of the land and the limited quantity of available land. Here at least is a return to the origin of rent; but this explanation does not take into account the varying fertility of the soil, just as the previous explanation leaves out competition.

Once more, therefore, we have two one-sided and hence only partial definitions of a single object. As in the case of the concept of value, we shall again have to combine these two definitions so as to find the correct definition which follows from the development of the thing itself and thus embraces all practice. Rent is the relation between the productivity of the land, the natural side (which in turn consists of *natural* fertility and *human* cultivation – labour applied to effect improvement), and the human side, competition. The economists may shake their heads over this 'definition'; they will discover to their horror that it embraces everything relevant to this matter.

The *landowner* has nothing with which to reproach the merchant.

He practises robbery in monopolizing the land. He practises robbery in exploiting for his own benefit the increase in population which increases competition and thus the value of his estate; in turning into a source of personal advantage that which has not been his own doing – that which is his by sheer accident. He practises robbery in *leasing his land*, when he eventually seizes for himself the improvements effected by his tenant. This is the secret of the ever-increasing wealth of the big landowners.

The axioms which qualify as robbery the landowner's method of deriving an income – namely, that each has a right to the product of his labour, or that no one shall reap where he has not sown – are not advanced by us. The first excludes the duty of feeding children; the second deprives each generation of the right to live, since each generation starts with what it inherits from the preceding generation. These axioms are, rather, consequences of private property. One should either put into effect the consequences or abandon private property as a premise.

Indeed, the original act of appropriation itself is justified by the assertion of the still earlier existence of *common* property rights. Thus, wherever we turn, private property leads us into contradictions.

To make land an object of huckstering – the land which is our one and all, the first condition of our existence – was the last step towards making oneself an object of huckstering. It was and is to this very day an immorality surpassed only by the immorality of self-alienation. And the original appropriation – the monopolization of the land by a few, the exclusion of the rest from that which is the condition of their life – yields nothing in immorality to the subsequent huckstering of the land.

If here again we abandon private property, rent is reduced to its truth, to the rational notion which essentially lies at its root. The value of the land divorced from it as rent then reverts to the land itself. This value, to be measured by the productivity of equal areas of land subjected to equal applications of labour, is indeed taken into account as part of the production costs when determining the value of products; and like rent, it is the relation of productivity to competition – but to *true* competition, such as will be developed when its time comes.

We have seen that capital and labour are initially identical; we see further from the explanations of the economist himself that, in the process of production, capital, the result of labour, is immediately transformed again into the substratum, into the material of labour; and that therefore the momentarily postulated separation of capital from labour is immediately superseded by the unity of both. And yet the economist separates capital from labour, and yet clings to the division without giving any other recognition to their unity than by his definition of capital as 'stored-up labour'. The split between capital and labour resulting from private property is nothing but the inner dichotomy of labour corresponding to this divided condition and arising out of it. And after this separation is accomplished, capital is divided once more into the original capital and profit – the increment of capital, which it receives in the process of production; although in practice profit is immediately lumped together with capital and set into motion with it. Indeed, even profit is in its turn split into interest and profit proper. In the case of interest, the absurdity of these splits is carried to the extreme. The immorality of lending at interest, of receiving without working, merely for making a loan, though already implied in private property, is only too obvious, and has long ago been recognized for what it is by unprejudiced popular consciousness, which in such matters is usually right. All these subtle splits and divisions stem from the original separation of capital from labour and from the culmination of this separation – the division of mankind into capitalists and workers – a division which daily becomes ever more acute, and which, as we shall see, is *bound* to deepen. This separation, however, like the separation already considered of land from capital and labour, is in the final analysis an impossible separation. What share land, capital and labour each have in any particular product cannot be determined. The three magnitudes are incommensurable. The land produces the raw material, but not without capital and labour. Capital presupposes land and labour. And labour presupposes *at least* land, and usually also capital. The functions of these three elements are completely different, and are not to be measured by a fourth common standard. Therefore, when it comes to dividing the proceeds among the three elements under existing conditions, there is no inherent standard; it is an entirely alien and with regard to them fortuitous standard that decides – competition, the cunning right of the stronger. Rent implies competition; profit on capital is solely determined by competition; and the position with regard to wages we shall see presently.

If we abandon private property, then all these unnatural divisions disappear. The difference between interest and profit disappears; capital is nothing without labour, without movement. The significance of profit is reduced to the weight which capital carries in the determination of the costs of production; and profit thus remains inherent in capital, in the same way as capital itself reverts to its original unity with labour.

Labour – the main factor in production, the 'source of wealth', free human activity – comes off badly with the economist. Just as capital has already been separated from labour, so labour is now in turn split for a second time: the product of labour confronts labour as wages, is separated from it, and is in its turn as usual determined by competition – there being, as we have seen, no firm standard determining labour's share in production. If we do away with private property, this unnatural separation also disappears. Labour becomes its own reward, and the true significance of the wages of labour, hitherto alienated, comes to light – namely, the significance of labour for the determination of the production costs of a thing.

We have seen that in the end everything comes down to competition, so long as private property exists. It is the economist's principal category – his most beloved daughter, whom he ceaselessly caresses – and look out for the Medusa's head which she will show you!

The immediate consequence of private property was the split of production into two opposing sides – the natural and the human sides, the soil which without fertilization by man is dead and sterile, and human activity, the first condition of which is that very soil. Furthermore we have seen how human activity in its turn was dissolved into labour and capital, and how these two sides antagonistically confronted each other. Thus we already had the struggle of the three elements against one another, instead of their mutual support; now we have to add that private property brings in its wake the fragmentation of each of these elements. One piece of land stands confronted by another, one capital by another, one labourer by another. In other words, because private property isolates everyone in his own crude solitariness, and because, nevertheless, everyone has the same interest as his neighbour, one landowner stands antagonistically confronted by another, one capitalist by another, one worker by another. In this discord of identical interests resulting precisely from this identity is consummated the immorality of mankind's condition hitherto; and this consummation is competition.

The opposite of *competition* is *monopoly*. Monopoly was the war-cry of the Mercantilists; competition the battle-cry of the liberal economists. It is easy to see that this antithesis is again a quite hollow antithesis. Every competitor *cannot but* desire to have the monopoly, be he worker, capitalist or landowner. Each smaller group of competitors cannot but desire to have the monopoly for itself against all others. Competition is based on self-interest, and self-interest in turn breeds monopoly. In short, competition passes over into monopoly. On the other hand, monopoly cannot stem the tide of competition – indeed, it itself breeds competition; just as a prohibition of imports, for instance, or high tariffs positively breed the competition of smuggling. The contradiction of competition is exactly the same as that of private property. It is in the interest of each to possess everything, but in the interest of the whole that each possess an equal amount. Thus, the general and the individual interest are diametrically opposed to each other. The contradiction of competition is that each cannot but desire the monopoly, whilst the whole as such is bound to lose by monopoly and must therefore remove it. Moreover, competition already presupposes monopoly – namely, the monopoly of property (and here the hypocrisy of the liberals comes once more to light); and so long as the monopoly of property exists, for so long the possession of monopoly is equally justified – for monopoly, once it exists, is also property. What a pitiful half-measure, therefore, to attack the small monopolies, and to leave untouched the basic monopoly! And if we add to this the economist's proposition mentioned above, that nothing has value which cannot be monopolized – that nothing, therefore, which does not permit of such monopolization can enter this arena of competition – then our assertion that competition presupposes monopoly is completely justified.

The law of competition is that demand and supply always strive to complement each other, and therefore never do so. The two sides are torn apart again and transformed into flat opposition. Supply always follows close on demand without ever quite covering it. It is either too big or too small, never corresponding to demand; because in this unconscious condition of mankind no one knows how big supply or demand is. If demand is greater than supply the price rises and, as a result, supply is to a certain degree stimulated. As soon as it comes on to the market, prices fall; and if it becomes greater than demand, then the fall in prices is so significant that demand is once again stimulated. So it goes on unendingly – a permanently unhealthy state of affairs – a constant alternation of over-stimulation and flagging which precludes all advance – a state of perpetual fluctuation without ever reaching its goal. This law with its constant adjustment, in which whatever is lost here is gained there, is regarded as something excellent by the economist. It is his chief glory – he cannot see enough of it, and considers it in all its possible and impossible applications. Yet it is obvious that this law is purely a law of nature and not a law of the mind. It is a law which produces revolution. The economist comes along with his lovely theory of demand and supply, proves to you that 'one can never produce too much', and practice replies with trade crises, which reappear as regularly as the comets, and of which we have now on the average one every five to seven years. For the last eighty years these trade crises have arrived just as regularly as the great plagues did in the past – and they have brought in their train more misery and more immorality than the latter. (Compare Wade: *History of the Middle and Working Classes*, London, 1835, p. 211.) Of course, these commercial upheavals confirm the law, confirm it exhaustively – but in a manner different from that which the economist would have us believe to be the case. What are we to think of a law which can only assert itself through periodic upheavals? It is certainly a natural law based on the unconsciousness of the participants. If the producers as such knew how much the consumers required, if they were to organise production, if they were to share it out amongst themselves, then the fluctuations of competition and its tendency to crisis would be impossible. Carry on production consciously as human beings – not as dispersed atoms without consciousness of your species – and you have overcome all these artificial and untenable antitheses. But as long as you continue to produce in the present unconscious, thoughtless manner, at the mercy of chance – for just so long trade crises will remain; and each successive crisis is bound to become more universal and therefore worse than the preceding one; is bound to impoverish a larger body of small capitalists, and to augment in increasing proportion the numbers of the class who live by labour alone, thus considerably enlarging the mass of labour to be employed (the major problem of our economists) and finally causing a social revolution such as has never been dreamt of in the philosophy of the economists.

The perpetual fluctuation of prices such as is created by the condition of competition completely deprives trade of its last vestige of morality. It is no longer a question of *value*; the same system which appears to attach such importance to value, which confers on the abstraction of value in money from the honour of having an existence of its own – this very system destroys by means of competition the inherent value of all things, and daily and hourly changes the value-relationship of all things to one another. Where is there any possibility remaining in this whirlpool of an exchange based on a moral foundation? In this continuous up-and-down, everyone *must* seek to hit upon the most favourable moment for purchase and sale; everyone must become a speculator – that is to say, must reap where he has not sown; must enrich himself at the expense of others, must calculate on the misfortune of others, or let chance win for him. The speculator always counts on disasters, particularly on bad harvests. He utilizes everything – for instance, the New York fire in its time – and immorality's culminating point is the speculation on the Stock Exchange, where history, and with it mankind, is demoted to a means of gratifying the avarice of the calculating or gambling speculator. And let not the honest 'respectable' merchant rise above the gambling on the Stock Exchange with a Pharisaic 'I thank thee, O Lord...', etc. He is as bad as the speculators in stocks and shares. He speculates just as much as they do. He has to: competition compels him to. And his trading activity therefore implies the same immorality as theirs. The truth of the relation of competition is the relation of consumption to productivity. In a world worthy of mankind there will be no other competition than this. The community will have to calculate what it can produce with the means at its disposal; and in accordance with the relationship of this productive power to the mass of consumers it will determine how far it has to raise or lower production, how far it has to give way to, or curtail, luxury. But so that they may be able to pass a correct judgment on this relationship and on the increase in productive power to be expected from a rational state of affairs within the community, I invite my readers to consult the writings of the English Socialists, and partly also those of Fourier.

Subjective competition – the contest of capital against capital, of labour against labour, etc. – will under these conditions be reduced to the spirit of emulation grounded in human nature (a concept tolerably set forth so far only by Fourier), which after the transcendence of opposing interests will be confined to its proper and rational sphere.

The struggle of capital against capital, of labour against labour, of land against land, drives production to a fever-pitch at which production turns all natural and rational relations upside-down. No capital can stand the competition of another if it is not brought to the highest pitch of activity. No piece of land can be profitably cultivated if it does not continuously increase its productivity. No worker can hold his own against his competitors if he does not devote all his energy to labour. No one at all who enters into the struggle of competition can weather it without the utmost exertion of his energy, without renouncing every truly human purpose. The consequence of this over-exertion on the one side is, inevitably, slackening on the other. When the fluctuation of competition is small, when demand and supply, consumption and production, are almost equal, a stage must be reached in the development of production where there is so much superfluous productive power that the great mass of the nation has nothing to live on, that the people starve from sheer abundance. For some considerable time England has found herself in this crazy position, in this living absurdity. When production is subject to greater fluctuations, as it is bound to be in consequence of such a situation, then the alternation of boom and crisis, over-production and slump, sets in. The economist has never been able to find an explanation for this mad situation. In order to explain it, he invented the population theory, which is just as senseless – indeed even more senseless than the contradiction of coexisting wealth and poverty. The economist *could not afford* to see the truth; he could not afford to admit that this contradiction is a simple consequence of competition; for in that case his entire system would have fallen to bits.

For us the matter is easy to explain. The productive power at mankind's disposal is immeasurable. The productivity of the soil can be increased *ad infinitum* by the application of capital, labour and science. According to the most able economists and statisticians (cf. Alison's *Principles of Population*, Vol. 1, Chs. 1 and 2), 'over-populated' Great Britain can be brought within ten years to produce a corn yield sufficient for a population six times its present size. Capital increases daily; labour power grows with population; and day by day science increasingly makes the forces of nature subject to man. This immeasurable productive capacity, handled consciously and in the interest of all, would soon reduce to a minimum the labour falling to the share of mankind. Left to competition, it does the same, but within a context of antitheses. One part of the land is cultivated in the best possible manner, whilst another part – in Great Britain and Ireland thirty million acres of good land – lies barren. One part of capital circulates with colossal speed; another lies dead in the chest. One part of the workers works fourteen or sixteen hours a day, whilst another part stands idle and inactive, and starves. Or the partition leaves this realm of simultaneity: today trade is good; demand is very considerable; everyone works; capital is turned over with miraculous speed; farming flourishes; the workers work themselves sick. Tomorrow stagnation sets in. The cultivation of the land is not worth the effort; entire stretches of land remain untilled; the flow of capital suddenly freezes; the workers have no employment, and the whole country labours under surplus wealth and surplus population.

The economist cannot afford to accept this exposition of the subject as correct; otherwise, as has been said, he would have to give up his whole system of competition. He would have to recognise the hollowness of his antithesis of production and consumption, of surplus population and surplus wealth. To bring fact and theory into conformity with each other – since this fact simply could not be denied – the population theory was invented.

Malthus, the originator of this doctrine, maintains that population is always pressing on the means of subsistence; that as soon as production increases, population increases in the same proportion; and that the inherent tendency of the population to multiply in excess of the available means of subsistence is the root of all misery and all vice. For, when there are too many people, they have to be disposed of in one way or another: either they must be killed by violence or they must starve. But when this has happened, there is once more a gap which other multipliers of the population immediately start to fill up once more: and so the old misery begins all over again. What is more, this is the case in all circumstances – not only in civilised, but also in primitive conditions. In New Holland,[3] with a population density of *one* per square mile, the savages suffer just as much from over-population as England. In short, if we want to be consistent, we must admit *that the earth was already over-populated when only one man*

[3] [The old name for Australia. (Tr.)]

existed. The implications of this line of thought are that since it is precisely the poor who are the surplus, nothing should be done for them except to make their dying of starvation as easy as possible, and to convince them that it cannot be helped and that there is no other salvation for their whole class than keeping propagation down to the absolute minimum. Or if this proves impossible, then it is after all better to establish a state institution for the painless killing of the children of the poor, such as 'Marcus' has suggested, whereby each working-class family would be allowed to have two and a half children, any excess being painlessly killed. Charity is to be considered a crime, since it supports the augmentation of the surplus population. Indeed, it will be very advantageous to declare poverty a crime and to turn poor-houses into prisons, as has already happened in England as a result of the new 'liberal' Poor Law. Admittedly it is true that this theory ill conforms with the Bible's doctrine of the perfection of God and of His creation; but 'it is a poor refutation to enlist the Bible against facts'.

Am I to go on any longer elaborating this vile, infamous theory, this hideous blasphemy against nature and mankind? Am I to pursue its consequences any further? Here at last we have the immorality of the economist brought to its highest pitch. What are all the wars and horrors of the monopoly system compared with this theory! And it is just this theory which is the keystone of the liberal system of free trade, whose fall entails the downfall of the entire edifice. For if here competition is proved to be the cause of misery, poverty and crime, who then will still dare to speak up for it?

In his above-mentioned work, Alison has shaken the Malthusian theory by bringing in the productive power of the land, and by opposing to the Malthusian principle the fact that each adult can produce more than he himself needs – a fact without which mankind could not multiply, indeed could not even exist; if it were not so how could those still growing up live? But Alison does not go to the root of the matter, and therefore in the end reaches the same conclusion as Malthus. True enough, he proves that Malthus' principle is incorrect, but cannot gainsay the facts which have impelled Malthus to his principle.

If Malthus had not considered the matter so one-sidedly, he could not have failed to see that surplus population or labour-power is invariable tied up with surplus wealth, surplus capital and surplus landed property. The population is only too large where the productive power as a whole is too large. The condition of every over-populated country, particularly England, since the time when Malthus wrote, makes this abundantly clear. These were the facts which Malthus ought to have considered in their totality, and whose consideration was bound to have led to the correct conclusion. Instead, he selected one fact, gave no consideration to the others, and therefore arrived at his crazy conclusion. The second error he committed was to confuse means of subsistence with [means of] employment. That population is always pressing on the means of employment – that the number of people produced depends on the number of people who can be employed – in short, that the production of labour-power has been regulated so far by the law of competition and is therefore also exposed to periodic crises and fluctuations – this is a fact whose establishment constitutes Malthus' merit. But the means of employment are not the means of subsistence. Only in their end-result are the means of employment increased by the increase in machine-power and capital. The means of subsistence increase as soon as productive power increases even slightly. Here a new contradiction in economics comes to light. The economist's 'demand' is not the real demand; his 'consumption' is an artificial consumption. For the economist, only that person really demands, only that person is a real consumer, who has an equivalent to offer for what he receives. But if it is a fact that every adult produces more than he himself can consume, that children are like trees which give superabundant returns on the outlays invested in them – and these certainly are facts, are they not? – then it must be assumed that each worker ought to be able to produce far more than he needs and that the community, therefore, ought to be very glad to provide him with everything he needs; one must consider a large family to be a very welcome gift for the community. But the economist, with his crude outlook, knows no other equivalent than that which is paid to him in tangible ready cash. He is so firmly set in his antitheses that the most striking facts are of as little concern to him as the most scientific principles.

We destroy the contradiction simply by transcending it. With the fusion of the interests now opposed to each other there disappears the contradiction between excess population here and excess wealth there; there disappears the miraculous fact (more miraculous than all the miracles of all the religions put together) that a nation has to starve from sheer wealth and plenty; and there disappears the crazy assertion that the earth lacks the power to feed men. This assertion is the pinnacle of Christian economics – and that our economics is essentially Christian I could have proved from every proposition, from every category, and shall in fact do so in due course. The Malthusian theory is but the economic expression of the religious dogma of the contradiction of spirit and nature and the resulting corruption of both. As regards religion, and together with religion, this contradiction was resolved long ago, and I hope that in the sphere of economics I have likewise demonstrated the utter emptiness of this contradiction. Moreover, I shall not accept as competent any defence of the Malthusian theory which does not explain to me on the basis of its own principles how a people can starve from sheer plenty and bring this into harmony with reason and fact.

At the same time, the Malthusian theory has certainly been a necessary point of transition which has taken us an immense step further. Thanks to this theory, as to economics as a whole, our attention has been drawn to the productive power of the earth and of mankind; and after overcoming this economic despair we have been made for ever secure against the fear of over-population. We derive from it the most powerful economic arguments for a social transformation. For even if Malthus were completely right, this transformation would have to be undertaken straight away; for only this transformation, only the education of the masses which it provides, makes possible that moral restraint of the propagative instinct which Malthus himself presents as the most effective and easiest remedy for over-population. Through this theory we have come to know the deepest degradation of mankind, their dependence on the conditions of competition. It has shown us how in the last instance private property has turned man into a commodity whose production and destruction also depend solely on demand; how the system of competition has thus slaughtered, and daily continues to slaughter, millions of men. All this we have seen, and all this drives us to the abolition of this degradation of mankind through the abolition of private property, competition and the opposing interests.

Yet, so as to deprive the universal fear of over-population of any possible basis, let us once more return to the relationship of productive power to population. Malthus establishes a formula on which he bases his entire system: population is said to increase in a geometrical progression – 1 + 2 + 4 + 8 + 16 + 32, etc.; the productive power of the land in an arithmetical progression – 1 + 2 + 3 + 4 + 5 + 6. The difference is obvious, is terrifying; but is it correct? Where has it been proved that the productivity of the land increases in an arithmetical progression? The extent of land is limited. All right! The labour-power to be employed on this land-surface increases with population. Even if we assume that the increase in yield due to increase in labour does not always rise in proportion to the labour, there still remains a third element which, admittedly, never means anything to the economist – science – whose progress is as unlimited and at least as rapid as that of population. What progress does the agriculture of this century owe to chemistry alone – indeed, to two men alone, Sir Humphry Davy and Justus Liebig! But science increases at least as much as population. The latter increases in proportion to the size of the previous generation, science advances in proportion to the knowledge bequeathed to it by the previous generation, and thus under the most ordinary conditions also in a geometrical progression. And what is impossible to science? But it is absurd to talk of over-population so long as 'there is enough waste land in the valley of the Mississippi for the whole population of Europe to be transplanted there', so long as no more than one-third of the earth can be considered cultivated, and so long as the production of this third itself can be raised sixfold and more by the application of improvements already known.

Thus, competition sets capital against capital, labour against labour, landed property against landed property; and likewise each of these elements against the other two. In the struggle the stronger wins; and in order to predict the outcome of the struggle, we shall have to investigate the strength of the contestants. First of all, labour is weaker than either landed property or capital, for the worker must work to live, whilst the landowner can live on his rent, and the capitalist on his interest, or, if the need arises, on his capital or on capitalised property in land. The result is that only the very barest necessities, the mere means of subsistence, fall to the lot of labour; whilst the largest part of the products is shared between capital and landed property. Moreover, the stronger worker drives the weaker out of the market, just as larger capital drives out smaller capital, and larger landed property drives out smaller landed property. Practice confirms this conclusion. The advantages which the larger manufacturer and merchant enjoy over the smaller, and the big landowner over the owner of a single acre, are well known. The result is that already under ordinary conditions, in accordance with the law of the stronger, large capital and large landed property swallow small capital and small landed property – i.e., centralisation of property. In crises of trade and agriculture, this centralisation proceeds much more rapidly.

In general large property increases much more rapidly than small property, since a much smaller portion is deducted from its proceeds as property-expenses. This law of the centralisation of private property is as immanent in private property as all the others. The middle classes must increasingly disappear until the world is divided into millionaires and paupers, into large landowners and poor farm labourers. All the laws, all the dividing of landed property, all the possible splitting-up of capital, are of no avail: this result must and will come, unless it is anticipated by a total transformation of social conditions, a fusion of opposed interests, an abolition of private property.

Free competition, the key-word of our present-day economists, is an impossibility. Monopoly at least intended to protect the consumer against fraud, even if it could not in fact do so. The abolition of monopoly, however, opens the door wide to fraud. You say that competition carries with it the remedy for fraud, since no one will buy bad articles. But that means that everyone has to be an expert in every article, which is impossible. Hence the necessity for monopoly, which many articles in fact reveal. Pharmacies, etc., *must* have a monopoly. And the most important article – money – requires a monopoly most of all. Whenever the circulating medium has ceased to be a state monopoly it has invariably produced a trade crisis; and the English economists, Dr Wade among them, do concede in this case the necessity for monopoly. But monopoly is no protection against counterfeit money. One can take one's stand on either side of the question: the one is as difficult as the other. Monopoly produces free competition, and the latter, in turn, produces monopoly. Therefore, both must fall, and these difficulties must be resolved through the transcendence of the principle which gives rise to them.

Competition has penetrated all the relationships of our life and completed the reciprocal bondage in which men now hold themselves. Competition is the great mainspring which again and again jerks into activity our aging and withering social order, or rather disorder; but with each new exertion it also saps a part of this order's waning strength. Competition governs the numerical advance of mankind; it likewise governs its moral advance. Anyone who has any knowledge of the statistics of crime must have been struck by the peculiar regularity with which crime advances year by year, and with which certain causes produce certain crimes. The extension of the factory system is followed everywhere by an increase in crime. The number of arrests, of criminal cases – indeed, the number of murders, burglaries, petty thefts, etc., for a large town or for a district – can be predicted year by year with unfailing precision, as has been done often enough in England. This regularity proves that crime, too, is governed by competition; that society creates a *demand* for crime which is met by a corresponding *supply*; that the gap created by the arrest, transportation or execution of a certain number is at once filled by others, just as every gap in population is at once filled by new arrivals; in other words, that crime presses on the means of punishment just as the people press on the means of employment. How just it is to punish criminals under these circumstances, quite apart from any other considerations, I leave to the judgment of my readers. Here I am merely concerned in demonstrating the extension of competition into the moral sphere, and in showing to what deep degradation private property has brought man.

In the struggle of capital and land against labour, the first two elements enjoy yet another special advantage over labour – the assistance of science; for in present conditions science, too, is directed against labour. Almost all mechanical inventions, for instance, have been occasioned by the lack of labour-power; in particular Hargreaves', Crompton's and Arkwright's cotton-spinning machines. There has never been an intense demand for labour which did not result in an invention that increased labour productivity considerably, thus diverting demand away from human labour. The history of England from 1770 until now is a continuous demonstration of this. The last great invention in cotton-spinning, the self-acting mule, was occasioned solely by the demand for labour, and rising wages. It doubled machine-labour, and thereby cut down hand-labour by half; it threw half the workers out of employment, and thereby reduced the wages of the others by half; it crushed a plot of the workers against the factory owners, and destroyed the last vestige of strength with which labour had still held out in the unequal struggle against capital. (Cf. Dr Ure, *Philosophy of Manufactures*, Vol. 2.) The economist now says, however, that in its final result machinery is favourable to the workers, since it makes production cheaper and thereby creates a new and larger market for its products, and thus ultimately re-employs the workers put out of work. Quite right. But is the economist forgetting, then, that the production of labour-power is regulated by competition; that labour-power is always pressing on the means of employment, and that, therefore, when these advantages are due to become operative, a surplus of competitors for work is already waiting for them, and will thus render these advantages illusory; whilst the disadvantages – the sudden withdrawal of the means of subsistence from one half of the workers and the fall in wages for the other half – are not illusory? Is the economist forgetting that the progress of invention never stands still, and that these disadvantages, therefore, perpetuate themselves? Is he forgetting that with the division of labour, developed to such a high degree by our civilisation, a worker can only live if he can be used at this particular machine for this particular detailed operation; that the change-over from one type of employment to another, newer type is almost invariably an absolute impossibility for the adult worker?

In turning my attention to the effects of machinery, I am brought to another subject less directly relevant – the factory system; and I have neither the inclination nor the time to treat this here. Besides, I hope to have an early opportunity to expound in detail the despicable immorality of this system, and to expose mercilessly the economist's hypocrisy which here appears in all its brazenness.

VIII
Karl Marx
1818–1883

Karl Marx

In a letter to his father of November 10, 1837, a nineteen-year-old Marx recounted the circumstances of his entry into the Berlin circle of Young Hegelians. He wrote that he had been ill, but

> during my illness, I had acquainted myself with Hegel from beginning to end, and most of his disciples as well. Through encounters with friends in Stralow [a section of Berlin] I became connected with a Doctor's Club, to which some instructors and my most intimate friend in Berlin, Dr Rutenberg, belong. In arguments many a conflicting opinion was voiced, and I was more and more chained to the current world philosophy [Hegelianism] from which I had thought to escape... Meanwhile, I have by no means abandoned the plan [to edit a journal of theatre criticism] all the more since all of the aesthetic notables of the Hegelian school have promised to co-operate, induced by instructor Bauer, who is important among them, and by my coadjutor, Dr Rutenberg.

This 'Doctor's Club' – which soon metamorphosed into the 'Free Ones' – was but one of the many informal groups that flourished in Berlin, clubs which accorded their like-minded participants a forum to criticize the continuing reactionary policies of King Friedrich Wilhelm III.

In the Doctor's Club, Marx was witness to and participant in the earliest expressions of Young Hegelianism. His association with this movement would last almost until its dissolution in the later 1840s. He was a representative member of the school, more talented than most – but in its context – less talented than some.

There were two sources from which every Young Hegelian drew his inspiration – Hegel and the other members of the school. The new truths were forged out of the solid metal of Hegelianism and then tempered in the heated debates that finally consumed the school itself. Marx's crucial encounters were first with Bauer and then, after leaving Berlin, Feuerbach. From one he learned to value the critical function of the intellect, from the other to value human goals over divine plans.

But in the course of time – and 1845 might be set as the date which terminates his philosophical apprenticeship – Marx finally established Marxism, and although it cannot be comprehended apart from its historic premises in Young Hegelianism, it is nevertheless not simply reducible to them. Marxism, just as all of the philosophical products that emerged out of the argumentative crucible of Young Hegelianism, is not merely an eclectic summation of post-Hegelianism, but a distinctive synthesis with its own character and unity.

The following two brief selections from Marx's early writings are merely intended to exemplify his attitudes during that period in his life in which he turned from being the mere critic of Hegel into the Marx of *The Communist Manifesto.*

Both the *Letter to Ruge* and *The Introduction to the Critique of Hegel's Philosophy of Right*, were first published in the *German–French Yearbooks*, which Marx and Ruge co-edited in the hope of fusing German and French liberalism.

Marx's *Letter to Ruge*, newly translated by the editor for this anthology, is but one of three letters written by Marx to Ruge which were published in the *Yearbooks.* It is the most interesting, for it reveals just how Hegelianism – left unmentioned – exercised a decisive influence not only upon Marx's rejection of the then-prevalent forms of utopian communism, but also upon his own final program of social reform. There is one item of interest in this new translation, the translation of the phrase 'die rücksichtslose Kritik alles Bestehenden'. This is perhaps the most important phrase of the letter, and the only one that Marx emphasized by italics. It has been sometimes translated as 'a ruthless criticism of everything existing', but this is incorrect if one considers both the context and the etymological basis of the term 'rücksichtslose'. In context and meaning the phrase seems best translated as 'the unrestrained [or uninhibited] criticism of everything established'. This reading renders Marx a bit less ferocious and a bit more clinical.

In March of 1842, Marx mentioned in a letter to Ruge that he was planning a criticism of Hegel's *Philosophy of Right.* But although the work was never completed, Marx nevertheless wrote out some 150 pages of a paragraph-by-paragraph analysis of the section in the *Philosophy of Right* which dealt with the internal constitution of the state. The *introduction* which appears in this anthology is the only part of the projected criticism that was fully prepared for publication. Marx, once having lost interest in the original project, found a place for the *introduction* in the *Yearbooks.*

The following translation of Karl Marx's *introduction* to this planned criticism of Hegel's *Philosophy of Right* is taken from *Karl Marx's Critique of Hegel's 'Philosophy of Right'*, translated by Annette Jolin and Joseph O'Malley (Cambridge University Press, 1970).

Letter to Arnold Ruge

Kreuznach, September 1843

I am happy you have made up your mind, and now turn your thoughts forward to a new undertaking, and away from a looking back upon the past. And so Paris, the old university of Philosophy – *absit omen* [let there be no omen]! and the new capital of the new world. What needs be will take care of itself. I have no doubt that all obstacles, whose gravity I do not ignore, will be overcome.

The undertaking may be successful or not, but in any case I will be in Paris at the end of this month, for here the air makes one servile, and I can see no room whatsoever for free action in Germany.

In Germany, everything is being forcibly crushed, a veritable anarchy of the Spirit, an army of ignorance has broken out, and Zurich obeys the orders of Berlin. It becomes ever clearer that a new rallying point must be sought out for the really thinking and independent minds. I am convinced that our plan would satisfy a real need, and real needs must indeed be able to find real fulfillment. I have, therefore, no doubts about the undertaking if it be taken seriously.

The inner difficulties seem almost to be greater than the outer obstacles. For even if there is no doubt about the 'whence', all the more dominates the confusion over the 'whither'. Apart from the eruption of general anarchy among the reformers, each must know that there is no exact view of what should be. But indeed in this the new direction has an advantage, for we do not dogmatically anticipate a new world, but will find it through the criticism of the old. Up to now philosophers had the solution of all riddles lying in their lecterns, and the ignorant world of the present had but to gape in order that the roasted dove of Absolute Knowledge fly directly into its mouth. Philosophy has made itself worldly, and the most striking proof of this is that the philosophic consciousness has not only externally, but internally as well, been pulled into the torment of the worldly struggle. If then it is not our concern to construct the future and to establish eternal answers, then it is all the more certain what we must now bring to fruition, I mean the *unrestrained criticism of everything established*, unrestrained not only in not fearing its own results, but even less of a conflict with whatever powers may be.

I am not at all concerned that we send up a dogmatic banner – quite the contrary – we must seek to help the Dogmatists come to an understanding of their own principles. In this light, even *Communism* is a dogmatic abstraction, and here I do not have in mind some imaginary and possible communism, but the actually existing and taught communism of Cabet, Dezamy, Weitling, etc. This communism is itself but a limited expression of a Humanism infected by its opposite principle, private being. This communism and the transcending of private property are in no manner identical, and it is not by chance that other socialistic doctrines, such as those of Fourier, Proudhon, etc., have arisen in opposition to it, for it is in itself but a one-sided and limited development of the socialist principle.

The total socialist principle expresses again only the one side, the *realistic* side, of true human existence. We, however, must concern ourselves just as much with the other side, the theoretical existence of man, to make religion, science, etc., the objects of our criticism. Beyond this we want to have an impact upon our contemporaries, and particularly upon our German contemporaries. The question here is: 'How is that to be effected?' Two kinds of facts cannot be avoided. First, religion, then politics are the objects which command the greatest interest in present Germany. We must, however, take these up as they are, and not set them against some completed system such as *The Voyage to Icaria* [Etienne Cabet's 1842 utopian novel].

Reason has always existed, but not always in a reasonable form. Hence, the critic can take up any form of the theoretical and practical consciousness, and then develop out of this *singular* form of actual reality the final goal and norm of true reality itself. Insofar as present life is concerned, the *political state* in all its modern forms, even when it is not yet conscious of socialist requirements, is yet filled with the requirements of reason. But the state does not stop at that. It envisions reason as everywhere actual. But exactly here there is everywhere a contradiction between its ideal determination and its present principles.

Out of this conflict of the political state with itself social truth in general will develop. As religion is the catalogue of the theoretical struggles of mankind, so the political state is to its practical struggles. Hence, within its form the political state expresses *sub specie rei publicae* [under the category of politics], all social struggles, needs, and truths. And so, it is not at all beneath the *hauteur des principles* to make the most specialized political questions – such as the difference between the corporative system [representation by class] and the representative system [representation by individuals] as an object of criticism. This question only expresses in a political manner the difference between the rule of private property and the rule of men. Hence, the Critic not only can but must enter into these political questions (which are considered by the crass kind of socialist as beneath anyone's dignity). In that he demonstrates the advantages of the representative system over the corporate, the Critic *practically interests* a large party. In that he abstracts the representative system out of its political form and elevates it into a general form, validating its fundamental meaning, he forces the political party to extend beyond its own limits, for here its very victory is at the same time its defeat.

And so, nothing stops our criticism from being a criticism of politics, a participation in politics, an engagement in *actual* struggles, and an identification with them. We do not then confront the world dogmatically with a new principle: 'Here is the Truth, kneel before it!' We develop new principles for the world out of the principles of the world. We do not say: 'Stop fighting, it is a waste of time, we want to tell you the true campaign-slogans', no, we are only showing you why you really fight, and consciousness is the thing which you must acquire – whether you want it or not.

The reform of consciousness *only* resides in letting the world perceive its own consciousness, to awaken it out of the dream of itself, to explain its actions to itself. Our whole purpose – as in the case of Feuerbach's critique of religion – is nothing else but the bringing of religious and political questions into self-conscious human form. Hence our maxim must be: do not reform consciousness through dogma, but through the analysis of the mystical, self-confused consciousness let it be explicated as either religious or political. It will then be revealed that is not a matter of dealing with a great dividing line between the past and the future, but rather of *completing* the thoughts of the past. And at last, it will be revealed that mankind brings forth no *new* work, but only the conscious completion of its old work.

And so, we can catch the direction of our journal in *one* word: the self-consciousness (critical philosophy) of the Age concerning its own struggles and desires. This is a task for the world and for us. It can only be the work of united powers. It is a matter of *confession*, nothing more. To have their sins forgiven, men need only understand what they are.

A Contribution to the Critique of Hegel's 'Philosophy of Right'

INTRODUCTION

For Germany, the critique of religion is essentially completed; and the critique of religion is the prerequisite of every critique.

Error in its profane form of existence is compromised once its celestial *oratio pro aris et focis* has been refuted. Man, who has found only his own reflection in the fantastic reality of heaven, where he sought a supernatural being, will no longer be disposed to find only the semblance of himself, only a non-human being, here where he seeks and must seek his true reality.

The foundation of irreligious criticism is this: man makes religion; religion does not make man. Religion is, in fact, the self-consciousness and self-esteem of man who has either not yet gained himself or has lost himself again. But man is no abstract being squatting outside the world. Man is the world of man, the state, society. This state, this society, produce religion, which is an inverted world-consciousness, because they are an inverted world. Religion is the general theory of this world, its encyclopedic compendium, its logic in popular form, its spiritualistic *point d'honneur*, its enthusiasm, its moral sanction, its solemn complement, its universal basis of consolation and justification. It is the fantastic realization of the human being because the human being has attained no true reality. Thus, the struggle against religion is indirectly the struggle against that world of which religion is the spiritual aroma.

The wretchedness of religion is at once an expression of and a protest against real wretchedness. Religion is the sigh of the oppressed creature, the heart of a heartless world and the soul of soulless conditions. It is the opium of the people.

The abolition of religion as the illusory happiness of the people is a demand for their true happiness. The call to abandon illusions about their condition is the call to abandon a condition which requires illusions. Thus, the critique of religion is the critique in embryo of the vale of tears of which religion is the halo.

Criticism has plucked the imaginary flowers from the chain, not so that man shall bear the chain without fantasy or consolation, but so that he shall cast off the chain and gather the living flower. The critique of religion disillusions man so that he will think, act, and fashion his reality as a man who has lost his illusions and regained his reason, so that he will revolve about himself as his own true sun. Religion is only the illusory sun about which man revolves so long as he does not revolve about himself.

It is the task of history, therefore, once the other-world of truth has vanished, to establish the truth of this world. It is above all the task of philosophy, which is in the service of history, to unmask human self-alienation in its secular forms, once its sacred form has been unmasked. Thus, the critique of heaven is transformed into the critique of the earth, the critique of religion into the critique of law, the critique of theology into the critique of politics.

The following exposition[1] – which is a contribution to this task – does not deal directly with the original, but with a copy, i.e., with the German philosophy of the state and of right, simply because it deals with Germany.

If we were to begin with the German *status quo* itself, even in the only appropriate way, which is negatively, the result would still be an anachronism. For even the negation of our political present is already a dusty fact in the historical junkroom of modern nations. If I negate powdered wigs, I still have unpowdered wigs. If I negate the German conditions of 1843, I am according to French chronology barely in the year 1789, and still less at the center of the present day.

Indeed, German history prides itself on a development which no other nation has previously achieved or will ever imitate in the historical firmament. We have shared in the restorations of modern nations without ever having shared in their revolutions. We have been restored, first because other nations ventured a revolution, and second because other nations endured a counter-revolution; in the first case because our leaders were afraid, and in the second case because they were not. Led by our shepherds, we have only once been in the company of liberty, and that was on the day of its interment.

One school of thought, which justifies the infamy of today by the infamy of yesterday, a school which interprets every cry of the serf under the knout as a cry of rebellion once the knout is time-honored, ancestral, and historical, a school to which history shows only its *a posteriori* as did the God of Israel to his servant Moses – the Historical School of Law – might well have invented German history were it not itself an invention of German history. A Shylock, but a servile

[1] [That is, the projected revision of the *Critique of Hegel's 'Philosophy of Right'* (§§261–313). (Tr.)]

Shylock, it swears by its bond, its historical bond, its Christian–Germanic bond, for every pound of flesh cut from the heart of the people.

On the other hand, good-natured enthusiasts, German nationalists by sentiment and enlightened radicals by reflection, seek our history of freedom beyond our history in the primeval Teutonic forests. But then how does our history of freedom differ from that of the wild boar, if it is only to be found in the forests? Besides, as the saying goes: what is shouted into the forests echoes back from the forest. So peace to the primeval Teutonic forests!

But war upon the conditions in Germany! By all means! They are beneath the level of history, beneath all criticism; yet they remain an object of criticism just as the criminal who is beneath the level of humanity remains an object of the executioner. In its struggle against them criticism is no passion of the brain, but is rather the brain of passion. It is not a scalpel but a weapon. Its object is its enemy, which it wishes not to refute but to destroy. For the spirit of these conditions is already refuted. They are not, in themselves, objects worthy of thought, but rather existences equally despicable and despised. Criticism itself needs no further self-clarification regarding this object, for criticism already understands it. Criticism is no longer an end in itself, but now simply a means. Indignation is its essential pathos, denunciation its principal task.

It is a matter of describing the stifling pressure of all the social spheres on one another, the universal, passive ill-feeling, the recognized yet misunderstood narrow-mindedness, all framed in a system of government which, living by the conservation of all this wretchedness, is itself wretchedness in government.

What a spectacle! The infinite division of society into the most diverse races confronting one another with their petty antipathies, bad conscience and crude mediocrity, and which, precisely because of their mutual ambiguous and suspicious disposition, are treated by their masters without distinction, though with differing formalities, as merely tolerated existences. And they are to recognize and acknowledge the very fact that they are dominated, ruled and possessed as a concession from Heaven! On the other hand there are the masters themselves, whose greatness is in inverse proportion to their number!

Criticism dealing with this situation is criticism in hand-to-hand combat; and in this kind of combat one does not bother about whether the opponent is noble, or of equal rank, or interesting; all that matters is to strike him. It is a question of permitting the Germans not a single moment of illusion or resignation. The burden must be made still more oppressive by adding to it a consciousness of it, and the shame made still more shameful by making it public. Every sphere of German society must be described as the *partie honteuse* of German society, and these petrified conditions must be made to dance by singing to them their own melody. The nation must be taught to be terrified of itself in order to give it courage. In this way an imperative need of the German nation will be fulfilled, and the needs of nations are themselves the final causes of their satisfaction.

This struggle against the limited content of the German *status quo* is not without interest even for the modern nations; for the German *status quo* is the overt perfection of the *ancien régime*, and the *ancien régime* is the hidden defect of the modern state. The struggle against the political present in Germany is the struggle against the past of the modern nations, who are still continually troubled by the reminiscences of this past. It is instructive for them to see the *ancien régime*, which experienced its moment of tragedy in their history, play its comic role as a German ghost. Its history was tragic so long as it was the privileged power in the world and freedom was a personal fancy; in short, so long as it believed, and necessarily so, in its own justification. So long as the *ancien régime*, as the existing world order, struggled against a new world coming into existence, it was guilty of a world-historical, but not a personal, error. Its decline was, therefore, tragic.

The present German régime, on the other hand – an anachronism, a flagrant contradiction of universally recognized axioms, the nullity of the *ancien régime* revealed to the whole world – only imagines that it believes in itself, and asks that the world imagine this also. If it believed in its own nature, would it hide that nature under the appearance of an alien nature, and seek its preservation in hypocrisy and sophistry? The modern *ancien régime* is nothing but the humbug of a world order whose real heroes are dead. History is thorough, and passes through many phases when it conveys an old form to the grave. The final phase of a world-historical form is its comedy. The Greek gods already once mortally wounded, tragically, in Aeschylus' *Prometheus Bound*, had to die once more, comically, in the dialogues of Lucian. Why does history proceed in this way? So that mankind will separate itself happily from its past. We claim this happy historical destiny for the political powers of Germany.

Meanwhile, the moment modern political and social actuality is subjected to criticism, the moment, therefore, criticism focuses on genuine human problems, either it finds itself outside the German *status quo* or it must treat its object under a different form. For example, the relationship of industry, of the world of wealth in general, to the political world is a major problem of modern times. Under what form does this problem begin to occupy the Germans? Under the form of protective tariffs, the system of prohibitions, national economy. German chauvinism has passed from men to matter, and so one fine morning our cavaliers of cotton and heroes of iron found themselves metamorphosed into patriots, Thus, in Germany the sovereignty of monopoly within the nation has begun to be recognized through its being invested with sovereignty *vis-à-vis* other nations. In Germany, therefore, we now begin with what in France and England is the end of a development. The old decayed state of affairs against which these nations are in theoretical revolt, and which they still bear only as chains are borne, is welcomed in Germany as the dawning of a glorious future as yet hardly daring to proceed from a cunning [*listigen*][2] theory to a pitiless practice. While in France and England the problem reads: political economy or the mastery of society over wealth; in Germany it reads: national economy or the mastery of private property over nationality. Thus, in France and England it is a question of abolishing monopoly, which has progressed to its final consequences, while in Germany it is a question of proceeding on to the final consequences of monopoly. There it is a question of the solution, here only a question of the collision. This is an adequate example of the German form of modern problems, an example of how our history, like a raw recruit, has until now only done extra drill on old historical matters.

If the whole of German development were at the level of German political development, a German could participate in contemporary problems no more than can a Russian. But if the single individual is not limited by the boundaries of the nation, still less is the nation as a whole liberated by the liberation of one individual. That a Scythian [Anacharsis] was numbered among the Greek philosophers did not enable the Scythians to advance a step toward Greek culture.

Fortunately, we Germans are not Scythians.

Just as ancient peoples lived their past history in their imagination, in mythology, so we Germans have lived our future history in thought, in philosophy. We are philosophical contemporaries of the present day without being its historical contemporaries. German philosophy is the ideal prolongation of German history. If, then, we criticize the *œuvres posthumes* of our ideal history, philosophy, instead of the *œuvres incomplètes* of our actual history, our criticism centers on the very questions of which the present age says: that is the question.

[2] [A punning reference to Friedrich List (1789–1846) whose economic theory was published under the title *Das nationale System der politischen Œkonomie* (1840). (Tr.)]

What for advanced nations is a practical break with modern political conditions is in Germany, where these conditions themselves do not yet exist, essentially a critical break with their philosophical reflection.

German philosophy of right and the state is the only German history that is *al pari* with official modern times. Thus, the German nation is obliged to connect its dream history with its present circumstances, and subject to criticism not only these circumstances but also their abstract continuation. Its future can be restricted neither to the direct negation of its real, nor to the direct fulfillment of its ideal, political and juridical circumstances; for the direct negation of its real circumstances is already there in its ideal circumstances, and it has almost outlived the direct fulfilment of these in its contemplation of neighboring nations. The practical political party in Germany is right, therefore, in demanding the negation of philosophy. Its error lies not in the demand, but in limiting itself to the demand which it neither does nor can fulfil. It believes that it can achieve this negation by turning its back on philosophy, averting its gaze, and murmuring a few irritable and trite phrases about it. In its narrow outlook it does not even count philosophy a part of German actuality, or it considers philosophy to be beneath the level of German practical life and its attendant theories. You [of the practical party] demand that actual germs of life be the point of departure, but you forget that the German nation's actual germs of life have until now sprouted only in its cranium. In short, you cannot transcend philosophy without actualizing it.

The same error, but with the elements reversed, was committed by the theoretical political party, which originated in philosophy.

This party saw in the present struggle only the critical struggle of philosophy against the German world. It failed to note that previous philosophy itself belongs to this world and is its complement, even if only an ideal complement. Critical of its counterpart, it remained uncritical of itself: it took its point of departure from the presuppositions of philosophy, and either accepted the conclusions reached by philosophy or else presented as directly philosophical demands and results drawn from elsewhere; even though these – assuming their validity – are obtainable only through the negation of previous philosophy, i.e., of philosophy as philosophy. We reserve until later a fuller account of this party. Its basic defect reduces to this: it believed that it could actualize philosophy without transcending it.

The criticism of the German philosophy of right and of the state, which was given its most logical, profound and complete expression by Hegel, is at once the critical analysis of the modern state and of the reality connected with it, and the definite negation of all the past forms of consciousness in German jurisprudence and politics, whose most distinguished and most general expression, raised to the level of a science, is precisely the speculative philosophy of right. If it was only in Germany that the speculative philosophy of right was possible – this abstract and extravagant thought about the modern state, whose reality remains in another world (even though this is just across the Rhine) – the German thought-version [*Gedankenbild*] of the modern state, on the other hand, which abstracts from actual man, was only possible because and in so far as the modern state itself abstracts from actual man, or satisfies the whole man only in an imaginary way. In politics the Germans have thought what other nations have done. Germany was their theoretical conscience. The abstract and presumptive character of its thinking was in step with the partial and stunted character of their actuality. If, then, the *status quo* of the German political system expresses the perfection of the *ancien régime*, the thorn in the flesh of the modern state, the *status quo* of German political thought expresses the imperfection of the modern state, the damaged condition of the flesh itself.

As the determined adversary of the prevailing mode of German political consciousness, criticism of the speculative philosophy of right does not remain within itself, but proceeds on to tasks for whose solution there is only one means – *praxis*.

The question arises: can Germany attain a praxis *à la hauteur des principes*, that is to say, a revolution that will raise it not only to the official level of modern nations, but to the human level which will be the immediate future of these nations?

The weapon of criticism certainly cannot replace the criticism of weapons; material force must be overthrown by material force; but theory, too, becomes a material force once it seizes the masses. Theory is capable of seizing the masses once it demonstrates *ad hominem*, and it demonstrates *ad hominem* once it becomes radical. To be radical is to grasp matters at the root. But for man the root is man himself. The manifest proof of the radicalism of German theory, and thus of its practical energy, is the fact of its issuing from a resolute positive transcendence [*Aufhebung*] of religion. The critique of religion ends in the doctrine that man is the supreme being for man; thus it ends with the categorical imperative to overthrow all conditions in which man is a debased, enslaved, neglected, contemptible being – conditions which cannot be better described than by the Frenchman's exclamation about a proposed tax on dogs: 'Poor dogs! They want to treat you like men!'

Even from the historical point of view, theoretical emancipation has a specific practical importance for Germany. Germany's revolutionary past is precisely theoretical: it is the Reformation. As at that time it was a monk, so now it is the philosopher in whose brain the revolution begins.

Luther, to be sure, overcame servitude based on devotion, but by replacing it with servitude based on conviction. He shattered faith in authority by restoring the authority of faith. He transformed the priests into laymen by changing the laymen into priests. He liberated man from external religiosity by making religiosity that which is innermost to man. He freed the body of chains by putting the heart in chains.

But if Protestantism was not the real solution it at least posed the problem correctly. Thereafter it was no longer a question of the layman's struggle with the priest outside of him, but of his struggle with his own inner priest, his priestly nature. And if the Protestant transformation of the German laity into priests emancipated the lay popes – the princes together with their clergy, the privileged and the philistines – so the philosophical transformation of the priestly Germans into men will emancipate the people. But just as emancipation is not limited to the princes, so the secularization of property will not be limited to the confiscation of church property, which was practiced especially by hypocritical Prussia. At that time, the Peasant War, the most radical event in German history, foundered because of theology. Today, when theology itself has foundered, the most unfree thing in German history, our *status quo*, will be shattered by philosophy. On the eve of the Reformation official Germany was the most abject servant of Rome. On the even of its revolution Germany is the abject servant of those who are inferior to Rome, of Prussia and Austria, of petty squires and philistines.

However, a major difficulty appears to stand in the way of a radical German revolution.

Revolutions require a passive element, a material basis. Theory will be realized in a people only in so far as it is the realization of their needs. Will the enormous discrepancy between the demands of German thought and the answers of German actuality be matched by a similar discrepancy between civil society and the state, and within civil society itself? Will theoretical needs be directly practical needs? It is not enough that thought strive to actualize itself; actuality must itself strive toward thought.

But Germany has not passed through the middle state of political emancipation at the same time as the modern nations. The very stages it has surpassed in theory it has not yet reached in practice. How is Germany, with a *salto mortale*, to surmount not only its own limitations, but also those of the modern nations, limitations which it must actually experience and strive for as the liberation from its own actual limitations? A radical revolution can only be a revolution of radical needs, whose preconditions and birthplaces appear to be lacking.

But if Germany accompanied the development of modern nations only with the abstract of thought, without taking an active part in the actual struggles of this development, it has still shared the pains of this development without sharing its pleasures or its partial satisfaction. The abstract activity on the one hand corresponds to the abstract pain on the other. One day Germany will find itself at the level of European decadence before it has ever achieved the level of European emancipation. It will be like a fetishist suffering from the illnesses of Christianity.

If we examine the German governments we find that the circumstances of the time, the situation in Germany, the viewpoint of German culture, and finally their own lucky instinct, all drive them to combine the civilized deficiencies of the modern political world, whose advantages we do not enjoy, with the barbaric deficiencies of the *ancien régime*, which we enjoy in full measure; so that Germany must participate more and more, if not in the rationality, at least in the irrationality of the political forms that transcend its *status quo*. For example, is there any country in the world which shares as naively as so-called constitutional Germany all the illusions of the constitutional régime without any of its realities? Wasn't it somehow necessarily a German government brain-wave to combine the torments of censorship with those of the French September Laws [of 1835], which presuppose the freedom of the press! Just as the gods of all nations were found in the Roman Pantheon, so the sins of all state-forms are to be found in the Holy Roman German Empire. That this eclecticism will attain an unprecedented level is assured by the politico-aesthetic *gourmanderie* of a German king [Frederick William IV], who intends to play all the roles of royalty – the feudal as well as the bureaucratic, absolute as well as constitutional, autocratic as well as democratic – if not in the person of the people at least in his own person, if not for the people at least for himself. Germany, as the deficiency of the political present constituted into an individual system, will be unable to demolish the specific German limitations without demolishing the general limitations of the political present.

It is not a radical revolution, universal human emancipation, that is a utopian dream for Germany, but rather a partial, merely political revolution, a revolution that leaves the pillars of the edifice standing. What is the basis of a partial, merely political revolution? It is this:

a section of civil society emancipates itself and achieves universal dominance; a determinate class undertakes from its particular situation the universal emancipation of society. This class emancipates the whole society, but only on the condition that the whole society shares its situation; for example, that it has or can obtain money and education.

No class of civil society can play this role unless it arouses in itself and in the masses a moment of enthusiasm, a moment in which it associates, fuses, and identifies itself with society in general, and is felt and recognized to be society's general representative, a moment in which its demands and rights are truly those of society itself, of which it is the social head and heart. Only in the name of the universal rights of society can a particular class lay claim to universal dominance. To take over this liberating position, and therewith the political exploitation of all the spheres of society in the interest of its own sphere, revolutionary energy and spiritual self-confidence do not suffice. For a popular revolution and the emancipation of a particular class to coincide, for one class to stand for the whole of society, another class must, on the other hand, concentrate in itself all the defects of society, must be the class of universal offense and the embodiment of universal limits. A particular social sphere must stand for the notorious crime of the whole society, so that liberation from this sphere appears to be universal liberation. For one class to be the class *par excellence* of liberation, another class must, on the other hand, be openly the subjugating class. The negative general significance of the French nobility and clergy determined the positive general significance of the bourgeoisie, the class standing next to and opposing them.

But every class in Germany lacks the consistency, the keenness, the courage, and the ruthlessness which would mark it as the negative representative of society. Moreover, every class lacks that breadth of soul which identifies it, if only for a moment, with the soul of the people; that genius which animates material force into political power; that revolutionary boldness which flings at its adversary the defiant phrase: I am nothing and I should be everything. The principle feature of German morality and honor, not only in individuals but in classes as well, is that modest egoism which asserts its narrowness and allows narrowness to be asserted against it. The relationship of the different spheres of German society is, therefore, not dramtic, but epic. Each of them begins to be aware of itself and to establish itself with its particular claims beside the others, not as soon as it is oppressed, but as soon as circumstances independent of its actions create a lower social stratum against which it can in turn exert pressure. Even the moral self-esteem of the German middle class is based merely on the consciousness of being the general representative of the philistine mediocrity of all the other classes. It is, therefore, not only the German kings who ascend the throne *mal à propos*. Each sphere of civil society suffers its defeat before it celebrates its victory, erects its own barrier before it overthrows its opposing barrier, asserts its narrow-minded nature before it can assert its generosity, so that the opportunity of playing a great role has passed before it ever actually existed, and each class, at the moment it begins to struggle with the class above it, is involved in the struggle with the class beneath. Hence, the princes are in conflict with the king, the bureaucracy with the nobility, the bourgeoisie with all of them, while the proletariat is already beginning its struggle against the bourgeoisie. The middle class hardly dares to conceive of the idea of emancipation from its own point of view, and already the development of social conditions and the progress of political theory show that this point of view itself is antiquated, or at least questionable.

In France it is enough to be something in order to desire to be everything. In Germany no one may be anything unless he renounces everything. In France partial emancipation is the basis of universal emancipation. In Germany universal emancipation is the *conditio sine qua non* for any partial emancipation. In France it is the actuality, in Germany the impossibility, of gradual emancipation which must give birth to full freedom. In France every national class is politically idealistic and considers itself above all to be not a particular class but the representative of the needs of society overall. The role of the emancipator thus passes in a dramatic movement to the different classes of the French nation, until it finally reaches the class which actualizes social freedom no longer on the basis of presupposed conditions which are at once external to man yet created by human society, but rather organizing all the conditions of human existence on the basis of social freedom. In Germany, on the other hand, where practical life is as little intellectual as intellectual life is practical, no class of civil society has the need and the capacity for universal emancipation until it is forced to it by its immediate situation, material necessity, and its very chains.

Where, then, is the positive possibility of German emancipation?

Our answer: in the formation of a class with radical chains, a class in civil society that is not of civil society, a class that is the dissolution of all classes, a sphere of society having a universal character because of its universal suffering and claiming no particular right because no particular wrong but unqualified wrong is perpetrated on it; a sphere that can claim no traditional title but only a human title; a sphere that does not stand partially opposed to the consequences, but totally opposed to the premises of the German political system; a sphere, finally, that cannot emancipate itself without emancipating itself from all the other spheres of society, thereby emancipating them; a sphere, in short, that is the complete loss of humanity and can only redeem itself through the total redemption of humanity. This dissolution of society existing as a particular class is the proletariat.

The proletariat is only beginning to appear in Germany as a result of the industrial development taking place. For it is not naturally existing poverty but artificially produced poverty, not the mass of men mechanically oppressed by the weight of society but the mass of men resulting from society's, and especially the middle class', acute dissolution that constitutes the proletariat – though at the same time, needless to say, victims of natural poverty and Christian–Germanic serfdom also become members.

When the proletariat announces the dissolution of the existing order of things it merely declares the secret of its own existence, for it *is* the *de facto* dissolution of this order of things. When the proletariat demands the negation of private property it merely elevates into a principle of society what society has advanced as the principle of the proletariat, and what the proletariat already involuntarily embodies as the negative result of society. The proletariat thus has the same right relative to the new world which is coming into being as has the German king relative to the existing world, when he calls the people his people and a horse his horse. In calling the people his private property the king merely expresses the fact that the owner of private property is king.

Just as philosophy finds its material weapons in the proletariat, so the proletariat finds its spiritual weapons in philosophy; and once the lightning of thought has struck deeply into this naive soil of the people the emancipation of the Germans into men will be accomplished.

Let us summarize:

The only practically possible emancipation of Germany is the emancipation based on the unique theory which holds that man is the supreme being for man. In Germany emancipation from the Middle Ages is possible only as the simultaneous emancipation from the partial victories over the Middle Ages. In Germany no form of bondage can be broken unless every form of bondage is broken. Germany, enamored of fundamentals, can have nothing less than a fundamental revolution. The emancipation of Germany is the emancipation of man. The head of this emancipation is philosophy, its heart is the proletariat. Philosophy cannot be actualized without the abolition [*Aufhebung*] of the proletariat; the proletariat cannot be abolished without the actualization of philosophy.

When all the intrinsic conditions are fulfilled, the day of German resurrection will be announced by the crowing of the Gallic cock.

IX
Max Stirner
1806–1856

Max Stirner

Johann Caspar Schmidt, better known under the *nom-de-guerre* of Max Stirner, was the enthusiastic devil's-advocate of the Young Hegelians. Although a companionable participant within the circle of 'Free Ones', Stirner yet found them just as deserving of criticism as the defenders of ossified Church and conservative state. Indeed, 'criticism' seems too mild a term to apply to Stirner's major work, *The Ego and His Own* [*Der Einzige und sein Eigentum*]. Its appearance, in the winter of 1844, was more of the order of a 'bombshell'–as Sidney Hook characterizes it–than a literary criticism. None were spared from its brilliant and vitriolic criticism, not the apparent revolutionaries and atheists of the time, nor the leader of the Berlin Young Hegelians, Bruno Bauer, nor Feuerbach, nor even the one-time editor of the redical *Rheinische Zeitung*, Karl Marx. Stirner turned on all, for he understood the 'new radicalism' to be in essence nothing more than the 'old orthodoxy', with the emerging Humanisms and Socialisms of his age being nothing more than the recrudence of the ancient delusions of religion. Stirner proposed a simple solution: the individual ego must be made conscious of its power over its own ideas. Ideas, once freed from the power of the individual mind by the perversion of that mind, were transformed into 'Ideals' which then turned–as Frankenstein's monster–upon their maker. Stirner's 'egoism' is but another name for a radically assertive self-consciousness that rejects self-generated slavery.

Stirner, along with Bauer and Feuerbach, shared the rare honor of having heard Hegel lecture, but unlike them did not gain an early recognition, and what recognition he finally did gain–with *The Ego and His Own*–was soon lost in the general shipwreck of Young Hegelianism. Nevertheless, this singular, and most stylistically and thematically striking of all their literature, has retained a small but constant readership. Stirner, who died in abject poverty with only Bruno Bauer and Adolph Rutenburg as his mourners, would hardly have imagined that his future was assured–particularly since *The Ego* had been out of print some years before his death; but since its publication in a small edition by Otto Wiegand, the daring radical publisher, it has appeared in over one hundred editions, and has been translated into eight languages.

In 1897, under the title of *Kleinere Schriften*, Stirner's minor writings were issued by his biographer John Henry Mackay. An expanded, but still incomplete edition of these short journal and newspaper articles was issued by Mackay in 1914. This second edition has been reissued.[1] Although various of these lesser writings have been translated, and a critical French translation of the full *Kleinere Schriften* has been undertaken,[2] the English-language reader has had the opportunity to read only one of these essays, *Das Unwahre Prinzip unser Erziehung*, which was given the title *The False Principle of our Education*.[3] And so, although the following translation from the *Kleinere Schriften* of 'Kunst und Religion' is not lengthy, it does represent a substantive expansion of Stirner's works now available to the English-language reader. The essay has been translated and annotated by the editor of this anthology. It is not only of interest in relating Stirner to Hegelianism, but also exemplifies an attempt on the part of Young Hegelianism, instanced particularly in Arnold Ruge and 'Young Germany', to tie art to politics.

The selections taken from *Der Einzige und sein Eigentum* are drawn from the excellent 1907 translation by Steven T. Byington, *The Ego and His Own*. This same translation has been employed in all of the eleven subsequent English language editions of this work, the last issue in 1995, by Cambridge University Press.

The selections in this text follow the order of their appearance in the original. That section entitled 'All Things are Nothing to Me' prefacing the first section of *The Ego and His Own*, with the section 'Ownness' comprising the third part of the work and that selection entitled 'The unique One' being the concluding section of the book. The annotations to the text are, if in parentheses, those of Byington. Stirner's notes are left unenclosed.

For the reader wishing to pursue a further study of Stirner, *The Nihilistic Egoist: Max Stirner* by R. W. K. Paterson (Oxford University Press, 1971) can be recommended. It is presently the only full-length study of Stirner available in English.

1 [Max Stirner: *Kleinere Schriften und seine Entgegnungen auf die Kritik seines Werkes 'Der Einzige und sein Eigentum'*, Faksimile-Neudruck (Stuttgart, 1976). (Ed./Tr.)]

2 [Editions l'Age d'Homme, Lausanne. (Ed./Tr.)]

3 [*Max Stirner: The False Principle of Our Education*, trans. Robert H. Beebe (Colorado Springs, 1967). (Ed./Tr.)]

Art and Religion[4]

Now, as soon as man suspects that he has another side of himself [*Jenseits*] within himself, and that he is not enough in his mere natural state, then he is driven on to divide himself into that which he actually is, and that which he should become. Just as the youth is the future of the boy, and the mature man the future of the innocent child, so that othersider [*Jenseitiger*] is the future man who must be expected on the other side of this present reality. Upon the awakening of that suspicion, man strives after and longs for the second other man of the future, and will not rest until he sees himself before the *shape* of this man from the other side. This shape fluctuates back and forth within him for a long time; he only feels it as a light in the innermost darkness of himself that would elevate itself, but as yet has no certain contour or fixed form. For a long time, along with other groping and dumb others in that darkness, the artistic genius seeks to express this presentiment. What no other succeeds in doing, he does, he presents the longing, the sought after form, and in finding its shape so creates the – Ideal. For what is then the perfect man, man's proper character, from which all that is seen is but mere appearance if it be not the Ideal Man, the Human Ideal? The artist alone has finally discovered the right word, the right picture, the right expression of that being which all seek. He presents that presentiment – it is the Ideal. 'Yes! that is it! that is the perfect shape, the appearance that we have longed for, the Good News – the Gospel. The one we sent forth so long ago with the question whose answer would satisfy the thirst of our spirit has returned!' So hail the people that creation of genius, and then fall down – in adoration.

Yes, adoring! The hot press of men would rather be doubled than alone, being dissatisfied with themselves when in their natural isolation. They seek out a spiritual man for their second self. This

[4] ['Kunst und Religion' appeared in June of 1842 in the radical *Rheinische Zeitung*, before Marx became its editor. In this translation, all italics and other important grammatical features are those of the original text. (Ed./Tr.)]

crowd is satisfied with the work of the genius, and their *disunion* is complete. For the first time man breathes easy, for his inward confusions are resolved, and the disturbing suspicion is now cast forth as a perceptible form. This Other [*Gegenüber*] is he himself and yet it is not he: it is his otherside to which all thoughts and feelings flow but without actually reaching it, for it is *his* otherside, encapsulated and inseparably conjoined with his present actuality. It is the inward God, but it is set without; and that is something he cannot grasp, cannot comprehend. His arms reach outward, but the Other is never reached; for would he reach it how could the 'Other' remain? Where would this disunion with all of its pains and pleasures be? Where would be – and we can speak it outright, for this disunion is called by another name – *religion*?

Art creates disunion, in that it sets the Ideal over and against man. But this view, which has so long endured, is called religion, and it will only endure until a single demanding eye again draws that Ideal within and devours it. Accordingly, because it is a viewpoint, it requires another, an Object. Hence, man relates himself religiously to the Ideal cast forth by artistic creation, to his second, outwardly expressed Ego as to an Object. Here lie all the sufferings and struggles of the centuries, for it is fearful to be *outside of oneself*, having yourself as an Object, without being able to unite with it, and as an Object set over and against oneself able to annihilate itself and so oneself.[5] The religious world lives in the joys and sorrows which it experiences from the Object, and it lives in the separation of itself. Its spiritual being is not of reason, but rather of understanding. Religion is a *thing of understanding* [*Verstandes-Sache*]![6] The Object is so firm that no pious soul can fully win it over to itself, but must rather be cast down by it, so fragile is its spirit when set against the Object of the understanding. 'Cold understanding!' – know ye not that 'cold' understanding? – Know ye not that nothing is so ardently hot, so heroically determined as understanding? 'Censeo, Carthaginem esse delendam' spoke the understanding of Cato, and he remained sane thereby.[7] The earth moves about the sun spoke the understanding to Galileo – even while the weak old man knelt adjuring the truth – and as he

[5] [A clearly similar conception is found in Bruno Bauer's *The Trumpet of the Last Judgement over Hegel the Atheist and Anti-Christ*. Stirner had reviewed this text for Gutzkow's *Telegraph für Deutschland* in January of 1842. (Ed./Tr.)]

[6] [Stirner's treatment of both understanding [*Verstand*] and reason [*Vernunft*] follows that as given by Hegel. (Ed./Tr.)]

[7] [In full, 'Ideoque, Censeo ego Carthaginem esse delendam [Therefore, I vote Carthage to be destroyed].' Cato usually concluded any of his addresses to the Roman Senate with this harsh statement. The repetition of this uncompromising sentence was highly irritating to the majority of Senators. (Ed./Tr.)]

rose up again he said 'and yet it moves about the sun'. No force is great enough to make us overthrow thought, that two times two is four, and so the eternal word of understanding remains this 'Here I stand, I can do naught else!'[8] The basis for such understanding is unshakable, for its object (two times two is four, etc.) does not allow itself to be shaken. Does religion have such understanding? Certainly, for it also has an unshakable Object to which it is fortified: the artist has created it for you and only the artist can regain it for you.

Religion itself is without genius. There is no religious genius, and no one would be permitted to distinguish between the talented and the untalented in religion. For religion, everyone has the same capacity, good enough for the understanding of the triangle and the Pythagorean theory as well. Of course, one does not confuse religion and theology, for not everyone has the same capacity here, just as with higher mathematics and astronomy, for these things require a particular level of – calculation.

Only the founder of a religion is inspired, but he is also the creator of Ideals, through whose creation any further genius will be impossible. Where the spirit is bound to an Object, its movement will henceforth be fully determined in respect to that Object. Were a definite doubt over the existence of God, over this transcendent object to emerge for the religious person, that person would stop being religious, somewhat as a believer in ghosts would no longer said to be a believer once he definitely doubted their existence. The religious person concerns himself only about the 'Proofs for God's Existence' because he, as bound fast within the circle of belief, inwardly reserves the free movement of the understanding and calculation. Here, I say, the spirit is dependent upon an object, seeks to explain it, to explore it, to feel it, to love it, and so forth . . . because it is not free, and since freedom is the condition of genius, therefore the religious spirit is not inspired. Inspired piety is as great an inanity as inspired linen-weaving. Religion is always accessible to the impotent, and every uncreative dolt can and will always have religion, for uncreativeness does not impede his life of dependency.

'But is not love the proper essence of religion, and is not that totally a matter of feeling and not of understanding?'[9] But if it is a matter of the heart, must it be less a matter of the understanding? If it takes

[8] [Luther's statement to the Diet at Worms in 1521. Stirner repeats it in *The Ego and His Own* (p. 61), and characterizes it as 'the fundamental maxim of all the possessed'. (Ed./Tr.)]

[9] [An obvious reference to the sentimental religiosity of dependency held by Hegel's rival Friedrich Schleiermacher (1768–1834). Stirner had attended his lecture series at the University of Berlin in the Spring of 1827. (Ed./Tr.)]

up my whole heart, then it is a concern of my heart – but that does not preclude it engaging my whole understanding as well, and that in itself is nothing particularly good, since hate and envy can also be concerns of the heart. Love is, in fact, only a thing of the understanding [*Verstandes-Sache*], but otherwise, it can retain unblemished its title as a thing of the heart. Love, in any case, is not a concern of reason [*Sache der Vernunft*], for in the Kingdom of Reason there is even less love than that which will be celebrated, according to Christ, in the Kingdom of Heaven. Of course it is permitted to speak of a love that 'passes understanding', but it is either so far beyond understanding as to be worthless – as that often called love by those enamoured by an attractive face – or it can appear in the future, a love that is presently beyond the expression of understanding, but yet to have expression. Childish love, without consciousness, is only understandable *in itself*, and taken alone is nothing without the given concerns of consciousness, going only so far as the maturation and growth of the child's understanding. As long as the child gives no sign of understanding, it shows – as anyone can learn from experience – no love. Its love begins in *fear* – or, if one wishes to say, in respect – of that Object which first separates itself from the general chaos that contains all, including men, and which then focuses itself upon it more than another. The child loves because it is drawn by a presence, or thing, and so a person, into its boundary of power or its magical circle. It clearly *understands* how the being of its mother is distinguished from another being even if it yet knows not how *to speak of this understanding*. No child loves before any *understanding*; and its most devoted love is nothing but that innermost understanding. Whoever has sensibly observed the love of a child will find this principle confirmed. But not only does the love of a child rise and sink with the understanding of its 'Object [*Gegenstandes*]' (as so often the loved one is significantly, but crudely, named) but rather every love. If a misunderstanding enters, so love more or less exists while it lasts, and one even uses the word 'misunderstanding' to exactly signify the discord which disturbs love. Love is gone and irretrievably lost whenever one has been totally *mistaken* about another: the misunderstanding is then complete, and the love extinguished.

The beloved thing is an indispensable Object, an 'Other [*Gegenstand*]'. It is this way with the understanding, that one and only proper spiritual act of religion, because understanding is only thought over and about an *object*, only meditation and devotion, and not free, undirected [*objectlose*] 'reasonable' thinking, which religion would rather consider and so condemn as 'philosophical chimeras'. Since to the understanding an object is necessary, it will always cease its activity whenever it finds nothing more to know. Its concern with a case expires with its activity upon the case, and for it to willingly dedicate itself and its powers to anything, that thing must be a *mystery* for it. This holds equally for the beloved as the lover. A marriage is only assured of a steady love when the couple discover themselves anew each day, and when each recognizes in the other an inexhaustible spring of life, that is, a mystery, unfathomed and incomprehensible. If they find nothing new in one another, so love dissolves inexorably into boredom and indifference. The *activity* of understanding, when unable to be exercised upon a mystery because its darkness has been dispelled, turns away from the completely understood and now insipid other. Who wishes to be loved must take care, like the clever woman, not to offer all charms at once. With something new every morning the love might endure centuries! The understanding is concerned with real mysteries which it develops into affairs of the heart: the *real* person is involved with matters of understanding, and so these are transformed into concerns of the heart.

Now as art has created the Ideal for man, and with this gives man's understanding an object to wrestle with, a wrestling match which will, in the course of time, give worth to those empty objects of the understanding, so is art the creator of religion, and in a philosophical system – such as Hegel's – it should not be placed after religion. Not only have the poets Homer and Hesiod 'made the gods of the Greeks', but others, as artists, have established religions, although one hesitates to apply the superficial name 'Artist' to them. Art is the beginning, the *Alpha* of religion, but it is also its end, its *Omega*. Even more – it is its companion. Without art and the idealistically creative artist religion would not exist, but when the artist takes back his art unto himself, so religion vanishes. However, in this return it is also preserved, for it is regenerated. Whenever art strides forth in its full energy, it creates a religion and stands at its source. On the other hand, philosophy is never the creator of a religion, for it never produces a *shape* that might serve as an Object of the understanding, and its insensible ideas do not lend themselves to being the revered objects of cultic worship. Art, other than philosophy, is compelled to draw forth from its seclusion within the concealing darkness of the *subject* the proper and best form of the spirit, the most completely idealized expression of the spirit itself, and to develop it and to release it as an *Object*. At that, man stands opposite to this Object, this creation of his spirit, to the God, and even the artist falls before it on his knees. In this engagement and involvement with the Object, religion pursues a course opposite of art. In art, the world of the artist is set before one's eyes as an Object, a world which the artist has brought forth and concentrated from the full power and richness of his own inwardness, a world which will satisfy every real need and longing. For its part, religion strives to recover this world once again for man's inwardness, to draw it back to its source, to make it again *subjective*. Religion endeavors to reconcile the Ideal, or God, with man, the subject, and to strip God of his hard Objectivity. God is to become inward – 'Not I, but Christ lives in me.' Man, sundered from the Ideal, strives to win God and God's Grace, and to finally transform God into his own being [*Gott ganz zu seinem Ich zu machen*], and God, separated from man, would only win him for the Kingdom of Heaven. Both sides seek and so complement each other. However, they will never find one another, and will never become united, for if they ever would then religion itself would vanish, for religion only exists in this separation. Accordingly, the believer hopes for nothing more than that he will someday have a 'face-to-face *view*'.

But still, art also accompanies religion, for the inwardness of man is expanded by its struggle with the Object, and in the genius of the artist it breaks forth again into a new expression, and the Object becomes yet further enhanced and illuminated. Thankfully, hardly a generation has been passed without such enlightenment by art. But, at the last, art will stand at the close of religion. Serene and confident, art will claim its own once again, and by so doing will rob the Object of its objectivity, its 'other-sidedness', and free it from its long religious imprisonment. Here, art no longer will enrich its Object, but totally destroy it. In reclaiming its creature, art rediscovers itself and renews its creative powers as well. It appears, at the decline of religion, as a trifling with the full seriousness of the old belief, a seriousness of content which religion has now lost, and which must be returned to the joyful poet. Hence, religion is presented as a ridiculous *comedy*.[10] Now, however, terrible this comedic destruction might be, it will nevertheless restore to actuality that which it thinks but to destroy. And so, we do not elect to condemn its horror!

Art creates a new Ideal, a new Object and a new religion. It never goes beyond the making of religion. Raphael's portrayal of Christ casts him in such a light that he could be the basis of a new religion – a religion of the biblical Christ set apart from all human affairs. From that first moment when the tireless understanding begins to pursue its long course of reflection upon a new Object, it steadily deepens in its thoughts until it finally turns upon itself in total inwardness. With

[10] [Cf. Hegel's similar treatment of Comedy which unmasks 'the pretentious claims of the universal abstract nature', in *Phenomenology of Mind*, trans. J. B. Baille (London, 1964), pp. 745ff. (Ed./Tr.)]

devoted love, it sinks into itself and attends to its own revelations and inspirations. But yet this religious understanding is so ardently in love with its own Object that it must have a burning hatred for all else – religious hatred is inseparable from religious love. Who does not believe in the Object, he is a heretic, and who is not truly godly, he tolerates heresy. Who will deny that Philip II of Spain is infinitely more godly than Joseph II of Germany, and that Hengstenberg[11] is truly godly, whereas Hegel[12] is quite not? In our times, the amount of hate has diminished to the extent that the love of God has weakened. A *human* love has infiltrated, which is not of godly piety but rather of social morality. It is more 'zealous' for the good of man than for the good of God. Truly, the tolerant Friedrich the Great cannot serve as a paragon of *godliness*, but can indeed well serve as a pattern for *manliness*, for humanity. Whosoever serves a God must serve him completely. It is, for example, a perverted and unreasonable demand of the *Christian* to have him lay no fetters upon the Jew – for even Christ, with the mildest heart, could do naught else, for otherwise he would have been indifferent to his religion, or would have been proceeding thoughtlessly. If the Christian were to reflect *understandingly* upon the ordinances of his religion, he would exclude the Jew from Christian rights, or, what is the same, from the rights of a Christian – and, above all, from the things of the State. This is so, for religion is for anyone other than a mere tepid hanger-on a relationship of *disunion*.

And so, this is the standing of art to religion. Art creates the Ideal and belongs at the beginning of religion; religion has in the Ideal a mystery, and would, by holding fast to the Object and making it dependent upon itself unite with it in inward godliness. But when the mystery is cleared up, and the otherness and strangeness removed, and established religion is destroyed, then comedy has its task to fulfill. Comedy, in openly displaying the emptiness, or better, the deflation of the Object, frees men from the old belief, and so their dependency upon this exhausted being. Comedy, as befitting its essence, probes into every holy area, even into Holy Matrimony, for this itself is no longer – in the actual marriage – Holy. It is rather an emptied form, to which man should no longer hold.[13] But even

[11] [Ernst W. Hengstenberg (1802–72), a determined and influential Lutheran pietist critic of Hegel and the Young Hegelians. (Ed./Tr.)]

[12] [Bauer's *Posaune des jüngsten Gerichts* had satisfied both the Berlin pietists and the Young Hegelians that Hegel was a covert atheist. (Ed./Tr.)]

[13] [This was written a year and a half before Stirner's own purposely irreverent and somewhat comical second marriage. See John Henry Mackay's *Max Stirner: sein Leben und sein Werk* (Berlin, 1910), p. 124ff. (Ed./Tr.)]

comedy, as all the arts, precedes religion, for it only makes room for the new religion, to that which are will form again.

Art makes the Object, and religion lives only in its many ties to that Object, but philosophy very clearly sets itself apart from both. It neither stands enmeshed with an Object, as religion, nor makes one, as art, but rather places its pulverizing hand upon all the business of making Objects as well as the whole of objectivity itself, and so breathes the air of *freedom*. Reason, the spirit of philosophy, concerns itself only with itself, and troubles itself over no Object. God, to the philosopher, is as neutral as a stone – the philosopher is a dedicated atheist. If he busies himself with God, there is no reverence here, only rejection, for he seeks only that *reason* which has concealed itself in every form, and that only in the light of *reason*. Reason only seeks itself, only troubles itself about itself, loves only itself – or rather, since it is not even an Object to itself – does not love itself but simply is with itself. And so, with a correct instinct, Neander[14] has proclaimed the destruction of the 'God of the philosophers.'

But as it lies outside of our theme, we have not undertaken to speak any further of philosophy as such.

[14] [Daniel A. Neander (1786–1850), Professor of Theology at the University of Berlin. He was a celebrated Church Historian. Stirner had attended his lectures. (Ed./Tr.)]

The Ego and his Own

ALL THINGS ARE NOTHING TO ME[1]

What is not supposed to be my concern![2] First and foremost, the Good Cause,[3] then God's cause, the cause of mankind, of truth, of freedom, of humanity, of justice; further, the cause of my people, my prince, my fatherland; finally, even the cause of Mind, and a thousand other causes. Only *my* cause is never to be my concern. 'Shame on the egoist who thinks only of himself!'

Let us look and see, then, how they manage *their* concerns – they for whose cause we are to labor, devote ourselves, and grow enthusiastic.

You have much profound information to give about God, and have for thousands of years 'searched the depths of the Godhead', and looked into its heart, so that you can doubtless tell us how God himself attends to 'God's cause', which we are called to serve. And you do not conceal the Lord's doings, either. Now, what is his cause? Has he, as is demanded of us, made an alien cause, the cause of truth or love, his own? You are shocked by this misunderstanding, and you instruct us that God's cause is indeed the cause of truth and love, but that this cause cannot be called alien to him, because God is himself truth and love; you are shocked by the assumption that God could be like us poor worms in furthering an alien cause as his own. 'Should God take up the causes of truth if he were not himself truth?' He cares only for *his* cause, but, because he is all in all, therefore all is *his* cause! But we, we are not all in all, and our cause is altogether little and contemptible; therefore we must 'serve a higher cause'. – Now it is clear, God cares only for what is his, busies himself only with himself, thinks only of himself, and has only himself before his eyes; woe to all that is not well-pleasing to him! He serves no higher person, and satisfies only himself. His cause is – a purely egoistic cause.

1 [*Ich hab' Mein' Sach' auf Nichts gestellt*, first line of Goethe's poem, *Vanitas! Vanitatum Vanitas!* Literal translation: 'I have set my affair on nothing.' (Tr.)]

2 [*Sache* (Tr.)]

3 [*Sache* (Tr.)]

How is it with mankind, whose cause we are to make our own? Is its cause that of another, and does mankind serve a higher cause? No, mankind looks only at itself, mankind will promote the interests of mankind only, mankind is its own cause. That it may develop, it causes nations and individuals to wear themselves out in its service, and, when they have accomplished what mankind needs, it throws them on the dung-heap of history in gratitude. Is not mankind's cause – a purely egoistic cause?

I have no need to take up each thing that wants to throw its cause on us and show that it is occupied only with itself, not with us, only with its good, not with ours. Look at the rest for yourselves. Do truth, freedom, humanity, justice, desire anything else than that you grow enthusiastic and serve them?

They all have an admirable time of it when they receive zealous homage. Just observe the nation that is defended by devoted patriots. The patriots fall in bloody battle or in the fight with hunger and want; what does the nation care for that? By the manure of their corpses the nation comes to 'its bloom!' The individuals have died 'for the great cause of the nation', and the nation sends some words of thanks after them and – has the profit of it. I call that a paying kind of egoism.

But only look at that Sultan who cares so lovingly for his people. Is he not pure unselfishness itself, and does he not hourly sacrifice himself for his people? Oh, yes, for 'his people'. Just try it; show yourself not as his, but as your own; for breaking away from his egoism you will take a trip to jail. The Sultan has set his cause on nothing but himself; he is to himself all in all, he is to himself the only one, and tolerates nobody who would dare not to be one of 'his people'.

And will you not learn by these brilliant examples that the egoist gets on best? I for my part take a lesson from them, and propose, instead of further unselfishly serving those great egoists, rather to be the egoist myself.

God and mankind have concerned themselves for nothing, for nothing but themselves. Let me then likewise concern myself for *myself* who am equally with God the nothing of all others, who am my all, who am the only one.[4]

If God, if mankind, as you affirm, have substance enough in themselves to be all in all to themselves, then I feel that *I* shall still less lack that, and that I shall have no complaint to make of my 'emptiness'. I am not nothing in the sense of emptiness, but I am

[4] [*der Einzige* (Tr.)]

the creative nothing, the nothing out of which I myself as creator create everything.

Away, then, with every concern that is not altogether my concern! You think at least the 'good cause' must be my concern? What's good, what's bad? Why, I myself am my concern, and I am neither good nor bad. Neither has meaning for me.

The divine is God's concern; the human, man's. My concern is neither the divine nor the human, not the true, good, just, free, etc., but solely what is *mine*, and it is not a general one, but is – unique,[5] as I am unique.

Nothing is more to me than myself!

Man is to man the supreme being, says Feuerbach.

Man has just been discovered, says Bruno Bauer.

Then let us take a more careful look at this supreme being and this new discovery.

At the entrance of the modern time stands the 'God-man'. At its exit will only the God in the God-man evaporate? And can the God-man really die if only the God in him dies? They did not think of this question, and thought they were through when in our days they brought to a victorious end the work of the Illumination, the vanquishing of God: they did not notice that Man has killed God in order to become now – '*sole* God on high'. The *other world outside us* is indeed brushed away, and the great undertaking of the Illuminators completed; but the *other world in us* has become a new heaven and calls us forth to renewed heaven-storming: God has had to give place, yet not to us, but to – Man. How can you believe that the God-man is dead before the Man in him, besides the God, is dead?

Ownness[6]

'Does not the spirit thirst for freedom?' – Alas, not my spirit alone, my body too thirsts for it hourly! When before the odorous castle-kitchen my nose tells my palate of the savory dishes that are being

[5] [*einzig* (Tr.)]

[6] [This is a literal translation of the German word *Eigenheit*, which, with its primitive *eigen*, 'own', is used in this chapter in a way that the German dictionaries do not quite recognize. The author's conception being new, he had to make an innovation in the German language to express it. The translator is under the like necessity. In most passages 'self-ownership', or else 'personality', would translate the word, but there are some where the thought is so *eigen*, that is, so peculiar or so thoroughly the author's *own*, that no English word I can think of would express it. It will explain itself to one who has read Part First intelligently. (Tr.)]

prepared therein, it feels a fearful pining at its dry bread; when my eyes tell the hardened back about soft down on which one may lie more delightfully than on its compressed straw, a suppressed rage seizes it; when – but let us not follow the pains further. – And you call that a longing for freedom? What do you want to become free from, then? From your hardtack and your straw bed? Then throw them away! – But that seems not to serve you: you want rather to have the freedom to enjoy delicious foods and downy beds. Are men to give you this 'freedom' – are they to permit it to you? You do not hope that from their philanthropy, because you know they all think like – you: each is the nearest to himself! How, therefore, do you mean to come to the enjoyment of those foods and beds? Evidently not otherwise than in making them your property!

If you think it over rightly, you do not want the freedom to have all these fine things, for with this freedom you still do not have them; you want really to have them, to call them *yours* and possess them as *your property*. Of what use is a freedom to you, indeed, if it brings in nothing? And, if you became free from everything, you would no longer have anything; for freedom is empty of substance. Whoso knows not how to make use of it, for him it has no value, this useless permission; but how I make use of it depends on my personality.[7]

I have no objection to freedom, but I wish more than freedom for you: you should not merely *be rid* of what you do not want; you should not only be a 'freeman', you should be an 'owner' too.

Free – from what? Oh! what is there that cannot be shaken off? The yoke of serfdom, of sovereignty, of aristocracy and princes, the dominion of the desires and passions; yes, even the dominion of one's own will, of self-will, for the completest self-denial is nothing but freedom – freedom, to wit, from self-determination, from one's own self. And the craving for freedom as for something absolute, worthy of every praise, deprived us of ownness: it created self-denial. However, the freer I become, the more compulsion piles up before my eyes; and the more impotent I feel myself. the unfree son of the wilderness does not yet feel anything of all the limits that crowd a civilized man: he seems to himself freer than this latter. In the measure that I conquer freedom for myself I create for myself new bounds and new tasks: if I have invented railroads, I feel myself weak again because I cannot yet sail through the skies like the bird; and, if I have solved a problem whose obscurity disturbed my mind, at once there await me innumerable others, whose perplexities impede my progress, dim my free gaze, make the limits of my *freedom* painfully

[7] [*Eigenheit* (Tr.)]

sensible to me. 'Now that you have become free from sin, you have become servants of righteousness.'[8] Republicans in their broad freedom, do they not become servants of the law? How true Christian hearts at all times longed to 'become free', how they pined to see themselves delivered from the 'bonds of this earth-life'! They looked out toward the land of freedom. ('The Jerusalem that is above is the freewoman; she is the mother of us all.' Gal. 4. 26.)

Being free from anything – means only being clear or rid. 'He is free from headache' is equal to 'he is rid of it'. 'He is free from this prejudice' is equal to 'he has never conceived it' or 'he has got rid of it'. In 'less' we complete the freedom recommended by Christianity, in sinless, godless, moralityless, etc.

Freedom is the doctrine of Christianity. 'Ye, dear brethren, are called to freedom.'[9] 'So speak and so do, as those who are to be judged by the law of freedom.'[10]

Must we then, because freedom betrays itself as a Christian ideal, give it up? No, nothing is to be lost, freedom no more than the rest; but it is to become our own, and in the form of freedom it cannot.

What a difference between freedom and ownness! One can get *rid* of a great many things, one yet does not get rid of all; one becomes free from much, not from everything. Inwardly one may be free in spite of the condition of slavery, although, too, it is again only from all sorts of things, not from everything; but from the whip, the domineering temper, of the master, one does not as slave become *free*. 'Freedom lives only in the realm of dreams!' Ownness, on the contrary, is my whole being and existence, it is I myself. I am free from what I am *rid* of, owner of what I have in my *power* or what I *control*. *My own* I am at all times and under all circumstances, if I know how to have myself and do not throw myself away on others. To be free is something that I cannot truly *will* because I cannot make it, cannot create it: I can only wish it and – aspire toward it, for it remains an ideal, a spook. The fetters of reality cut the sharpest welts in my flesh every moment. But *my own* I remain. Given up as serf to a master, I think only of myself and my advantage; his blows strike me indeed, I am not *free* from them; but I endure them only for *my benefit* perhaps in order to deceive him and make him secure by the semblance of patience, or, again, not to draw worse upon myself by contumacy. But, as I keep my eye on myself and my selfishness, I take by the forelock the first good opportunity to trample the slaveholder into the dust. That I then become *free* from him and his whip is only the consequence of my antecedent egoism. Here one

[8] [Rom. 6. 18. (Tr.)]

[9] [Gal. 5. 13. (Tr.)]

[10] [James 2. 12. (Tr.)]

perhaps says I was 'free' even in the condition of slavery – to wit, 'intrinsically' or 'inwardly'. But 'intrinsically free' is not 'really free', and 'inwardly' is not 'outwardly'. I was own, on the other hand, my own, altogether, inwardly and outwardly. Under the dominion of a cruel master my body is not 'free' from torments and lashes; but it is *my* bones that moan under the torture, *my* fibres that quiver under the blows, and *I* moan because *my* body moans. That *I* sigh and shiver proves that I have not yet lost *myself*, that I am still my own. My leg is not 'free' from the master's stick, but it is *my* leg and is inseparable. Let him tear it off me and look and see if he still has my leg! He retains in his hand nothing but the – corpse of my leg, which is as little my leg as a dead dog is still a dog: a dog has a pulsating heart, a so-called dead dog has none and is therefore no longer a dog.

If one opines that a slave may yet be inwardly free, he says in fact only the most indisputable and trivial thing. For who is going to assert that any man is *wholly* without freedom? If I am an eye-servant, can I therefore not be free from innumerable things, from faith in Zeus, from the desire for fame, and the like? Why then should not a whipped slave also be able to be inwardly free from un-Christian sentiments, from hatred of his enemy, etc.? He then has 'Christian freedom', is rid of the un-Christian; but has he absolute freedom, freedom from everything, as from the Christian delusion, or from bodily pain?

In the meantime, all this seems to be said more against names than against the thing. But is the name indifferent, and has not a word, a shibboleth, always inspired and – fooled men? Yet between freedom and ownness there lies still a deeper chasm than the mere difference of the words.

All the world desires freedom, all long for its reign to come. Oh, enchantingly beautiful dream of a blooming 'reign of freedom', a 'free human race'! – who has not dreamed it? So men shall become free, entirely free, free from all constraint! From all constraint, really from all? Are they never to put constraint on themselves any more? 'Oh yes, that, of course; don't you see, that is no constraint at all?' Well, then at any rate they are to become free from religious faith, from the strict duties of morality, from the inexorability of the law, from – 'What a fearful misunderstanding!' Well, *what* are they to be free from then, and what not?

The lovely dream is dissipated; awakened, one rubs his half-opened eyes and stares at the prosaic questioner. 'What men are to be free from?' – From blind credulity, cries one. What's that? exclaims another, all faith is blind credulity; they must become free from all faith. No, no, for God's sake – inveighs the first again – do not cast all faith from you, else the power of brutality breaks in. We must have the republic – a third makes himself heard – and become – free from all commanding lords. There is no help in that, says a fourth: we only get a new lord then, a 'dominant majority'; let us rather free ourselves from this dreadful inequality. – O, hapless equality, already I hear your plebeian roar again! How I had dreamed so beautifully just now of a paradise of *freedom* and what – impudence and licentiousness now raises its wild clamor! Thus the first laments, and gets on his feet to grasp the sword against 'unmeasured freedom'. Soon we no longer hear anything but the clashing of the swords of the disagreeing dreamers of freedom.

What the craving for freedom has always come to has been the desire for a *particular* freedom, such as freedom of faith; the believing man wanted to be free and independent; of what? of faith perhaps? no! but of the inquisitors of faith. So now 'political or civil' freedom. The citizen wants to become free not from citizenhood, but from bureaucracy, the arbitrariness of princes, and the like. Prince Metternich once said he had 'found a way that was adapted to guide men in the path of *genuine* freedom for all the future'. The Count of Provence ran away from France precisely at the time when she was preparing the 'reign of freedom', and said: 'My imprisonment had become intolerable to me; I had only one passion, the desire for *freedom*; I thought only of it.'

The craving for a *particular* freedom always includes the purpose of a new *dominion* as it was with the Revolution, which indeed 'could give its defenders the uplifting feeling that they were fighting for freedom', but in truth only because they were after a particular freedom, therefore a new *dominion*, the 'dominion of the law'.

Freedom you all want, you want *freedom*. Why then do you higgle over a more or less? *Freedom* can only be the whole of freedom; a piece of freedom is not *freedom*. You despair of the possibility of obtaining the whole of freedom, freedom from everything – yes, you consider it insanity even to wish this? – Well, then leave off chasing after the phantom, and spend your pains on something better than the – *unattainable*.

'Ah, but there is nothing better than freedom!'

What have you then when you have freedom – for I will not speak here of your piecemeal bits of freedom – complete freedom? Then you are rid of everything that embarrasses you, everything, and there is probably nothing that does not once in your life embarrass you and cause you inconvenience. And for whose sake, then, did you want to be rid of it? Doubtless *for your* sake, because it is in *your* way! But, if something were not inconvenient to you; if, on the contrary, it were quite to your mind (such as the gently but *irresistibly commanding* look of your loved one) – then you would not want to be rid of it and free from it. Why not? For *your sake* again! So you take *yourselves* as measure and judge over all. You gladly let freedom go when unfreedom, the 'sweet service of love', suits *you*; and you take up your freedom again on occasion when it begins to suit *you* better – that is, supposing, which is not the point here, that you are not afraid of such a Repeal of the Union for other (perhaps religious) reasons.

Why will you not take courage now to really make *yourselves* the central point and the main thing altogether? Why grasp in the air at freedom, your dream? Are you your dream? Do not begin by inquiring of your dreams, your notions, your thoughts, for that is all 'hollow theory'. Ask yourselves and ask after yourselves – that is *practical* and you *know* you want very much to be 'practical'. But there the one hearkens what his God (of course what he thinks of at the name God is his God) may be going to say to it, and another what his moral feelings, his conscience, his feeling of duty, may determine about it, and a third calculates what folks will think of it – and, when each has thus asked his Lord God (folks are a Lord God just as good as, nay, even more compact than, the other-worldly and imaginary one; *vox populi, vox dei*), then he accommodates himself to his Lord's will and listens no more at all for what *he himself* would like to say and decide.

Therefore turn to yourselves rather than to your gods or idols. Bring out from yourselves what is in you, bring it to the light, bring yourselves to revelation.

How one acts only from himself, and asks after nothing further, the Christians have realized in the notion 'God'. He acts 'as it pleases him'. And foolish man, who could do just so, is to act as it 'pleases God' instead. – If it is said that even God proceeds according to eternal laws, that too fits me, since I too cannot get out of my skin, but have my law in my whole nature, in myself.

But one needs only admonish you of yourselves to bring you to despair at once. 'What am I?' each of you asks himself. An abyss of lawless and unregulated impulses, desires, wishes, passions, a chaos without light or guiding star! How am I to obtain a correct answer, if, without regard to God's commandments or to the duties which morality prescribes, without regard to the voice of reason, which in the course of history, after bitter experiences, has exalted the best and most reasonable thing into law, I simply appeal to myself? My passion would advise me to do the most senseless thing possible. – Thus each deems himself the – devil; for, if, so far as he is unconcerned about religion, he only deemed himself a beast, he would easily find that the beast, which does follow only *its* impulse (as it were, its advice), does not advise and impel itself to do the 'most senseless' things, but takes very correct steps. But the habit of the religious way of thinking has biased our mind so grievously that we are – terrified at *ourselves* in our nakedness and naturalness; it has degraded us so that we deem ourselves depraved by nature, born devils. Of course it comes into your head at once that your calling requires you to do the 'good', the moral, the right. Now, if you ask *yourselves* what is to be done, how can the right voice sound forth from you, the voice which points the way of the good, the right, the true? What concord have God and Belial?

But what would you think if one answered you by saying: 'That one is to listen to God, conscience, duties, laws, and so forth, is flim-flam with which people have stuffed your head and heart and made you crazy'? And if he asked you how it is that you know so surely that the voice of nature is a seducer? And if he even demanded of you to turn the thing about and actually to deem the voice of God and conscience to be the devil's work? There are such graceless men; how will you settle them? You cannot appeal to your parsons, parents, and good men, for precisely these are designated by them as your *seducers*, as the true seducers and corrupters of youth, who busily sow broadcast the tares of self-contempt and reverence to God, who fill young hearts with mud and young heads with stupidity.

But now those people go on and ask: For whose sake do you care about God's and the other commandments? You surely do not suppose that this is done merely out of complaisance toward God? No, you are doing it – *for your sake* again. – Here too, therefore, *you* are the main thing, and each must say to himself, *I* am everything to myself and I do everything *on my account*. If it ever became clear to you that God, the commandments, and so on, only harm you, that they reduce and ruin *you* to a certainty you would throw them from you just as the Christians once condemned Apollo or Minerva or heathen morality. They did indeed put in the place of these Christ and afterward Mary, as well as a Christian morality; but they did this for the sake of *their* souls' welfare too, therefore out of egoism or ownness.

And it was by this egoism, this ownness, that they got *rid* of the old world of gods and became *free* from it. Ownness *created* a new *freedom*; for ownness is the creator of everything, as genius (a definite ownness), which is always originality, has for a long time already been looked upon as the creator of new productions that have a place in the history of the world.

If your efforts are ever to make 'freedom' the issue, then exhaust freedom's demands. Who is it that is to become free? You, I, we. Free from what? From everything that is not you, not I, not we. I, therefore, am the kernel that is to be delivered from all wrappings and – freed from all cramping shells. What is left when I have been freed from everything that is not I? Only I; nothing but I. But freedom has nothing to offer to this I himself. As to what is now to happen further after I have become free, freedom is silent – as our governments, when the prisoner's time is up, merely let him go, thrusting him out into abandonment.

Now why, if freedom is striven after for love of the I after all – why not choose the I himself as beginning, middle, and end? Am I not worth more than freedom? Is it not I that make myself free, am not I the first? Even unfree, even laid in a thousand fetters, I yet am; and I am not, like freedom, extant only in the future and in hopes, but even as the most abject of slaves I am – present.

Think that over well, and decide whether you will place on your banner the dream of 'freedom' or the resolution of 'egoism', of 'ownness'. 'Freedom' awakens your *rage* against everything that is not you; 'egoism' calls you to *joy* over yourselves, to self-enjoyment; 'freedom' is and remains a *longing*, a romantic plaint, a Christian hope for unearthliness and futurity; 'ownness' is a reality, which *of itself* removes just so much unfreedom as by barring your own way hinders you. What does not disturb you, you will not want to renounce; and, if it begins to disturb you, why, you know that 'you must obey *yourselves* rather than men!'

Freedom teaches only: Get yourselves rid, relieve yourselves, of everything burdensome; it does not teach you who you yourselves are. Rid, rid! so call, get rid even of yourselves, 'deny yourselves'. But ownness calls you back to yourselves, it says 'Come to yourself!' Under the aegis of freedom you get rid of many kinds of things, but something new pinches you again: 'you are rid of the Evil One; evil is left'. As *own* you are *really rid of everything*, and what clings to you *you have accepted*; it is your choice and your pleasure. The *own* man is the *free-born*, the man free to begin with; the free man, on the contrary, is only the *eleutheromaniac*, the dreamer and enthusiast.

The former is *originally free* because he recognizes nothing but himself; he does not need to free himself first, because at the start he rejects everything outside himself, because he prizes nothing more than himself, rates nothing higher, because, in short, he starts from himself and 'comes to himself'. Constrained by childish respect, he is nevertheless already working at 'freeing' himself from this constraint. Ownness works in the little egoist, and procures him the desired – freedom.

Thousands of years of civilization have obscured to you what you are, have made you believe you are not egoists but are *called* to be idealists ('good men'). Shake that off! Do not seek for freedom, which does precisely deprive you of yourselves, in 'self-denial'; but seek for *yourselves*, become egoists, become each of you an *almighty ego*. Or, more clearly: Just recognize yourselves again, just recognize what you really are, and let go your hypocritical endeavors, your foolish mania to be something else than you are. Hypocritical I call them because you have yet remained egoists all these thousands of years, but sleeping, self-deceiving, crazy egoists, you Heautontimorumenoses, you self-tormentors. Never yet has a religion been able to dispense with 'promises', whether they referred us to the other world or to this ('long life', etc.); for man is *mercenary* and does nothing 'gratis'. But how about that 'doing the good for the good's sake' without prospect of reward? As if here too the pay was not contained in the satisfaction that it is to afford. Even religion, therefore, is founded on our egoism and – exploits it; calculated for our *desires* it stifles many others for the sake of one. This then gives the phenomenon of *cheated* egoism, where I satisfy, not myself, but one of my desires, such as the impulse toward blessedness. Religion promises me the – 'supreme good'; to gain this I no longer regard any other of my desires, and do not slake them. – All your doings are *unconfessed*, secret, covert, and concealed egoism. But because they are egoism that you are unwilling to confess to yourselves, that you keep secret from yourselves, hence not manifest and public egoism, consequently unconscious egoism – therefore they are *not egoism* but thraldom, service, self-renunciation; you are egoists, and you are not, since you renounce egoism. Where you seem most to be such, you have drawn upon the word 'egoist' – loathing and contempt.

I secure my freedom with regard to the world in the degree that I make the world my own, 'gain it and take possession of it' for myself, by whatever might, by that of persuasion, of petition, of categorical demand, yes, even by hypocrisy, cheating, etc.; for the means that I use for it are determined by what I am. If I am weak, I have only weak means, like the aforesaid, which yet are good enough for a considerable part of the world. Besides, cheating, hypocrisy, lying, look worse than they are. Who has not cheated the police, the law? Who has not quickly taken on an air of honorable loyalty before the sheriff's officer who meets him, in order to conceal an illegality that may have been committed? He who has not done it has simply let violence be done to him; he was a *weakling* from – conscience. I know that my freedom is diminished even by my not being able to carry out my will on another object, be this other something without will, like a rock, or something with will, like a government, an individual; I deny my ownness when – in presence of another – I give myself up, give way, desist, submit; therefore by *loyalty*, *submission*. For it is one thing when I give up my previous course because it does not lead to the goal, and therefore turn out of a wrong road; it is another when I yield myself a prisoner. I get around a rock that stands in my way, till I have powder enough to blast it; I get around the laws of a people, till I have gathered strength to overthrow them. Because I cannot grasp the moon, is it therefore to be 'sacred' to me, an Astarte? If I only could grasp you, I surely would, and, if I only find a means to get up to you, you shall not frighten me! You inapprehensible one, you shall remain inapprehensible to me only till I have acquired the might for apprehension and call you my *own*; I do not give myself up before you, but only bide my time. Even if for the present I put up with my inability to touch you, I yet remember it against you.

Vigorous men have always done so. When the 'loyal' had exalted an unsubdued power to be their master and had adored it, when they had demanded adoration from all, then there came some such son of nature who would not loyally submit, and drove the adored power from its inaccessible Olympus. He cried his 'Stand still' to the rolling sun, and made the earth go round; the loyal had to make the best of it; he laid his axe to the sacred oaks, and the 'loyal' were astonished that no heavenly fire consumed him; he threw the pope off Peter's chair, and the 'loyal' had no way to hinder it; he is tearing down the divine-right business, and the 'loyal' croak in vain, and at last are silent.

My freedom becomes complete only when it is my – *might*; but by this I cease to be a merely free man, and become an own man. Why is the freedom of the peoples a 'hollow word'? Because the peoples have no might! With a breath of the living ego I blow peoples over, be it the breath of a Nero, a Chinese emperor, or a poor writer. Why is it that the G...[11] legislatures pine in vain for freedom, and are lectured for it by the cabinet ministers? Because they are not of the 'mighty'! Might is a fine thing, and useful for many purposes; for 'one goes further with a handful of might than with a bagful of right'. You long for freedom? You fools! If you took might, freedom would come of itself. See, he who had might 'stands above the law'. How does this prospect taste to you, you 'law-abiding' people? But you have no taste!

The cry for 'freedom' rings loudly all around. But is it felt and known what a donated or chartered freedom must mean? It is not recognized in the full amplitude of the word that all freedom is

[11] [Meaning 'German'. Written in this form because of the censorship. (Tr.)]

essentially – self-liberation – that I can have only so much freedom as I procure for myself by my ownness. Of what use is it to sheep that no one abridges their freedom of speech? They stick to bleating. Give one who is inwardly a Mohammedan, a Jew, or a Christian, permission to speak what he likes: he will yet utter only narrow-minded stuff. If, on the contrary, certain others rob you of the freedom of speaking and hearing, they know quite rightly wherein lies their temporary advantage, as you would perhaps be able to say and hear something whereby those 'certain' persons would lose their credit.

If they nevertheless give you freedom, they are simply knaves who give more than they have. For then they give you nothing of their own, but stolen wares: they give you your own freedom, the freedom that you must take for yourselves; and they *give* it to you only that you may not take it and call the thieves and cheats to an account to boot. In their slyness they know well that given (chartered) freedom is no freedom, since only the freedom one *takes* for himself, therefore the egoist's freedom, rides with full sails. Donated freedom strikes its sails as soon as there comes a storm – or calm; it requires always a – gentle and moderate breeze.

Here lies the difference between self-liberation and emancipation (manumission, setting free). Those who to-day 'stand in the opposition' are thirsting and screaming to be 'set free'. The princes are to 'declare their peoples of age', that is, emancipate them! Behave as if you were of age, and you are so without any declaration of majority; if you do not behave accordingly, you are not worthy of it, and would never be of age even by a declaration of majority. When the Greeks were of age, they drove out their tyrants, and, when the son is of age, he makes himself independent of his father. If the Greeks had waited till their tyrants graciously allowed them their majority, they might have waited long. A sensible father throws out a son who will not come of age, and keeps the house to himself; it serves the noodle right.

The man who is set free is nothing but a freed man, a *libertinus*, a dog dragging a piece of chain with him: he is an unfree man in the garment of freedom, like the ass in the lion's skin. Emancipated Jews are nothing bettered in themselves, but only relieved as Jews, although he who relieves their condition is certainly more than a churchly Christian, as the latter cannot do this without inconsistency. But, emancipated or not emancipated, Jew remains Jew; he who is not self-freed is merely an – emancipated man. The Protestant State can certainly set free (emancipate) the Catholics; but, because they do not make themselves free, they remain simply – Catholics.

Selfishness and unselfishness have already been spoken of. The friends of freedom are exasperated against selfishness because in their religious striving after freedom they cannot – free themselves from that sublime thing, 'self-renunciation'. The liberal's anger is directed against egoism, for the egoist, you know, never takes trouble about a thing for the sake of the thing, but for his sake: the thing must serve him. It is egoistic to ascribe to no thing a value of its own, an 'absolute' value, but to seek its value in me. One often hears that pot-boiling study which is so common counted among the most repulsive traits of egoistic behavior, because it manifests the most shameful desecration of science; but what is science for but to be consumed? If one does not know how to use it for anything better than to keep the pot boiling, then his egoism is a petty one indeed, because this egoist's power is a limited power; but the egoistic element in it, and the desecration of science, only a possessed man can blame.

Because Christianity, incapable of letting the individual count as an ego,[12] thought of him only as a dependent, and was properly nothing but a *social theory* – a doctrine of living together, and that of man with God as well as of man with man – therefore in it everything 'own' must fall into most woeful disrepute: selfishness, self-will, ownness, self-love, and the like. The Christian way of looking at things has on all sides gradually re-stamped honorable words into dishonorable; why should they not be brought into honor again? So *Schimpf* (contumely) is in its old sense equivalent to jest, but for Christian seriousness pastime became a dishonor,[13] for that seriousness cannot take a joke; *frech* (impudent) formerly meant only bold, brave; *Frevel* (wanton outrage) was only daring. It is well known how askance the word 'reason' was looked at for a long time.

Our language has settled itself pretty well to the Christian standpoint, and the general consciousness is still too Christian not to shrink in terror from everything un-Christian as from something incomplete or evil. Therefore 'selfishness' is in a bad way too.

Selfishness,[14] in the Christian sense, means something like this: I look only to see whether anything is of use to me as a sensual man. But is sensuality then the whole of my ownness? Am I in my own senses when I am given up to sensuality? Do I follow myself, my *own* determination, when I follow that? I am my *own* only when I am master of myself, instead of being mastered either by sensuality or by anything else (God, man, authority, law, State, Church); what is of use to me, this self-owned or self-appertaining one, my selfishness pursues.

12 [*Einzige* (Tr.)]

13 [I take *Entbehrung*, 'destitution', to be a misprint for *Enteh*-rung. (Tr.)]

14 [*Eigennutz*, literally 'own-use'. (Tr.)]

Besides, one sees himself every moment compelled to believe in that constantly-blasphemed selfishness as an all-controlling power. In the session of February 10, 1844, Welcker argues a motion on the dependence of the judges, and sets forth in a detailed speech that removable, dismissable, transferable, and pensionable judges – in short, such members of a court of justice as can by mere administrative process be damaged and endangered – are wholly without reliability, yes, lose all respect and all confidence among the people. The whole bench, Welcker cries, is demoralized by this dependence! In blunt words this means nothing else than that the judges find it more to their advantage to give judgment as the ministers would have them than to give it as the law would have them. How is that to be helped? Perhaps by bringing home to the judges' hearts the ignominiousness of their venality, and then cherishing the confidence that they will repent and henceforth prize justice more highly than their selfishness? No, the people does not soar to this romantic confidence, for it feels that selfishness is mightier than any other motive. Therefore the same persons who have been judges hitherto may remain so, however thoroughly one has convinced himself that they behaved as egoists; only they must not any longer find their selfishness favored by the venality of justice, but must stand so independent of the government that by a judgment in conformity with the facts they do not throw into the shade their own cause, their 'well-understood interest', but rather secure a comfortable combination of a good salary with respect among the citizens.

So Welcker and the commoners of Baden consider themselves secured only when they can count on selfishness. What is one to think, then, of the countless phrases of unselfishness with which their mouths overflow at other times?

To a cause which I am pushing selfishly I have another relation than to one which I am serving unselfishly. The following criterion might be cited for it; against the one I can *sin* or commit a *sin*, the other I can only *trifle away*, push from me, deprive myself of – commit an imprudence. Free trade is looked at in both ways, being regarded partly as a freedom which may *under certain circumstances* be granted or withdrawn, partly as one which is to be held *sacred under all circumstances*.

If I am not concerned about a thing in and for itself, and do not desire it for its own sake, then I desire it solely as a *means to an end* for its usefulness; for the sake of another end, as in oysters for a pleasant flavor. Now will not every thing whose final end he himself is, serve the egoist as means? And is he to protect a thing that serves him for nothing – for example, the proletarian to protect the State?

Ownness includes in itself everything own, and brings to honor again what Christian language dishonored. But ownness has not any alien standard either, as it is not in any sense an *idea* like freedom, morality, humanity, and the like: it is only a description of the – *owner*.

The Unique One

Pre-Christian and Christian times pursue opposite goals; the former wants to idealize the real, the latter to realize the ideal; the former seeks the 'holy spirit', the latter the 'glorified body'. Hence the former closes with insensitiveness to the real, with 'contempt for the world'; the latter will end with the casting off of the the ideal, with 'contempt for the spirit'.

The opposition of the real and the ideal is an irreconcilable one, and the one can never become the other: if the ideal became the real, it would no longer be the ideal; and, if the real became the ideal, the ideal alone would be, but not at all the real. The opposition of the two is not to be vanquished otherwise than if some one annihilates both. Only in this '*some one*', the third party, does the opposition find its end; otherwise idea and reality will ever fail to coincide. The idea cannot be so realized as to remain idea, but is realized only when it dies as idea; and it is the same with the real.

But now we have before us in the ancients adherents of the idea, in the moderns adherents of reality. Neither can get clear of the opposition, and both pine only, the one party for the spirit, and, when this craving of the ancient world seemed to be satisfied and this spirit to have come, the others immediately for the secularization of this spirit again, which must forever remain a 'pious wish'.

The pious wish of the ancients was *sanctity*, the pious wish of the moderns is *corporeity*. But, as antiquity had to go down if its longing was to be satisfied (for it consisted only in the longing), so too corporeity can never be attained within the ring of Christianness. As the trait of sanctification or purification goes through the old world (the washings, etc.), so that of incorporation goes through the Christian world: God plunges down into this world, becomes flesh, and wants to redeem it, that is, fill it with himself; but, since he is 'the idea' or 'the spirit', people (Hegel, for example) in the end introduce the idea into everything, into the world, and prove 'that the idea is, that reason is, in everything'. 'Man' corresponds in the culture of to-day to what the heathen Stoics set up as 'the wise man'; the latter, like the former, a – *fleshless* being. The unreal 'wise man', this bodiless 'holy one' of the Stoics, became a real person, a bodily 'Holy One', in God *made flesh*; the unreal 'man', the bodiless ego, will become real in the *corporeal ego* in me.

There winds its way through Christianity the question about the 'existence of God', which, taken up ever and ever again, gives testimony that the craving for existence, corporeity, personality, reality, was incessantly busying the heart because it never found a satisfying solution. At last the question about the existence of God fell, but only to rise up again in the proposition that the 'divine' had existence (Feuerbach). But this too has no existence, and neither will the last refuge, that the 'purely human' is realizable, afford shelter much longer. No idea has existence, for none is capable of corporeity. The scholastic contention of realism and nominalism has the same content; in short, this spins itself out through all Christian history, and cannot end *in* it.

The world of Christians is working at *realizing ideas* in the individual relations of life, the institutions and laws of the Church and the State; but they make resistance, and always keep back something unembodied (unrealizable). Nevertheless this embodiment is restlessly rushed after, no matter in what degree *corporeity* constantly fails to result.

For realities matter little to the realizer, but it matters everything that they be realizations of the idea. Hence he is ever examining anew whether the realized does in truth have the idea, its kernel, dwelling in it; and in testing the real he at the same time tests the idea, whether it is realizable as he thinks it, or is only thought by him incorrectly, and for that reason unfeasibly.

The Christian is no longer to care for family, State, etc., as *existences*; Christians are not to sacrifice themselves for these 'divine things' like the ancients, but these are only to be utilized to make the *spirit alive* in them. The *real* family has become indifferent, and there is to arise out of it an *ideal* one which would then be the 'truly real', a sacred family, blessed by God, or, according to the liberal way of thinking, a 'rational' family. With the ancients, family, State, fatherland, is divine as a thing *extant*; with the moderns it is still awaiting divinity, as extant it is only sinful, earthly, and has still to be 'redeemed', that is, to become truly real. This has the following meaning: the family, etc., is not the extant and real, but the divine, the idea, is extant and real; whether *this* family will make itself real by taking up the truly real, the idea, is still unsettled. It is not the individual's task to serve the family as the divine, but, reversely, to serve the divine and to bring to it the still undivine family, to subject everything in the idea's name, to set up the idea's banner everywhere, to bring the idea to real efficacy.

But, since the concern of Christianity, as of antiquity, is for the *divine*, they always come out at this again on their opposite ways. At the end of heathenism the divine becomes the *extramundane*, at the end of Christianity the *intramundane*. Antiquity does not succeed in putting it entirely outside the world, and, when Christianity accomplishes this task, the divine instantly longs to get back into the world and wants to 'redeem' the world. But within Christianity it does not and cannot come to this, that the divine as *intramundane* should really become the *mundane itself*: there is enough left that does and must maintain itself unpenetrated as the 'bad', irrational, accidental, 'egoistic', the 'mundane' in the bad sense. Christianity begins with God's becoming man, and carries on its work of conversion and redemption through all time in order to prepare for God a reception in all men and in everything human, and to penetrate everything with the spirit: it sticks to preparing a place for the 'spirit'.

When the accent was at last laid on man or mankind, it was again the idea that they '*pronounced eternal*'. 'Man does not die!' They thought they had now found the reality of the idea: *Man* is the I of history, of the world's history; it is he, this *ideal* that really develops, *realizes*, himself. He is the really real and corporeal one, for history is his body, in which individuals are only members. Christ is the I of the world's history, even of the pre-Christian; in modern apprehension it is man, the figure of Christ has developed into the *figure of man*: man as such, man absolutely, is the 'central point' of history. In 'man' the imaginary beginning returns again; for 'man' is as imaginary as Christ is. 'Man', as the I of the world's history, closes the cycle of Christian apprehensions.

Christianity's magic circle would be broken if the strained relation between existence and calling, that is, between me as I am and me as I should be, ceased; it persists only as the longing of the idea for its bodiliness, and vanishes with the relaxing separation of the two: only when the idea remains – idea, as man or mankind is indeed a bodiless idea, is Christianity still extant. The corporeal idea, the corporeal or 'completed' spirit, floats before the Christian as 'the end of the days' or as the 'goal of history'; it is not present time to him.

The individual can only have a part in the founding of the Kingdom of God, or, according to the modern notion of the same thing, in the development and history of humanity; and only so far as he has a part in it does a Christian, or according to the modern expression human, value pertain to him; for the rest he is dust and a worm-bag.

That the individual is of himself a world's history, and possesses his property in the rest of the world's history, goes beyond what is Christian. To the Christian the world's history is the higher thing, because it is the history of Christ or 'man'; to the egoist only *his* history has value, because he wants to develop only *himself* not the mankind-idea, not God's plan, not the purposes of Providence, not liberty, and the like. He does not look upon himself as a tool of the idea or a vessel of God, he recognizes no calling, he does not fancy that he exists for the further development of mankind and that he must contribute his mite to it, but he lives himself out, careless of how well or ill humanity may fare thereby. If it were not open to confusion with the idea that a state of nature is to be praised, one might recall Lenau's *Three Gypsies*. What, am I in the world to realize ideas? To do my part by my citizenship, say, toward the realization of the idea 'State', or by marriage, as husband and father, to bring the idea of the family into an existence? What does such a calling concern me! I live after a calling as little as the flower grows and gives fragrance after a calling.

The ideal 'Man' is *realized* when the Christian apprehension turns about and becomes the proposition, 'I, this unique one, am man'. The conceptual question, 'what is man?' – has then changed into the personal question, 'who is man?' With 'what' the concept was sought for, in order to realize it; with 'who' it is no longer any question at all, but the answer is personally on hand at once in the asker: the question answers itself.

They say of God, 'names name thee not.' That holds good of me: no *concept* expresses me, nothing that is designated as my essence exhausts me; they are only names. Likewise they say of God that he is perfect and has no calling to strive after perfection. That too holds good of me alone.

I am *owner* of my might, and I am so when I know myself as *unique*. In the *unique one* the owner himself returns into his creative nothing, of which he is born. Every higher essence above me, be it God, be it man, weakens the feeling of my uniqueness, and pales only before the sun of this consciousness. If I concern myself for myself, the unique one, then my concern rests on its transitory, mortal creator, who consumes himself, and I may say:

All things are nothing to me.

X

Moses Hess

1812–1875

Moses Hess

Unlike the other major representatives of Young Hegelianism, Moses Hess never shared in the strictures of German academic life. Having little experience with either Gymnasium or University, he was – in the words of his biographer Edmund Silberner – 'an autodidact in the truest sense of the word'. Indeed, perhaps it was because he was self-taught and free from the fixed and often stifling academic world of his day which allowed Hess to develop his eclectic originality of thought, a seminal vision which in time earned him two honored but now half-forgotten titles: 'The Father of German Socialism' and 'The Founder of Theoretical Zionism'. The practical talents of both Karl Marx and Theodore Herzl would have to follow upon a path first laid out by Hess before they could gain their own, and higher fame.

Hess's first book, *The Holy History of Mankind* [*Die heilige Geschichte der Menscheit*] was published anonymously – by 'a disciple of Spinoza' – in 1837. The slender book attracted little notice, although it was later acknowledged as being the first socialist treatise written in German for Germans. It set both the tone and perspective for the rest of Hess's socialistic treatises – a tone charged with a heated concern for social justice, and a perspective fixed upon an ideal future of human equality. This essentially programmatic first work was followed, in 1841, by a more popular effort, *The European Triarchy* [*Die europäische Triarchie*], which immediately established his reputation among the Young Hegelians. In it, he expressly joined Cieszkowski in criticising the passivity and retrospective character of 'right-wing' Hegelianism, and proposed a revolutionary 'Philosophy of Action' which would generate a communist society. In that same portentous year, Hess was also successful in founding the *Rheinische Zeitung* and first encountered Karl Marx. From that time, until Marx, in the *Communist Manifesto*, broke doctrinally with Hess's 'True Socialism', they worked in concert and shared a common view as to the needs of their age, a sharing clearly evident if, for example, Marx's 1844 essay 'On the Jewish Question' is compared with Hess' essay – of the same year – 'On the Essence of Money'.

Certainly, not all liberal German intellectuals shared Heine's opinion that Hess was 'one of the most outstanding of our political writers', but none could deny that Hess' 'Philosophy of Action' had exercised a powerful role in transforming Hegelian theory into a program of radical social action.

For the reader wishing to know something more of Moses Hess, Isaiah Berlin's excellent *The Life and Opinions of Moses Hess* (1959) can be recommended.

Late in 1844, Hess obtained a press copy of Stirner's *The Ego and His Own*. He read it, and then sent it along to his friend Engels, who read it and passed it along to Marx. It was not until 1846 that Marx and Engels – along with some help from Hess – had time to prepare an exhaustive rejection of 'Saint Max' and other Young Hegelians in *The German Ideology*. Hess, however, had immediately prepared a small brochure critical of Stirner and other unsocialistic Hegelians which he entitled *The Recent Philosophers* [*Die letzten Philosophen*].

This short essay, significant not only in itself as an expression of Hess' socialistic theory, but also as an interesting prelude to *The German Ideology*, is here presented in its entirety. It has been annotated and for the first time translated into English by the editor of this anthology.

The Recent Philosophers

Anyone who had not already passed through the historical development of Christianity and German Philosophy might be of the opinion that recent German Philosophers have published their writings at the instigation of reactionaries. – I would have hardly expected to declare such an opinion of a man who earlier stood at the pinnacle of Young Hegelianism along with Bruno Bauer, although at that time the writings of Bauer were far removed from their later 'consequence', to say nothing of that cynicism recently expressed in Stirner's writings – but in spite of all this, it is nevertheless true that neither Bruno Bauer nor Stirner ever allowed themselves to be influenced from *without*. It is rather the case that this 'insanity' emerged directly from the *inner* living development of this philosophy – and so it is that exactly in this manner, and no other, must the progeny of the Christian ascetics take their departure from the world.

I

It would not occur to anyone to maintain the astronomer to be at one with the Solar System he observes, but according to our recent German philosophers, the singular human being, who has observed nature and history, should be the 'species', the 'All'. In Buhl's *Monthly*[1] it is said that every person is the State, Mankind – and, as the philosopher Julius[2] has lately written, every man is the species, the Whole, Mankind. For Stirner, 'As the individual is the whole of

[1] [The *Berliner Monatsschrift* of Ludwig Buhl (1814–1882), one of the short-lived Young Hegelian journals. It was established in 1843 and ceased publication in 1845, at the time of Hess' article. In 1841, in another Berlin journal, the *Athenaum*, Buhl had critically reviewed Hess' second book, *Die europäische Triarchie*. (Ed./Tr.)]

[2] [Gustav Julius was the editor of the *Berliner Zeitung-Halle* who later revenged himself on Hess by reporting that Hess was involved with publishing criticisms of Friedrich Wilhelm IV. This set the police upon Hess, forcing him to leave Cologne for Paris in 1847. (Ed./Tr.)]

nature, so he is the whole of the species too.'[3] Since the rise of Christianity men have worked to resolve the difference between the Father and the Son, the Divine and Human – in a word, between the 'Species-Man [*Gattungsmenschen*]' and the 'bodily' man. But as little has come of this effort as has come to Protestantism in its annulment [*Aufhebung*] of the visible Church – for the invisible Church (Heaven) and the invisible Priest (Christ) endure – and so a new clergy is permitted to rise up. The recent philosophers will gain just as little by casting off [*aufhoben*] this invisible Church and establishing the 'Absolute Spirit',[4] 'Self-consciousness',[5] and 'Species-Being [*Gattungswesen*]'[6] in the place of Heaven. All of these attempts to *theoretically* resolve the difference between the particular man and the human species must miscarry, for even if the singular man does indeed comprehend the world and mankind, nature and history, he yet in actuality remains only a sundered man [*Vereinzelung*][7] as long as the division of man is not *practically* overcome. But this separation of man will only be practically resolved through Socialism – that is, if men unite themselves in community life and activity, and surrender private gain. So long as they are separated in actual life, i.e., in social life, so long as the difference between the singular man and mankind be only theoretically, in 'consciousness' resolved, men will remain not only separated from one another in actual life, but the individual man will remain divided in his 'consciousness'. He must feel and think of himself as other than he is in actuality, in life. The longing, as isolated individuals to become as we feel, imagine, and think of ourselves, has brought forth all of the illusions which have occupied our heads since the rise of Christianity to the present day. Instead of honestly confessing to ourselves, that we will only be something through a social union with our neighboring men, we have wanted to believe that our misery could be cast out, that the divisiveness of our social isolation could be pushed aside, that we could be divinized, and humanized by mere theoretical knowledge alone. We yet

[3] [Max Stirner in *The Ego and His Own* (New York: Dover Publications, 1973), p. 183. This Dover edition follows the same pagination as the earlier 1963 Libertarian Book Club edition. The above citation is found on p. 125 of the somewhat abridged German edition of *Der Einzige und sein Eigentum* (Munich: Hanser Verlag, 1968) edited by H. G. Helms. It will hereafter be referred to as *Helms*. (Ed./Tr.)]

[4] [The '*absoluten Geist*' of Hegel. (Ed./Tr.)]

[5] [The '*Selbstbewusstsein*' of Bauer. (Ed./Tr.)]

[6] [Feuerbach's term. (Ed./Tr.)]

[7] [In an 1840 *German-English Dictionary* (Philadelphia: Mentz and Son) the term '*Vereinzelung*' not only connotes 'dismembering' but 'retailing; selling in single portions', a usage undoubtedly known and appreciated by Hess. (Ed./Tr.)]

believed that through simple knowledge, through philosophical comprehension, through religious feeling, that we could become loving, moral, godly, virtuous, pious and blessed – indeed, upon this, we even imagined our nature to be religious, or thought it philosophical – although we yet remained in actual life loveless, worldly, miserable, impious, torn and sundered Egoists and inhuman men.

The rupture between theory and praxis,[8] Godliness and worldliness – however one chooses to name it – this Christian dualism is to be found throughout the whole Christian era, and the modern, philosophical, atheistical Christians are just as subject to it as the old, believing Christians. The history of modern Christianity has had the same course as that of the old. The old Christianity, as a teaching, a theory, must institute a Church, a doctrine, a priesthood. This Church, once set into life, must pervert itself, that is, it will set itself in opposition to its established purpose. The Church, created to overcome the dichotomy between Godliness and worldliness, theory and praxis, to heal and to sanctify the world, to fill the chasm between the individual and the species, to reconcile the emnity between men, now brings forth these divisions in their sharpest forms. In response to clergy and laity arose Medieval lordship and bondage: the practical Egoism of the world against the theoretical Egoism of religion. We have the Church itself to thank for transforming the consciousness of man from the pantheism fundamental to the theory of Christianity into one of deep and abrupt contradictions between Heaven and Earth, this world and the other, spirit and body. In the course of Church history Christianity has reformed itself, and would restore its fundamental thought; it turns back to its primal sources, becomes protestant, rationalistic, philosophical, atheistic – but it always remains what it was according to its principle: an expression of the separation between theory and praxis. In like manner the modern Christian, as the old, must institute a teaching doctrine, a Priesthood, a *philosophical* clergy, for it yet holds to the position that Mankind is to be taken up and taught only theoretically. Modern Christianity, this new religion, must have the same fate as the old religion – it must, once entered into life, lose itself and be transformed into its opposite.

The modern Christian Church is the Christian – State. We do not mean by this that mongrel being that can not break away from the old Church and so stands between it and the State, nor that fantastic

[8] [The term '*praxis*' has here ceased to play the mediating role between theory and practice as earlier envisioned by Cieszkowski and has merely replaced the term 'practice'. (Ed./Tr.)]

image of our Romantics which floats in the air between the Medieval heaven and the actuality of this earth, in short, not 'German Christendom' but the modern, the 'free' State, as it really exists in France, England and North America, but which exists only as an *Ideal* for us Germans. This State is the modern Church, just as philosophy is the modern religion. The State is but only the actualized form of philosophy, just as the Church was but the actualized form of religion. But the 'Free State' as well, which originated in order to resolve the divisions of the Medieval world, has only called forth into life a newer and sharper antithesis between theory and praxis, for it has only replaced the old Heaven and old earth with a new Heaven and a new earth – it has only brought Christianity to its fulfillment.

The sundering of theory and praxis was still not universally and in principle carried out by the Medieval Church, by Medieval life. At that time consciousness moved itself within both the sacred world and this godless world, just as in that life the Clergy and laity, nobility and peasantry moved separately and side by side. One excluded the other. The layman could not at the same time be a Priest, the serf could not at the same time be a Lord, the Earth could not be Heaven, the Body not Spirit, Man could not be God, and the individual could not at the same time be the generic being. That would be unChristian – for Christianity, this theoretical pantheism, certainly wants this duality in unity; the God-Man in one person is indeed the Christian ideal. Once again the attempt is being made to theoretically bring about within Christianity this enchanted condition, and hence to allow the divisiveness of actual human life to exist at a distance; to sanctify, to humanize, to elevate into general humanity these individual men, and – as in Heaven so on earth – to sanction separation and divisiveness.

And look! the enchantment is perfectly accomplished. The beatific spirits of the Christian Heaven now wander about on earth; they are – the 'free citizens'! Heaven is no longer in the beyond, but here and now; it is – the 'State'.

Now are the 'citizens' actual men? – No, they are but the spirits of actual men. The bodies of these spirits are in the – *civil society* [*bürgerlichen Gesellschaft*].

The bodiless Idealism of the Christian Heaven is come from Heaven unto earth, to become the State. But yet near it also exists the spiritless Materialism of the Christian World, existing in the civil society. The modern state has only sharpened the opposition between the individual and the species, and certainly, it has brought it for the first time into its *perfection*!

But now, the stronger, the more intensively and more universally this present contradiction exists between individual and species, and indeed the more men are violently seized by this contradiction, then all the more rapidly will history take its course, and all the greater will be the longing for a better reality, but a reality which is no longer sought in another world, but must be sought in present social life. Attempts to reform our society will repeat until they suit our innermost consciousness, that consciousness derived from our lives. We now live in this reforming or revolutionary time.

But, as it has been said and recognized, Germany has not brought about – in reality – the modern free State. But even if this modern Church has not become practically existent for us, we still have brought it forth in all respects according to its theoretical actuality. Recent German philosophers have fallen out among one another for the reason that one holds the principle of the State without civil society to be consistent, the other holds that the principle of civil society is consistent without the State – and finally the third holds to the Whole, and therefore in principle advocates a *contradiction* between the State and civil society.

Feuerbach's *Philosophy of the Future*[9] is nothing other than a philosophy of the present, but a present which to the German still appears as a future, an Ideal. The *Principles of the Philosophy of the Future* would discuss philosophically and theoretically what in England, France, North America and elsewhere is a present reality – the modern state confronted with its supplementary civil society, and under 'actuality' the 'base actuality' with *its* rights, *its* marriage, and *its* property – he appeals at one time to a narrow-minded egoism, at another time – contrariwise – he anticipates the social man, the 'species-man', the 'essence of man', and takes it that these essences are self-consciously present in the individual. What a philosophical fraud and a bit of modern state sagacity it is when the generic-human can only exist in a society in which all men self-seekingly cultivate and posit themselves. This contradiction will only be solved by Socialism. It takes the termination and negation of philosophy seriously, it will set aside philosophy as well as the state, and will write no philosophical books over the negation of philosophy, for Socialism does not merely assert this or that, but it will tell *how* to deny philosophy as mere teaching, and *how* to finish it off in social life. However, *consistent* theoreticians still come to us out of the philosophical school, pure theoretical egoists who stand 'solitary' [*einsam*] on the most extreme peak of theoretical wisdom and look down with contempt upon the lesser doings of the *practical* Egoists, the base

[9] [Published in 1843, this work appears in a translation by Manfred H. Vogel, *Principles of the Philosophy of the Future* (Indianapolis, 1966). (Ed./Tr.)]

'mass'. On this peak stands, for example, Bruno Bauer, lonely – as he puts it – as a modern pillar-saint. Most recently, there has arisen opposite Bauer another peak, which exactly reverses Bauer's position and defends the 'mass', the 'base actuality', the practical Egoist. This is Stirner, the 'Unique One [*der Einzige*]'.[10] Let us now pay particular attention to him.

At first glance, it is already seen that the both aforementioned philosophers are but the two sides of the sundered man. The 'Solitary' and the 'Unique One' are opposing sides that presuppose one another, and we must – if only in passing – discuss the 'Solitary [*Einsamen*]' in order to illuminate the 'Unique One'.

As Philosophy itself has pointed out, the crassest egoism slumbers in the background of religion.[11] But what is *philosophical* egoism other than private egoism? Is the consistent Philosopher, as he appears in Bruno Bauer, not the self-satisfied egoist, the solitary who is blissful and all-powerful in his self-consciousness? Has he not devoured, consumed, dissolved and digested the whole of nature and the human species? Is he not but as the pious Christian who has been elevated and consoled by his communion feast and so separated from this evil and fallen world? Has he anything other to do in the world except – to learn to despise it? – Read Bruno Bauer! No Church Father and no statesman has ever more cynically expressed their scorn of the world of the 'mass' than this recent philosopher – why not! For is the 'Critic'[12] unlike the national police which would hold the people in check? And what would this authority do if no vulgar, base, miserable rabble were to exist?[13] As *philosophical* communism exhibits the same theoretical egoism as *religious* humanism, why should it not also have the same practical egoism in its background? As soon as it is revealed to the Monk that there is nothing to his Heavenly Egoism, his *blessedness*, he will become an animal directly, and collapse completely into Earthy Egoism, and thenceforth instead of striving for his alienated theoretical essence, for God and Heavenly Beatitude, he will strive for his alienated practical essence, money and happiness. Even so the Philosopher, for as soon as it develops that there is nothing to the 'Spirit', and it turns out that his 'imaginary

[10] [Stirner's self-designation in *Der Einzige und sein Eigentum* (*The Ego and His Own*). (Ed./Tr.)]

[11] [An obvious reference to Feuerbach's *The Essence of Christianity*. (Ed./Tr.)]

[12] [A reference to the brothers Bauer, whose identification with the 'Critic' appears most fully in Edgar Bauer's 1844 work, *Der Streit der Kritik mit Kirche und Staat*. (Ed./Tr.)]

[13] [A common Young Hegelian conceit, inspired by Hegelian dialectics, that appears even in later works such as Marx's 1863 *Theorien über den Mehrwert* in which 'The criminal produces not only crime but also the criminal law.' (Ed./Tr.)]

essence' was quite unnecessary, he falls directly into a practical egoism, and casts aside transcendental Humanity along with all *real* humanity as well.

II

According to Stirner, the whole fault of previous egoists resided simply in the fact that they had no consciousness of their egoism – that they were not Egoists out of principle, but always affected to pay homage to Humanity, that the war of all against all – even in free competition – was not followed through consistently.

'Take hold, and take what you require!' With this the war of all against all is declared. I alone decide what I will have.

'Now, that is truly no new wisdom, for self-seekers have acted so at all times!' Not at all necessary either that the thing be new, if only consciousness of it is present. But this latter will not be able to claim great age, unless perhaps one counts in the Egyptian and Spartan law; for how little current it is appears even from the structure above, which speaks with contempt of 'self-seekers'. One is to know just this, that the procedure of taking hold is not contemptible, but manifests the pure deed of the egoist at one with himself.

Only when I expect neither from individuals nor from a collectivity what I can give to myself, only then do I slip out of the snares of – love; the rabble ceases to be rabble only when it *takes hold*. Only the dread of taking hold, and the corresponding punishment thereof, makes it a rabble. Only that taking hold is *sin*, crime – only this dogma creates a rabble. For the fact that the rabble remains what it is, it (because it allows validity to that dogma) is to blame as well as, more especially, those who 'self-seekingly' (to give them back their favorite word) demand that the dogma be respected. In short, the lack of *consciousness* of that 'new wisdom', the old consciousness of sin, alone bears the blame.[14]

Hence 'consciousness' is the only thing which we still lack in order for us to become perfect egoists, and with it 'the rabble ceases to be rabble'.

Not the mutual alienation of men, but rather the theoretical expression of this alienation: religion and philosophy; not the war of all against all, which emerges from the isolation and estrangement of men in life, but the bad consciousness which accompanies it; not the crime from above and the crime from beneath, not, in short, the rabble and its tyrants which egoism has brought forth in the world, but – says Stirner – the *consciousness of sin* which came with it bears all the guilt!

[14] [See *The Ego*, pp. 257–8. (Ed./Tr.)]

If you break a leg, and it causes pain, and the doctor places the leg in a cast, so it is – according to our philosopher – not the *break*, but rather the painful *sense* of the broken leg and the *cast on the leg* which is the cause of your troubles!

If you are *sick*, and have a *doctor*, and if you would be *healthy* again – so send the doctor away!

This is the logic of the 'new wisdom'. Now how does it apply itself to what remains?

Not directly – complains Stirner – 'but only through money can one come out ahead of another, as, for example, the rich over the poor and the impoverished'. Now, Stirner has no complaint over this usual exploitation of one over the other if this only mutual exploitation is simply direct and personal. Stirner is not opposed to free competition because it is murder and theft [*Raubmord*], but only because it is not *directly* murder and theft.

But is *indirect* murder and theft something other than *conscious* murder and theft – and has not Stirner earlier complained that our Egoists lack an egoistic *consciousness*?

Stirner has nothing at all to object against the usual form of practical egoism except that it lacks 'consciousness'. It will become clear, however, that it is not the usual egoism which lacks the consciousness of egoism, but only the *fancied* Egoist.

Simply, and in general, what is Egoism? – and wherein stands the difference between the egoistical life and the life of love?

To love, to create, to work, to produce, is directly pleasurable; I can not love without at the same time to live, to live *well* – I can not produce without at the same time to consume, to *enjoy*. The Egoist also wants enjoyment! Now through what does Egoism distinguish itself from the life of love? Through this: that the Egoist would have life without love, enjoyment without work, and consume without producing – he takes only unto himself and never gives from himself, that is, he never gives himself over to anything. As an Egoist, he knows himself but yet does not know himself; he has no content, and so must always strive to seize upon a foreign content – for the Egoist stands over and against himself as a strange other. He can not create, for he has no content. He must forever hunt after pleasure, for he can never come upon 'the full enjoyment of life', and he comes not thereto for he can not create.

'Therefore do you not create and love only to obtain pleasure?'

No, you precocious child, in no way do I create and love for pleasure, but rather do I love out of love, create out of creative desire, out of the vitality of life, out of direct natural energy. If I love for the sake of enjoyment, then not only do I not love, but I also have no enjoyment – and if I work, act, in order to gain something, I am thence not freely acting, and not only have no joy and love in the work, but in fact nothing is gained for me: I exhaust only myself in this 'work', in this 'industriousness [*Erwerbstätigkeit*]'.[15]

The egotistical life is the self-divisive and self-consuming life of the animal world. The animal world is but the natural history of self-disintegrating and self-destroying life in general, and our whole history – up to this point – is nothing but the history of the *social* animal world.

But through what is the *social* animal world distinguished from the *wild* animal world? – Through nothing but *consciousness*. The history of the *social* animal world is but the history of the *conscious* animal world, and just as the natural animal world finds its highest expression in *the beast of prey* [*das Raubtier*], so the social animal world finds its highpoint in the *conscious beast of prey*.

Civilized barbarism begins exactly where uncivilized wilderness stops. The savage is still the beast of prey, whose estrangement in life is but 'immediate', 'personal', that is to say life is set over against him as natural or physical; whereas, with the barbarian, *spiritual* no less than physical life – his visible self (*physical individuality*) – stands opposed and foreign to him.

Just as unconscious Egoism, so conscious Egoism has its own history of development. And so as it has come about in the history of the animal world, so must it also happen in the history of man: the sundering of the species into hostile individuals, societies, peoples, and races – for this sundering, this mutual estrangement, is but the *first* form of existence of the species. In order to come into existence, the species must *individualize* itself. Through this opposition and struggle of individuals consciousness is first awakened in mankind. The first consciousness is the egoistic consciousness. Man could not begin to say 'I' without considering you, his *alter ego*, his neighboring humans and nature as foreign to him, and appearing to himself as being among hostile circumstances and powers. The *social* world of animals, with all of its egoistical desires, was first present in the awakening consciousness of men. Even then, the individual stood isolated, for in his *consciousness* all others stood opposed to him. As Egoism is the mutual estrangement of the Species, so then *religious* consciousness is the *consciousness* of this estrangement. The animal world of the wild simply has no religion, for it lacks the consciousness of its estrangement, that is, it lacks the *consciousness of sin*. And so, the *first* consciousness in man is the *consciousness of sin* – this being otherwise

[15] [A general theme in Marx's *Economic and Philosophic Manuscripts of 1844*. (Ed./Tr.)]

expressed in the myth of the 'Fall'.[16] This is the beginning, the first emergence of 'conscious' Egoism.

In the beginning, only individuals stood over and against the singular man as alien beings; the particular things of nature as well as men surrounded him as unique natural powers. But indeed, the more he now gained in knowledge, the more his egoism, his religiosity, his consciousness of sin expanded, until finally he discovered that the whole of mankind was set against him, and then this estranged Being of Mankind, this whole Species became for him his Godly Man, his God-Man, his *Christ*.

Egoism cannot create, and has no content, as its content is alienated from it – hence it can only 'consume' and 'enjoy' others. Equally, the conscious Egoist can only consume, and even Christ, the God-Man, will only 'consume', and 'partake' of Holy Communion. In like manner, the human species, the 'Spirit' of mankind, the 'Essence' of man, can only be acquired, taken up, held, broken up, consumed, digested, partaken of, and 'enjoyed' by the Egoist. 'Critical Philosophy' is just as much an egotistical institution as Holy Communion. It is the religion of Spiritual and theoretical Egoism, and thus the *consciousness* of Egoism. As such it lacks, just as religion in itself, the practical side of the egoistical consciousness – egotistical praxis. Egotistical consciousness is but the theoretical expression of egotistical praxis, without which this consciousness is unthinkable, as unthinkable as the consciousness of sin without sin.

As egotistical theory and consciousness have reached their most exalted point in religion and philosophy, so egotistical praxis must reach its highest point; and now it has, in the modern, Christian – commercial world [*Krämerwelt*].

What is our commercial world? It is the acme of the animal social world, and as the beast of prey was the high point of the native and wild world of animals, so the commercial world is the supreme attainment of the conscious and social animal world. In the self-enclosed existence of the animal body, in *blood*, the beast of prey enjoys his own self-enclosed existence. In the isolated life of the social body, in *gold*, the commercial world enjoys its own isolated existence. The *thirst for wealth* in the mercenary world is the *blood lust* of the beast of prey – the mercantile world is *avaricious*, and the bestial world is *preying*. The money-hungry possesive animal consumes not only its alienated theoretical essence – its God – but above all it consumes its estranged practical essence: money. To satisfy its egotistical needs, it not only attends its *Holy* Mass, but above all attends to the *profane*

[16] [Cf. Hegel's similar treatment of the Fall in his *Encyclopedia*, Appendix to Para. 24. (Ed./Tr.)]

Mass (the Mercenary Mass)[17] held in the market place. And if this world knows how to revere the Church and God as its *Sunday meal*, so must it also take into account the stock-market and the cult of wealth (money making) as its *daily bread*.

Egoism and the egotistical consciousness always go hand in hand in the social animal world. Indeed, the more cultivated the theoretical estrangement, the more cultivated is the practical as well, and – conversely – the more cultivated the practical the more cultivated the theory, the consciousness of egoism. Not only is the beast of prey perfected in our mercenary world, but the *consciousness* of this highest expression of the animal world is perfected as well. What, until now, has always been more or less allowed to happen without either consciousness or will – the mutual exploitation of men – will now be consciously carried out with a will. Privileged plundering comes to an end; the *arbitrary exercise of power* is now *universal human right*. The rights of man are now identical to those of the human animal, that is, the rights of all isolated and so-called 'independent' and 'free'[18] toward the alienated essence of all; here, the war of all against all is *sanctioned*. The celebrated declaration of 'The Rights of Man' is celebrated in that henceforth all preying beasts are equally justified, justified – as the 'Constitutionalists' of the 'free States' say – because they are autonomous and free beings, justified because they, as Egoists, as 'independent individuals', are now *recognized* and legally *acknowledged*.

The 'free competition' of our modern mercenary world is not only the perfected form of *rapacious robbery*, but it is also the perfected *consciousness* of the complete diversity of human estrangement. The prehistorical wild, classical slavery, roman bondage, were all more or less unfitted to the essence of this estrangement. They still had limited perspectives, and so had not attained to the universality and general justification of rapacity now found in our commercial world. The present mercenary world is the developed, essentially befitting, 'conscious', and 'principle' form of Egoism.

And now we can also understand what Stirner really wants – unconsciously wants – since existing egoism does not attract him in that he is unconsciously at one with it. I am sorry to have to declare, in spite of Stirner's protests, that his 'wisdom' is 'out of date', and I can give him only the comfort of knowing that 'critical' wisdom is even older.

What is the 'new wisdom' of Stirner?

17 [A fine word play, as the German *Messe* can denote either the religious Mass of the Catholic or the commercial trade-fair. (Ed./Tr.)]

18 [A reference to the Berlin Young Hegelians, the 'Free Ones'. (Ed./Tr.)]

In order to escape from the *religious* animal world, Stirner calls upon us to return once again to the world of wild animals: *retournons à la nature*!

On the other hand, what does 'critical' wisdom desire?

The High Priest of 'Criticism' says that the world is a vulgar and base 'mass', and it must be transcended by the 'Critic'. Only spirits without bodies exist in the Critical Heaven, lonely, conscious Egoists, without egotistical praxis, without egotistical needs. Now, is it yet necessary for me to tell you that the classical base of these solitary Egoists less egotistical praxis, these self-satisfied beatific Egoists, is the Christian Heaven, the *sinless paradise*? But I would tell you where this garden with its innocent populace *really* is – in the world beyond the city gate.

The 'consequence' of the 'Unique One' rationally expressed is the categorical imperative – become animals!

The 'consequence' of the 'solitary' rationally expressed is the categorical imperative – become plants!

Stirner's *Ideal* is the *civil society*, in which the State – as the world of animals – takes up into itself the world of plants.

Bauer's *Ideal* is the *State*, in which the civil society – *the world of plants* – takes up into itself the world of animals.

III

In recent times so much has been said of the 'bodily' individual, of 'actual' men, of the 'realization' of the Idea, that it should cause no wonder if news of it has also reached Berlin, and because of this 'philosophical heads' have been roused out of their beatitude.

However, the philosophical heads have understood the matter *philosophically*. Indeed, the *living individual* should step into the place of the spiritualized man, but not that *self-estranging*, isolated, heartless, spiritless, soulless, dead body given by the Egoist, that which the Egoist has displaced from himself in order to 'enjoy'. If this were to be the case, then we would only have the estranged *invisible* Ego in place of the estranged *visible* Ego, theoretical in place of practical Egoism, in place of 'spiritual' alienation the alienation of our 'natural' life, and in place of the philosophical 'in-and-for-itself' its so-called 'otherness'. But we want *being-for-another*, the '*for-one-another*' of men – the active and *creative* individual. However, in so far as human qualities are primarily our general property when developed through a social *upbringing*, so then the property of the individual will first complete itself, become his real property, only when he can manifest it through cultivated social qualities *worked out* in social life. But just as universal human qualities – in so far as they are not cultivated – are not *actual* but merely the *possibility* of our universal property, so also, if our socially conditioned qualities remain unmanifested in life, they are not actual but merely the possibility of our personal, social property. Or, philosophically expressed: so long as their 'spiritual' property is not real, men are in fact 'in-themselves', but in so far as they do not possess their spiritual property they are not 'for-themselves.' Further, that these persons are still less *social owners*, humans-for-one-another, self-actualizing, creative, and living is something self-evident – but this cannot be philosophically expressed. Philosophy, which has so many 'categories' is not acquainted with the category of '*for-one-another*'. It cannot bring itself to go beyond the category of the 'in-and-for-itself'.

Now Stirner does note that the 'in-and-for-itself' of philosophy is but an abstraction, but instead of proceeding to the 'being-for-one-another' he rather turns back to the 'other-being' of nature, to preying, to the unspiritual. Out of pure anguish, out of his 'physical' individuality he then loses sight of all human understanding and feeling.

Stirner is under the illusion that he, the 'Unique One', is the headless and heartless *rear-end*, but in fact he is nothing more than his illusion, for he is not only 'spiritless' but bodiless as well. It is the same with the 'Critical Head' – Bauer's 'Solitary' is not only bodiless but heartless and headless as well.

How does the 'Unique One' criticize liberalism, humanism, and socialism? On the grounds that reason, humanity, and love are, to *philosophy*, but abstractions and hence have no reality *in general*. Again, as we are now *brought up* to personality, we are not allowed to develop, cultivate, work out, or manifest our character from within ourselves. And so, because our essence up until now was to us but an *estranged and holy thing*, so we should *consume* this holy thing: 'If you *devour the sacred*, you have made it your own! Digest the sacramental wafer, and you are rid of it!'[19]

As if we no longer consumed our 'holy' property! As if the estranged 'holy' property would become *personal* through our consumption of it! And if our *actual* property would now step forth and replace the previous *illusion*, would it be something other than the manifest culmination of our qualities? Would it be something other than the *production* of our lives instead of the *consumption* of our lives?

Socialism is unconcerned with the State, for it rests upon totally

[19] [The *Ego*, p. 97; *Helms*, p.72. (Ed./Tr.)]

other grounds. Stirner knows only of the first beginnings of socialism, which still rest upon the premises of politics and political economy. He knows of such as Babeuf, the French and Worker forms of communism only by hearsay, for otherwise he must know, for example, that even communism which stands the ground of politics has already long passed beyond the conflicting poles of Egoism (*intérêt personnel*) and Humanism (*dévouement*). Of 'society' he knows only as much as the 'Critic' knows. His opposition to the State is the completely commonplace opposition of the open-minded Bourgeois, who likewise blame the State if the people are impoverished and starving.

It has also come to the attention of our Berlin philosophers that people have been talking a great deal about 'Anarchy'. He likewise desires 'Anarchy'. But with a view to declare a 'new wisdom', he not only sets out with this category of Proudhon[20] against the sovereignty of every external authority, but against the 'sovereignty of Reason' itself. However, this wisdom is so little new, that to encounter it one must turn back to the beginning of history, to the source of our social world of animals; whereas, in order to encounter the Anarchy of Proudhon, one need but turn back to the religious and political revolutions of our newest and most recent history.

Every page of his writings makes it clear that the 'Unique One' is not only serious in his opposition to certain forms of reasoning and morality, but is absolutely set against the *reasonable content* of all previous forms of morality. As an example, he would ignore the canonization of the 'human' by 'humane liberalism' if the 'human' were taken as a human possibility, since the error of the 'humanists' would then be but a logical one, and not a real mistake, but – 'Do you suppose the humane liberal will be so liberal as to aver that everything possible to man is *human*? On the contrary! He does not, indeed, share the Philistine's moral prejudice about the prostitute, but "that this woman turns her body into a money-getting machine" makes her despicable to him as "human being". His judgement is, the prostitute is not a human being; or, so far as a woman is a prostitute, so far is she unhuman, dehumanized.'[21] Now, this is what Stirner has set forth regarding Humanism – but he would agree with Humanism in respect to its *content* if it would catch sight of something human in the 'money-getting machine'! – This then is what Stirner expresses regarding Humanism. Certainly, Stirner would find Human-

[20] Proudhon was the first to accept and apply the term 'Anarchy' as a definite political category. (Ed./Tr.)]

[21] [The *Ego*, p. 126. Stirner is citing Bauer. (Ed./Tr.)]

ism in accord with the *content* of his own thought were it but to catch sight of something still human in the money-making machine!

Humanism, to Stirner, is not in error because it turns men into merely a 'principle', that is to say, because it has as a content only the theoretical abstraction of men – and so an illusion – but rather because (hear! hear!) 'Criticism, among social theories is indisputably the most complete, because it removes and deprives of value everything that *separates* man from man...How can you be truly single so long as even one connection still exists between you?'[22]

Hence, in order to transcend and annul the contradiction between the human 'Idea' and inhuman reality, we should not seek to develop and perfect men, but rather 'turn away' from ourselves and return to the 'beast'. The man who takes himself for 'a beast, would easily find that the beast, which follows its own impulse – its own advice, as it were – does not impel itself to do the most senseless things, but takes very correct steps'.[23] *Retournons à la nature*!

Socialism declares: you should not be *idealists*, but *real* men. Stirner, to the contrary, declares: 'Thousands of years of culture have obscured to you what you are, have made you believe you are not egoists but are *called* to be idealists – good men. Shake that off!'[24]

A Socialist establishes the proposal that we should become *real species-being* [*wirkliche Gattungswesen*],[25] and thereby proposes a society in which everyone can cultivate, exercise and perfect their human qualities. Stirner wants to know nothing of *this* actual man. He presents his opposing view of actual men in the following manner: 'Real man is only – the un-man.'[26] Again, 'I, the egoist, have not at heart the welfare of this "human society", I sacrifice nothing to it, I only utilize it; but to be able to utilize it completely I transform it rather into my property and my creature; that is, I annihilate it, and form in its place the *Union of Egoists* [*Verein von Egoisten*].'[27]

Unique one, you are certainly an original and amusing celebrity! But I would have preferred to have seen your 'Union of Egoists' exist only on paper. Now, if it is not permitted of me, then I must allow myself to characterize the real ideas of your 'Union of Egoists'.

Our whole history up to now has been nothing but the history of egotistical unions, whose fruits are known to all of us – ancient slavery,

[22] [The *Ego*, p. 134; *Helms*, p. 101. (Ed./Tr.)]
[23] [The *Ego*, p. 134; *Helms*, p. 101. (Ed./Tr.)]
[24] [The *Ego*, p. 191; *Helms*, p. 110. (Ed./Tr.)]
[25] [The exact phrase that Stirner attributes to Marx in the *Ego*, p. 176. (Ed./Tr.)]
[26] [The *Ego*, p. 177; *Helms*, p. 121. (Ed./Tr.)]
[27] [The *Ego*, p. 179; not in *Helms*. (Ed./Tr.)]

Roman bondage, and our modern principled and universal serfdom. And now, after the circular course of this egotistical union is completed and has died out, Egoism – in its despairing confusion – is proposing all sorts of combinations of already historically obsolete forms of egoistical associations. In these days this despair has already brought many foolish thoughts into the world. But no one would have even allowed himself to dream that it would take a fancy to the most brutal form of Egoism – *fierce savagery* – and then desire to introduce this into the world. But it is precisely this thought which dominates the 'Unique One'. In all seriousness, Stirner desires to see once again the establishment of the most fundamental form of egotistical intercourse – totally direct murder and robbery!

'Stirner wants that?' Well, you have reason not to believe that the 'Unique One' wants that – and so I must take back my words. Stirner wants, in general, nothing. He is only making boastful noises.

Now, it is possible to consider the 'Unique One' excused on the ground that he himself does not know what he wants. He is of a mind to struggle against the 'Critic', but he is merely the *slave* of the 'Critic'. He wants to annihilate the continuity of the 'State' but remains standing constantly upon this *ground*. He sings the praises, in all keys, of a return to the world of the beast, but in the last analysis he simply intends to return to being a *peaceful vegetable*.

'The last and most decided opposition, that of unique against unique, is at bottom beyond what is called opposition, but without having sunk back into "unity" and unison. As unique you have nothing in common with the other any longer, and therefore nothing divisive or hostile either;... The opposition vanishes in complete – *severance* or singleness [*Einzigkeit*].'[28]

Certainly it vanishes – as light to the blind man, as a mistake in the face of stupidity, as life before death! And thus to evade every collision, every life-struggle, he finally returns back to the womb of the earth, and there – vegetates! The grand braggadocio of brutality has simply coursed back but yet again to the *peaceful* insensitivity of the 'Solitary'!

Is there yet anything more to Stirner's struggle against Bauer? Is Stirner fully the practical Egoist he imagines himself to be? Is he such a stubborn sinner as he thinks?

As he is set against every 'calling', every 'determination', one could believe that he himself must be beyond every 'determination' and 'calling'. This is far from being the case, for he is constantly surveyed by *the secret police of his own critical conscience*. His lack of

[28] [The *Ego*, p. 208; *Helms*, pp. 135–6. (Ed./Tr.)]

constraint is a lie, his toughness an affectation. He has not forgotten that 'the program of the critic will allow no stability to any part of our possessions, and would only cast aside our welfare'. He always remains behind the back of his egotistical 'Ideal'. The Egoist continually calls forth his critical consciousness out of his mind, and allows nothing to be of such interest to him as that he would give himself totally over to it. He is as Luther, and must call out 'Here I stand, I cannot do otherwise! and that is the fundamental maxim of the possessed.'[29] Yes, 'anxiety' would likely 'fix' something in him, and leave this prematurely old child of nature not a moment of peace! He can never fulfill his 'determination' as an Egoist. He must question himself every time – 'Do I follow myself, my *own* determination'[30] if I give myself completely over to this or to that?

We have already seen in the introduction that Stirner agrees with the philosophers in principle: the single person is the species. We have further seen that Bauer is as much an Egoist as Stirner, and that Stirner is as much an Idealist as Bauer. Again, that Stirner, with all of his brutal talk, simply intends to be a peaceful vegetable, and that in the last instance he cannot free himself from the surveillance of the 'critical' secret police. What then is finally the distinction between the egotistical 'Unique One' and the critical 'Solitary'?

The 'Solitary' is an Egoist with grey hair, a childish old man; the 'Unique One' is a precocious child. The 'Solitary' is a *slave on the throne*; the 'Unique One' is a *slave who has broken his bonds*. Bauer has set up a foolish *theoretical* Egoism in his head; Stirner a foolish *practical* Egoism. As in our case, and that of their philosophical representative Feuerbach, they would of necessity have to unite in order to engage in a further advance, and one might even have the hope to see them sometime resurrected as Socialists – after they have expiated their inner contradictions. But as they are *separated*, they remain alone, lonely, without life, without death, and are unable to rise up into existence. They are, and remain – philosophers.

[29] [The *Ego*, p. 61; *Helms*, p. 57. (Ed./Tr.)]

[30] [The *Ego*, p. 169; *Helms*, p. 118. (Ed./Tr.)]

XI
Karl Schmidt
1819–1864

Karl Schmidt

The last significant, and the most obscure participant in the Young Hegelian movement was Karl Schmidt, whose singular work of 1846 *The Realm of the Understanding and the Individual* [*Das Verstandestum und das Individuum*] logically exhausted the philosophical potential of Hegelianism and so went even beyond the exhaustive criticisms of Stirner to criticise Stirner himself. *The Realm of the Understanding* is a critical *tour de force* in which Schmidt, who well knew and was well known by the Young Hegelians, pulverized every remaining positive position within the movement, and thus was consciously left with only the immediate world of commonplace practice as a field of activity.

Unhappily for his future reputation, Schmidt's criticism was published anonymously, and although the author was privately known within the circle of Young Hegelians, his name was lost to subsequent historians of the movement. Indeed, Schmidt was not associated with *The Realm of the Understanding* until most recently, when his brief – and unpublished – autobiography revealed him to be the author of this extraordinary work.

In 1841, Schmidt began his career as a theology student at the University of Halle. And, as so many young theologians of his time, soon fell under the spell of Strauss' *Life of Jesus*. It was but a short step from Strauss to Hegel, and so – as he remarks – 'Hegelian philosophy took the place of religion for me'. In 1844, Schmidt left Halle to study at the University of Berlin. It was, significantly, the same year in which Kierkegaard – with whom Schmidt shares a spiritual kinship – published his *Concept of Dread* and *Philosophical Fragments*. Schmidt soon joined Bruno Bauer's Berlin Circle, and then pursued the path of Young Hegelianism to what he perceived to be its pathetic yet logical conclusion. To Schmidt, the valid course of Hegelianism seemed inexorably to lead into a desert of egoism. In his *Autobiography*, Schmidt retraced the line of thought he had taken during his two philosophically eventful years in Berlin:

> If someone has once heard of Hegel, he must proceed to Strauss, from Strauss to Feuerbach, and from Feuerbach to Bruno Bauer. I accomplished the consequence of this thought in myself, but soon came to the further conclusion... that Stirner makes more sense than Bruno Bauer and that one must proceed beyond Stirner to arrive at the most abstract individualism.

In sum, *The Realm of the Understanding* is the chronicle of Schmidt's *via dolorosa*, a steep dialectical path which began with Strauss' Hegel and terminated beyond Stirner, in the arid emptiness of 'the most abstract individualism'. The compulsive logic of Karl Schmidt would mark the dead end of critical Young Hegelianism.

Once having 'settled accounts with his philosophic conscience' – to borrow a phrase from Marx and Engels – Schmidt methodically proceeded to gain a moderate but secure reputation as an educationalist. With *The Realm of the Understanding*, he not only had left Young Hegelianism theoretically, but practically as well, and he entered upon the pursuit of concrete bourgeois rewards with not a hint of either remorse or resignation. In 1862, he finally secured his reputation with the publication of a four-volume *History of Pedagogy*. For this, he was spared the obscurity and poverty which dogged the later lives of most of the Young Hegelians, and died in surroundings of moderate success – just after being appointed to school inspector and director of teachers' education at Gotha. Nevertheless, for the few who have knowledge of his earlier writings, it is not inconceivable that Schmidt, as educationalist, was merely an ironic creation of Schmidt, the Young Hegelian.

The last two chapters of the first part of *The Realm of the Understanding* appear here for the first time in any language since the original edition of 1846. These chapters summarize the critical first part of the work, which fixed upon a destructive *reductio ad absurdum* of the theories of the Bauers, Feuerbach, Stirner and the Communists.

The selections have been translated and annotated by Eric von der Luft.

The most valuable work done on Karl Schmidt to this date comprises the third chapter (pp. 39–52) of Ernst Barnikol's fine scholarly study of Bruno Bauer, *Das Entdeckte Christentum im Vormärz: Bruno Bauers Kampf gegen Religion und Christentum und Erstausgabe seiner Kampfschrift*, (Jena: Eugen Diederichs, 1927).

The Realm of the Understanding and the Individual
Part I, Chapters IV and V

IV. THE WAR AGAINST CRITIQUE

'Critique' celebrates its golden age and its consummation as 'history'; but what is consummated must be annihilated; the annihilation of what is consummated lies at the same time in its consummation; fullness and wholeness is at the same time the end. 'Pure critique' is summoned to the battlefield and challenged to fight. It takes its stand. The slaughter begins.

1. *The Critique of Critical Critique*

'The struggle between *Strauss* and *Bauer* concerning substance and self-consciousness is a struggle within Hegelian speculation. There are three elements in Hegel, Spinozistic substance, Fichtean self-consciousness, and Hegelian *absolute spirit*, the necessarily contradictory unity of the two. The first element is *nature*, metaphysically parodied, in *separation* from man; the second is *spirit*, metaphysically parodied, in *separation* from nature; the third is *actual man* and the actual *human species*, the metaphysically parodied *unity* of the two. *Strauss* has led Hegel to a Spinozistic standpoint; Bauer has led Hegel to a Fichtean standpoint thoroughly consistent within the theological domain. Both have *criticized* Hegel insofar as, for him, each of the two elements is *falsified* through the other; whereas they have developed each of the elements into its *one-sided*, and thus consistent, realization. Both proceed beyond *Hegel* from this point in their critique, but both also remain firmly within Hegel's speculation, and each represents only *one side* of Hegel's system' [Marx–Engels, p. 147].[1] 'Also, for

[1] [Because Schmidt's work is a skillfully wrought satirical mosaic, depending largely upon the precise way in which its citations are stylistically combined with his own words, I have thought it best to use my own translations of the quoted passages, whether or not a better translation exists, in order to preserve the fluidity and grace of expression which is evident in the original German. I have thus inserted in the text bracketed references to the following editions of Schmidt's sources: Marx' and Engels' *Die heilige Familie*, abbreviated 'Marx-Engels', in

Bauer as for Hegel, who discloses and elevates to self-consciousness the reservedness of substance,[2] self-consciousness is substance elevated to self-consciousness or self-consciousness as substance; self-consciousness is transformed from a predicate of man to a self-reliant subject. It is the metaphysical-theological caricature of man in his separation from nature. The essence of this self-consciousness is thus not man, but the idea whose actual existence it is. It is the idea-become-human and therefore also *infinite*. All human properties transform themselves thence in a mysterious way into properties of the imaginary infinite self-consciousness' [Cf. Marx–Engels, p. 146]. 'Mr Bauer, who is now accomplishing in *all* areas *his* opposition to *substance*, his philosophy of self-consciousness or of spirit, must therefore in all areas have to deal only with his own phantoms. Critique is, in his hand, the instrument to sublimate into mere pretense and pure thought anything which still maintains a finite, material existence outside of infinite self-consciousness. He does not combat the metaphysical illusion in substance, but rather the worldly kernel – nature; nature, not only as it exists outside of man, but also as it is his own nature. Presupposing substance in no area – he still speaks in this language – thus means for him to recognize: no being different from thinking, no natural energy different from spiritual spontaneity, no power of human essence different from understanding, no suffering different from activity, no impression left by others different from the impression effected by oneself, no feeling and willing different from knowing, no heart different from head, no

Bd. II of their *Werke* (Berlin: Dietz Verlag, 1962); Max Stirner's *Der Einzige und sein Eigentum*, abbreviated 'Stirner', hrsg. von Ahlrich Meyer (Stuttgart: Philipp Reclam, 1972); Stirner's *Kleinere Schriften und seine Entgegnungen auf die Kritik seines Werkes 'Der Einzige und sein Eigentum'*, abbreviated 'Stirner KS' (Stuttgart: Frommann, 1976); and the Barnikol edition of Bauer's *Das entdeckte Christentum*, abbreviated 'Barnikol' (where the original page numbers appear in the margins). Also inserted in brackets are section or paragraph numbers for Feuerbach's *Grundsätze der Philosophie der Zukunft* and for other, miscellaneously cited passages, e.g., from Shakespeare, Goethe, etc. In general, either Schmidt or his editor was very careless in the placement of quotation marks and in the transcription of passages. I have tried to correct the use of punctuation *in situ*. Against what is now common practice, but following Schmidt, lengthy prose quotations are not set off by indentation. Where major discrepancies in the citations occur, I have indicated this either by footnotes or by simply inserting 'Cf.' in the bracketed references in the text, thus inviting the interested reader to make the comparison himself. In all cases of such discrepancy, it is Schmidt's erroneous version, rather than the correct original, which is translated. All notes in the text are Schmidt's; all footnotes are my own. (Tr.)]

[2] [Schmidt's paraphrase of Hegel as misquoted by Marx; Cf. *Phänomenologie des Geistes*, hrsg. von Johannes Hoffmeister (Hamburg: Felix Meiner, 1952), p. 13. (Tr.)]

object different from subject, no praxis different from theory, no man different from the critic, no actual community different from abstract universality, no *Thou* different from the *I*. It is accordingly consistent when Mr Bauer continues further to identify himself with infinite self-consciousness and with spirit, i.e., to set their creator in the place of these his creations. It is just as consistent to disavow as stubborn mass and material the rest of the world which obstinately persists in being something different from his product. And now he hopes:

> It will not endure long
> And it will perish with bodies.
> [Goethe, *Faust*, Part I, lines 1357–8]

Hitherto not being able to get close to 'something of this gross world', he likewise constructs his own discord consistently for himself as a self-discord of this world, and constructs the rebellion of his critique of the development of mankind as an enormous rebellion of mankind against his critique, against spirit, against Mr Bruno Bauer and his associates. Mr Bauer has been a theologian from birth, but not an average one, rather a critical theologian or a theological critic. As the outermost extreme of old-Hegelian orthodoxy, as a speculative organizer of all religious and theological nonsense, he has already pronounced critique to be constantly his personal property. At that time he designated Straussian critique as human critique, and explicitly asserted the right of divine critique in opposition to that of Strauss. He later picked out of the religious masquerade the great self-esteem or self-consciousness which was the hidden kernel of this godliness, granted it autonomy as a special essence, and exalted it to the principle of critique under the sign of 'infinite self-consciousness'. In his own movement he then fulfilled the movement which the 'philosophy of self-consciousness' describes as an absolute act of life. He again removed the 'difference' of 'the product', *infinite self-consciousness*, from the producer, from *himself*, and recognized that in its movement there '*was only he himself*', and that thus the movement of the universe just becomes *genuine* and *actual* in his ideal self-movement. Divine critique in its return into itself has been restored in a rational, conscious, critical way; being-in-itself has changed into being-in-and-for-itself; and the performed, actualized, revealed beginning has just become the conclusion. Divine critique, in contradistinction to human critique, has revealed itself as *the critique*, as the *pure critique*, as *the critical critique*. In the place of apologetics for the Old and New Testaments have apeared apologetics for the old and new works of Mr Bauer. The theological opposition of God and man, of spirit and flesh, of infinity and finitude, is transformed into the critical theological opposition of spirit, critique, or Mr Bauer, and the material of mass, or the profane world. The theological opposition of faith and reason has dissolved itself in the critical theological opposition of *common sense* and pure critical thinking. The '*Journal for Speculative Theology*' has been transformed into the newspaper of critical literature. The *religious redeemer of the world* is finally actualized in the *critical redeemer of the world*, Mr Bauer. The last phase of Mr Bauer's development is no anomaly; it is the *return* of this development *into* itself out of *its alienation.* It is obvious that the moment in which *divine* critique *alienated* itself and emerged from itself coincides with the moment in which it became partially untrue to itself and created something *human. Absolute critique*, having reverted to its starting point, has finished its *speculative circular course* and with it the course of its *life.* Its further movement is a pure, prominent *circulating within itself*, concerned with every *massive* interest, and therefore without any further interest in mass' [Marx–Engels, pp. 149–51]. Even absolute critique has its dogma. 'Absolute critique emanates from the *dogma* of the absolute justification of "*spirit*". Absolute critique emanates further from the *dogma* of the *extra-worldly* existence of spirit, i.e., existence outside of the teeming mass of mankind. Absolute critique finally transforms, on the one side, "spirit" and "progress", and on the other side, "mass", into fixed essences, into concepts, and refers them then to one another as such given, firm extremes. It does not occur to absolute critique to inquire into spirit itself, to investigate whether or not "the catch-word", "self-deception", or "kernel-lessness" are grounded in spirit's own spiritualistic nature, in spirit's frivolous "pretension". On the contrary, spirit is *absolute*, but, unfortunately, at the same time it is constantly turning over into *spiritlessness*: It is constantly overlooking the most vital factor. It must therefore have an *adversary* which plots against it. Mass is this *adversary*. The same is the case with "progress". Despite the pretensions of "progress", *retrogressions* and *circular movements* are constantly becoming evident. Absolute critique, far removed from surmising that the category of "progress" is fully worthless and abstract, is rather clever enough to acknowledge "progress" as absolute, in order to insinuate that *mass* is the explanation of retrogression and a "personal enemy" of progress. Because "mass" is nothing but the "*antithesis of spirit*", of progress, of "critique", it can thus also only be determined through this imaginary antithesis; and, disregarding this opposition, critique knows only that which is *meaningless* concerning the *meaning* and the being-there of mass, and it knows, since mass is fully undetermined, to speak of it in *that sense* in which the "word" *even* includes the *so-called* cultured world. An "even" and a "so-called" are sufficient for a critical definition. *Mass* is thus distinguished from *actual* masses, and exists as "*mass*" only for the sake of "critique"' [Marx–Engels, pp. 87–8]. 'The relationship between "spirit and mass" *discovered* by Mr Bauer nevertheless still has a *hidden* sense. It is, of course, nothing else but the *critically caricatured consummation* of the *Hegelian apprehension of history*, which again is nothing else but the *speculative* expression of the *Christian*, *Germanic* dogma of the opposition of *spirit* and *material*, of *God* and the *world*. This opposition, to be sure, expresses itself within history, within the human world itself, in such a way that a few select *individuals*, as the *active* spirit of the rest of mankind, stand over against that mankind which is just *spiritless mass* and *material*. *Hegel's* apprehension of history presupposes an *abstract* and *absolute* spirit which so develops itself that mankind is only a *mass* which upholds this spirit either more unconsciously or more consciously. He thus allows a *speculative*, esoteric history to take precedence within empirical, exoteric history. The history of mankind transforms itself into the history of the *abstract spirit* of mankind, spirit which is thus *ulterior* with respect to actual man' [Cf. Marx–Engels, pp. 89–90]. 'Surely, for Hegel, the *absolute spirit* of history has its material in *mass* and its appropriate expression first in *philosophy*. *The philosopher*, meanwhile, appears only as the organ in which absolute spirit, the maker of history, comes to consciousness,[3] *almost as an afterthought*, after a completion of the movement. The philosopher's share in history reduces itself to his supplementary consciousness, for absolute spirit achieves the actual movement *unconsciously*. The philosopher thus arrives *post festum*. Hegel is guilty of a twofold incompleteness, first by pronouncing philosophy to be the being-there of absolute spirit, but then at the same time restraining himself from pronouncing the *actual*, *philosophical individual* to be *absolute* spirit; second, however, by allowing absolute spirit as absolute spirit to produce history only for *show*. Because absolute spirit, of course, just comes to *consciousness* in the philosopher *post festum* as creative world-spirit, thus its fabrication of history exists only in consciousness, in the opinion and mental imagery of the philosopher, only in speculative imagination. Mr Bauer preserves, cancels, and uplifts Hegel's incompleteness. *Now* he pronounces *critique* to be absolute spirit, and pronounces *himself* to be *critique*. As the element of critique is exiled from mass, so is the element of mass exiled from critique. Thus critique does not know itself in a *mass*, but rather in a trifling *little band* of chosen men,

[3] [Richard Dixon and Clemens Dutt mistranslate *Bewusstsein* as 'self-consciousness'; cf. *The Holy Family* in volume IV of Marx' and Engels' *Collected Works* (New York: International Publishers/London: Lawrence and Wishart, 1975), p. 85. (Tr.)]

exclusively incarnated in Mr Bauer and his disciples. Mr Bruno preserves, cancels, and uplifts Hegel's other incompleteness further as he no longer makes history in fantasy *post festum*, as does Hegelian spirit, but instead, with *consciousness* in opposition to the mass of the rest of mankind, plays the role of *world-spirit*, appears in a contemporary dramatic relation to this mass, and, intentionally and after mature, careful deliberation, invents and fulfils history. On the one side stands mass as the passive, spiritless, history-less, *material* element of history. On the other side stands *spirit*, *critique*, Mr Bauer and company, as the active element from which all *historical* action proceeds. Society's act of metamorphosis reduces itself to the *cerebral activity* of critical critique' [Cf. Marx–Engels, pp. 90–91]. 'Even *history*, like *truth*, becomes a singular person, a metaphysical subject, whose sole supporters are actual, human individuals. Absolute critique thus helps itself to these catchwords: "*History* does not let itself be mocked, *history* has spent its greatest exertions in this direction, *history* has been busy; why should history be so busy? *History* explicitly furnishes us with proof, *history* introduces truths, etc., etc."' [Cf. Marx–Engels, pp. 83–84]. Indeed: 'History does *nothing*, it "*owns* no colossal wealth", it "fights no battles!" Rather, it is *man*, actual, living man, who does everything, who owns and fights; it is not "history" which needs man as the means to work through *its* ends – as if it were a singular person – on the contrary, history is *nothing* but the activity of man in pursuit of his ends' [Marx–Engels, p. 98]. Critique, because of its utterly theological tendency, must handle its past apologetically. Critique wanted to become acquainted with mass and preserve, cancel, and uplift it, thus it already knew in advance the gap which separates the critic from mass, the gap which just consists in being preserved, cancelled, and uplifted by the critic [Cf. Marx–Engels, p. 105]. 'Now since everyone is himself his own neighbor, "critique" busies itself chiefly with preserving, cancelling, and uplifting its own *massive enormity*, just like the Christian ascetics who begin the campaign of spirit against flesh by mortifying their *own* flesh. The "flesh" of absolute critique is its *actually massive* – covering twenty or thirty volumes – literary *past*. Mr Bauer must therefore liberate the literary biography of "critique" – which exactly coincides with his own literary biography – from its *massive illusion*, subsequently *improve* and *interpret* it, and "provide authority for critique's earlier works" through this *apologetic* commentary' [Marx–Engels, p. 105]. 'The self-apology of absolute critique has at its disposal an entire *apologetical* dictionary: "not even proper", "only not marked", "there was besides", "not yet complete", "nevertheless...nonetheless", "not only...but especially", "but only just as proper", "critique should have...", "if it had been possible for me and if it, on the other side, ...", "if...then one will surely concede at the same time...", "now if it is natural, if it is not inevitable, etc., etc.", "not even". Not very long ago absolute critique expressed its opinion of similar apologetic windings as follows: "'Although' and 'nonetheless', 'certainly' and 'however', a heavenly Yes and an earthly No,[4] are the pedestals of modern theology, the stilts on which it moves along, the trick in which all of its wisdom is contained, the winding which returns into all of its windings, its alpha and omega."' (*Discovered Christianity*, p. 162).[5] [Barnikol, p. 153; Marx–Engels, p. 112].

The critics of critical critique have readily grasped the points in which critique has been vulnerable, and they have shown its weakness and one-sidedness, the weakness of pure spirit and the one-sidedness of the defense of this spirit. But because *Engels* and *Marx* are blinded by the gleam of another new ideal and captivated and stupefied by the delirium of another new idea, because they approach critique with spiritual prejudices and with an imaginary and thoroughly pondered heaven, they must step forth as fanatics, dressing their words with the holy light of their idea, they may not apprehend and comprehend critique clearly, and they must be dumbstruck by the superiority of 'critique', *of spirit par excellence*. Their motto is: real humanism. 'And in Germany "real humanism" has no opponent more dangerous than spiritualism, or the speculative idealism which sets "self-consciousness" or "spirit" in the place of the actual, individual man and, with the evangelist, teaches: "Spirit is that which makes something alive, flesh is useless." It is obvious that this fleshless spirit has spirit only in its fancy. What we resist in *Bauerian* critique is speculation simply reproducing itself as a caricature. We consider it to be the most nearly consummated expression of the Christian, Germanic principle which is now performing its swan song while it transforms "critique" itself into a transcendent power' [Marx–Engels, p. 7]. Engels and Marx thus do not combat critique at all, neither critique in and for itself, nor critique for its own sake, or for the sake of its own inner deficiency; they do not analyse critique as long as they salvage the elements of

4 [Bauer's text, according to Barnikol, reads, 'ein himmlisches Nein und ein irdisches Ja', while Schmidt's text, which is here translated, reads, 'ein himmlisches Ja und ein irdisches Nein'. (Tr.)]

5 [Schmidt, in one of his few specific references to a cited passage, has misidentified its source. It actually occurs on p. 102 of *Das entdeckte Christentum*, while Schmidt, copying the printer's error in the first edition of Marx, has placed it on p. 162. (Cf. Barnikol, p. 44). (Tr.)]

the analysis themselves; rather, they wage a *holy* war against critique because critique is their enemy, the most dangerous enemy of the 'real humanism' of a determined spiritual formula.

'Real humanism' is the presupposition and the basis on which stands 'the critique of critical critique'. 'Real humanism' is the discovered philosopher's stone because it creates the 'actual, individual man'. – The critique of critical critique could not strike critique dead.

2. *Ludwig Feuerbach*

The founder of 'real humanism' fixes, 'I am an actual, sensuous essence: my body belongs to my essence, indeed the body in its totality is my I, my essence itself' [Cf. Feuerbach, § 36] as the starting point of 'modern philosophy'. Therefore 'only what requires no demonstration, what is certain immediately through itself, what supports and accepts itself immediately, what is immediately followed by the affirmation that it is, is true and divine – the simply decided, the simply indubitable, the crystal clear. But only the sensuous is crystal clear; only where sensuousness begins does all doubt and strife cease. The mystery of immediate knowing is sensuousness' [Feuerbach, §38]. However, 'to the senses, not only "external" things are an object. Man himself is only given to himself through sense – he is himself an object as a sense object. The identity of subject and object, abstract thought only in self-consciousness, is truth and actuality only in the sensuous viewing of man by man. We feel not only stones and wood, not only flesh and bone, we also feel feelings as we press the hands or lips of a feeling essence; we perceive through our ears not only the roaring of water and the whispering of leaves, but also the soulful voice of love and wisdom; we see not only mirrored surfaces and colored apparitions, we also glance into the eyes of man; thus not only the external – but also the internal, not only flesh – but also spirit, not only the thing – but also the I, is an object of sense. Everything is therefore sensuously perceptible, if not immediately, then surely mediately, if not with the raw, plebeian senses, then surely with the refined senses, if not through the eyes of the anatomist or the chemist, then surely through the eyes of the philosopher' [Feuerbach, §41]. The sensuous is thus 'not immediate in the sense that it is profane, tremendously obvious, thoughtless, or self-evident' [Cf. Feuerbach, §43]. 'The actual, in its actuality and totality, the object of modern philosophy, is only an object for an actual and complete man.[6] Modern philosophy thus holds as its

[6] [Feuerbach reads, 'Wesen'; Schmidt reads, 'Menschen'. (Tr.)]

principle of knowledge, as its subject, not the I, not absolute spirit, i.e., not abstract spirit, in short not reason *in abstracto*,[7] but rather the actual and entire essence of man. Reality, the subject of reason, is only man. Man thinks, not the I, not reason. Modern philosophy is thus founded on the Godhead, i.e., a truth of the whole man; or, it is even well founded on reason, but on the reason whose essence is human essence, thus not on an essence-less, colorless, and nameless reason, but rather on the reason which is saturated with the blood of man. Therefore if the old philosophers said, "Only the rational is true and actual", then modern philosophy responds to them by saying, "Only the human is true and actual, for only the human is rational; man is the measure of reason"' [Cf. Feuerbach, §50]. 'Truth does not exist in thinking, or in knowing for itself. Truth is only the totality of human life and essence' [Feuerbach, §58]. 'The individual man for himself does not have the essence of man in himself, neither in himself as the moral essence nor in himself as the thinking essence. The essence of man is comprised only in the community, in the unity of man with man – a unity which however is only founded on the reality of the difference between I and Thou' [Cf. Feuerbach, §59]. 'Solitude is finitude and narrowness; communal solidarity is freedom and infinity. Man for himself is man (in the usual sense); man with man, the unity of I and thou, is God' [Feuerbach, §60]. 'The highest and final principle of philosophy is accordingly the unity of man with man. All essential relationships – the principles of the various sciences – are only various types and modes of this unity' [Feuerbach, §63]. 'Modern philosophy, as the philosophy of man, is also essentially the philosophy for man – it has, without detriment to the dignity and independence of the theory, indeed in the most intimate harmony with this theory, an essentially practical tendency, to be sure, practical in the highest sense; it replaces religion, it has the essence of religion within it, it is, in truth itself, religion' [Cf. Feuerbach, §64].

However, 'to the senses' is indeed only 'sense'; 'the sensuous' is only 'object'. 'Man' is not given through 'the senses', but through 'thinking', because man is a 'thought', an 'abstraction'. Thus, in the end, even Feuerbach may not and can not be content with the usual, actual, stalwart sensuousness, the sensuousness which is nothing but sensuousness, this determined sensuousness; but instead he needs the 'refined sense', the 'philosophical eye', i.e., the sense and the eye which are no longer sense and eye, but rather the sense and eye which peer through the thick cloud-cover of spirit and proceed, privileged

[7] [Feuerbach reads, 'für sich allein'; Schmidt reads, '*in abstracto*'. (Tr.)]

and authorized, out of the spiritual wash; he thus needs 'philosophy' and 'thought'. How could sense, this determined sensuousness, ever apprehend 'man'? Is not 'essence' a matter of thought? Does not 'the totality of human essence' exist only in 'thought' alone? And this totality must and may, even for Feuerbach, appear only in thought, not in hard actuality. He must both wish and not wish it to make an appearance, i.e., he must make it into an exclusive object of yearning and hope. The sensuousness and the being of Feuerbach are not this determined sensuousness or this individual and exclusive being, but they are universal sensuousness and universal being – an abstraction. Feuerbachian man is a worthy essence of 'modern philosophy', and modern philosophy is, 'in truth itself, religion'. Feuerbachian man is Feuerbachian fantasy. Feuerbach's 'philosophy' could not annihilate 'critique'.

3. *Max Stirner*

Stirner takes up the fight. His first victim is *the middle class*. 'The middle class is nothing other than the thought that the state is, all in all, the true man, and that the human value of the individual consists in being a citizen of the state. The true man is the nation, but the individual is forever an egoist. Therefore strip off your individuality or your isolation, in which egoistical inequality and dissension swarm, and dedicate yourselves completely to the true man, the nation, or the state. Then you will be considered as a man and have everything which makes a man; the state, the true man, will authorize you as its own and give you your "human rights": Man gives you his rights!' [Cf. Stirner, p. 108]. So runs the speech of political liberalism. 'Man's freedom in political liberalism is freedom from *persons*, from personal mastery, from the *lord*; it is personal freedom securing each individual person against other perspns. Nobody commands, the law alone commands. But if people have become *equal*, certainly their *possessions* have not. And indeed the poor *need* the rich as the rich *need* the poor, the one needs the money of the rich as the other needs the work of the poor. Thus nobody needs anybody as a *person*, but he needs him as a *giver*, and consequently as someone who has something to give, as a proprietor or an owner. Thus what a man *has* is what makes the *man*. And in *having* or in "property" people are not equal. – Accordingly, *social liberalism* concludes that *nobody* must *own*, as in political liberalism *nobody* should *command*, i.e., as to this point the *state* alone has maintained command, so now *society* alone should maintain ownership' [Stirner, pp. 127–8]. 'Through the principle of work, to be sure, what pertains to fortune or competition in the state[8] is outdone. But at the same time the worker retains in his consciousness that what is essential for him is to be "the worker", far from egoism, and submits to the supreme majesty of a workers' society, as the middle class citizen has adhered with devotion to the competition state. The beautiful dream of a "social duty" still continues to be dreamed. We again suppose that society *gives* us what we need, and that on this account we are *obliged* to it, we are all indebted to it. We insist upon wanting to *serve* a "highest giver of all goodness". The social liberals do not think that society is not at all an I which could give, lend, or vouchsafe, but rather an instrument or a medium which we may use to our advantage; or that we do not have societal duties, but rather only interests which society must help us to pursue; or that we are not bound to make offerings to society, but rather, if we make offerings, we expect offerings to us in return; because the social liberals – as liberals – are imprisoned in the religious principle after which they zealously strive, the religious principle which hitherto was the state – holy society. Society, by which we have everything, is a new mistress, a new spectre, a new "highest essence" which takes us "into service and duty"!' [Stirner, p. 135]. '*Humane consciousness* despises middle-class consciousness as much as it despises worker consciousness, because the middle-class citizen is only "provoked" by the tramp and his immorality, and because the *lazy sluggard* and his principles, which are "unethical" because they are impoverishing and unsocial, enrage the worker. Against them the humanitarian retorts, "The unsettledness of many is alone your product, Philistine! But that you, Proletarian, demand *grinding toil* of everyone, and want to make *drudgery* universal, further insinuates your subsequent status as a pack ass"' [Cf. Stirner, pp. 136–7]. 'Of course it is necessary that man be without any master, but rather than that the egoist should again be the master of man, man should become the master of the egoist. Of course man must have leisure time, but if the egoist turns it to his own advantage, then it eludes man; therefore you must give leisure time a human significance. But you workers even undertake your work out of egoistical motives, because you want to eat, drink, and live; how should you be any less egoistical in your leisure time? You only work because it is good to be idle after work is done, and however you spend your leisure time is left to *chance*. But should every door be barred to egoism, then a completely "disinterested" commerce, *total* disinterestedness, must be sought. This is only human, since only man is disinterested; the egoist is always

[8] [Schmidt adds, 'im Staate'. (Tr.)]

interested' [Stirner, p. 137]. 'And do you not notice that your disinterestedness, again, like religious disinterestedness, is a heavenly interestedness? The profit of individuals certainly leaves you cold, and you can proclaim abstractly: *fiat libertas, pereat mundus*, i.e., Let there be liberty, though the world perish. You do not even provide for the next day and generally do not have any serious concern for the needs of the individual, neither for your own good living nor for that of others; but, out of all of these things, exactly none are of consequence to you, because you are a – visionary' [Cf. Stirner, p. 138].

Max Stirner has a rightful claim against critique, the claim of the negative pole against the positive, of one moment of the opposition against the other moment. *The Unique Individual and his Property* is the negation, opposition, and contradiction of critique, but because it is merely the negation, it is also itself critique and the completion of critique. Stirner represents 'the mass' of 'critique'; he asserts the 'right' of the 'mass' which 'critique' holds to be 'illegitimate' against the 'spirit' which 'critique' has sanctified.

'I have made my affairs dependent on nothing' [Stirner, p. 3] – thus the unique individual begins the song of himself and of his life, and thus he shows at the same time that he is aware of enough strength in himself to be, all in all, himself. He proclaims enthusiastically: 'I am the creative nothing, the nothing out of which I myself, as creator, create everything' [Cf, Stirner, p. 5]. And what then does the unique individual know to create out of himself? What then is the creation of this creator?

Let us just consider his creations.

The course of his life – that is his first creation.

He gazes into and out of the world of his ancestors and finds therein the 'ancients' who 'lived in the feeling that the world and worldly relations were the truth before which their swooning I must humble itself' [Cf. Stirner, p. 16]. 'But even the ancients struggled to make their truth into a lie' [Stirner, p. 17]. In Sophism 'Greece made sport of that which till then had been for it a matter of enormous seriousness' [Cf. Stirner, p. 17]. 'Do not be amazed', say the Sophists with calm audacity, 'and use your understanding, your wit, your spirit, against everything. With a good and skilled understanding one fares best in the world, one prepares the best share, the most agreeable life' [Cf. Stirner, p. 17]. – this is their theory; and *understanding* is thus the heartening word against the enslaving force of steadfast, fatherly existents. – 'Do not merely cultivate your understanding, but also[9] your heart', said *Socrates*, the founder of

[9] [Schmidt omits Stirner's 'besonders'. (Tr.)]

ethics [Cf. Stirner, p. 18]. Here commences the period of the purity of the heart. The Sophists had proclaimed only the omnipotence of the understanding, but the heart was disposed toward the mundane, a servant of the world, having always remained affected by worldly desires. This crude heart had to be refined: the age of the *education of the heart*. Everything worldly must therefore come to disgrace before the heart; family, public affairs, fatherland, etc. must be given up for the sake of the heart, i.e., *bliss*, the bliss of the heart; for nothing more may the heart beat. This war from Socrates onward reaches its peaceful conclusion just on the day of the death of the ancient world [Cf. Stirner, pp. 18–19] – through the *Skeptics*. 'The sentiments and thoughts which we create out of the world contain no truth' – says Timon. 'There is nothing either good or bad, but thinking makes it so' [Shakespeare, *Hamlet*, II, ii, 252–3] [Cf. Stirner, pp. 24–5]. There is in the world no truth to apprehend, things contradict themselves, thoughts about things are indiscriminate; the apprehension of truth is done for, 'and only the man who is unable to apprehend, the man who finds nothing in the world to apprehend, remains, and this man just leaves the world empty of truth and does nothing with it' [Cf. Stirner, p. 25]. 'The man who is led by no more than his heart's desire, his sympathy, pity, his *spirit*, is the innovator,[10] the – *Christian*' [Cf. Stirner, p. 25]. 'Until the time preparatory to the Reformation the *understanding* was imprisoned by the dominion of Christian dogmas, when it arose sophistically in the Reformation[11] century and played a heretical game with all the propositions of faith' [Cf. Stirner, p. 26]. Humanism is Christian Sophism: 'If only the heart remains convinced of Christianity, the understanding may well do as it likes' [Cf. Stirner, p. 26]. 'But the Reformation seriously addressed the heart itself, and since then hearts have become noticeably – more unchristian' [Cf. Stirner, p. 26]. 'The heart, daily more unchristian, loses the content with which it is occupied until at last nothing is left for it except empty *cordiality*, the wholly universal love of men, the love *of man*, the consciousness of freedom, "self-consciousness". Thus Christianity is just consummated because it has become naked, paralyzed, and void of content. There is now no more content against which the heart does not rebel, unless it is unconsciously or without "self-consciousness" infiltrated by this content. The heart criticizes to death with relentless *cruelty* everything that wants to intrude upon it, and is capable of no friendship, no love.

[10] [Stirner reads, 'der Neue', i.e., 'the modern one'; Schmidt reads, 'der Neuerer', i.e., 'the innovator'. (Tr.)]

[11] [Stirner has this event in the *pre*-Reformation century. (Tr.)]

Whatever could there be to love in men, since they are altogether "egoists", not one *man* as such, i.e., not one who is *only spirit*? The Christian loves only the spirit; but how could there be anyone who is actually nothing but spirit?' [Cf. Stirner, p. 27]. 'For pure theory men are only there to be criticized and most thoroughly despised: They are, for it, no less than for the fanatic priest, only "dung" and other such clean things. Driven to the outermost point of disinterested cordiality, we must at last perceive that the spirit which the Christian loves alone, is nothing, or that spirit is a – lie' [Cf. Stirner, p. 27]. Thus begins the unique individual's second day of creation.

'I must oppose Christian "freedom" to idiosyncrasy.' That is the 'I become' of the unique individual. 'Must I?' Yes indeed, the unique individual *must*, because he always '*must*', because the '*must*' is his despotic lord and he its servile slave. '*Oppose*?' Yes, 'oppose', for out of the 'opposing', and thus out of the 'opposition', and thus from his 'opposite', and thus from the world which he wants to conquer, the unique individual can not escape. He *must* oppose Christian freedom to idiosyncrasy, '-ness' against '-ness', for 'one can get *rid* of quite a lot, but surely not everything; one becomes free of much, but not everything' [Cf. Stirner, p. 173]. 'Against Christian freedom, idiosyncrasy is my whole essence and being-there, it is I myself' [Stirner, p. 173]. 'I am *my own* at all times and in all circumstances, if I understand how to have myself and not waste myself on others' [Stirner, p. 173]. 'The urgent pursuit of a *determined* freedom always includes the intention of a new command' [Stirner, p. 176]. 'Freedom you all want, you want *freedom*. Why then do you haggle over more or less? Freedom can only be complete freedom; a bit of freedom is not freedom. You despair of winning complete freedom, freedom from everything, indeed, you hold it to be madness even just to wish it? – Now, stop chasing after the phantom and use your effort toward something better than the – *unattainable*' [Stirner, p. 176]. 'My freedom just becomes perfected when it is my – *force*; but through this I cease to be merely free, and I become my own. Why is the freedom of the people a "hollow expression"? Because the people have no force! I blow down the people with a puff from the living I, be it the puff of a Nero, a Chinese emperor, or a poor author' [Stirner, pp. 183–4]. 'Force is a beautiful thing, and very useful; for one goes further with a hand full of force than with a sack full of right' [Stirner, p. 184]. 'Whoever has force stands above the law' [Stirner, p. 184]. 'Behave as if you were mature, thus you are without any other declaration of majority; if you do not behave accordingly, you are not worthy of it, and would never be mature even by a declaration of majority. The mature Greeks chased their tyrants out, and the mature son makes himself independent of his father. If the Greeks had waited until their tyrants had most graciously granted them their majority, they could have waited long. The intelligent father throws the son who does not want to be mature out of the house and maintains the house himself; it serves the pup right' [Cf. Stirner, p. 185]. 'Idiosyncrasy involves everything owned and again honors what was dishonored by Christian speech. Idiosyncrasy, however, has no strange standards, as it is not at all an *idea* like freedom, ethical order, humanity, etc.; it is only a description of the – *owner*' [Stirner, p. 188]. 'My power is my property.' [Stirner, p. 203] – That is the property of the owner. 'I am only not entitled to what I do not do with free courage, i.e., what I do not entitle myself to. I decide if it is right in me; there is no right *outside* me. If it is right *for me*, it is right. Possibly that is therefore not yet right for the others; that is their worry, not mine: They may defend themselves. If there were something not right for the whole world, but right for me, i.e., if I wanted it, then I would not ask anything about the whole world. Everyone who knows to treasure *himself* does so, each to the degree that he is an egoist, because force goes before right, and indeed – with full right' [Stirner, p. 208]. Perhaps you say, 'Of course everything would go in utter confusion if everyone could do whatever he wanted!' 'But whoever told you that everyone can do everything? Then why are you there, you who do not need to stand for everything? Guard yourself, and nobody will do anything to you! Whoever wants to break your will has to deal with you, and is your *enemy*. Treat him as such. If millions more stand behind you for protection, then you are an imposing power and will have an easy victory. But even if you impress your adversary as a power, you are thereby still not a sanctified authority for him, unless he is a scoundrel. He does not owe you respect and attention, even though he will pay attention in the face of your force' [Cf. Stirner, pp. 215–16]. 'Right is a spanner in the works, thrown in by a spectre. Power – I am that myself, I am the powerful one and the owner of power. Right is above me, is absolute, and exists in something higher, by the grace of which it flows into me: Right is a gift of the grace of the judge; power and force exist only in me, the powerful and forceful' [Stirner, pp. 230–1]. For me in *my business* 'no majesty, nothing holy, is a barrier, nothing which I know how to overcome. Only what I can not overcome still restricts my force, and I of restricted force am temporarily a restricted I, not restricted by the force *outside* me, but rather restricted by *my own* still deficient force, by my own *powerlessness*.

Yet, "the guard dies, but does not surrender!"[12] Above all, only a physical adversary!

> I want any foe
> That I can see and fix in my eye,
> Who, himself full of courage, enflames my courage too, etc.'
> [Stirner, pp. 233–4]

'What is *my* property? Nothing but what is under my *force*! To what property am I entitled? To every property to which I – *empower* myself. I give myself the right to property by taking property, or I give myself the power of the property owner, full power, empowerment. Whatever cannot be snatched away from me by force remains my property; very well, let force decide property, and I choose to expect everything from my force! Strange force, force which I leave to another makes me a bondman; so may my own force make me an owner. Let me then retract the force which I have yielded to others out of ignorance about the strength of my *own* force! Let me say to myself that whatever my force reaches is my property, and let me claim as property everything which I feel strong enough to gain, and let me extend my actual property as far as I entitle, i.e., – empower, myself to seize it' [Stirner, pp. 284–5]. 'Egoism does not think of sacrificing anything, of compromising itself; it simply decides that what I need I must have and I will provide' [Stirner, p. 285]. 'Grab and take what you need!' – That is the rule of the egoist and 'thus the war of all against all is declared. I alone determine what I want to have. "Now"', the Philistines of love will cry, '"truly that is not new wisdom, for the selfish have always behaved in this way!" It is not at all necessary that the matter be new, if only the *consciousness* of it is present. But this consciousness cannot claim to be of an advanced age, unless perhaps one considers here Egyptian and Spartan law; for how unfamiliar it is follows from the above reproach, which speaks of the selfish with contempt. One should just

[12] [At Waterloo, General Pierre Jacques Étienne, Comte Cambronne, supposedly replied 'La Garde meurt, mais ne se rend pas!' to demands that he surrender his hopelessly cornered Garde Impériale. Although Cambronne denied having said any such thing, although his more probable reply was simply 'Merde!', and although he was actually taken prisoner in the battle, this line, which was probably just a fiction of the journalist Rougement, became Cambronne's epitaph, inscribed on his monument in Nantes. The 'mot de Cambronne' was certainly freshly in the mind of both Stirner and Schmidt, since the Frenchman had died only recently, in 1842. In later years, Cambronne's alleged defiance may have inspired another commander on a Belgian battlefield, General Anthony Clement McAuliffe, who, on 23 December 1944, to Nazi demands that he surrender his 101st Airborne Division, replied 'Nuts!' (Tr.)]

know that that process of grabbing is not contemptible, but manifests the pure act of the egoist who is at one with himself' [Cf. Stirner, p. 286]. Later the cheated will pull up their courage, certainly from the egoistic standpoint, with the question: '"By what is your property safe, you who are privileged?" – and they answer themselves: "By us, who refrain from usurpation. And therefore by our protection! And what do you give us for it? Boots and scorn you give to the 'common people'; police surveillance and a catechism with the main point: 'Respect what is *not yours*, what belongs to *others*! Respect others, especially your superiors!' But we retort: 'If you want our respect, *then buy* it for the price which we approve. We want to leave you your property, if you compensate us properly for leaving it'"' [Cf. Stirner, p. 300]. '"With what do you compensate us for chewing potatoes while we calmly watch you slurp oysters? Buy the oysters as expensively from us as we must buy the potatoes from you, then you may continue to eat them. Or do you mean that the oysters do not belong to us as much as they belong to you? You would scream out against *force* if we reached out to devour them, and you would be right. Without force we do not get them, as you do not have them unless you use violent force on us."' [Stirner, p. 300]. '"We want nothing given by you, but we also want to give you nothing. For centuries we have bestowed alms upon you out of obliging – stupidity, we have contributed the mite of the poor, and we have given to the lord what is – not the lord's; now just once open your purse, for from now on the price of our wares increases most enormously. We want to take nothing at all from you, only you should pay better for what you want to have. Then what do you have?" "I have an estate of a thousand acres." "And I am your farmhand and I will only plow your field hereafter for a Thaler a day." "Then I will hire someone else." "You will not find anyone else, for we farmhands no longer do things differently, and if one announces that he will take less, then he had best beware of us. There is the housemaid who is now also demanding as much, and you will no longer find one below this price." "Oh, then I will be ruined." "Not so rash! You will surely take in as much as we do, and if not, then we will reduce our share so that you may live like us." "But I am used to better living." "We have nothing against that, but it is not our problem; if you can make more, then do it. Why should we work for less than our price so that you can live in luxury?"' [Stirner, pp. 301–2]. '"But you uneducated people surely do not need so much." "Now, we are taking something more so that we can provide for ourselves the education which we perhaps need". "But if you thus reduce the rich, who will then sustain the arts and sciences?" "Well now, the multitude must manage it; we all donate to make a nice little sum; besides, you rich now buy only the most insipid books and lachrymose portraits of the Virgin, or a nimble pair of dancer's legs." "Alas, accursed equality!" "No, my good old sir, nothing of equality. We only want to be considered for what we are worth, and if you are worth more, then you should after all be considered more worthy. We only want to be *worth our price*, and we intend to show ourselves worthy of the price that you will pay"' [Cf. Stirner, p. 302]. 'Above the gate of our time stands not that Apollonian "Know yourself!" but instead a "Make use of yourself!"' [Stirner, p. 353]. Thus, 'I no longer *submit* to any power and I recognize that all powers are only my power, which I instantly have to subjugate if they threaten to become a power *against* or *over* me; each of them is allowed to be only one of *my means* to succeed, as a hound is our power against the game, but if he attacks us ourselves, then we kill him. I then degrade all powers which govern me so that they serve me. Idols exist through me; I need only not create them anew, then they exist no more; "higher powers" exist only through my elevating them while I render myself inferior' [Stirner, p. 357]. 'My business with the world consists in my enjoying it, and so exhausting it for my self-enjoyment. *Business* is *enjoying the world*, and appertains to *my – enjoying myself*' [Stirner, p. 358]. 'From now on sounds the question, not how man can acquire life, but how he can waste it and enjoy it; or not how man is to establish the true I in himself, but how he is to disintegrate himself and live to the hilt' [Stirner, p. 359]. 'A person is "called" to nothing, and has no "burden", no "determination", no more of a "calling" than has a plant or a beast. The flower follows no calling to consummate itself, but spends all its energies to consume and enjoy the world as well as it can, i.e., it sucks in as much of the earth's juices, as much of the ether's air, as much of the sun's light, as it can get and retain. The bird does not live according to any calling, but it uses its energies, as much as it can, to catch beetles and sing to its heart's delight. But the energies of the bird and the flower are meager compared to those of a man, and a man who applies his energies will intervene in the world much more forcefully than will a flower or a beast. He has no calling, but he has energies which make themselves felt where they are because their being indeed consists only in their making themselves felt, and they are as little able to remain idle as life, which, if it "stood still" even for a second, would no longer be life' [Stirner, p. 366]. 'Therefore, because energies always prove themselves active of themselves, the command to use them would be superfluous and senseless. To use his energies is not man's *calling* and burden, but rather it is his ever actual, present *act*' [Cf. Stirner, p. 367]. 'The true man does not dwell in the future, an object of yearning, but rather he dwells, actually and existing-ly, in the present. However and whoever I may be, joyful and sorrowful, a child or a senile old man, in confidence or in doubt, asleep or awake, I am this, I am the true man' [Stirner, p. 367]. 'We are altogether perfect, and on the whole earth there is not one person who is a sinner! There are madmen who imagine themselves to be God the Father, God the Son, or the Man in the Moon, and so also the world[13] abounds with fools who fancy themselves sinners; but as the former are not the Man in the Moon, so the latter are not – sinners. Their sin is imaginary' [Stirner, p. 404]. 'You have never seen a sinner, you have only – dreamed him' [Stirner, p. 405]. 'I no longer serve any idea, any "higher essence", thus it is obvious that I also no longer serve any man except – under all circumstances – *me*. But thus I am, not only by my act and my being, but also for my consciousness, the *unique individual*' [Stirner, pp. 405–6]. 'I am not an I along with other I's, but the only I: I am unique. Therefore my requirements are also unique, as are my acts; in short, everything which is mine is unique. And only as this unique I do I take everything as mine to own, as only as this do I get busy and develop myself. Not as a man and not for man[14] do I develop, but as I, do I develop – myself' [Cf. Stirner, p. 406]. 'The ideal "man" is *realized* if the Christian view is turned over into the proposition: "I, this unique individual, am man." The conceptual question, "What is man?" has then changed into the personal question, "Who is man?" By "what", the concept is sought, in order to realize it; by "who", it is no longer a question at all, but the answer is instantly, personally present in him who asks the question; the question answers itself. It is said of God, "Names name thee not." That is true of me; no *concept* expresses me, nothing assigned as my essence exhausts me; they are only names' [Stirner, pp. 411–412]. 'In the unique individual the nakedness and barrenness of concepts and ideas come to light in his nakedness and barrenness, in his shameless uprightness; vain pomp is revealed as his enemy; it becomes clear that the greatest "catchword" is that which appears to be the slogan with the most content. The unique individual is the upright, undeniable, revealed catchword; he is the keystone of our world of catchwords, of this world in whose "beginning was the Word".[15] The unique individual is the declaration by which it is

[13] [Stirner reads, 'es'. (Tr.)]

[14] [Stirner's text is ambiguous regarding accusative singular or dative plural; Schmidt has removed, and perhaps 'solved', the ambiguity by substituting the dative singular. (Tr.)]

[15] [Cf. John 1.1. (Tr.)]

conceded with all frankness and honesty that it declares – nothing' [Cf. Stirner KS, p. 347]. 'It[16] ought to be nothing but the common catchword, only so that through this it[16] is actually that which the bombastic catchwords of enemies are unable to be, and so that it[16] thus brings to shame the making of catchwords' [Cf. Stirner KS, p. 347]. 'The unique individual is a slogan without thought; it has no content of thought. But then what is his content, if not thought? One who can not exist for the second time accordingly also can not be *expressed*; for if he could be expressed, actually and completely expressed, then he would be there for the second time, would be there in the "expression"' [Stirner KS, p. 348]. 'The judgment, "You are unique", signifies nothing else than "You are you", a judgment which the logician calls a nonsensical judgment because it judges *nothing*, says nothing, because it is empty, or a judgment which is not a judgment' [Stirner KS, p. 349]. 'You, the unthinkable and unspeakable, are the content of the catchword, the owner of the catchword, the embodied catchword; you are the *who*, the *he* of the catchword. In the unique individual science can come forth as life, since for life[17] the *it* becomes the *he*, and the *he* who then seeks himself no longer in the word, in the *logos*, in the predicate' [Cf. Stirner KS, p. 350]. The unique individual recognizes all relations in the present world, only divests it of its illusion of holiness. His egoism 'is not an opposition to love, not an opposition to thinking, not an enemy of a sweet life of love, not an enemy of surrender and sacrifice, not an enemy of the most inward cordiality, not even an enemy of critique, not an enemy of socialism, in short, not an enemy of an *actual interest*; he does not exclude any interest. He is only directed against disinterestedness and against what is uninteresting, not against love, but against holy love, not against thinking, but against holy thinking, not against the socialists, etc.' [Cf. Stirner KS, p. 375]. 'It is said of God that he is perfect and has no calling to strive for perfection. That is also true of me alone. I am the *owner* of my force, and I am that when I know myself as *the unique individual*. In the *unique individual* the owner reverts even to his creative nothing out of which he is born. Each higher essence over me, be it God, be it man, weakens the feeling of my unique individuality, and fades only before the sun of this consciousness. If I set myself toward myself, the unique individual, my affair then stands on the ephemeral one, on its mortal creator,

16 [Stirner reads, 'er', i.e. 'he', the unique individual; Schmidt reads, 'es'. (Tr.)]

17 [Stirner reads, 'in dem ihr...' i.e., 'in which (life) its (science's)...' or 'in which (life) for it (science)...'; Schmidt reads, 'indem ihm...' i.e., 'while (or since) for it (i.e., life)...' (Tr.)]

who consumes himself, and I may say that I have set my affair on nothing' [Cf. Stirner, p. 412].

That is the unique individual and his property. That is the act of the unique individual, a unique act.

The unique individual is the first attempt to escape from the dominion of spirit. The tribute he must pay is that he himself comes to be the most spiritual of spirits, the ghost of ghosts, the fanatic of fanatics, the holy of holies, the god of gods, or rather the devil of devils. The unique individual knows that there is nothing to the world of spirits, that it is only the *universal* shadow of the shadows, called men, floating around the world, that spirit is only the tyrannizing chimera of man. He has sought the incantation before which spirit flees and collapses in its exhalation, but – he has himself, because he was short-sighted, erred along the way and has died in error. The unique individual has not consumed the world of spirits, on the contrary, he is consumed by it. He has chewed it, but not digested it; he has swallowed it, but – Misfortune! – it lies too hard in his stomach: He dies of the world of spirits and in the world of spirits. He is '*pure Being*', the immutable, dead existence – the abstract abstraction. The critique of the unique individual is therefore the last critique of critique: 'Critique' defeats the unique individual, but the victory over him is costly: It must pay him with its existence.

The unique individual is the conclusion of the world; he fed and fostered the communists, communists, i.e., universal men, general men, common men, and communal men, men who under the cloak of communism maintain, and must maintain, egoism, because egoism is their own essence, egoism is the truth of communism. The communist opposes and confronts the egoist: Communism can not live without egoism. In just this way the communist must remain opposed to the egoist, because without him the egoist does not exist. The love, the deep sigh of the heart of the egoist, is the communist. The egoist is the frantic communist, the dionysian, orgiastic song of the communist, the truth, the unveiled and brazen shame and form of the communist. He is devil against God, the evil one who belongs to the holy spirit, the hell which is the discovered heaven. The communist belongs to the egoist and the egoist to the communist: Both are only thinkable and actual in and with each other, both stand and fall together: Egoist and communist are *basically* one, but fight *on account of* their unity and *in* their unity with each other. – It is not an accidental, but a necessary, designation when the unique individual chooses 'egoist' as his name. He wants therewith to refer always and everywhere in himself to himself and to escape from spirit. Indeed, 'he who flees is not yet free, for in fleeing he is still conditioned by that before which he flees'. The egoist is for him and with him the power which limits, suppresses, and shatters everything, even the individual, the entire embodied man; *the egoist* – naturally not the ordinary, not the profane egoist, in the sense and in the meaning in which one is trained from infancy, but rather the egoist for whom one must imagine 'the identical judgment' [Cf. Stirner KS, p. 349, p. 354], the egoist who is not an enemy of a sweet life of love, not an enemy of surrender and sacrifice, not an enemy of the most inward cordiality, not an enemy of critique, not an enemy of socialism, not an enemy of an actual interest [Cf. Stirner KS, p. 375], but rather he who wants to annihilate only 'holiness' and who has sworn eternal enmity to disinterestedness and to the uninteresting, thus the egoist who, under the sign of mere thought, hallows holy thought, i.e., universal, exclusive thought, the thought which because of its holiness alone can claim the name of thought, who with his unholy socialism lifts socialism in general into heaven, who thereby, to preserve an actual interest, turns love into a chaste daughter of heaven and a coveted nun, who, through his actual interest, makes his stand opposed to the uninteresting, the non-actual, the illusory, the diabolical interest, and thus venerates the actual interest as God. – The unique individual is altogether consumed by spirit and therefore needs *spirit* for his foremost axiom and leading principle: He wants, through thoughtlessness, to end thinking. But what does thoughtlessness begin when thought attacks it? The poor thing, where can it flee? Indeed, thoughtlessness is not so thoughtless as you may well believe; it is the opposite of thought, hence itself a thought, and can on this account, in spite of its thoughtlessness, rightfully mean and say that it itself should distinguish the robberies of the unique individual through the *consciousness* of robbery from all other, ordinary robberies, and that one should just *know* that the process of seizing is not contemptible – it can rightfully mean and say this because it is *meaning* and *thought*. – He wants, through lack of respect, to end respect. I respect nothing – he says. I respect nothing – is, however, also respect, even if respect for – nothing. – He wants, through praxis, through action, to end theory. His highest category is thus the will; he is intoxicated by the liquor of the will, and as a drunkard who does not stand on his own feet, but reels and staggers, and before whom the actual makes a wry face, has become faint, impotent, unsteady, spineless, in order to become actually an individual, a unique individual. He *wants* to retract everything into himself; he *wants* to do what he *wants*; he arrives, however, at wanting, and can never go beyond it. 'Wanting' is his God, the catchword he adores, his happiness and his salvation, his dream of a better time – his idea.

The unique individual *wants*, i.e., he *ought*: 'In the ought always lies the weakness that something is recognized as justified, and yet, it is not able to assert itself.'[18] He is the objectified will, *the* will in human configuration – the phantom, *the* spirit. – He wants, through the unspiritual world, through nature, to end the world of spirits. He calls for whomever will listen to him to be like the flower of the field or like the sheep and the ox. Nature is thus his universality. As nature does, so ought man to do, i.e., man ought to be and become 'man'; man ought to mold himself to 'nature', i.e., to a new spirit. He wants to get rid of spirit, since he despises it. But in and with this despising he remains stuck in spirit, which is for him still an object worthy of despising, which is thus for him still something worthy, which he still must, and wants to, make into a thing, which is still his own shadow, his unavoidable ghost.

The unique individual can not get away from his opposition. He needs privileged robbers' states in order to rob, he needs stupidity in order to cheat the stupid, he needs spirit in order to be able to be spiritless. He is a Brahmin and differs from the Indian Brahmins only in that they say their 'Om' all their life long, but the unique individual says 'Un'. 'Un' is his principle and his highest bliss, the moment in which he cries out 'Un' in ecstasy and in mystic delirium: '*un*sayable', '*un*spiritual', '*un*true', '*un*holy', '*un*ethical', '*un*just', '*un*fair', etc.

The unique individual stands on the same ground as his foes. He is, as well as they, an idealist. He luxuriates in his ideal and dreams therefore, also consistently, of a world full of egoists, of an egoistic world which should then come to be. 'The cheated will later step forward with an egoistic consciousness' [Cf. Stirner, p. 300]. What he, the unique individual, thinks and is, the rest of the human creations which exist in his head should also think and be. As if then the unique individual were not sunk down and thrown down into the abyss of nothingness, as if he then were among all others what he would be as an egoist among egoists. As if these 'egoists' differed from 'men'. As if the egoists were not as good '-ists' as the pantheists and communists, i.e., a fantastic universality. The egoist must pretend a world of egoists because he himself is not enough. The unique individual must give a commission to his time, must write 'Make use of yourself!' above the gate[19] of his time in order to introduce a new spirit and a new misery, a new hunt and a new madness. He must fashion a new chimera, but the chimera which

[18] [This sentence, enclosed in quotation marks by Schmidt, epitomizes thoughts found in Stirner, p. 307, pp. 326–7, and pp. 332–3. (Tr.)]

[19] [I assume 'Phorte' is a misprint for 'Pforte'. (Tr.)]

gives 'humanity' its true expression, with which he leads this 'humanity' on and away, he, the robber – his gang of robbers.

The unique individual does not produce uniqueness. 'We could, if he were entirely, as he says, the "*unique individual*", no longer quarrel with him, indeed if only *he* existed and we did not. But we are not yet at that stage. What then is he? He is at most an *individual*, as I am, insofar as he is an egoist. What could we in this form, he and I, do with each other? We could jostle and use force on each other; we have in common only that we are both these brittle, completely *detached* individuals. But then why does the egoist write his book? Why does he put himself to useless trouble with language, with thought and other universalities? Through that he does not become what he wants to become, the "unique individual"; rather, he becomes public property. He even duplicates his book, he diffuses his thoughts about others; he becomes "transcendent", he has put a "phantom" into the world, and the more spirit spouts forth in his executions, the more mischievous is the goblin which he produces. This "unique individual" could not be born without becoming a man for all the world, as he launches himself, the "unique individual", he moves unfeelingly like a drop into the universal sea. That we have him is already enough to annihilate him; that we can speak with him is already his refutation.'[20] The unique individual does not know that he creates 'universalities' through 'thoughts' – the 'form of the unique individual' should be a mere shell into which all 'content' can be stuffed; he also does not know that content collapses with form and that he, *pure* form, is also *pure* content.

Therefore, unique individual, do you also dream? Do you also make yourself, 'a madman', into the 'Kaiser', the 'Pope', and the 'Lord God'? Egoist – are you also spiritual, spiritualized, and spiritually sanctified? Now, just dream on, dogmatic dogmatist, on until the Last Judgment, where, with the resurrection of all, even your ideal and your idea will attain reality. Then the war of all against all will break out. Then one will revolt against the other and one will strike the other dead in the holy strife in order to be nearest to the great egoist – Max Stirner. Then the farmhands will be unanimous and the housemaids will do a dance entwined around one another and will mutually confirm with eternal vows that henceforth they choose to work only for a Thaler a day. Then nectar and ambrosia will flow and roasted pigeons will fly into the gaping, snapping mouth of the egoist. Then God will be all in all. – Farewell, unique individual.

[20] [This passage is probably excerpted from a contemporary critique of Stirner's work. (Tr.)]

V. THE AUDITING OF CRITIQUE

'Critique' was the unique and exclusive power 'of the world'. 'Critique' brings to 'self-consciousness' the immobile and the motionless, absorbing and negating everything, entangling everything in its womb, in the grave of the 'substance' which admits a silent universality: It makes the full, lifeless, color-faded, and color-fading pictures of 'substance' into definite, resolute, and animated configurations. 'Critique' steals[21] the fire from the 'species' and imparts the spark of life to man, 'the spirit of his travels', 'the reformation of illusions', 'of dogmas', 'of the contradictions in man's brain', 'of the human head', through which he learns to be independent of critique, to exist in himself, to stop and go by himself. For 'critique', 'spirit' is no longer a dead, abstract beyond which persists in itself, insists upon itself, and does not exceed its once assumed form and figure; instead, critique is *in 'the world'*. [Critique is] that which is coming to be, that which eternally works and lives, a new shaping and a new shape, perpetual progress, a conversion and a metamorphosis of the realm of spirit, the process of development, the principle of movement, 'the law of the development' of the spirit of the world and of the time. In 'critique' spirit opens its workshop and shamelessly displays its true being, shows how it continues and advances and how it furthermore is nothing but this continuing and advancing, shows how it criticizes anew and solves anew each acquired result, i.e., itself, how it only and alone is only this chasing after itself with itself, – how it works and creates and lives and moves and struggles. Critique is of an elastic nature, to be characterized nowhere in a 'spiritual' field comprehensibly and vulnerably and just now at its end and in its consummation of the total, personal, individual negation of its consummation – to be presented and portrayed as it has destroyed and dissolved this determined standpoint and this determined form of world-spirit, even while it still appears to be working within this form – as it corrects itself, whatever it admits and accepts originally as accurate and legitimate it allows to stand and later to fall, lets its own decisions, assertions, and proofs gradually elapse in its own invalidity and waste away through itself, – as it generates itself in its annihilation – the world of spirits until it has subjugated everything under it and has become 'world-spirit itself'.

'Critique' has succeeded in overturning the hitherto prevailing world-view and in freely suppressing the hitherto dominant spiritual

[21] [I read 'stiehlt' for 'stielt'. (Tr.)]

powers; with it 'could the ceaseless vultures cease to prey / On self-condemning bosoms' (Byron, *Childe Harold*, III, [59]);[22] what *Bacon* asserted about philosophy is true of critique, that it, with only a little trouble, leads away from 'God', but, exhaustively driven, leads back to God. In critique was the fulfillment of the prophetic words of the poets first possible, Shakespeare's 'there is nothing either good or bad, but thinking makes it so' [*Hamlet*, II, ii, 252–3], and Byron's:

> The Mind which is immortal makes itself
> Requital for its good or evil thoughts, –
> Is its own origin of ill and end –
> And its own place and time: its innate sense,
> When stripped of this mortality, derives
> No colour from the fleeting things without,
> But is absorbed in sufferance or in joy,
> Born from the knowledge of its own desert.
> [*Manfred*, III, iv, 129–36]

'Critique will involuntarily remind one of the three well-known axioms of the loafer Nante,[23] which read: "Do not be amazed"; "Fear means nothing to me"; and "Lot is dead", i.e., all solemnity is ridiculous. Critique was the piercing eye by which whatever anyone hitherto believed could be placed above man as a transcendent power was simply glanced at and, through the mere glance, was reduced to "personality", as to the author of personality; critique looked things sharply in the face and – see here! – not things, but rather only this sharp glance of critique remained as that which was "alone significant" of them. In short, the combined spiritual powers, which hitherto had sustained the history of mankind, staggered before this omnipotence of "personality".'

'The critics' were the victors in the 'Olympic Games' of spirit. In them bloomed 'the elite of mankind'. In them 'the aristocracy of mankind caroused at a small table'.

'Critique' was 'great', 'monstrously great'. It has stormed the 'heaven of religion' with the sharp sword of '*man*' and of the 'infinite self-consciousness'. It has allowed 'the sanctuary of the state' to collapse before 'mankind'. It has sacrificed the 'inhuman' to 'mankind', 'spiritlessness' to 'spirit', 'mass' to the 'critic', and, after a clarifying and an enlightening of the contradictions in the predominant mental images, after a preserving, cancelling, uplifting, and evacuating of the hitherto prevalent development of the human

[22] [Schmidt has misidentified the stanza in *Childe Harold* as III, 19. (Tr.)]

[23] [*Der Eckensteher Nante* is a Berlin folk character who was popularized by Ludwig Lenz (1813–96) and Adolf Glasbrenner, or Glassbrenner (1810–76). (Tr.)]

race toward the false, illusory foundation of humanity, has arrived at the abstraction: 'Development!' Critique has not allowed any thought to ascend beyond it unless it has plucked the feathers out of that thought; it has beaten one 'idea' with another, overthrown one 'privilege' of spirit with another, dispelled one 'dogma' with another...

But –

It has not overthrown the 'original privilege', the 'original idea', the 'original dogma', and it cannot overthrow them without overthrowing itself. 'Critique' lets itself proceed and stand 'uncritically' and 'uncriticized'. 'Critique' wants to liberate the world from 'dogma', and yet it forces upon the world 'the dogma of dogmas', the dogma of critical infallibility, the dogma that critique itself is all, that the rest is nothing, that critique is the heaven and saviour of mankind, that everything left outside of it is Satan with his hell. Critique wants to annihilate heaven and hell, and makes itself into heaven, and makes the world of masses and the world-mass into hell. Critique wants to strike transcendence dead, yet it cries: 'I am, that is, *spirit* is eternal, *spirit* is all, *spirit* must remain – even if the body dies.'

'Critique' is 'for critique' an 'idea', a 'feeling', a 'heart-stirring mental image' – the yearning and hoping, the luxurious feeling of bliss, the worthy object of devotion and reverence.

Hegel has liquefied the whole world in all of its forms and contrasts with his 'not only... but also' which always preceded and supported the 'neither... nor'. He held these contrasts and contradictions to be rational, declared them to be the idea itself, and allowed them to endure and proceed after their critique and alignment in and along the thread of dialectic; he is the personified reason of the world of spirits. Critique has placed self-consciousness, spirit, the author of the Hegelian dialectic, at the head of all; it has taken contrasts and contradictions at their word as contrasts and contradictions, has found them to be null and void, and has dissolved them with 'critique' and with 'self-consciousness'; it is the understanding of the world of spirits, the understanding which by itself and through itself ruins all actual configurations because they are not it itself, a pure, actual, true understanding; it is the understanding which does not achieve understanding in the presence of sheer understanding, which further is nothing but understanding, and which further retains nothing but *the* understanding, the understanding which represents the state of the understanding in a specific highest person – *the realm of the understanding*.

But critique, as well as Hegel, has remained responsible for demonstrating that this its objective dialectic, this eternal process, lacking individuals, is the true and the absolute; both critique and Hegel have rather presumed that dialectic and process were as such. Critique wants, through thinking, to decompose thought. Therefore no determined thought endures before critique, which undermines, lacerates, dissects[24] every determined and solid thought through another thought, another mental image, another fantasy and so on to *progressus in infinitum*, until it itself has reached *the* thought. But before '*the* thought', before the 'objective world', before 'humanity', before 'self-consciousness', before the 'concept' – there the understanding, which is 'holy' to critique, brings critique to a standstill. 'Spirit', 'development', 'truth' as the power of critique, and 'freedom' as the essence of the critic, must remain firmly 'the universal', thus, 'the absolute', and are inviolable. Because '*critique*' is '*spirit*' and has a 'principle' – and as long as spirit rules, the principle rules also, and with it the dogmatism which is just spirit, and even if the principle of critique were anxiety in the face of the principle, the principlelessness and its dogmatism would be only the flight, within dogmatism, from dogmatism – critique is transcendental, having emerged, not out of transcendence, but out of beyondness, and it must grow dumb at its conclusion and write its resignation on its banner. At its zenith, godless individuality is not permitted to rule in 'history', but rather history must develop itself 'purely' and 'objectively'. 'Not I! Not I' – says the ogre of critique – 'The talk is not of me! I do not make history, but only say what exactly are the interests and intentions of history in each period.' The critic is, even in history, only 'a servant of thought who, as honorably and as truly as possible, seeks to articulate what critique says to him'. The critic can not and is not allowed to know that perpetual process and 'presuppositionlessness' are a 'presupposition' before which he must castigate himself, fast, kneel, and pray, which tortures him and drives him incessantly further, so that it is *he* who writes these histories thus and not otherwise, so that *he* first creates 'objectivity' and then organizes his creations, so that '*history*' is an 'illusion', a 'phantom of spirit', a 'spiritual folly', an 'absurd fancy'. Then 'spirit', 'the universal', 'that which embraces the whole world', 'that which dwells in heaven', 'that which hangs over the individual', 'the essence', 'the concept', 'the idea', would be annihilated and 'the critic' as such, and with him critique, would be killed.

The critic has *himself* portrayed *himself* everywhere, and through this, through his individuality, '*he himself*' has become 'great'. Or tell

[24] [I read 'zerlegert' for 'zerledert'. (Tr.)]

me, critic, have you in all of your works presented anything else except yourself? Indeed, I do not even want to ask – yourself, but only something other than *your* thoughts, *your* opinions, *your* fantasies? Have you worked for the sake of anything else, or has your own individuality forced and driven you, have you left yourself no peace until you have found yourself, the *pure* critic? You mean that you have worked for 'humanity' and have not taken yourself into consideration, that you are therefore *great* because you have done much work and are, through that, 'the critic'. Surely *your* work for 'humanity' was *your* interest for *yourself*. And *your* greatness? 'In what, then, consists *your* greatness?' Exactly in this, that you are more than other people (the 'mass'), are more, since *people* are ordinary, are more than 'ordinary people'; exactly in your elevation over people. Before other people you do not distinguish yourself by being a person, on the contrary, because you are a 'unique' person. You show well what a person can accomplish, but because you, a person, accomplish it, therefore others, also people, can never accomplish it by any means. You have achieved it only as a unique person and are therein unique. Man does not constitute your greatness, but you create it, because you are more than man, and more forceful than other people.

The process of history, development as a category, is the last illusion of the holy, behind which spirit has taken refuge and with which it has veiled itself, the most extreme consequence of bondage and, conjointly, of egoism – the self-surrendering self-externalization. With 'history' critique has disclosed and constituted itself as the realm of spirits, its and *the* most nearly perfect and most nearly universal form and formula, set in the place of old, not yet precise, forms and formulas; and by itself, the absolute, has dislodged the earlier, still unclear, absolute. 'Critique', 'the thinking' which thinks itself, 'the development' which develops itself, has, as 'history', stepped into its improved holy cathedral, where it sings a *Te Deum* in the most holy holiness. 'Critique' from now on has no more to revolutionize, because 'history', 'world-spirit', 'providence', 'does all for the best'.

Because of the substantial character of 'critique', the individual critic has had to and must surround himself with glory, hypostatize his thoughts, transform his individuality into objectivity, his judgment into universal truth – become religious and theological. He must defend all of his higher declarations with the courage and the fiery zeal of apologetics. He is not allowed ever to err or ever to have erred, because he is not a separate thing, not something independent, not something particular, not something individual, because he denies himself and does not participate in his declaring, because he has abandoned all finitude and narrowness and has yielded and surrendered himself to the holy goddess, '*Critique*'.

'The critic' was the gravedigger of ancient times, the promulgator of death, of that which had no more life. He was not strangled by the universal death which went around the globe, until death had seized everyone, and the critic died because he had nothing left to bury. Critique is the death which devours all old and decayed life; when death has devoured it, then death itself is no more. Critique is the road which must be travelled to reach the seventh heaven, spirituality in person, holiness in its full pathos, the realm of spirits and of the understanding in its full extent, and therewith and thereby solid ground; but whoever travels this road, never arrives –

Stop!

Young Hegelianism: A Bibliography of General Studies, 1930 to the present

BOOKS

Adorno, Theodor W. *Aspekte der Hegeleschen Philosophie.* Frankfurt (Main), 1957.

Balser, Frolinde. *Die Anfänge der Erwachsenenbildung in Deutschland in der ersten Hälfte des 19. Jhs.* Stuttgart, 1959.

Barth, Hans. *Wahreit und Ideologies.* Zürich, 1945.

Barth, Karl. *Die protestantische Theologie im 19. Jahrhundert.* Zürich, 1947. (E.t. *Protestant Theology in the Nineteenth Century.* London, 1972.)

Benz, Ernst von. *Der Übermensch. Eine Diskussion.* Zürich–Stuttgart, 1961.

Bockmühl, Klaus Erich. *Leiblichkeit und Gesellschaft: Studien zur Religionskritik und Anthropologie im Frühwerk von Ludwig Feuerbach und Karl Marx.* Göttingen, 1961.

Brazill, W.J. *The Young Hegelians.* London, 1970.

Bultmann, Rudolf. *Geschichte und Eschatologie.* Tübingen, 1958.

Cornu, Auguste. *Moses Hess et la Gauche Hégélienne.* Paris, 1934.

Gasciogne, R. *Religion, Rationality and Community: Sacred and Secular in Thought of Hegel and His Critics.* Dordrecht, 1985.

Gebhardt, Jürgen. *Politik und Eschatologie. Studien zur Geschichte der Hegelschen Schule in den Jahren 1830–1840.* München, 1963.

Hecker, Konrad. *Mensch und Masse. Situation und Handeln der Epigonen, gezeigt an Immermann und den Jungdeutschen.* Berlin, 1933.

Heer, Friedrich. *Europäische Geistesgeschichte.* Stuttgart, 1953.

Hook, Sidney. *From Hegel to Marx.* New York, 1958.

Keil, Wilhelm ed. *Deutschland 1848–1948.* Stuttgart, 1948.

Klutentreter, Wilhelm. *Die Rheinische Zeitung 1842/43 in der geistigen und politischen Bewegung des Vormärz.* Phil. Diss. F.U. Berlin, 1956.

Kobylinski, Hanna. *Die französische Revolution als Problem in Deutschland 1840 bis 1848* (Histor. Studien, ed. Emil Ebering, H. 237). Berlin, 1933.

Kornetzki, Heinz. *Die revolutionäre dialectische Entwicklung in den Hallischen Jahrbüchern.* Phil. Diss. München, 1955.

Lange, Marx Gustav. *Der Junghegelianismus und die Anfänge des Marxismus.* Phil. Dissertation. Jena, 1946.

Marxismus–Leninismus–Stalinismus. Stuttgart, 1955.

Lobkowicz, Nicholas. *Theory and Practice: History of a Concept from Aristotle to Marx.* Notre Dame, Ind., 1967.

Löwith, Karl. *Die Hegelsche Linke.* Stuttgart, 1962.

Von Hegel zu Nietzsche. Stuttgart, 1956.

Lubac, Henri de. *Affrontements mystiques.* Paris, 1950.

Le drame de l'humanisme athée. Paris, 1959.

Lübbe, Heinrich. *Die Hegelsche Rechte,* Stuttgart, 1962.

Mah, H. *The End of Philosophy, The Origin of "Ideology": Karl Marx and the Crisis of the Young Helegians.* University of California, 1987.

McLellan, David. *The Young Hegelians and Karl Marx.* London, 1969.

Mende, Georg. *Karl Marx' Entwicklung vom revolutionären Demokraten zum Kommunisten.* Berlin, 1955.

Moog, Willy. *Hegel und die Hegelsche Schule.* München, 1930.

Nigg, Walter. *Geschichte des religiösen Liberalismus.* Zürich–Leipzig, 1937.

Popitz, Heinrich. *Der entfremdete Mensche: Zeitkritik und Geschichtsphilosophie des jüngen Marx.* Basel, 1953.

Quispel, Gilles. *Gnosis als Weltreligion.* Zürich, 1951.

Reding, Marcel. *Der politische Atheismus.* Köln, 1957.

Rehm, Walter. *Der Untergang Roms im abendländischen Denken.* Leipzig, 1930.

Sass, Hans-Martin. *Untersuchungen zur Religionsphilosophie in der Hegelschule,* 1830–1850. Phil. Diss. Münster, 1963.

Schoeps, Hans-Joachim. *Vorläufer Spenglers,* Leiden, 1955.

Das andere Preussen. 1957.

Seeger, Reinhart. *Friedrich Engels. Die religiöse Entwicklung des Spätpietisten und Frühsozialisten.* Halle, 1935.

Sens, Walter. *Karl Marx: Seine irreligiöse Entwicklung und antichristliche Einstellung.* Halle, 1935.

Stadelmann, Rudolf. *Soziale und politische Geschichte der Revolution von 1848.* München, 1948.

Stuke, Horst. *Philosophie der Tat: Studien zur "Verwirklichung der Philosophie" bei den Junghegelianern und den Wahren Sozialisten,* Stuttgart, 1963.

Talmon, J. L. *Political Messianism: The Romantic Phase.* London, 1960.

The Origins of Totalitarian Democracy. London, 1955.

Toews, John E. *Hegelianism: The Path Toward Dialectical Humanism,* 1805–1841. Cambridge, 1980.

ARTICLES

Barnikol, E. 'Das ideengeschichtliche Erbe Hegels bei und seit Strauss und Bauer im 19. Jahrhundert', *Wissenschaftliche Zeitschrift der Martin-Luther Universitat Halle-Wittenberg,* x, 1961 pp. 281–306.

Benz, Ernst. '*Hegels Religionsphilosophie und die Linkshegelianer', Zeitschrift für Religions- und Geistesgeschichte,* VII (1955).

'Johann Albrecht Bengel und die Philosophie des Deutschen Idealismus', *Deutsche Vierteljahrsschrift für Literaturwissenschaft und Geistesgeschichte,* 27, 1953.

Conze, Werner. 'Staat und Gesellschaft in der frührevolutionaren Epoche Deutschlands'. *Historische Zeitschrift,* 186, 1958.

Droz, J. & Ayfoberry, P. 'Structures sociales et courants idéologiques en Allemagne prérévolutionnaire', in *Annali,* VI, 1963, pp. 164–236.

Hertz-Eichenrode, Dieter. '"Massenpsychologie" bei den Junghege-lianern', *International Review of Social History* VII, 1962, pp. 231–59.

Kesting, Hanno. 'Utopie und Eschatologie', *Archiv für Rechts- und Sozialphilosophie* XLVI, 2, 1960.

Krauss, Werner. 'Karl Marx im Vormärz', *Deutsche Zeitschrift für Philosophie*, 1, 1953.

Kuhler, Otto. 'Sin Bedeutung und Auslegung der Heiligen Schrift in Hegels Philosophie. Mit Beiträgen zur Bibliographie über die Stellung Hegels (und der Hegelianer zur Theologie, insbesondere) zur Heiligen Schrift', *Studien und Bibliographien zur Gegenwartisphilosophie* 8, 1934.

Kupische, Karl. 'Vom Pietismus zum Kommunismus'. *Der Anfang*, 18, 1953.

Lauth, Reinhard. 'Einflusse slawischer Denker auf die Genesis der Marxschen Weltanschauung', *Orientalia Christiana Periodica*, 1, 1955.

'Die verwirtschaftete Humanität'. *Neue Deutsche Hefte. Beiträge zur europäischen Gegenwart*, 2, 1955/56.

Löwith, Karl. 'Die philosophische Kritik der christlichen Religion im 19. Jahrhundert', *Theologische Rundschau*, n.F., 5, 1933.

Lukács, Georg. 'Zur philosophischen Entwicklung des jungen Marx', *Deutsche Zeitschrift für Philosophie*, 2, 1954.

Lutz, Rolland Ray Jr. 'The "New Left" of Restoration Germany', *Journal of the history of Ideas*, 21 (Apr.–June 1970).

Mayer, George, 'Die Anfänge des politischen Radikalismus in vormärzlichen Preussen', *Zeitschrift für Politik*, 6 (1931).

Müller, Gustav E. 'Die Entwicklung der Religionsphilosophie in der Hegelschen Schule', *Schweizerische Theologische Umschau*, 18, 1948.

Rosenberg, Hans. 'Theologischer Rationalismus und vormärzlicher Vulgärliberalismus', *Historische Zeitschrift*, 141, 1930.

Sandberger, Jorg F. 'Spekulative Philosophie und Historischkritische Bibelauslegung', *Evangelischen Theologie*, 1, 1971.

Schlawe, Fritz. 'Die Berliner Jahrbucher für wissenschaftliche Kritik', *Zeitschrift für Geistes- und Religions-geschichte*, 11, 1959.

'Die junghegelische Publizistik', *Die Welt als Geschichte*, 20, 1960.

Wartofsky, M.; Sass, H-M., eds., *The Philosophical Forum*, 8, no. 2–4 (1978). Special issue on the Young Hegelians and Marx.

Wiese, Benno v. 'Zeitkrisis und Biedermeier in Laubes "Das junge Europa" und in Immermanns "Epigonen",' *Dichtung und Volkstum*, 36, 1935.

Index of names